The New Eighteenth Century

The New Eighteenth Century
Theory • Politics • English Literature

edited by
Felicity Nussbaum and
Laura Brown

Methuen   New York and London

For Donna Jay Guy
and in memory of Arthur Raymond Cohen

First published in 1987 by
Methuen, Inc.
29 West 35th Street, New York, New York 10001

Published in Great Britain by
Methuen & Co. Ltd.
11 New Fetter Lane, London EC4P 4EE

© 1987 Methuen, Inc.

Printed in the United States of America

Library of Congress Cataloging-in-Publication Data

The New eighteenth century.

Includes bibliographies and index.
1. English literature—18th century—History and criticism.   2. Canon (Literature)   3. Criticism.
I. Nussbaum, Felicity.   II. Brown, Laura, 1949–
PR442.N48   1987   820'.9'005   87-2757
ISBN 0-416-01631-6
ISBN 0-416-01641-3 (pbk.)

British Library Cataloguing in Publication Data

The New Eighteenth Century ; theory,
    politics, English literature.
    1. English literature—18th century—
    History and criticism
    I. Nussbaum, Felicity   II. Brown, Laura
    820.9'005   PR441

    ISBN 0-416-01631-6
    ISBN 0-416-01641-3 Pbk

CONTENTS

ACKNOWLEDGMENTS

The following colleagues and friends have provided advice and comments in the course of this project—John Bender, Steve Cohan, Walter Cohen, Jean Howard, Margaret Ferguson, Donna Landry, Janice Price, and John Richetti. We are grateful for their help. We must also acknowledge the support of Syracuse University and Cornell University for assistance in preparation of the typescript.

REVISING CRITICAL PRACTICES:
An Introductory Essay

Felicity Nussbaum and Laura Brown

I

This volume represents itself as "new" in part to call attention to the resistance to contemporary theory that has largely characterized the study of eighteenth-century English literature. Such resistance is worth documenting and analyzing at the outset of this collection in order to provide a full account of the context that will shape the future of the field. We will turn to that future in the last section of this essay, but we begin with an attempt to provide an interventionist reading of the present and the past.

The resistance to theory in eighteenth-century English studies has been characterized by a basic definitional problem. The word "theory" has held a series of connected but conflicting meanings for those scholars and critics in the field who have sought to resist its incursions or to distance themselves from its questions, and in this context "theory" has become not only an occasion for a certain amount of confusion, but a location of ideological struggle. Of course "theory" is no simple category in literary studies at large: at some times it seems to mean a science, at others a master discourse, and at times—as in the sense in which we use it here—a systematic method of inquiry without closure that is always subject to revision, a mode of questioning the status quo. But for many critics in this field, "theory" calls up an apparently protean enemy that requires a variety of contradictory defenses.

One defense is simple dismissal: if theory is what we all do naturally, as some scholars in the eighteenth century have suggested, then it can be said to refer to any methodology, however vague, that attaches to literary study. This definition binds the field to the status quo by dismissing what are described as unnecessary neologisms and obfuscation without undertaking an examination of the conceptual problems or issues that might be raised by revisionist or "theoretical" work. On the other hand, for some eighteenth-century scholars "theory" seems to refer specifically to Derridean deconstruction, with its focus on linguistic interplay and its apparent lack of interest in history or culture. In this view, "theory" represents an arid formalism, and the field can defend the dominant critical assumptions by alluding to the long-standing strength of historical work in eighteenth-century literary studies, much as it defended itself against the powerful formalist model of the New Criticism two decades ago. This historicist attack on theory for being reductively formalist depends, of course, on a definition of "theory" that excludes the specifically historical models of contemporary theory—Marxist, Foucauldian, new historical, or feminist. But yet another definition of "theory," one that is particularly tenacious and pervasive, attacks recent work for being *in*sufficiently formalist and for neglecting "literary pleasure." In this case, an appreciative formalism uses a notion of the aesthetic as a bludgeon against revisionist readings; and thus in this context the definition of "theory," while it includes poststructuralism, emphasizes Marxist or other historicist methods, which are all classed together as anti-"literature." The attitudes toward theory and its uses are by these means subtly legislated, and the kinds of work that can be written, published, and reviewed are regulated by what is acceptable in the academy. This systematic inconsistency and lack of clarity in the way some eighteenth-century critics have chosen to define "theory" suggest not only a certain amount of ignorance and misinformation, but an opportunistic—if not conscious or concerted—manipulation of the term in order to marshall an omnibus defense of eighteenth-century literary studies, traditionally defined. Whatever one's political or institutional program, such reactionary reasoning and its influence on the field must be carefully assessed.

Though it proposes to defend a particular method of critical analysis, this multifaceted attack on theory is often linked to an attack on particular materials of study as well. One strong statement of these coordinate sentiments is represented in the concluding paragraph of a recent review:

> The balkanization of literary studies continues. As scholars take the time to learn more about the history of women, popular culture, sexuality, or

the latest version of a derivative critical theory, they take less time to learn about literary texts themselves and the dominant cultures that produced them. Consequently, the periphery becomes the center, and important distinctions become blurred—whether dissenter and Anglican, baronet and peer, standard and outmoded editions, works published before or after one another, and theories that are imposed on a text rather than rise from it. The concept of literary pleasure thus is in danger of being replaced by competing nonliterary ideologies, often transmogrified to personal psychotherapeutic or political agendas.[1]

This passage might have served as a negative epigraph to this essay, since it compactly joins method and material, "theory" and "the periphery," the "dominant cultures" and "literary pleasure." In contrast, the essays in this volume systematically link the study of "women, popular culture, sexuality," and literary theory, and they consistently question issues of literary pleasure, aesthetic unity, and coherence. And of course *The New Eighteenth Century* takes the opposite side from this reviewer on the value and significance of a study of the oppositional and the problematic—textual, cultural, and political. Though "theory" and "the periphery" are our central concerns, such a focus does not entail ignorance or neglect of the "dominant cultures." Textual contradiction or incoherence arises as a divergence from aesthetic unity, and marginal social groups or cultural forms are necessarily situated in relation to centers of power. Far from neglecting the dominant culture, *The New Eighteenth Century* places it in its necessary relation to the periphery, in a theoretical context designed to broaden and sharpen our perspectives on the period and its critical tradition as well. In this sense the "new" readings presented here supply a more inclusive view of the period than those which are limited to the dominant culture alone. The partial view is the one that can see only the pleasures and the positions of power, and that dismisses the problematic, the popular, the female, the political, or the self-consciously theoretical to an irrelevant periphery.

It is, of course, from our position within the academic profession and its institutions that we urge the revision of present practices. Yet we wish to point to the exclusions that are inevitably inherent in that context, to the ways in which institutions authorize certain kinds of knowledge and empower those who reproduce them. Our claims for this volume must also be circumscribed by the current state of theoretical practice within our discipline, where the attack on "theory," though influential, has not gone unanswered. Thus, we seek to play a strongly revisionist role, but one that is attentive to its debts and its institutional limits, and responsible—even in opposition—to the work it undertakes to revise.

Though the essays in this volume do not authorize a single reading of the period, they do share a commitment to critical and political self-consciousness, to the unspoken of their texts, to the foregrounding of theoretical assumptions, not only for the sake of clarity but also for the purpose of acknowledging the writers' own cultural and historical positions. And relatedly, they all take perspectives that involve a rejection of either purely theoretical or purely scholarly enterprises as a debilitating division; and they all entail a corresponding commitment to an understanding of the relationships between reading texts and the larger conceptual issues in eighteenth-century studies and in cultural and literary studies in general. A collection such as this offers not a synthesis and distillation of prior work with the aim of consolidating and simplifying an already existing consensus, but various specimens of recent efforts to formulate new critical practices, the consequences and implications of which are not yet entirely clear. We say this in order to suggest what might be the most appropriate way of using this volume: not as the last word on the subject, but as one of the first.

II

Current work in critical theory, represented in the United States in journals like *Critical Inquiry, Cultural Critique, Diacritics, New Literary History,* and *Representations,* has enabled critics to ask new and urgent questions about texts, contexts, and the act of reading. In contrast, the most respected journals in eighteenth-century studies remain relatively untouched by recent developments in critical theory. In comparison with current studies of the Renaissance, the Romantic period, or the Victorian novel, work in eighteenth-century literary studies relies more heavily on appreciative formalist readings that seek to describe a stable core of meaning in the text, or on a positivist historicism, unreflective about its theoretical grounds or its political implications. Leading journals in the field such as *Eighteenth-Century Studies, Modern Language Review, Philological Quarterly,* and *Studies in English Literature,* for example, tend to publish essays that provide New Critical readings of canonical texts, new textual or editorial evidence, or new intellectual contexts. These articles occasionally make initial reference to a relevant theorist—Iser, Bakhtin, Barthes, or Foucault, for example—but without pursuing the implications of those modes of inquiry for their own project. Most often, however, they assume that their methodology is natural or consensual, that it need not be explained or justified. Though of course all these journals occasionally include essays that build upon recent theoretical developments, there has been no concerted impulse or occasion for eighteenth-century scholars to confront the issues that contemporary theories raise or to engage in a systematic debate on those issues.

Why has eighteenth-century English literary studies often ignored or resisted new theoretical approaches, and why, in turn, have theorists neglected the materials of the eighteenth century? What can we learn from this lack of interest and response? Here we would like to propose some possible answers to these complex questions.

Contemporary eighteenth-century studies received its definition from major critics of the middle third of the twentieth century such as R. S. Crane, William K. Wimsatt, Earl Wasserman, and Reuben Brower.[2] Crane's position is complicated, since he started out as a traditional albeit distinguished historical scholar, before moving to neo-Aristotelian formalism rather late in his career. Wimsatt, of course, is one of the central figures in the definition and popularization of New Criticism, and his work on Johnson helped legitimize that interpretive mode in the period. Wasserman and Brower confined themselves more narrowly to the eighteenth century, and thus their writings perhaps had a more profound impact on critical practice in the field than the more theoretically oriented work of Crane and Wimsatt. Both Wasserman and Brower combined skillful New Critical analysis of seminal texts with formidable scholarship, in Wasserman's case augmented by references to intellectual history. All of these critics, then, were formalists, and whatever their stance on intellectual history, they were in no position to propose or to challenge a particular historical narrative of the age. Indeed, they came to a field already constrained by political predilections that represent a heritage from the Whig historians of the nineteenth century, which viewed the eighteenth century as the tranquil haven of political stability in modern English history. And even after the twentieth-century revisions of that interpretation, the prominence of political analysis in modern historiography has continued to support the stereotype of pervasive and long-term stability in the period, a political stability linked to an image of equivalent social and cultural coherence, to a sense of an unchallenged class hierarchy represented and perpetuated in a literary culture where aesthetics, ethics, and politics perfectly mesh.[3] Thus, the eighteenth century has fostered a criticism whose ultimate concern is the preservation and elucidation of canonical masterpieces of cultural stability. This protection of a stable canon and culture is only a more powerful version or prototype of the ideology that has dominated Anglo-American literary studies during much of this century, and especially during the first twenty-five years after World War II, but it has made challenges to the status quo—both theoretical and political—particularly difficult and threatening.

The perpetuation of the argument for political stability in English history helps explain why eighteenth-century studies has such a different profile outside of English literature, even in the work of the major American literary critic of the last two decades, Paul de Man. De Man's essay on Rousseau in *Blindness and Insight* (1971) pioneered a major new mode of reading for an American audience, but, significantly, has had no impact on readings of English texts in the period. Within the English eighteenth century, a few substantial but scattered studies have had some influence. Beyond essays by Wolfgang Iser on Fielding and Sterne, and Edward Said on Swift, there have been only diffuse examples of theoretically engaged full-length studies in the field.[4] These include an early Foucauldian study by W. B. Carnochan, *Confinement and Flight* (California, 1977), and William Dowling's *Language and Logos in Boswell's "Life of Johnson"* (Princeton, 1981), called on the flyleaf "the first deconstructionist interpretation of a major eighteenth-century work." But much of the theoretically informed work has concentrated on the novel, including Lennard J. Davis's *Factual Fictions: The Origins of the English Novel* (Columbia, 1983), as well as feminist work in Nancy K. Miller's *The Heroine's Text: Readings in the French and English Novel, 1722–1782* (Columbia, 1980) and Mary Poovey's *The Proper Lady and the Woman Writer: Ideology as Style in the Works of Mary Wollstonecraft, Mary Shelley, and Jane Austen* (Chicago, 1984). The spate of books on Richardson— *Reading Clarissa: The Struggles of Interpretation* (Yale, 1979) by William Warner, Terry Castle's *Clarissa's Ciphers: Meaning and Disruption in Richardson's "Clarissa"* (Cornell, 1982), and Terry Eagleton's *Rape of Clarissa: Writing, Sexuality, and Class Struggle in Samuel Richardson* (Minnesota, 1982)—suggest on the one hand the gradual opening up of the field, and on the other the limited range of theoretical references in eighteenth-century studies. Books which are more specifically dedicated to a particular methodology include Murray Cohen's poststructuralist *Sensible Words: Linguistic Practice in England, 1640–1785* (Johns Hopkins, 1977), James Swearingen's phenomenological study of *Reflexivity in 'Tristram Shandy': An Essay in Phenomenological Criticism* (Yale, 1977), Joel Weinsheimer's hermeneutical approach in *Imitation* (Routledge & Kegan Paul, 1984), and G. Douglas Atkins's deconstruction of Dryden and Pope in *Reading Deconstruction, Deconstructive Readings* (Kentucky, 1983). These ventures have been important among those that indicate the beginnings of a shift in the field's orientation and in encouraging further theoretical work, but they have thus far been anomalous contributions, and in that regard they have only served as a tentative preamble to the more extended debate that we hope *The New Eighteenth Century* will help to initiate.

As early as 1974 the relation of the new and the old was becoming a subject of attention, as scholars apparently felt intellectual pressure from the ideas of structuralism and, in particular, from Foucauldian revisions of eighteenth-century history. In that year *New Approaches to Eighteenth-Century Literature*, a volume edited by Philip Harth from papers delivered at the English Institute (Columbia, 1974), signaled an occasion for definition and reflection. Harth identifies two directions among his contributors: a concern with greater exactitude in methodology, and a movement away from a New Critical attention to the text isolated from culture toward a more socio-anthropological emphasis. The two most speculative essays in the collection are those by Donald Greene and Lawrence K. Lipking. Greene urges the eighteenth-century literary scholar "to resolve to try to keep up with current scholarship in the other areas of eighteenth-century cultural and intellectual history with which his work overlaps."[5] He calls for a new interdisciplinarity, to be institutionalized in the recently formed American Society for Eighteenth-Century Studies (ASECS).

In "The History of the Future" in the same volume, Lipking also encourages more interdisciplinary work, to propel scholars out of the isolation of disciplines, as well as a countermove toward a fact-finding scholarship that will fill the lacunae in our knowledge. Lipking seems caught between his passion for the new and his fear of it: "Fashion makes strange canons. But eighteenth-century studies can hardly exist unless they resist such canons, and draw part of their impetus from *within* the period."[6] He sets up a dichotomy between two critical methods, "the kind of pedantic historicism I have called Retrenchment, and on the other side, . . . the desperate up-to-the-minuteness I have called Fashion"; and he then identifies a third and more desirable alternative represented by Michel Foucault's *Madness and Civilization* (1961, trans. 1965). Following Foucault, Lipking maps out an early version of what has now come to be called "new historicism"[7] as a model for the future of eighteenth-century studies: "To define the unspoken assumptions of another age, apparently one must also define one's own assumptions: the structures of thought, mysteriously silent, so pervasive and automatic that few men recognize the need to justify them" (170). This earlier volume of new approaches, like the present collection, emphasizes the special relevance of interdisciplinary work in eighteenth-century studies, and seeks to define a series of critical methods that would take account of both current and past scholarship.

The conservative tendencies of eighteenth-century literary scholars have been oddly reinforced over the past two decades by the formation of ASECS in 1969. Partly a reaction against the New Critical antagonism to history, authorial biography, and political context, ASECS sought to consolidate an alternative position by which critics in the field could defend themselves against what was still felt to be a hegemonic formalism. Dominated largely by literary scholars, ASECS nevertheless has substantial representation from various other disciplines. History, philosophy, fine arts, religion, and science have often been valued as providing the "background" and "context" for literary works. Such approaches are informed by the discipline of history as it was until recently practiced in the United States, with its strong bias toward political and intellectual history, and its empiricist and implicitly antitheoretical assumptions. These versions of history support the search for allusions and sources that editors, bibliographers, and textual scholars seek. And though as a response to New Criticism the institutionalization of interdisciplinarity was belated, this approach readily lends itself to a defense against subsequent movements in contemporary theory.

In helping to enforce an unexamined antitheoretical disposition in the field, ASECS has been more than a casual influence. In an important account of the profession of eighteenth-century studies in America, William H. Epstein suggests that the establishment of ASECS and the subsequent proliferation of allied regional organizations represented the process by which the discursive practice of eighteenth-century studies—the production of knowledge, the definition of appropriate objects of inquiry, and the production of possible modes of discourse—was institutionalized. Epstein exemplifies the practice of eighteenth-century studies through an account of the editorial cornerstone of the Age of Johnson, the Yale Boswell "industry," an editorial project "on the model of American corporate enterprise," funded by the Mellon banking fortune.[8] Following the model of the Boswell "industry," the dominant source for the production of professional power in the field, Epstein argues, is the publication of directories, newsletters and conference proceedings, the annual bibliography, and the journal *Eighteenth-Century Studies*. Thus, while ASECS served at its founding moment as a significant agent for revitalizing the field by emphasizing its links with other disciplines, it has not encouraged other timely, political, and intellectually challenging approaches. New work in the eighteenth century thus must confront not only the predilection among established critics for a critical status quo, but "one of the most well recognized and institutionalized areas of period specialization" (21).

In short, ASECS has in effect institutionalized the traditional relationship between literary and historical study. In large part, interdisciplinary work as it is usually practiced in the field employs history as background or defines literature as reflection in a narrow sense. This, added to the residual influence of Whig historiography that we have already noted, begins to explain the conservative nature of the field. In addition, it seems possible that eighteenth-century scholars often uncritically enter the ethos of the privileged and canonical in the period—

Pope's "Whatever is, is right" or Johnson's kicking the stone to refute Berkeley's idealism. In other words, they adopt the eighteenth-century's liberal humanism, empiricism, or Enlightenment ideals—including hope, progress, and the pursuit of individual happiness—as their own commonsensical position without much reflection on the ends for which they are employing these philosophies in our criticism. But avoiding confrontation with the methodologies scholars use and the ideologies that inform them does not exempt eighteenth-century studies from producing work within a recognizable ideological discourse. The effect of new poststructuralist and Marxist theories is to require that a liberal humanism or a belief in the universal moral value of "literature" must now be argued rather than assumed.

In this volume, then, we want to place the terms of our intellectual pursuits and the politics at stake in them under renewed scrutiny. The "new" that we define in this volume has its roots in recent renewed attention to interdisciplinary work and in particular the relationship of literature and history. But if the new has much in common with the old, it also makes radical breaks with the past in its confrontation with theory and politics, especially new feminisms, Marxisms, and historicisms. We will turn now, however, to the reactions to these new theories in *The Eighteenth Century: Theory and Interpretation*, and the last decade's "Year's Work in the Eighteenth Century" in *Studies in English Literature*. We will end by arguing that approaches to literature informed by recent theoretical and political criticisms enable powerful new modes of reading and writing about eighteenth-century literature and culture. This moment of articulation, the historical moment of this volume, is possible only because a number of eighteenth-century scholars are beginning to believe that contemporary theory is now particularly productive for their work. Finally, in writing our version of the recent history of the field, and describing the place of this volume in the trajectory that we see for the future, we hope to point toward the theoretical and political controversies, the fertile issues of debate, that are most urgent for a new kind of eighteenth-century studies.

III

In addition to the founding of ASECS and the publication of the *New Approaches* volume, an important turning point came in the late 1970s, when *Studies in Burke and His Time* changed its name to *The Eighteenth Century: Theory and Interpretation* (ECTI). This change marked a recognition, on the part of the editors at least, that there was a void in the creation of knowledge about the eighteenth century that other journals were not filling. Originally devoted to a study of a "great man" and his period, the journal's editors felt impeded "by its limitation less to one discipline than to one hazily defined but identifiable approach to all disciplines represented in its pages." They continued: "Whether this approach be called 'historical empiricism' or something equally vague, it is clear that alternative approaches have already proved their interest and value."[9] In spite of the ferment over contemporary French theory, no specific modes of inquiry are mentioned. Instead the new editorial policy resolved on a *via media*: "Our aim . . . will be to provide a forum not only for fruitful integrations among disciplines but also for fruitful clashes among methodologies." On the one hand, the declaration of an editorial policy shift directed contributors and readers to be reflective about their methodologies: the editors urged a move beyond "historical empiricism." On the other hand, they found themselves unable to suggest specific approaches except "our fundamental assumption . . . that no methodology is 'natural'" (195). Remarkably, the word "theory" is never used. In the inaugural issue the editors retreat from the purportedly revisionist shift to "theory," hesitantly suggesting only that "historical empiricism or something equally vague" cannot be assumed as the "right" or "only" methodology and hastening to assure their readership that the new policy does not represent "a radical break with the journal's past" and that "the journal professes no ideology" (5). In practice, then, the early numbers of *ECTI* may have unwittingly discouraged polemical essays on theoretical topics by this dissociation from the innovative, the radical, and the ideological. While the journal has provided an occasion for the publication of essays representing diverse methodologies, only in the most recent numbers has this debate begun to take place.

One essay published in *ECTI*, however, stands out as a harbinger of the concerns of our volume. In 1979 Murray Cohen argued that while "formalist critical assumptions still reign in eighteenth-century studies," he would like to encourage engagement with recent theoretical developments to infuse "a new energy in literary study" that derives in part from scholarly self-reflexivity.[10] Distressed at the lack of a public debate over methodology, he writes, "These central tenets of the new methodologies—that texts, like ideas, persons, and perceptions, are not simply denotative, or naturally well ordered, but are compilations of how people tried to make sense at a particular time—can help us return to the historical, materially dense, and multiply connected world in which eighteenth-century writings can still exist" (11). He concludes with a hope that "we might try for a time to reread our subjects . . . less with a compulsion to find either completed forms, or unified identities, or well-documented traditions than with a willingness to make do with the lively problematics generated by competing claims on language" (23). The field has proven slow to respond to Cohen's critique. In a series of recent review essays in *Eighteenth-Century Life* (a journal founded in 1974 to foster interdisciplinary ties), historians themselves— responding to methodological shifts in their own field—have drawn attention to the theoretical approaches of the books under review. For example, F. S. Schwarzbach in "London and Literature in the Eighteenth Century" notes that a view of history "as a stable monolithic entity, which can be drawn upon when necessary," is too prevalent in "inter-disciplinary studies of a literary nature" with its concomitant "shallow sense of historicity."[11] There is an assumption, he notes, "that history, which deals with hard evidence, produces certain equally hard conclusions about things which actually happened in the 'real' world." Literature is not, he argues, simply a response to or reflection of a hard reality. Apparently adopting Hayden White's argument, he notes, "What critics should be stressing is the value of literary texts as historical and cognitive events in their own right, no more or less 'real' than any others" (112).[12] Here major contemporary shifts in the discipline of history are brought to bear on eighteenth-century literary studies, and the discipline that had previously played a conservative, positivist role provides the basis for a critique of that very positivism.

Why have eighteenth-century scholars largely resisted appeals such as those just outlined? The year's review of work, "Recent Studies in the Restoration and Eighteenth Century" in *Studies in English Literature*, affords an occasion to describe the attitudes that have worked against "theory." We rehearse this narrative of reviews not to single out any individual critic's claims (for many of these scholars may not wish to be fixed in their positions of some years past), but because taken collectively such comments have discouraged change and have served to protect a conservative assumption of objective consensus. They have produced the contradictory definitions of "theory" that we outlined above, and in the process they have excused eighteenth-century critics from learning about theoretical and political methodologies. In each year's review, "theory" is only infrequently mentioned, but we can detect a series of implicit and explicit assumptions about theory and its relation to the period.[13] First, though theory is never defined, the word functions interestingly as a place where the struggles over meaning are fought. These review essays consistently imply that we all know and do "theory," and hence that there is nothing very new about it. Paul Korshin, for example, in the most recent *SEL* review (1986), indicates that after surveying the field of books published in 1985, he finds no lack of theory, though in the course of his summary he rarely mentions the theoretical approaches of the books under discussion. Similarly, Maximillian Novak claims in his survey of the year's work that he "found no critic ignorant of theory" (*SEL* 22, 1982, 553). Now that the heated arguments over New Critical method have receded into the past for a generation of eighteenth-century scholars, they assume that methodology needs little explanation. The notion that theory too is self-evident marks the logical extension of this assumption.

A second assumption, which contradicts the first claim that theory is ubiquitous and natural, is that theoretical models are useless. The *SEL* review for 1981 by Richard Schwartz is quickly dismissive of a Marxist reading of children's literature (21, 532). Similarly, though Schwartz finds flaws in Irvin Ehrenpreis's *Literary Meaning and Augustan Values*, the reviewer congratulates him on recapitulating "an already established method (one that will easily survive the challenges of so-called 'theoretical' methods)" (533). And another book that employs an explicit theoretical model is chided for its "jargon, cant, and twisted syntax" (529). This complaint about neologisms is frequent among critics dismissive of theoretical work (G. S. Rousseau, 1978, 555). The reviews often ask whether the best books of the year require their complex theoretical vocabulary to achieve their excellence, or whether the books are good *in spite* of theory. For example, J. Paul Hunter (1980) gives high praise to a recent book for its detailed editorial commentary, its erudition, and its sophisticated grasp of recent theory, only to steal the power away from the theory that informs it: "His [William Warner's] reading is essentially a deconstructionist reading based upon post-structuralist theory, and he allies himself with the philosophical and political allegiances of his method, neither of which I support, and I imagine he would think that the strength of his accomplishment comes from his method. I disagree" (534). This disagreement is apodictic; Hunter does not explain how the same results could be derived from another method (542).

The most pervasive and passionate assertion in recent reviews is that of the destructive despotism of theory. This claim has become a familiar one in literary studies in general, as new modes of criticism contest the long-held New Critical status quo. But in eighteenth-century studies in particular, the anxiety takes a special turn. Even during the hegemony of New Criticism, eighteenth-century scholars maintained a strong connection with history—political and social—and with biography. In this sense, the field's resistance to change has been consistent, long-standing, and ecumenical. Thus eighteenth-century scholars today, who discern a new attack on the critical status quo, recall their position during a prior period of embattlement, and remind us of the time when—in their recollection—the New Critics controlled the discourse and the economics of the profession. Apparently unaware of the variety of contemporary theoretical models, they claim that theory will produce a similarly

monist view, finding only one meaning, one truth in literary works. In
1984 Morris Brownell, remarking on the frequent reference to ideology
in the year's work, carries this concern to modern Marxist theory's "ideological imperialism" (603). Maximillian Novak (1982) worries about the
tyranny of monolithic theory, the power of strongly held ideas to destroy
departments and careers. He wants to avoid a repetition of the time
when "New Criticism became a tyranny in the university. Those who
dared speak of the intentions of an author were likely to be scorned and
eventually fired. Those who brought historical knowledge to enlighten
poems and novels were considered to be in violation of the law of autonomous texts" (551).

A corollary and extension of this concern about intellectual domination is the association of all theory with ahistoricism or anachronism.
The problem as it is conceptualized in these reviews is whether, since
eighteenth-century literary studies has for so long defined itself in relation to eighteenth-century history, modern philosophers and theo-
reticians can have anything of worth to say about the period. While
Novak professes the "highest respect for deconstructive criticism from
Derrida to Paul de Man" (1982, 551), he protests that "the only work
on the eighteenth century that is not adding to our knowledge and
understanding of the period is occurring where those 'invisible theorists
are hurling lightning bolts at one another'" (554). And Brownell, acknowledging the problematic relationship between history and literature, voices a concern about the way "this year's more doctrinaire studies
. . . [do not] refrain from imposing a modern bias on the past" (1984,
604).

And finally, perhaps the least convincing of these arguments against
an alteration of the critical status quo is the fear that theory will distract
us from what matters and make us ignore or even forget the aesthetic
value of "literature." This definition of literature as something universally acknowledged and transhistorical, as we have argued, represents
an identification with the elite culture of the eighteenth century. Thus,
Howard D. Weinbrot, in the passage cited earlier, quite explicitly associates the "dominant culture" with "literary pleasure," excluding from
that perfect union the "marginal," the "popular," and the "female," in
the same breath with "critical theory." And G. S. Rousseau is concerned
that in the "urgency to scientize criticism [we have] forfeited the most
basic function of the critic: to keep literature alive" (1978, 556–57). These
critics rely on a traditional humanist definition of literature as a timeless
rather than an historically produced category.

Ronald Paulson's *SEL* review of 1983 stands out among these others
as one of the few instances of a serious consideration of texts that use
theory. Paulson seeks to define the ways in which theory may encourage

us to rethink our assumptions about classic texts. He, himself the author of work informed by structuralist and psychoanalytic positions, singles out for particular attention the power of Michel Foucault's ideas on discourse and knowledge in the work on prose fiction for 1983, an important year for theoretically informed studies of the novel—including Davis's *Factual Fictions*, Castle's *Clarissa's Ciphers*, and Eagleton's *Rape of Clarissa*. Paulson begins by describing the methodological frame for the books he discusses, citing their indebtedness to Ian Watt's "realism," the Chicago School, or Foucault. Readily acknowledging that this is an age of poststructuralism, he refers to Barthes and Derrida, but also to Marx. He even reprimands one author for omitting "post-new critical developments and focusing on the retrograde reactions of" earlier critics (508). In short, while Paulson does not dismiss the old, he displays considerable respect for and understanding of the power of new theoretical models to enliven the illuminate eighteenth-century texts.

IV

Our project, then, is the revision or problematization of period, canon, tradition, and genre in eighteenth-century literary studies, and the individual essays included here, taken collectively, embody a variety of theoretical practices which have in common their commitment to reflecting on their own methodologies as well as an engagement with eighteenth-century history, politics, and culture. John Bender and Jill Campbell focus on social and cultural institutions and the texts they produce. For Bender, in "Prison Reform and the Sentence of Narration in *The Vicar of Wakefield*," Goldsmith's novel provides a paradigm for the ideological significance of the rise of the penitentiary in eighteenth-century society, a phenomenon that can be linked both to the bureaucratization of social control and to the development of formal realism in the novel. Campbell, in "'When Men Women Turn': Gender Reversals in Fielding's Plays," treats the institution of the theater during the 1730s, where the pervasive cross-dressing in Fielding's plays serves as a site of gender identification and confusion. Using as cultural points of reference cross-dressing and the ambiguous position of the contemporary castrati, as well as the pervasive commodification of women, she documents the age's consistent transgression of gender boundaries.

For Fredric Bogel and Terry Castle, psychoanalytic categories open up texts to new kinds of readings, and vice versa. In "Johnson and the Role of Authority," Bogel uses the category of narcissism to question the boundaries of Johnson's authority with reference to plagiarism and intertextuality; by this means he reads the canonical texts through the noncanonical or "ghost written" works, to re-evaluate the status of both. In "The Spectralization of the Other in *The Mysteries of Udolpho*," Castle finds a bizarre "ghostliness" in the most domestic and least sensational scenes of Radcliffe's novel, and she uses Philippe Ariès' account of death in modern culture to address the Freudian account of the "ghosts" of the unconscious.

Feminist critics writing in the eighteenth century, working at the margins of the canon and the field, have engaged in important archival retrieval of women's texts, and they have isolated the ideologies of gender at work in the "major authors" of the period. Among the first to bring political concerns to a broad academic audience, these scholars interested in gender have often been forced to confront the vexed relationships among literary form, history, and feminist politics. The feminist essays here question the significance of a tradition of women's writing and the relevance of women's experience to its representation in texts, as well as the extent to which a given work can be said to possess an ideology. Beyond this, they urge that "woman" must be read as an historically and culturally produced category that is situated within specific material conditions and is interactive with the complicated problems of class and race. They indicate how certain regimes of truth, of discourse, and of subjectivity are limited by the category of gender. In this sense some of the feminist essays in *The New Eighteenth Century* can be seen to move toward the formation of a feminist cultural politics.

Aside from Campbell's study of the drama, the feminist contributions to this volume include essays by Felicity Nussbaum, Laura Brown, and Donna Landry. Nussbaum, in "Heteroclites: The Gender of Character in the Scandalous Memoirs," focuses on some of the first published women writers, the scandalous memoirists, as subjects in history and culture rather than as whole autonomous beings who "express themselves." She notes in particular the way the memoirs were produced and consumed by readers who sought to confine "woman" to a recognizable category. Brown uses a woman's colonialist romance to approach the problem of slavery in "The Romance of Empire: *Oroonoko* and the Trade in Slaves," where the conjunction of race and gender provides a means of reading the history of the oppressed in the texts of the dominant culture. And in "The Resignation of Mary Collier: Some Problems in Feminist Literary History," Landry attends to the suppressed voice of a working class poet, using the category of class to raise questions about feminist literary history.

Class and the dialectical process of history receive attention from John Richetti and Michael McKeon as well. Asking why the under class is such a consistent object of comedy in *Joseph Andrews* and *Tom Jones*, Richetti's "Representing an Under Class: Servants and Proletarians in

Fielding and Smollett" argues that the novels efface the social actuality of that class to reclaim it for the category of the aesthetic, with significant ideological consequences. And McKeon uses a dialectical method to show how Marxism can transform the meaning of literature—a familiar poem like Dryden's *Absalom and Achitophel*, but also a familiar critical category like "the aesthetic"—by returning it to its historical context.

If *The New Eighteenth Century* attends to the voices of the laboring classes and the African slave, it gives at least equal space to the class that gains hegemony by the middle of the century: the bourgeoisie. Bourgeois ideology is variously demystified in this collection, in essays by Robert Markley, John Barrell and Harriet Guest, and Carole Fabricant. Markley, in "Sentimentality as Performance: Shaftesbury, Sterne, and the Theatrics of Virtue," reads *A Sentimental Journey* by way of Shaftesbury's moral philosophy, and finds that sentimentality can be seen as a bourgeois rationalization of economic inequalities, where materialism underwrites a purportedly aesthetic sensibility. Barrell and Guest, in "On the Use of Contradiction: Economics and Morality in the Eighteenth-Century Long Poem," trace similar contradictions in the form and function of the major long poems of the period by Pope, Young, Thomson, and Goldsmith. They argue that these poems are defined generically by the contradiction between the incompatible discourses of theodicy and mercantile amoralism, and that they function to allow the reader to ignore one of the fundamental ideological contradictions of the age. And finally, Fabricant's essay, "The Literature of Domestic Tourism and the Public Consumption of Private Property," questions traditional disciplinary boundaries and the ways they have been constituted in historical and cultural studies. She examines the discourse of tourism and domestic travel as an index of the contradictory forces implicit in bourgeois literary culture, where admiration and emulation of the property of one's "betters" could serve as either a form of social control or a source of discontent.

Broadly speaking, the essays we include address a number of issues now current: the ways subjectivity is historically constructed, and whether such constructs support "false consciousness" or, alternatively, representations of our relation to reality that vindicate political domination; the ways in which gender is an economic, social, political, historical, and cultural construct; the problem of the canon and the ideological status of works by major writers like Dryden, Pope, Thomson, Fielding, Sterne, Goldsmith, and Johnson; the nature and the authority of received modes of representation such as epic, realism, sentimentalism, and autobiography; the function of affect or sensibility; the status of history and culture and their relation to "literature"; the conceptualization of ideology, particularly in its application to genre; and the problematics of readers and reading in history.

Our breaks with traditional treatments of eighteenth-century literary culture are both material and methodological. Collectively, we open up texts and issues that have been infrequently discussed: tourist literature, working-class women's poetry, scandal chronicles, and Johnson's "ghost written" hack works, as well as race and slavery, the under class, transvestism, and the penitentiary. These concerns—largely invisible to the previous generation—present themselves with a fresh urgency to the new generation of eighteenth-century critics. And in this context, the volume must also be situated in relationship to contemporary trends in theory, which provide the new context and the conceptual rationale for this revisionist enterprise. Within and among these essays, feminist, Marxist, new-historical, deconstructive, and psychoanalytic theories are combined, juxtaposed, and contrasted. Bogel joins deconstruction and psychoanalysis, while Castle argues that Freudian theories of the unconscious are as subject to historicization and demystification as the literary texts of the period, and Nussbaum uses an account of character to argue against transhistorical psychoanalytic descriptions of female identity. While Campbell merges feminist and new-historicist methods, Landry describes the tension of Marxism and Anglo-American feminism. While Brown, claiming to define a systematic conjunction of Marxist and feminist methods, argues against the conclusions of an American Foucauldian position, Bender uses a strongly Foucauldian approach to the social institution of the penitentiary. Even those essays that utilize Marxist theory must be distinguished from one another: Fabricant emphasizes the false consciousness enforced by the dominant bourgeois ideology and Markley the systematic polyvalence of that ideology; Barrell and Guest focus on the dynamic of ideological contradiction; and McKeon on the dialectical nature of historical contextualization.

In short, this collection does not recite a single story about the period, the texts, or the methods used to examine them. Part of our task, as we see it, is to foreground our differences, in theory and interpretation, not just to stir things up, but to suggest the political value of a critical pluralism—that is, of systematic and strongly argued modes of inquiry in confrontation with one another—at least in the current volatile era of literary studies. The recent adaptations of poststructuralist analysis by Marxists, or of feminist perspectives by psychoanalytic critics, or of Marxist theory by Anglo-American feminists, all suggest the potential uses of a critical pluralism; not to dilute critical writing or to dissolve difference, but to promote a vigorous revisionism characterized by informed debate, productive disagreement, and, at times, innovative synthesis. Taken together, then, these essays begin to make an argument for new conjunctions and exclusions in tracing relationships among literature, culture, and society, especially along the lines of gender, class, and race. The prospects for a Marxist feminism, or an historicized psychoanalysis, or a political poststructuralism are as yet unclear, but the current state of eighteenth-century studies—tentatively theoretical, traditionally historical—seems to us to provide the potential for a clearer conceptualization of its modes of inquiry, and in this context our field might well provide an unusually fertile arena for such theoretical and political controversies.

In this volume, most though not all of the contributors would see historical analysis as crucial to their enterprise. They address the issues of their essays as an intellectual and political imperative; they read the past in the ways they do *because* of their commitments in the present historical moment. That is, they recognize the political implications of their theoretical positions. But even among these critics, it is easy to detect divergences that are in fact important disagreements. A number of the contributors, particularly those reliant in some fashion on the Marxist tradition, would acknowledge their indebtedness to the earlier school of British cultural Marxism represented in eighteenth-century literary studies by Christopher Hill's work with Marvell, Milton, Bunyan, and Richardson. Other contributors, particularly those indebted to the writings of Foucault and American new historicists like Stephen Greenblatt, would seek to distance themselves from the humanism and especially the commitment to the knowability of historical process that has characterized the heritage represented by Hill, E. P. Thompson, and Raymond Williams.

Carole Fabricant's essay, the last of the volume, ends with the claim that her reading of bourgeois thought is significant, "not as a matter of theoretical sophistication or trendiness, but as a political act no less liberating for our existence in the present as it is revolutionary in its implications for our understanding of the past." The British cultural Marxist tradition has consistently subordinated theory to politics, just as it has maintained what it understands as the humanist ideal of liberation in a prominent place in its endeavor. This tradition indicates the implicit priority, for some of our contributors, of political practice over theoretical vanguardism, and of the truth value of history over historical relativism. With the rise of postmodernist theory, British and especially American Marxist critics have often been cut off from the prior radical tradition, with an inevitable loss of momentum and historical experience. Hill's work with major cultural materials of the Restoration and eighteenth century supplies a vital continuity between one generation and the next, and between a liberationist criticism that reconstructs a radical past, on the one hand, and a demystifying criticism that exposes

oppression in the dominant culture, on the other. Indeed, for some of
our contributors, Hill's most important contribution to the study of this
period is arguably the recovery of a radical political past, and the revelation both of its impact at the time and of its continuing meaningful-
ness today.

Other contemporary versions of political criticism, including some
strains of Marxism, question whether one can ever discuss questions of
the economy and class without accounting for the places of gender, race,
and culture. Similarly, such critics see ideology as itself a site of contestation. For them, particular ideologies, located in material practices
at a given historical moment, are identified as contradictory, and the
conflicts come to rest in human subjects who are themselves summoned
into place by ideologies. From this perspective, the complexities of the
formation and perpetuation of the dominant ideology take on greater
significance, along with questions about the function of ideology in reproducing the conditions of its own production, and the discursive and
the nondiscursive aspects of ideology.

Still other versions of contemporary political criticism, including the
positions of some of the authors here, would emphasize the difference
between the tradition of an older "humanistic" Marxism primarily focused on social history and with connections to working-class movements, and the forms of cultural critique informed both by the anti-
humanist Marxist tradition represented by Louis Althusser and the
poststructuralist historiography represented by Foucault and by redactions of Foucauldian criticism. These critics have been influenced by
Marxist notions, particularly the importance of the social, the category
of the historically constituted subject, the connection between socioeconomic and cultural forces in the reproduction of relations of power, and
a hermeneutics of suspicion. But this perspective would call into question several of the categories and arguments of previous Marxist his-
toriographical models, especially the notion of the ultimate knowability
of history and the relevance of historical process, but also the relative
significance of social class and class consciousness, the proposition of
an ultimate economic determinant, and the oppositional position of marginal ideological formations. Following Foucault in rejecting the notion
of a fixed historical ground, these critics describe history as a discursive
formation, and their commitment is to the problematization of truth
value, either in historical or in literary interpretation. Thus, no monolithic historical or political criticism dominates *The New Eighteenth
Century*.

While there has been much discussion recently about just what the
new historicism is, certain critical practices might be said to distinguish
it from older forms of Marxist cultural analysis and from "old" histo-

ricism. One difficulty is that the term is itself still ambiguous, though several common tendencies can be identified. In the first place, in new historicism, distinctions between a privileged category of the literary and other, nonliterary forms of cultural practice no longer hold. New historicists read the texts of legal, political, historical, and popular-cultural discourse alongside literary texts, as well as the texts of such sociopolitical events as revolutions. Some critics privilege the analysis of complex systems of power and control within dominant ideologies. And there is no assumption of a value-free objectivity prevailing in historical investigation; new historicism reflects upon its own priorities and assumptions as ideologically constructed while seeking to analyze the workings of ideological production in the cultural documents of the past. If previous historicist models assumed the unity and integrity of the dominant ideologies of the past, new historicism reads historical texts for gaps, fissures, and possibilities of incompletely articulated but emergent counterideologies.

Perhaps one danger in the "rise" of new historicism in America lies in its potential establishment as a new orthodoxy, particularly if it comes to be perceived as a flight from the theoretical possibilities of other poststructuralist movements such as deconstruction, or as an alternative to the more explicit political commitments of Marxism, feminism, and antiracist, postcolonial critiques. We would do well to ponder why American scholars have preferred the term "new historicism" to describe their enterprise, while in Britain there is discussion instead of cultural materialism. The most important work, we would argue, always insists on the relations between ideology, gender, race, and class, and on the functions of the oppressed and excluded in texts and cultural formations.

V

We see, then, among the most productive new directions for eighteenth-century studies, first, the formation of a broad and systematic critique of ideology, and second, a new interdisciplinarity concurrent with and attendant upon such a critique. The critique of ideology would be fully situated in history and culture, and informed by debates concerning class, gender, and race. Certainly feminists have long recognized the implications of sexual politics in the canon, the classroom, and critical practice. Now especially, materialist feminists are questioning the extent to which gender should compete for privilege over class and race. In addition, in working toward a politicized theoretical model that steps away from the essentialized "woman," feminists have found the new historicist attention to gender insufficient or apolitical. New historicism, however, is beginning to have a significant impact on many fields of literary study in its recognition of the way scholars partially invent the texts and cultures they study, and in noting the ways texts in history are actively made pertinent to present dilemmas. New historicism makes the category of the real problematic, and, in its various versions, places different degrees of emphasis on the relation of texts to history and material culture. In short, the current articulation of material feminisms with versions of Marxism and new historicism makes possible, we think, a convergence of various diffuse versions of political and historical criticism in ideology critique. And indeed, ideology in its many definitions is a locus of interest for nearly all our contributors.[14] Whether ideology means "false consciousness" (Marx), the "manifestation of the intimate contradictions by which society is lacerated" (Gramsci), the representation of our imaginary, lived relation to the real (Althusser), or an effect of the multiple forces that fashion an object (Eagleton), the essays included here in their various combinations of Marxism, new historicism, and feminism, acknowledge that our literary critical endeavors have uses and consequences. They serve implicit political purposes, often without our recognition of them, as we seek to isolate and identify the ideologies within which we are placed.

Such an acknowledgment forms the basis of the new interdisciplinarity toward which we hope this volume can point, an interdisciplinarity which would attempt to interrupt the established divisions among disciplines and remap the territory of the production of knowledge about the eighteenth century.[15] If eighteenth-century literary studies is to forge such a theoretically informed interdisciplinarity, it will have to become more skeptical about the traditional boundaries of the disciplines, largely formed in the nineteenth century, which confine the approaches and investigations of the eighteenth. As we have seen, eighteenth-century literary studies is traditionally interdisciplinary in one sense, and critics in the field, as well as the institution of ASECS, have often turned to history, continental literatures, and the fine arts. But this has been largely a juxtaposition of materials within an assumed theoretical consensus, rather than a systematic questioning of the methodologies that govern these disciplines and the boundaries that restrict them. If eighteenth-century literary studies is to recognize its own constraints, it will have to become more informed about the theoretical assumptions in other disciplines in order to subject them to careful scrutiny and revision—not only in the humanities, but in the social, physical, and life sciences as well.[16] The exact nature of a theoretically sophisticated crossing of disciplinary lines remains to be debated, but the confrontation with these questions holds the potential for disrupting past practices and creating a critique beyond disciplines that would be particularly applicable to eighteenth-century studies and that would have implications for other interdisciplinary fields of endeavor as well. Such a reformulation will require rigorous collaborative efforts of fresh and inventive kinds; it will require reconstructing writing, research, and teaching as truly collective activities. This reconfiguration of the field will also place pressure on current practices in the classroom and the profession; it will influence the way critics and teachers, as producers of syllabi and curricula, profess the eighteenth century. We think these new openings for a critique of ideology and for a revised and radical interdisciplinarity are signs of a renewed confidence in the efficacy of our own critical practices to influence the students we teach and to change the culture we inhabit. In the possibilities engendered by these unfamiliar conjunctions and contradictions we find new energy and new direction for eighteenth-century literary studies.

1

HISTORICIZING *ABSALOM AND ACHITOPHEL*

Michael McKeon

The aim of this essay is to demonstrate, within a brief compass, a Marxist method of literary criticism. My text will be *Absalom and Achitophel* (1681), generally regarded as John Dryden's greatest poem. My technique will be to "historicize" Dryden's poem by elaborating for it an increasingly inclusive historical context whose several stages augment the intelligibility of *Absalom and Achitophel* by successively enlarging the field in which it is able to become intelligible. By dividing this historicizing process into four separate stages—the "literary," the "religious," the "political," and the "socioeconomic"—my reading may (rightly) be felt to reflect the customary limits of disciplinary knowledge, our habit of distinguishing the study of "history" into its semiautonomous "parts." As the reading unfolds, however, it will become clear that these separate stages are also analogous to each other: that they are in a sense different "versions" of one another that repeat, in their "own" terms, a common theme or process; and that in this respect, the separate "parts" are also inseparable parts of a greater "whole."

This element of doubleness in the historicizing method—the simultaneous pursuit of parts and wholes—amounts to a dialectical method of knowledge that is central to Marxism. Beginning with what is conventionally understood as an autonomous whole—a poem, an object, a doctrine, an institution—according to the definitive terms of a limiting discourse (like those of the several disciplines), dialectical method sit-

uates that whole within a broader frame of reference so as to compre-
hend also its "partiality," its participation in a historical context on which
it fully depends for its significance. In the following attempt to historicize
Absalom and Achitophel, I will expand the context of the poem's intelligibility by explicitly invoking, as far as possible, the work of previous
critics of the poem. The special utility of this act of documentation will
become clear at my conclusion.

I Literary Succession

The dimension of history that is customarily available and pertinent
to literary criticism is, of course, that of literary history. Although Dryden himself situated *Absalom and Achitophel* within the line of Varronian
satire,[1] critics have long responded to the way the poem appears to place
itself within the epic or heroic tradition.[2] This is first of all the tradition
of Homer and Virgil; but attention has focused especially on Dryden's
allusive indebtedness to his great contemporary John Milton. And the
common estimate of this indebtedness has been rather straightforward:
Dryden imitates his master by invoking a Miltonic scheme of values that
validates his own, more limited exercise in poetic valuation. Central to
this Miltonic inheritance is what has been called Dryden's "mock-heroic" critique of Achitophel and his followers by the normative standard
of King David: for it is borrowed from Milton's own mock-heroic treatment of Satan, whose efforts to imitate God instead enact a parodic
negation of divine power.[3]
But despite the insistent Miltonisms ("Him Staggering so when Hells
dire Agent found" [373] being only the most ostentatious), more than
one critic has wondered at the eccentricity of Dryden's contribution to
the heroic line. Can a work so attenuated in structure and so deficient
in narrative movement really qualify as an epic poem? The question
throws Dryden's indebtedness into a more problematic light. At the very
least, are we not justified in extending the term "mock-heroic" from the
analogous relationships that subsist *within* the works of Milton and Dryden, to the instability of the relationship *between* the two poets? The
premise of mock-heroic is not succession but its impediments, and Dryden's attitude toward his own status as a poetic successor was never
simple. With respect to Milton, Dryden's critical judgments and poetic
practice combine an elevated esteem for the Puritan poet with a nagging
apprehension that he may already have been prevented in his own
accomplishments.[4]
Nor is this the full dimension of instability. Some critics have asked
if Dryden is likely to have engaged in so deferential an imitation of a

poet whose political and religious principles he thoroughly rejected.[5] Quite apart from matters of political difference, moreover, the parodic mechanism of mock-heroic is complicated enough to demand further thought. For despite attempts to simplify its workings,[6] mock-heroic is a profoundly unstable form that flourishes especially in periods of radical cultural crisis, when efforts to criticize the present by the absent authority of a precursor are intensified, but also stealthily subverted by the tendency of the critique to take in the putative authority as well. This subversive tendency is evident throughout the mock-heroic literature of the period; how much more inevitable must it be in poetry that self-consciously undertakes to accommodate the pagan tradition of heroic poetry to a Christian culture? If a case can be made that this is the undertaking of *Absalom and Achitophel*,[7] it is preeminently the project of *Paradise Lost*, whose explicit premise is not only the continuation but also the critique of the heroic tradition.[8] But this is then to say that Dryden's ambivalence about poetic "succession" is fully anticipated by Milton's. The kernel of truth in Blake's "satanist" reading of *Paradise Lost* is its recognition that the poem is charged with Milton's apprehension that his project is not Christian but Satanic in its ambition both to follow the false authority of the pagan fathers and to emulate the true Authority of the Father.[9] Anticipating Blake in the argument that Satan rather than Adam is the hero of *Paradise Lost*, Dryden himself acknowledged misgivings about Milton's position in the line of heroic poetry.[10]

So Dryden "succeeds" Milton most of all, perhaps, in having doubts about his own place in the poetic succession that may also be entertained (he believed with good reason) about Milton's. Like *MacFlecknoe* and a great deal more in Dryden's canon, *Absalom and Achitophel* evinces a fully "mock-heroic" ambivalence about its relation to its literary precursors.[11] The pattern of complication that is evident in this initial encounter with readings of *Absalom and Achitophel*—Dryden both invites and disturbs our expectations of a literary "succession"—will be fundamental to the following stages in its historicization.

II Spiritual Succession

Although his allusive relationship to the tradition of heroic poetry is one important dimension of Dryden's concern with succession, it is far less dominant in *Absalom and Achitophel* than the "religious" argument of succession that proceeds through his use of biblical typology. Indeed, the poem seems first of all to be "about" not English but Old Testament history. Scholars have shown that Dryden's identification of the Jewish with the English Nation, a commonplace of Protestant typology, is a departure from the earlier, pre-Reformation, typological tradition. In the traditional scheme, New Testament "antitype" succeeds Old Testament "type"—as Christ does Moses—in the sense of providing its spiritual completion and fulfillment. Protestant thought did not inaugurate the extension of this scheme of fulfillment beyond the scope of sacred history to the realm of contemporary events, but it made that extension common, even normative.

The importance of this Protestant innovation in typological argument is undeniable. Some scholars have seen the principal effect of correlating sacred with modern figures—with "correlative types" or "neotypes," as they have been called—as an intensification of personal and political expression, an investment of contemporary experience with the spiritualizing power of the sacred.[12] Others, however, have emphasized on the contrary the secularizing effects of the Protestant innovation.[13] Once the typological mode is extended to include not only sacred but modern secular history, the antitype occupies a position that is chronologically but not spiritually conclusive, and the mechanism of typological fulfillment is divided against itself. Sacred history loses its status as the central, overarching story into which all else fits, and becomes instead a past narrative like Roman history, useful in verifying and legitimating the events of our own, implicitly autonomous, period, which now occupies center stage.

How do these disparate views of Protestant typology influence the interpretation of its use in *Absalom and Achitophel*? Most critics note the numerous asymmetries in Dryden's correlation of Jewish and English history, the way he chooses to stress features of one narrative that have no equivalent in the other. This effect has encouraged a number of influential critics to recognize, in different ways, the centrality to Dryden's purpose of an "awareness of an incongruity" in the historical correlation on which *Absalom and Achitophel* is based, and they have tended to speak of his typology less as a method of spiritual ascription than as a technique of rhetorical persuasion, one among several systems of metaphor.[14] Many critics have also observed that Dryden's highly selective construction of the Jewish story from scattered elements of Old Testament history results in a narrative that is internally and ostentatiously anachronistic. This effect has been rationalized, unproblematically, as the sign of an aim to "establish a broad biblical framework"[15]; but it may also be felt to undermine the authority of Dryden's central text, 2 Samuel, as an integral and coherent history, let alone as sacred Scripture.

Perhaps the most compelling evidence, however, that Dryden would not have us take with utter seriousness the notion of a "typological succession" between Old Testament Jews and modern English people

is his early denial that the Jebusites, or Roman Catholics, had plotted
to kill the king:

> Some thought they God's Anointed meant to Slay
> By Guns, invented since full many a day:
> Our Author swears it not; but who can know
> How far the Devil and *Jebusites* may go?
>
> (130–33)

Here the anachronism is ostentatious not only in the way it is explicitly
asserted, but also because it consists in nothing less than the disruption
of sacred by secular history. Pushed "too far," the fiction of a typological
fulfillment suddenly explodes in our faces. Even the argument of a
merely secular historical succession or analogy is momentarily incapa-
citated, replaced instead by a self-conscious and playful skepticism that
insists that Israel is one thing and England quite another. At such a
moment, Dryden seems most interested in having us understand the
present in its essential autonomy and integrity, in having us judge the
current crisis (surprisingly enough) on its own terms.

The controversial appeal of reformed typology was of course irre-
sistible, since it allowed contemporaries to enlist the profoundly normative types and antitypes of sacred history in partisan defense of their
own favored "neotypes." The result was that over time, typological
interpretation became as plural and competitive as modern, secular
opinion itself. Dryden was as sensitive as any to the political exploitation
of typology, and *Absalom and Achitophel* might be said to reenact, in
miniature, the relativizing reduction of typological argument that had
been the fruit of the preceding several decades of intense political debate. It reenacts this debate by incorporating rival typologists whose
interpretations cannot be reconciled with one another. The principal
exegete is of course Dryden's speaker, among whose typological iden-
tifications are the succession that runs from the fallen fiends of Isaiah
and Jude to the rebels against David to the rebels against English monarchy; and the complementary succession from Satan to Achitophel to
Shaftesbury (144–45, 228–39). And the speaker's principal rival is Achitophel, who propounds a contrary typological succession that runs from
Lucifer to David and on to Charles (273–74).

Now, common sense may seem to argue that the effect of this exe-
getical contradiction is not at all to destabilize the authority of typological
argument, but rather to reinforce, by the implausibility of the false,
Whiggish exegete, the perspicuity of the true, Tory one.[16] The problem
with this is only in part that Achitophel's eloquent equations are not at
all implausible. It is also that in important respects, the rival exegetes

also agree in their readings. For on the one hand, Dryden's depiction
of Achitophel as the tempting Satan echoes especially the Miltonic temptation scene in *Paradise Regained*, and its corollary is therefore a typological succession of the tempted—running from Christ to Absalom to
Monmouth—that invites us to see the latter as a figure of Christ. Achitophel's interest in the Satan figure, on the other hand, focuses on
Charles's fallen state rather than on his rhetorical wiles, and this encourages a view of Monmouth not as one tempted toward sin, but as
the true and unfallen savior (230–40). But despite this difference, Achitophel's typological chain ends at the same point as Dryden's: for by
creating a succession from Moses to Christ to Absalom—and by implication on to Monmouth—he concurs with Dryden in his typological
identification of Monmouth as a Christ figure (as does "the Croud,"
727).

The effect of this odd concurrence—the unexpected dovetailing of
supposedly antithetical lines of advocacy—is unsettling, because it
seems momentarily to obscure and relativize the difference between
Dryden's and Shaftesbury's political positions. For a moment we are
made to feel a disturbing conjunction between the "studied arts" and
"plots" (208, 228)—both typological and conspiratorial—of the poet and
of his ostensible antagonist that is analogous to the disquieting proximity
of Milton and Satan in *Paradise Lost*.[17] What is actually relativized, I
believe, is not the substance of the political conflict but the mode of
typological advocacy, which is shown to be capable not only of supporting either side with equal plausibility, but even of reducing obvious
difference to identity. In fact, if we are fully satisfied with Dryden's
typological argument, we only repeat the credulity of Absalom—in effect
"fulfilling" his type—since Dryden portrays Monmouth's ambition as
blinding him, finally, to the ambiguity and vulnerability of Shaftesbury's
oratory. The effect of Dryden's oratory is instead to distance us both
from its tropes and from biblical history: to disclose the typological
framework *as* a trope rather than a transparent truth, an instrumental
use of religious argument that invites us to make a knowing engagement
in its fictionality without expecting from us a full-scale investment of
belief.

It is therefore going too far, no doubt, to say that *Absalom and Achitophel*
entails a "debasement" of Scripture and its typological exegesis, although the argument has been made with force and originality.[18] Closer
to the spirit of the poem, and to the "wit" that many critics have found
in its management of the typological succession, would be the notion
that in *Absalom and Achitophel* Dryden achieves a self-conscious *aesthe-
ticization* of typology. Several decades later, the deist Anthony Collins
would reflect the altered status of typological argument in language that

suggestively evokes Dryden's own stance: "For what is a *Poetick De-scription* fulfill'd, but a Typical Prophesy *fulfill'd?*"[19] Dryden's procedure insures that if we are persuaded by *Absalom and Achitophel*, it is not of a neotypological succession of the spirit that we are persuaded, but of a neotypological argument self-consciously and candidly deployed.

III Political Succession

To some critics, the political argument of *Absalom and Achitophel* has seemed clearly to depend on a notion of sovereignty as founded in the royal succession. The Exclusion Crisis of 1678–1681 challenged the con-tinuity of the Stuart monarchy by threatening to end in the exclusion of the rightful heir, the Duke of York, from succession. *Absalom and Achitophel* rebuts this challenge, it has been argued, by showing that the lawfulness of sovereignty requires the maintenance of the genealogical line of succession. In this view, the sovereignty argument that becomes explicit in Dryden's "passage on government" (759–810) is reinforced by the implicit argument of typological succession that suffuses the poem, and is scarcely separable from the emphasis on the authority of succession that is evident in Dryden's reliance on the theory of the divine right of kings and the patriarchal theory of political obligation.[20] Other critics, however, have found in the passage on government an argument not of lawful sovereignty but of expedient and skeptical "pragmatism." According to this very different reading, patriarchalism makes no ap-pearance in Dryden's program; in so far as he invokes the divine right of kings, it is given a "thoroughly pragmatic justification."[21] Finally, there is a third and mediating position that acknowledges the absence of a theory of sovereignty based on the authority of succession, but describes what is present in terms—"the conservative myth"—that do not clearly distinguish it from a position fully buttressed by notions of genealogical, patriarchal, and divine authority.[22]

I have already argued that Dryden "aestheticizes" the authority of typological succession even as he evokes its aura. As in that argument, it will be useful now to historicize Dryden's treatment of political sov-ereignty during the Exclusion Crisis by placing it in the context of a larger cultural crisis that had for some time been extending the appli-cation and destabilizing the meaning of "sovereignty."

At the beginning of the seventeenth century, divine right and the doctrine of the king's two bodies variously asserted the sempiternal existence of monarchal authority in ways that were quite compatible with the view that sovereignty was transmitted through a continuous royal succession. But parliament, having developed a theory of its own immemorial succession, broke the royal succession in the most dramatic means imaginable—by killing Charles I—and the ensuing experiments in Cromwellian kingship only weakened, for many people, the authority of the institution itself. The Restoration of Charles II was accompanied by the sanguine fiction that the Stuart succession had never lapsed. But by undermining the idea of parliament's historical continuity, royalist lawyers of the 1670s helped discredit the general principle of historical succession as fully as the regicides had done. The most telling events of the constitutional upheaval in which the Exclusion Crisis participated, however, are those that directly followed it. Seven years after the attempt to exclude the Duke of York from the succession had been defeated, royalists and parliamentarians joined together to depose him from the throne—also passing over fifty-seven more immediate heirs—in order to crown one whose Protestantism (and its pragmatic political implications) seemed far more important than his genealogical legitimacy or the "divinity" conventionally associated with it. At the very time when patriarchalist theory was receiving its fullest airing in England, divine right was being rearticulated so as to accommodate not only hereditary succession to, but also practical possession of, monarchal power. As William Sherlock, Dean of St. Paul's, put it, "It is all but Providence still, and I desire to know why the Providence of an [hereditary] Entail is more Sacred and Obligatory than any other Act of Providence, which gives a Setled possession of the Throne?"[23]

How does this context of crisis in the theory of royal sovereignty illuminate the political position of *Absalom and Achitophel*? Dryden's anticipation there of some of the "revolution principles" that would surface at the end of the decade is well described, I think, as that of "a proleptic intelligence."[24] The historicizing of the crisis may suggest, however, that his exercise of intelligence is less an anticipation of the future than a sensitivity to what is already there, already present in the contradictory development that thought undergoes at times of change before crystallizing and stabilizing into clearly delineated "doctrines." One way to attend to this contradictory presence is to acknowledge—as on the level of typological argument—the degree to which Dryden's stance on questions of political sovereignty approximated that of his opponent, Achitophel-Shaftesbury.

Now, we tend to remember best those passages in which Achitophel argues a contractual theory of government that would seem to be fundamentally incompatible with the principle of historical succession:

> And Nobler is a limited Command,
> Giv'n by the Love of all your Native Land,
> Than a Successive Title, Long, and Dark,

Drawn from the Mouldy Rolls of *Noah*'s Ark.
(299–302)

But Achitophel's contractual theory is not really incompatible with the legitimacy of succession. It simply "limits" or subordinates succession to the more basic principle of popular sovereignty. As Achitophel puts it, "Succession, for the general Good design'd,/In its own wrong a Nation cannot bind" (413–14). It is important to recognize that Achitophel's memorable lecture on the rights of the people has a basically secondary status, since it is occasioned by his acknowledgment to Absalom that a fuller theory of government may be required in the event that his primary plan for deposing York should fail. And the primary plan, fully appreciative of the instrumental value of succession, is to deny the king financial support "Till time shall Ever-wanting *David* draw,/To pass your doubtfull Title into Law" (407–8). In the same spirit, Achitophel reminds Absalom that if the movement against David can be led by "a Chief of Royal Blood," the cause will gain "Not barren Praise alone, . . . but solid Power" (294, 297–98). Thus succession remains an important principle in Achitophel's thinking, not because it really justifies political power but because it is conventionally allowed to do so.

How do Achitophel's arguments compare with those that Dryden speaks in his own voice? Despite claims that I have already cited, the patriarchalist argument is absent from *Absalom and Achitophel*. Adam enters the passage on government as the chronological ancestor not of kingly authority but of human depravity, which is entailed on us by his Original Sin (770–71). The relation between this act of entailment and matters of kingship is not chronological but analogical: just as Adam bound his future race in divine damnation, so the people bound their posterity in kingly subjection (765–76). Dryden's argument is not that royal sovereignty derives from the patriarchal power of Adam, but that the "Sovereign sway" of the people (780), once given up, cannot be resumed at will. And this is very important, because it means that Dryden is speaking within the basic assumptions of contractual rather than patriarchalist theory. Throughout the passage on government he argues in the conditional and the interrogative, entertaining Achitophel's contractual theory as a working hypothesis and dissenting only on the matter of whether such contracts between king and people are able (as he implicitly claims they are) to bind posterity beyond its will.

This is, of course, an important dissension: for it denies the popular limitation that Achitophel would impose upon the authority of royal succession once authority has been delegated, even as (for the sake of argument) it allows the original source of authority to lie with the people. Yet rather than pursue this relatively emphatic account of the authority of succession, Dryden now steps back, ironically granting his antagonist the full limits he would place upon the royal succession, and by this gesture shifting his defense of succession to the prudential and instrumental register.

> Yet, grant our Lords the People Kings can make,
> What Prudent men a setled Throne would shake?
> For whatsoe'r their Sufferings were before,
> That Change they Covet makes them suffer more.
> All other Errors but disturb a State;
> But Innovation is the Blow of Fate.
> If ancient Fabricks nod, and threat to fall,
> To Patch the Flaws, and Buttress up the Wall,
> Thus far 'tis Duty; but here fix the Mark:
> For all beyond it is to touch our Ark.
>
> (795–804)

Dryden's "setled Throne" is not the same as Sherlock's "Setled possession of the Throne," since it refers to an heir who is in the immediate line of succession rather than to one who disrupts it.[25] Nevertheless the climax of the passage on government has radically reconceived the principle of succession on what are aptly called "pragmatic" and prudential grounds. In these terms, the value of succession is not any essential authority it may possess or transmit, but its literal and sheer "successiveness," its synonymity with what is stable and "settled." Dryden defends the status quo most profoundly not on ethical or spiritual grounds, but because it is the status quo: a known rather than an unknown quantity. This does not preclude an appeal to the value-laden ideas of genealogical, patriarchal, and divine succession, as the rest of Dryden's poem demonstrates. It defines the enormous utility of such an appeal by delicately denying succession the status, beyond all utility, of a value in itself. The delicacy of the distinction is crucial: what in Achitophel-Shaftesbury is depicted as the artifice of cynical opportunism becomes in Dryden himself the consummate art of political poetry. But the delicate conjunction is also crucial: for a moment liberalism and the modern version of conservatism cross paths at their origins before parting ways.

David's concluding address extends the emphasis achieved by the passage on government, although in other terms. The king's refrain—his dual access to "Law" and to "Power"—invites us to see his prophesied exercise of power as legitimated by law while leaving the actual, effective relationship between the two in some uncertainty (see 991–94, 999–1003, 1023–24). Which is it, power or the law, that rationalizes and justifies the other? Is "law" equivalent to "legitimacy," or to the power of legal enforcement? In David's concluding speech it is not easy to answer these questions. In fact, his most consistent tone in this speech is less that of studied moderation or rueful regret, than the self-consciously droll and waggish air of one who dutifully invokes (like all other actors in the crisis) the several models of legitimate rule, while transparently pursuing the underlying pragmatics of power:[26]

> A King's at least a part of Government,
> And mine as requisite as their Consent:
> . . .
> My Pious Subjects for my Safety pray,
> Which to Secure they take my Power away.
> . . .
> What then is left but with a Jealous Eye
> To guard the Small remains of Royalty?
> (977–78, 983–84, 989–90)

Thus the king responds to political crisis as the poet does, by relaxing the relationship between policy and its legitimation, between advocacy and its persuasive tropes, into an instrumental one that ostensibly saves appearances in order to get the job done.

In Dryden's eyes, the "job" that must be done is not to convince his readers that the political polarization achieved by the Exclusion Crisis represents an absolute ethical (let alone spiritual) choice. It is rather to provide them with a compelling model of decisive action whose ethical empowerment is quite sufficient to the task but in the end unnecessary to its achievement, which after all will require a very different show of power. Dryden's muted insistence on the difference between these two sorts of power recalls the strategic movement that I have found constant in his several engagements with the idea of "succession"—that is, the distinction between its essential or immanent value, which is subject to skeptical questioning, and its instrumental or "aesthetic" value, which requests our suspended disbelief in the fiction. In the concluding section of the poem, the compelling model before us is the king, whose "Sword of Justice" will now supply the real power that was heretofore only implicit in, and obstructed by, the ethical power of his "Mercy" (1002, 1004). But Charles is also the most important of Dryden's readers, and the poet hopes to make him take to heart the model he has constructed, to become a sophisticated reader whose belief in the fiction of royalty's absolute ethical empowerment is not so total that it usurps the place of real power.

From another perspective, however, the compelling model of decisive action is also Dryden himself. If artful Achitophel-Shaftesbury is the dangerous, negative reflection of the poet, the prophet David-Charles is his positive foil. In the preface to *Absalom and Achitophel*, Dryden uses the figure of the body politic to argue a parallel between the king's and the poet's management of crisis. Thus the end of the poet is *"the amendment of Vices by correction,"* much as the physician might prescribe *"harsh Remedies to an inveterate Disease"* ("To the Reader," 5). By the same token, Dryden later observes that Charles's counsellors have shown him "that no Concessions from the Throne woud please,/But Lenitives fomented the Disease" (925–26). Dryden is one of those counsellors both by advice and by example, and the counsel of *Absalom and Achitophel* is an approach to poetry and politics that effectively demystifies both by disclosing the instrumental role of pleasing myths and fictions in each pursuit. To be effective, poetry and politics must emulate the harshness of the practices they would amend. This requires not the total abandonment of "lenitives" and pleasing fictions, but the self-conscious and pragmatic use of them as a means toward an end. And Dryden poetically exemplifies this advice at the conclusion of *Absalom and Achitophel* when he shows how the pleasing and movingly allusive invocation of the muse (854, 898) can deepen the pathos of the crisis without obviating the call for bloody vengeance that alone can end it.

IV   Socioeconomic Succession

The superiority of York's over Monmouth's claim lies in the fact that Monmouth, being the bastard son of the king, can provide no "True Succession" to the throne, whereas York, the king's younger brother and first in the "Collateral Line," in the absence of a "Lawfull Issue" must be the "next Successor" (16, 351, 352, 401). More than one critic has observed how vital the theme of familial inheritance is to the political argument of *Absalom and Achitophel* as well as to its larger scheme of values.[27] The poem is centrally "about" fathers and sons: not only Charles and Monmouth, but also Shaftesbury and his son and Ormonde and his son (169–72, 829–39). Matters of inheritance are stressed in the accounts of both of these familial relationships, and each (it has been argued) may be understood to define, respectively, the negative and positive poles of legitimate inheritance between which Charles and Monmouth are suspended in uneasy mediation. Is it plausible to see genealogical legitimacy as the normative foundation of value in *Absalom and Achitophel*? How is our answer to this question, and our reading of the poem, affected by historicizing its undoubted concern with matters of genealogy and legitimacy?

"Aristocratic" cultures assume a general correspondence between birth and worth, "status" and "virtue," genealogical and "internal" nobility. Seventeenth-century England experienced a breakdown in this aristocratic fiction, a major crisis in attitudes toward the relation between individual capacity and external validation (and one that is important to the contemporaneous constitutional crisis regarding the idea of political sovereignty). The crisis has several dimensions—demographic, socioeconomic, and intellectual. Early in the century, the Stuart monarchy multiplied so heedlessly the sale of titles of nobility to wealthy commoners that it precipitated an "inflation of honors" that seriously challenged the presumed consistency of birth and worth. In the middle decades, a sharp population decline threatened so severely the norm of direct male descent that patrilineal principles could be maintained only by resort to obvious fictions that underscored the artificiality of the genealogical line.

During the same period, inheritance laws were reformed by the invention of the device of the "strict settlement," which in seeking to adjudicate the several competing interests of life tenant, male heir, younger sons and daughters, and the estate itself, inevitably accentuated the fact of intrafamilial competition and the deeply problematic nature of the idea of a just inheritance. Moreover, growing skepticism about the purity of aristocratic blood and the continuity of aristocratic successions was fueled by evidence, generated through widespread and rapid social mobility, that the relationship between power, wealth, and genealogical status was not a social given but a complex variable. One consequence of these changes may be the extraordinary increase in illegitimate births in England from the later seventeenth to the later eighteenth century. As a percentage of all first births, the illegitimacy rate rose during this period from twelve to an astonishing fifty percent. And the rising toleration of bastardy implies a corollary skepticism regarding genealogical standards of legitimacy. It is not surprising that the traditional values of aristocratic rank, nobility, and honor were profoundly destabilized by this crisis, nor that there arose enormous interest in a spectrum of social types—bastards, younger sons, possessors of "true" but not inherited nobility—whose "status inconsistency" crystallized the injustice of aristocratic culture, and whose popularity bespoke its concurrent demise.[28]

The opening of *Absalom and Achitophel*, whose witty acknowledgment of David's vulnerability to criticism has engaged and divided critics, economically achieves two related but divergent ends. It announces at the outset the crucial fact that Absalom could not participate in a "True Succession," and it suggests that this condition nonetheless does not contain the whole "truth" of succession. "With secret Joy, indulgent

David view'd/His Youthfull Image in his Son renew'd" (31–32). Absalom
is a bastard, a "Natural" son whose natural "grace," Dryden says, proclaims the presence of a natural if not a legal succession (28–29). In
emphasizing this perspective on Absalom, as he does throughout the
poem, Dryden identifies him as an exemplar of status inconsistency, a
culture hero who advertises the arbitrary nature of aristocratic assumptions and the poignant separation, in the real world, of virtue and status,
"nature" and "law," inward capacity and outward legitimacy. As Dryden depicts him, the bastard prince is very like the protagonist of family
romance, the divided product of two incommensurate familial lines:

> I find, I find my mounting Spirits Bold,
> As *David*'s Part disdains my Mothers mold.
> Why am I Scanted by a Niggard Birth?
> My Soul Disclaims the Kindred of her Earth.
>
> (367–70)

Absalom sees the inconsistency of his birth and his worth as the perversely arbitrary trick of fate:

> Yet oh that Fate Propitiously Enclind,
> Had rais'd my Birth, or had debas'd my Mind;
> To my large Soul, not all her Treasure lent,
> And then Betray'd it to a mean Descent.
>
> (363–66)

And Dryden's speaker, although he does not quite echo Absalom's
youthful self-regard, is yet in substantial and sympathetic agreement:
"How happy had he been, if Destiny/Had higher plac'd his Birth, or
not so high!" (481–82).

Of course, Absalom is no more the "hero" of *Absalom and Achitophel*
than is Achitophel. The seventeenth-century critique of aristocratic culture denied the essential value of aristocratic birth, its presumed and
automatic signification of personal worth. But the detachment of birth
from worth could have very different ideological implications. Dryden's
conservatism denies birth and the principle of succession any essential
value, but grants them an instrumental value in the rationalization of
the social order. And he distinguishes this attitude from what might be
called the liberal alternative, which refuses the pragmatic revaluation of
birth and succession and consigns them to the realm of the utterly val-
ueless. It is from this liberal perspective that Absalom might be made
to possess heroic stature, the mere commoner who triumphantly dem-

onstrates his inner virtue by extraordinary achievement. In *Absalom and Achitophel*, the figure of Corah (Titus Oates) serves to parody this peculiarly modern sort of heroism. "What tho his Birth were base," asks Dryden. "By that one Deed" of concocting the Popish Plot he "Enobles all his Bloud" (636, 641). "Prodigious Actions may as well be done/By Weavers issue, as by Princes Son" (638–39).The falsity of this liberal heroism Dryden links to that of Calvinism, whose devotees, "Born to be sav'd," in effect invent a new method of signifying "worth" by "birth" that is far more insidious than that of patrilineal succession since its signifying mechanism is nothing but belief itself (539–40). Succession at least has the sanction of "laws" that, however arbitrary they ultimately may be, are still external to the subjective convictions of the individual, who always will be prepared to feel his special virtue and to demonstrate it through worldly achievement.

This is the sort of opportunism that Dryden depicts by playing on the word "successful" in Achitophel's voice. For Achitophel, David attained the throne not because he was in the line of succession but because "his successfull Youth" seized the opportunity when it fleetingly presented itself in 1660 (266). By the same token, Achitophel boasts that "All sorts of men by my successful Arts" have been estranged from David and his royal succession (289), hoping even with these words to alienate Absalom himself from the necessity of a "Successive Title" (301). So the opposition between the royal "succession," and personal "success" unconstrained by any external system of legality, is an important means by which Dryden limits the instability of his instrumental valuation of succession. That the instability cannot be eradicated, however, is clear from the fact—evident on all levels of the poem's procedure—that Dryden is firmly tied to his antagonist in questioning the argument of succession that has seemed to some to underwrite the entire value system of *Absalom and Achitophel*.

V Conclusion

What are the fruits of this exercise in historicizing *Absalom and Achitophel*? To historicize a literary work is not just to situate it "against" a "background," since this would be only to provide a static focus on the work with a static historical setting. The aim of historicizing is instead to remind us that the literary "work" itself partakes of historical process: that it is a strenuous and exacting labor of discourse that seems thereby to detach itself from its historical medium, but that bears within its own composition the distinguishing marks of its continuity with the world it has ostensibly left behind. From one perspective, this dialectical dis-

covery—the literary work as historical process—may seem to imply a
view of the work as "partial," one fleeting "part" of a more comprehensive movement, and therefore "partial" also in the sense of ideological limitation or bias. The notion of the literary work as ideology,
partial to a particular view of things (whether or not it has, like *Absalom
and Achitophel*, an immediately "political" relevance), is accurately associated with Marxist criticism. But the connection between ideological
and dialectical "partiality" can also shed light "in the other direction,"
as it were, by illuminating the dialectical fluidity that inheres in Marx's
idea of ideological bias.

For ideology, rightly understood, does not simply "distort" and "conceal." Its purpose is to resolve difficult problems so as to make them
not simple but comprehensible, to provide an explanation of reality
whose plausibility will depend on the degree to which it appears to do
justice to the reality it explains. Ideology "works" simultaneously to
conceal and to represent with plausibility, to distort and to naturalize
by moderating its effects. My reading of *Absalom and Achitophel* suggests
several ways in which this contradictory aspect of ideology can be discerned. I have shown, for example, that Dryden's unquestionable advocacy of the Stuart succession—its biased "partiality"—is deepened
throughout the poem by the subtle and disarming acknowledgment that
the foundation of royalist advocacy, "succession," is under "part-own-
ership," a rhetorical commonplace shared by a spectrum of political
causes. In a pamphlet published in the same year as *Absalom and Achitophel*, Dryden remarked of his Whig antagonists: "How many, and
how contradicting Interests are there to be satisfied!"[29] A historicized
reading of *Absalom and Achitophel* shows that it, too, encloses a set of
"contradicting interests" within its ostensibly single-minded unity. Perhaps the most striking sign of this contradiction is the way the boundaries between Dryden's speaker and his antagonist Achitophel are
blurred at crucial moments, so that the discrete and antithetical
"wholes" of Whig and Tory are for an instant experienced as correlative
parts of a larger historical movement.

But the foregoing account of Dryden's poem also provides, in its dependence on the combined and often contradictory interpretations of
many critics, another access to the nature of ideological "partiality." In
seeking to construct a fuller, because more historicized, interpretation
of *Absalom and Achitophel* out of the seemingly incompatible readings of
others, I have been guided by the assumption that these readings are
not "wrong" but partial. I have seen them, that is, as contributory components of a dialectical whole whose interpretive value depends entirely
on the fact of its inner contradictions, which bespeak the nature not only
of literary, but also of literary-critical, composition.

A final way of appreciating the contradictory, ideological nature of *Absalom and Achitophel* is to observe that its "biased" defense of particular "interests" is occasioned, and necessarily colored, by their critical endangerment. The dangerously shifting ground of crisis is inseparable from the effort at ideological stabilization it evokes, which proclaims its persistent affiliation to crisis in the very attempt to overcome and negate it. Marxism would have us see all of history as "unstable" and "in crisis," a contradictory unity divisible into antagonistic periods each of which replicates, in its "own" domain, the tensions of dialectical process. At the same time, it encourages us to discriminate those crucial historical moments when crisis seems to be redoubled and intensified. Such moments can be known by the way the deep and perpetual contradictions of historical process force themselves to the surface of historical consciousness in the palpable form of warfare, social disruption, or the sort of cultural crisis—so evident in Dryden's delicate deployment of "succession"—that entails the transformation of an entire system of cultural values.

I have already said enough, perhaps, about the character of the cultural revolution that Dryden mediates with such virtuosity in *Absalom and Achitophel*. But it may be useful to end with a few remarks on its more specifically literary implications. I have suggested that at every stage of his argument, Dryden may be said to "aestheticize" the terms of his advocacy, to dislodge the value of "succession" from the essentialist realm of absolute value and implicit belief and offer it instead as a pleasing fiction in which we are asked to make a self-conscious investment. This spirit of detachment can be seen as well in Dryden's approach to the genre of his poem. So far from subscribing to a "traditionalistic" attitude toward generic identity as definitive and exclusive in its prescriptions, he playfully entertains all possibilities—the poem is both an impartial history and an invented satire, its subject is both ancient Jews and modern Whigs and Tories—in such a way as to suggest that the larger purposes of the poem may be served well enough by a sophisticated and well-modulated species of assent to its central fiction ("To the Reader," 3–5). The aestheticizing detachment that controls the procedure of *Absalom and Achitophel* is by no means typical of its period, but I believe it is prescient not only of the modern decay of the strict system of genre, but also of the modern rise of the belief in aesthetic detachment and autonomy. In *Absalom and Achitophel*, Dryden proposes a model of a new sort of poetry, which draws power and value from the realms of religious faith, political allegiance, and historical factuality while evading subservience to them all. The realm of the aesthetic, an invention of the Enlightenment, came into being in the interstices of those other realms, imitating them and internalizing versions of their disparate modes of authority as its own, unique amalgam.[30] One of our great "political" poems, *Absalom and Achitophel* also helps inaugurate the distinctively modern conviction that "politics," and the aesthetic autonomy of "poetry," are by their very nature incompatible.

2

THE ROMANCE OF EMPIRE:
Oroonoko and the Trade in Slaves

Laura Brown

> Our victims know us by their scars and by their chains, and it is this that
> makes their evidence irrefutable. It is enough that they show us what we
> have made of them for us to realize what we have made of ourselves.
>
> Jean-Paul Sartre, Preface to Frantz Fanon's *The Wretched of the Earth*[1]

I

Aphra Behn's novella *Oroonoko: Or, the Royal Slave*, written and published in the summer of the year of the 1688 revolution in England,[2]
no longer needs an extensive introduction for students of Restoration
and eighteenth-century literature, or even for many critics in other
fields. *Oroonoko* has almost entered the canon, as works by Behn and
other women writers have been recovered by Anglo-American feminist
criticism. The novella *Oroonoko* and the dramatic satire *The Rover*,
Behn's two most important works, both saw new printings in the late
1960s and early 1970s.[3] And Behn herself has recently been the subject
of two critical biographies, by Maureen Duffy and Angeline Goreau—
the first significant studies since George Woodcock's *Incomparable Aphra*

I would like to thank Walter Cohen, Judy Frank, Jeff Nunokawa, Felicity Nussbaum,
and Mark Seltzer for their help with early versions of this article.

in 1948.[4] But Woodcock was clearly an anomaly: an anarchist critic in
the early stages of the Cold War, exploring issues of feminism and racism
while others in the field were consolidating the New Critical paradigm.
The only prior attention to Behn had been a brief skirmish initiated by
Ernest Bernbaum in 1913 about the historical question of Behn's trip to
Guiana, the geographical setting of *Oroonoko*.[5]

Now we can find *Oroonoko* even in the undergraduate curriculum on
occasion, and according to the *MLA Bibliography* two or three articles on
Behn appear each year—treating matters of gender and genre.[6] Feminist
criticism has opened up *Oroonoko* to readers who twenty-five years ago
would have stuck to Dryden, Rochester, or Congreve. But even though
that feminist revision has been significant—especially for projects in
political criticism like this one—the recovery of *Oroonoko* was quite unnecessary. In another tradition of cultural criticism apparently inacces-
sible to the feminist revisionists who "recovered" Behn for students of
literature, *Oroonoko* has long held a prominent place. The novella has
been recognized as a seminal work in the tradition of antislavery writings
from the time of its publication down to our own period. The story of
Behn's "royal slave" occupied the English stage for almost a century,
in dramatic redactions by Thomas Southerne (*Oroonoko*, 1696) and John
Hawkesworth (a revision of Southerne's play, 1759). And its sentimental
authenticity was confirmed and augmented by the famous occasion in
1749 when an African "prince" and his companion, previously sold into
slavery but ransomed by the British government and received in state
in London, attended a performance of Southerne's *Oroonoko*: affected
"with that generous grief which pure nature always feels, and which
art had not yet taught them to suppress; the young prince was so far
overcome, that he was obliged to retire at the end of the fourth act. His
companion remained, but wept the whole time; a circumstance which
affected the audience yet more than the play, and doubled the tears
which were shed for *Oroonoko* and *Imoinda*."[7] Historians of slavery have
never neglected *Oroonoko*. In the two most important accounts of literary
treatments of slavery that deal with eighteenth-century England, Wylie
Sypher's *Guinea's Captive Kings* (1942) and David Brion Davis's *The Problem of Slavery in Western Culture* (1966), Oroonoko figures prominently
as a significant and even prototypical character in "a vast literature depicting noble African slaves" (Davis, 473), a crucial early text in the
sentimental, antislavery tradition that grew steadily throughout the
eighteenth century.[8]

Perhaps the feminist failure to attend to the primary concern of *Oroonoko* is partially due to the general neglect of race and slavery among
critics of eighteenth-century literature. This is the period of the largest
slave trade in history, when at least six million human beings were

forcibly transported across an ocean, to produce a massive new work force on two continents and in the islands of the West Indies. England's economic participation in the slave trade, especially after the Peace of Utrecht in 1713 and the acquisition of the Asiento—the exclusive right to supply slaves to the West Indies—has been extensively documented.[9] For over forty years literary critics have had access to Sypher's exhaustive description of the pervasive references to slavery in the literature of the period, from William Dodd and Thomas Bellamy to Daniel Defoe and James Thomson. If critics in the field have been almost universally oblivious to race, feminists have only followed suit.

Thus, while *Oroonoko* is certainly a crucial text in the tradition of women's literature and in the development of the novel; while it supplies us with an interesting early example of the problematic stance of a self-consciously female narrator; and while it demonstrates almost programmatically the tensions that arise when romance is brought together with realism; it demands at this conjuncture a broader political reevaluation. *Oroonoko* can serve as a theoretical test case for the necessary connection of race and gender—a model for the mutual interaction of the positions of the oppressed in the literary discourse of its own age, and a mirror for modern criticism in which one political reading can be seen to reflect another, one revisionist school a plurality of revisions. Sartre's juxtaposition in the epigraph to this essay—"what we have made of them" and "what we have made of ourselves"—suggests the reciprocal movement necessary for such a political revisionism, both within the treatment of specific texts and in the discipline of literary studies at large. In Sartre's reading of Fanon, that reciprocity is the prerequisite for a relationship of mutual knowledge between the colonizer and the colonized. In this reading of *Oroonoko*, the figure of the woman in the imperialist narrative—a sign of "what we have made of ourselves"—provides the point of contact through which the violence of colonial history—"what we have made of them"—can be represented.

The conjunction of race and gender in the study of ideology and literary culture might seem almost automatic, since recent work on colonial and third-world literature has been so strongly dependent on the same analytical category that has underwritten much contemporary feminist theory: the notion of the "other." The staging of the relationship of alterity has taken many forms in contemporary theory. Beginning perhaps with the Hegelian scenario—and the paradigmatic play between master and slave—the "other" can be internalized as a dimension of the psychological dynamic, or externalized as an account of social forms—producing, on the one hand, psychic models like that of the conscious and unconscious or the imaginary and symbolic, or sociological or anthropological paradigms like that of the in-group and the out-group or the cooked and the raw. Feminist critics have drawn widely from these interconnected dualisms to describe the position of women in patriarchal culture. More recently, third-world critics have consistently utilized the category of the "other" in accounts of the relationship of colonizer and colonized, Occident and Orient, European and native, white and black. But with the exception of Gayatri Chakravorty Spivak, neither group has used the concurrence of terms as the occasion for a congruence of critiques. The force of Spivak's work, in this context, has been in her insistence on the distortions that occur when a feminist approach fails to take cognizance of colonialism and, reciprocally, in her reading of the literary culture of colonizer and colonized through the figure of the woman.[10] For most recent critics of colonial and neocolonial literature, however, gender enters not at all into the analysis of imperialist ideology. Such a striking irony is perhaps symptomatic of a constraint implicit in these dualisms—a binary logic that militates against the dialectical argument at which this essay aims.

In addition to forestalling the conjunction of critical accounts of race and gender, the category of the "other" works to hold apart the historical categories of imperialist and native. This dualism is in part politically necessary: it enables Edward Said to detail the massive, diffuse spectrum of discursive power controlled by the colonizer, and gives Frantz Fanon a powerful terminology in which to advocate revolutionary struggle. For Said "Orientalism" is a discourse of power, a "distribution of geopolitical awareness" into various cultural forms—"aesthetic, scholarly, economic, sociological, historical, and philological"—by which the Occident creates and concurrently intends to understand, "control, manipulate, even to incorporate" the Oriental "other."[11] His study, then, documents and demystifies the discourse of the Occident from the perspective of the Third World, just as, from the same perspective but with the alternative strategy, Fanon's writings articulate the interests of the colonized—recounting, theorizing, and ultimately advocating a struggle to the death, through the absolute and violent conflict in the colonial world between the settler and the native.[12]

Following Fanon, Abdul JanMohamed provides perhaps the most schematic model for the role of the "other" in the critique of colonialism. He argues that "the dominant model of power- and interest-relations in all colonial societies is the manichean opposition between the putative superiority of the European and the supposed inferiority of the native."[13] For JanMohamed, colonialist ideology and literary culture are constituted by a choice of identity with or difference from the "other." and Tzvetan Todorov, in his account of "the conquest of America"— an account, in his words, of "the discovery the *self* makes of the *other"*[14]—depends, perhaps more systematically than any other critic of colonialism, upon the argument from alterity. For Todorov, Columbus, like "every colonist in his relations to the colonized," conceives of the native according to the "two component parts" of alterity, absolute identity or absolute difference (42).

Said, Fanon, JanMohamed, and Todorov locate the "other" in the historical struggle between the colonizer and the native. Homi Bhabha focuses instead upon an intrinsic otherness, the difference within the colonial subject, whether colonizer of colonized. When the dominant discourse of colonialism attempts the representation of the native, "other 'denied' knowledges enter upon the dominant discourse and estrange the basis of its authority."[15] Thus although Bhabha argues directly against a "power struggle between self and Other, or . . . mother culture and alien cultures" (153), he does posit within the colonial subject a division that reproduces the dualism we have already observed. This position raises the problem of the status of opposition for some critics who adopt the perspective of alterity. Though Bhabha claims that "the discursive conditions of dominance [turn] into the grounds of intervention" (154), his argument suggests that opposition is contained within the production of colonial power, that the only autonomy that remains for the native "other" resides within the dominant colonial discourse. This notion of the pervasive, preemptive nature of power is often evoked by American Foucauldian critics and is defined by Stephen Greenblatt in a recent essay on Shakespeare's second *Henriad*. Discussing the "alien voices," the "alien interpretations" encountered by the first English settlers in Virginia, Greenblatt claims that "subversiveness, as I have argued, was produced by the colonial power in its own interest."[16] Here the category of the "other" privileges the position of power while minimizing the possibility of resistance.

Productive and important as this binary opposition has proven, then, it seems nevertheless to have stymied a genuinely dialectical critique of colonial culture. It forecloses an approach that works through alterity to the interaction that may occur even in an oppressive relationship. And it sometimes also precludes finding a place for the struggles of the native in the complex edifices of power that seem to contain all resistance.[17] But the ideal of moving beyond absolute difference has been raised repeatedly by recent critics. Todorov ends with the hopeful assertion that "self-knowledge develops through knowledge of the Other" (254). He seeks ultimately to locate a position beyond difference: "We need not be confined within a sterile alternative: either to justify colonial wars . . . or to reject all interaction with a foreign power . . . Nonviolent communication exists, and we can defend it as a value" (182). Jan-Mohamed too imagines a "syncretic possibility," theoretically available through the dialectic upon which his manichean opposition is founded, but present in practice only as an unrealized negative example ("Economy," 65), symptomatic of the difficulty of transcending alterity. In the same way, Said turns to the "human" at the end of *Orientalism*: "I consider Orientalism's failure to have been a human as much as an intellectual one . . . Orientalism failed to identify with human experience, failed also to see it as human experience." "Without 'the Orient' there would be scholars, critics, intellectuals, human beings, for whom the racial, ethnic, and national distinctions were less important than the common enterprise of promoting human community" (328). "Communication," "syncretic possibility," "human community"—however it is named, this gesture outside the "other" is at best an adjunctive, utopian moment, attractive but obviously extraneous to the argument from alterity. It gives us a sentiment without a method; we can derive from these examples inspiration, but not critical practice.

My treatment of *Oroonoko* is extensively indebted to these critics, but it seeks to avoid what I see as the theoretical pitfalls of the "other" and to substitute the dialectical notion of what Johannes Fabian, in a critique of modern anthropological writing, calls "radical contemporaneity" (xi). Focusing on the discipline's constitutive use of time as a distancing mechanism, on temporalizations placing the native in the "primitive" past or in a "passage from savagery to civilization, from peasant to industrial society" (95), Fabian argues that this systematic "denial of coevalness" (31) has operated in the ideological service of colonialism and neocolonialism by concealing the fact that "anthropology's Other is, ultimately, other people who are our contemporaries" (143). Fabian proposes that anthropologists "seek ways to meet the Other on the same ground, in the same Time" (164). His notion of radical contemporaneity is based on the Marxian theory of history as embodied in the formations of the present, on a view of "the totality of historical forces, including their cotemporality at any given time" (158). Radical contemporaneity serves "as the condition for truly dialectical confrontation between persons as well as societies. It militates against false conceptions of dialectics—all those watered-down binary abstractions which are passed off as oppositions: left vs. right, past vs. present, primitive vs. modern. . . . What are opposed, in conflict, in fact, locked in antagonistic struggle, are not the same societies at different stages of development, but different societies facing each other at the same Time" (155). For Fabian "the anthropologist and his interlocutors only 'know' when they meet each other in one and the same cotemporality" (164).

The critic of literary culture can rarely argue that either she or the colonialist author and her characters "meet the Other on the same ground, in the same Time" (164). But from the perspective of radical contemporaneity, the texts of colonialism reveal signs of the dialectical confrontations embodied in the historical formations of the period. Though the colonialist and the native may never "know" one another or their historical present, we can perhaps come to know something of both. The aim of this critical project, then, is to demonstrate the contemporaneity of issues of race and gender in a particular stage in the history of British capitalism associated broadly with commodity exchange and colonialist exploitation. Their conjunction in this particular text is sufficient to demonstrate the value of a pragmatic dialectical criticism, and indeed the political importance of refusing to posit any opposition as absolute.

II

As a test case for "radical contemporaneity," *Oroonoko* may seem at first to provide a rather recalcitrant model: the novella lends itself with great readiness to the argument from alterity. Indeed, Behn's opening description of "royal slave," Oroonoko, is a *locus classicus* of the trope of sentimental identification, by which the native "other" is naturalized as a European aristocrat. In physical appearance, the narrator can barely distinguish her native prince from those of England:

> [Oroonoko] was pretty tall, but of a Shape the most exact that can be fancy'd: The most famous Statuary cou'd not form the Figure of a Man more admirably turn'd from head to foot . . . His Nose was rising and *Roman*, instead of *African* and flat. His mouth the finest shaped that could be seen; far from those great turn'd Lips, which are so natural to the rest of the Negroes. The whole Proportion and Air of his Face was so nobly and exactly form'd, that bating his Colour, there could be nothing in Nature more beautiful, agreeable and Handsome. (8)

If this account of Oroonoko's classical European beauty makes it possible to forget his face, the narrator's description of his character and accomplishments further elaborates the act of absolute identity through which he is initially represented:

> Nor did the Perfections of his Mind come short of those of his Person; and whoever had heard him speak, wou'd have been convinced of their Errors, that all fine Wit is confined to the white Men, especially to those of Christendom . . . 'twas amazing to imagine . . . where 'twas he got that real Greatness of Soul, those refined Notions of true Honour, that absolute Generosity, and that Softness that was capable of the highest Passions of Love and Gallantry. . . . the most illustrious Courts could not have produced a

braver Man, both for Greatness of Courage and Mind, a Judgment more
solid, a Wit more quick, and a Conversation more sweet and diverting. He
knew almost as much as if he had read much: He had heard of and admired
the *Romans*: He had heard of the late Civil Wars in *England*, and the deplorable Death of our great Monarch; and wow'd discourse of it with all
the Sense and Abhorrence of the Injustice imaginable. He had an extreme
good and graceful Mien, and all the Civility of a well-bred great Man. He
had nothing of Barbarity in his Nature, but in all Points address'd himself
as if his Education had been in some *European* Court. (8, 7)

Oroonoko is thus not only a natural European and aristocrat, but a
natural neoclassicist and Royalist as well, an absurdity generated by the
desire for an intimate identification with the "royal slave." Like Columbus in Todorov's account, Behn's narrator seems to have only two
choices: to imagine the "other" either as absolutely different and hence
inferior, or as identical and hence equal. The obvious mystification involved in Behn's depiction of Oroonoko as a European aristocrat in
blackface does not necessarily damage the novella's emancipationist reputation: precisely this kind of sentimental identification was in fact the
staple component of antislavery narratives for the next century and a
half, in England and America. But the failure of Behn's novella to see
beyond the mirror of its own culture here raises the question of Behn's
relationship with the African slave.

For not only is the novella's protagonist an aristocratic hero, but his
story is largely constructed in the tradition of heroic romance. Briefly,
Oroonoko, a noble African prince, falls in love with Imoinda, the daughter of his aristocratic foster-father. The two are divided first by the intervention of the King, Oroonoko's grandfather, who covets Imoinda
for himself, and then by their independent sale into slavery. Reunited
in Suriname, the British colony in Guiana where Behn was a visitor,
Oroonoko and Imoinda are at first promised their freedom, then lead a
slave rebellion, and finally die—Imoinda at the hands of Oroonoko,
Oroonoko (known, as a slave, by the name of Caesar) executed by the
colonists. Oroonoko's exploits follow closely the pattern outlined by
Eugene Waith for the "Herculean hero," the superhuman epic protagonist who plays a major role in heroic form from the classical period
through the Renaissance.[18] Oroonoko is invincible in battle, doing sin-
glehandedly "such things as will not be believed that Human Strength
could perform" (30). He is also a man of wit and address, governed
absolutely by his allegiance to the conventional aristocratic code of love
and honor. When he declares his love to Imoinda, for instance, it is
voiced entirely in the familiar terms of heroic romance: "Most happily,
some new, and, till then, unknown Power instructed his Heart and

Tongue in the Language of Love. . . . his Flame aim'd at nothing but Honour, if such a distinction may be made in Love" (10).

This formula is typical of the dramatic heroic romances by Davenant, Orrery, Dryden, and Lee that were prominent on the English stage especially from the Restoration through the 1670s. Behn made her own contribution to this genre in *Abdelazer*, a heroic tragedy produced and published in 1677. The main direct source of heroic convention in *Oroonoko*, then, is the aristocratic coterie theater of the Restoration. When Oroonoko swears his loyalty to "his charming Imoinda" (71):

> they mutually protested, that even Fetters and Slavery were soft and easy, and would be supported with Joy and Pleasure, while they cou'd be so happy to possess each other, and to be able to make good their Vows. *Caesar* swore he disdained the Empire of the World, while he could behold his *Imoinda*. (44)

This abdication of empire for love is one of the most persistent motifs of late heroic drama, exemplified most prominently by Dryden's Anthony in *All for Love* (1677): "Give to your boy, your Caesar,/This rattle of a globe to play withal, . . . I'll not be pleased with less than Cleopatra."[19]

The hierarchical and rigic conventions of heroic romance made it particularly useful in the representation of the alien scenes of West Indian slavery. In a discussion of nineteenth-century travel writing, Mary Louise Pratt analyzes the strategy of "reductive normalizing," through which the alien figure of the native is textualized and contained by the imperialist observer. She finds this textual device typical of writing about the imperial frontier, "where Europeans confront not only unfamiliar Others but unfamiliar selves," and where "they engage in not just the reproduction of the capitalist mode of production but its expansion through displacement of previously established modes."[20] In Behn's text "reductive normalizing" is carried out through literary convention, and specifically through that very convention most effectively able to fix and codify the experience of radical alterity, the arbitrary love and honor codes of heroic romance.

Emerging directly from this mystification is the persistent presence of the figure of the woman in *Oroonoko*. In heroic romance, of course, the desirable woman serves invariably as the motive and ultimate prize for male adventures. As this ideology evolved in the seventeenth-century French prose tradition, dominated by women writers like Madeleine de Scudéry and Madame de LaFayette, women became increasingly central to the romantic action. Behn's novellas, like other English prose works of the Restoration and early eighteenth century, draw extensively upon this French material, and the foregrounding of female authorship in *Oroonoko* through the explicit interventions of the female narrator signals the prevalent feminization of the genre.

This narrative must have women: it generates female figures at every turn. Not only is the protagonist represented as especially fond of the company of women (46), but female figures—either Imoinda or the narrator and her surrogates—appear as incentives or witnesses for almost all of Oroonoko's exploits. He fights a monstrous, purportedly immortal tiger for the romantic approval of his female admirers: *"What Trophies and Garlands, Ladies, will you make me, if I bring you home the Heart of this ravenous Beast . . .* We all promis'd he should be rewarded at all our hands" (51). He kills the first tiger in defense of a group of four women— who "fled as fast as we could" (50)—and an unidentified, symptomatically faceless Englishman, who effaces himself further by following the ladies in their flight (50). On the trip to the Indian tribes over which Oroonoko presides as expedition leader, the female figure is again the center of attention. Along with the narrator and her "Woman, a Maid of good Courage" (54), only one man agrees to accompany Oroonoko to the Indian town, and once there, the *"White* people," surrounded by the naked natives, stage a scene of cultural difference in which the fully clothed woman is the central spectacle:

> They were all naked; and we were dress'd . . . very glittering and rich; so that we appear'd extremely fine: my own Hair was cut short, and I had a taffety Cap, with black Feathers on my Head. . . . from gazing upon us round, they touch'd us, laying their Hands upon all the Features of our Faces, feeling our Breasts and Arms, taking up one Petticoat, then wondering to see another; admiring our Shoes and Stockings, but more our Garters, which we gave 'em, and they ty'd about their Legs. (55)

Even at the scene of Oroonoko's death, the narrator informs us, though she herself was absent, "my Mother and Sister were by him" (77).

The narrator herself makes it still more evident that the romantic hero is the production and expression of a female sensibility, of "only a Female Pen" (40). The narrator's act of modest self-effacement here, and again on the last page of the novella, signals the special relevance she claims for the female figure, in contrast to the "sublime" masculine wit that would have omitted the crucial naturalness and simplicity (1) of the tale for which the female pen has an innate affinity:

> Thus died this great Man, worthy of a better Fate, and a more sublime Wit than mine to write his Praise: Yet, I hope, the Reputation of my pen is considerable enough to make his glorious Name to survive to all Ages, with that of the brave, the beautiful, and the constant *Imoinda*. (78)

As the female narrator, along with the proliferative female characters who serve as her proxies, produces Oroonoko's heroic drama, so that they become in turn its consumers, Oroonoko also is represented as a consumer of the romantic form he enacts. He keeps company with the women in the colony, in preference to the men, and in their conversations he and Imoinda are "entertained . . . with the Loves of the *Romans*" (46), a pastime that incidentally serves to forestall Oroonoko's complaints about his captivity. In the end, then, even Oroonoko himself is feminized, incorporated into the circular system by which the figure of the woman becomes both object and beneficiary of romantic form.

III

But the "normalizing" model of heroic romance does not account for all the material in Behn's representation of West Indian slavery. In fact, neither the theme of slavery nor the romantic action would seem to explain the extended account of the Caribs, the native Americans of Guiana, with which Behn begins. This opening description deploys another set of discursive conventions than those of romance: the natives are the novella's noble savages. The notion of natural innocence, which civilization and laws can only destroy, is obviously incompatible with the hierarchical aristocratic ideology of heroic form; Oroonoko, educated by a Frenchman, is admirable for his connection with—not his distance from—European civilization. The account of the Indians belongs partly to the tradition of travel narrative, by Behn's period a popular mode describing voyages and colonial expeditions to the new world and including detailed reports of marvels ranging from accurate botanical and ethnographic records to pure invention.[21]

Behn's opening description of the Indians establishes her credibility in this context, but in its almost exclusive emphasis on trade with the natives, it also indicates the economic backdrop of the history of the "royal slave":

trading with them for their Fish, Venison, Buffalo's Skins, and little Rarities; as *Marmosets* . . . *Cousheries*. . . . Then for little *Paraketoes*, great *Parrots*, *Muckaws*, and a thousand other Birds and Beasts of wonderful and surprizing Forms and Colours. For Skins of prodigious Snakes . . . also some rare Flies, of amazing Forms and Colours . . . Then we trade for Feathers, which they order into all Shapes, make themselves little short Habits of 'em, and glorious Wreaths for their Heads, Necks, Arms and Legs, whose Tinctures are unconceivable. I had a Set of these presented to me, and I gave 'em to the King's Theatre, and it was the Dress of the *Indian Queen*, infinitely admired by Persons of Quality; and was unimitable. Besdies these, a thousand little Knacks, and Rarities in Nature; and some of Art, as their Baskets, Weapons, Aprons. (2)

The marvels here are all movable objects, readily transportable to a European setting, where they implicitly appear as exotic and desirable acquisitions. Behn's enumeration of these goods is typical of the age's economic and literary language, where the mere act of listing, the evocation of brilliant colors, and the sense of an incalculable numerousness express the period's fascination with imperialist accumulation.[22] But the Indians' goods are at best a small factor in the real economic connection between England and the West Indies; they serve primarily as a synecdoche for imperialist exploitation.

This opening context is centered upon the feathered habit which the narrator acquires, and which, she claims, became upon her return to England the dress of the Indian Queen in Dryden's heroic play of the same name (1664), an artifact of imperialism displayed in the most spectacular manner possible—adorning the female figure of a contemporary actress on the real stage of the Theatre Royal in Bridges Street. The foregrounding of female dress parallels the scene of the expedition to the Indian village, where the spectacle of the narrator's clothing is similarly privileged. And in general, the items in the opening account of imperialist trade reflect the acquisitive instincts of a specifically female sensibility—dress, skins, and exotic pets. Pets, indeed, in particular birds, were both sign and product of the expansion and commercialization of English society in the eighteenth century.[23] Even more important, the association of women with the products of mercantile capitalism, and particularly the obsession with female adornment, is a strong cultural motif in this period of England's first major imperial expansion.[24] Addison's image of the woman fitted out in the fruits of empire evokes the ideology to which Behn's account belongs:

> I consider woman as a beautiful, romantic animal, that may be adorned with furs and feathers, pearls and diamonds, ores and silks. The lynx shall cast its skin at her feet to make her a tippet; the peacock, parrot, and swan shall *pay contribution* to her muff; the sea shall be searched for shells, and the rocks for gems; and every part of nature furnish out its share towards the embellishment of a creature that is the most consummate work of it.[25]

Dressed in the products of imperialist accumulation, women are, by metonymy identified not only with those products, but ultimately with the whole fascinating enterprise of trade itself.

And of course the substantial trade and real profit was not in the

Indians' buffalo skins, *Paraketoes*, or feathers, but in sugar and slaves. Behn's description of the slave trade, highly accurate in many of its details, is the shaping economic and historical context of *Oroonoko*. A letter written in 1663 to Sir Robert Harley—at whose house at St. John's Hill (49) the narrator claims to have resided—from one William Yearworth, his steward, may describe the arrival of the slave ship which Behn would have witnessed during her visit to the colony:[26]

> Theare is A genney man [a slave ship from the Guinea Coast] Ariued heare in This riuer of ye 24th of [January] This Instant att Sande poynt. Shee hase 130 nigroes one Borde; ye Comanders name [is] Joseph John Woode; shee has lost 54 negroes in ye viage. The Ladeyes that are heare liue att St Johnes hill.[27]

Behn recounts the participation of African tribal leaders in collecting and selling slaves to European traders, the prearranged agreements for lots in the colonies, the deliberate dispersal of members of the same tribe around the plantations, the situation of the Negro towns, the imminence of rebellion, and the aggressive character of the Koromantyn (in Behn, Coramantien) slaves—the name given to the Gold Coast tribes from which Oroonoko comes.[28]

Behn's account of the black uprising—an obvious consequence of the slave trade—has no specific historical confirmation, but the situation is typical. Revolts and runaways, or marronage, were commonplace in the West Indies and Guiana throughout this period. In Jamaica rebellions and guerrilla warfare, predominantly led by Koromantyn ex-slaves, were virtually continuous from 1665 to 1740.[29] Marronage was common in Guiana as well during the period when *Oroonoko* is set: while Behn was in Suriname a group of escaped slaves led by a Koromantyn known as Jermes had an established base in the region of Para, from which they attacked local plantations.[30] And Wylie Sypher has documented several cases like Oroonoko's, in which the offspring of African tribal leaders were betrayed into slavery, often on their way to obtain an education in England.[31]

The powerful act of "reductive normalizing" performed by the romantic narrative is somewhat countered, then, by a similarly powerful historical contextualization in Behn's account of trade. Not that the representation of trade in *Oroonoko* is outside ideology; far from it. As we have seen, the position it assigns to women in imperialist accumulation helps rationalize the expansionist impulses of mercantile capitalism. We could also examine the novella's assumption—partly produced by the crossover from the code of romantic horror—that blacks captured in war make legitimate objects for the slave trade. We cannot read Behn's colonialist history uncritically, any more than we can her heroic romance. But we can read them together, because they are oriented around the same governing point of reference—the figure of the woman. In the paradigm of heroic romance, women are the objects and arbiters of male adventurism, just as, in the ideology of imperialist accumulation, women are the emblems and proxies of the whole male enterprise of colonialism. The female narrator and her proliferative surrogates connect romance and trade in *Oroonoko*, motivating the hero's exploits, validating his romantic appeal, and witnessing his tragic fate. Simultaneously they dress themselves in the products of imperialist acquisition, enacting the colonialist paradigm of exploitation and consumption, not only of the Indians' feathers and skins, and the many marvels of the new world, but of slaves as well, and the adventure of the "royal slave" himself.

These two paradigms intersect in Oroonoko's antislavery speech:

> *And why* (said he) *my dear Friends and Fellow-sufferers, should we be Slaves to an unknown People? Have they vanquished us nobly in Fight? Have they won us in Honourable Battle? And are we by the Chance of War become their Slaves? This wou'd not anger a noble Heart; this would not animate a Soldier's Soul: no, but we are bought and sold like Apes or Monkeys, to be the sport of Women, Fools and Cowards.* (61)

The attack on slavery is voiced in part through the codes of heroic romance: the trade in slaves is unjust only if and when slaves are not honorably conquered in battle. But these lines also allude to the other ideology of *Oroonoko*, the feminization of trade that we have associated primarily with the Indians. Oroonoko's resentment at being "bought and sold like Apes or Monkeys . . . the sport of women" is plausible given the prominent opening description of the animals and birds traded by the Indians, in particular of the little "Marmosets, a sort of Monkey, as big as a Rat or Weasel, but of a marvellous and delicate shape, having Face and Hands like a Human Creature" (2). In conjunction with the image of the pet monkey, Oroonoko's critique of slavery reveals the critique of colonialist ideology in one of its most powerful redactions— the representation of female consumption, of monkeys and men.

In grounding the parallel systems of romance and trade, the female figure in Behn's novella plays a role like that outlined by Myra Jehlen, the role of "Archimedes' lever"—the famous paradoxical machine that could move the earth, if only it could have a place to stand.[32] Though they are marginal and subordinate to men, women have no extrinsic perspective, no objective status, in this narrative, either as the arbiters of romance or as the beneficiaries of colonialism. But though they have no independent place to stand, in their mediatory role between heroic romance and mercantile imperialism, they anchor the interaction of these two otherwise incompatible discourses. They make possible the superimposition of aristocratic and bourgeois systems—the ideological contradiction that dominates the novella. And in that contradiction we can locate a site beyond alterity, a point of critique and sympathy produced by the radical contemporaneity of issues of gender with those of romance and race.

IV

On the face of it, the treatment of slavery in *Oroonoko* is neither coherent nor fully critical. The romance motifs, with their elitist focus on the fate of African "princes," entail an ambiguous attack on the institution of slavery, and adumbrate the sentimental antislavery position of the eighteenth century. But the representation of trade and consumption, readily extended to the trade in slaves and the consumption of Oroonoko himself, and specifically imagined through a female sensibility, renders colonialism unambiguously attractive. This incoherence could be explored in further detail: in the narrative's confusion about the enslavement of Indians and the contradictory reasons given for their freedom; in the narrator's vacillation between friendship with and fear of the "royal slave"; in the dubious role she plays in "diverting" Oroonoko with romantic tales so as to maintain his belief that he will be returned to Africa, her collusion in the assignment of spies to attend him in his meetings with the other slaves, and the quite explicit threat she uses to keep him from fomenting rebellion; and even in the fascination with dismemberment that pervades the novella's relation with the native "other"—both Indian and African—and that suggests a perverse connection between the female narrator and Oroonoko's brutal executioners.

A deeper critique of slavery emerges at the climactic moment in the ideological contradiction that dominates the novella. This insight originates in the hidden contemporary political referent of the narrative: the party quarrels in the West Indies and Guiana at the time of Behn's visit. Though the novella's account is sketchy, Behn names historical persons and evokes animosities traceable to the political tensions that emigrated to the colonies during the revolution and after the Restoration.[33] The relative political neutrality of the West Indies and Guiana attracted Royalists during the revolution and Parliamentarians and radicals after the Restoration. The rendering of the colonists' council (69), and the account of the contests for jurisdiction over Oroonoko reflect the reigning atmosphere of political tension in Suriname during the time of Behn's visit in 1663 and 1664, though without assigning political labels to the disputants. In fact, the Lord Governor of Suriname to whom the novella refers is Francis, Lord Willoughby of Parham, intimate of the royal family and of Lord Clarendon and constant conspirator against the Protectorate, who had received his commission for settlements in Guiana and elsewhere in the Caribbean from Charles II, at his court in exile. Willoughby is absent during Behn's narrative, but the current governor of the colony, William Byam, who orders Oroonoko's execution, was a key figure in the Royalist struggle for control of Barbados in the previous decade, and likewise in Suriname engaged in a continuous battle with the contingent of Parliamentarians in the colony. In 1662, immediately before Behn's arrival, Byam had accused a group of Independents, led by Robert Sandford, of conspiracy, summarily trying and ejecting them from the colony. Sandford was the owner of the plantation neighboring Sir Robert Harley's, St. John's Hill, the narrator's residence. Harley also was a Royalist and had been a friend of Willoughby, though a quarrel between the two during Harley's chancellorship of Barbados resulted in Willoughby's expulsion from that colony in 1664. There were few firm friendships beyond the Line in this tumultuous period of colonial adventurism. Indeed in 1665, shortly after Behn left Suriname, Willoughby himself, in a visit to Guiana meant to restore orderly government to the colony, was nearly assassinated by John Allen, who resented his recent prosecution for blasphemy and duelling.

Behn herself may have been engaged with these volatile politics through an alliance with a radical named William Scot, who went to the colony to escape prosecution for high treason in England, and whose father Thomas figured prominently on the Parliamentary side during the revolution and Commonwealth.[34] The radical connection makes some sense in that Byam, the notoriously ardent and high handed Royalist, is clearly the villain of the piece, and Colonel George Martin, Parliamentarian and brother to "*Harry Martin* the great *Oliverian*" (50), deplores the inhumanity of Oroonoko's execution. But its relevance need not be directly personal. The first substantial antislavery statements were voiced by the radical Puritans in the 1660s;[35] there was a Quaker colony in Suriname during this period; and George Fox made a visit to the West Indies in 1671, where he urged the inclusion of blacks at Friends' meetings.[36] Though as a group the Quakers in the New World were ambivalent about slave ownership and often profited from the slave trade themselves, individual Friends throughout this period enlarged upon Fox's early example. William Edmundson spoke against slavery in both the West Indies and New England.[37] Planters in Barbados charged that Edmundson's practice of holding meetings for blacks in

Quaker homes raised threats of rebellion, and in 1676 the colonial government passed a law to prevent "Quakers from bringing Negroes to their meetings" and allowing slaves to attend Quaker schools.[38] Though modern readers often assume that the early attack on slavery voiced in *Oroonoko* arose from a natural humanitarianism, the Puritan precedent suggests that Behn's position had an historical context. Such sentiments were "natural" only to a specific group.

But there is no simple political allegory in Behn's novella. Though the Royalist Byam is Oroonoko's enemy, Behn describes Trefry, Oroonoko's friend, as Willoughby's overseer in Suriname; although he has not been historically identified, Trefry must have been a Royalist. His open struggle with Byam over Oroonoko's fate might allude to divisions within the Royalist camp, divisions which were frequent and intense in Barbados, for instance, when Willoughby came to power in that colony. More important than direct political correspondences, however, is the tenor of political experience in the West Indies and Guiana in this period. For Behn and others, the colonies stage an historical anachronism, the repetition of the English revolution, and the political endpoint of Behn's narrative is the reenactment of the most traumatic event of the revolution, the execution of Charles I.

From almost the instant of his beheading, the King's last days, and the climactic drama of his death, were memorialized by Royalist writers in a language that established the discourse of Charles's suffering as heroic tragedy. *The Life of Charles I*, written just after the Restoration and close to the year in which Oroonoko's story is set, suggests the tenor of this discourse:

> He entred this ignominious and gastly Theatre with the same mind as He used to carry His Throne, shewing no fear of death . . . [Bloody trophies from the execution were distributed among the King's murderers at the execution and immediately thereafter] . . . some out of a brutish malice would have them as spoiles and trophees of their hatred to their Lawfull Sovereign . . . He that had nothing Common in His Life and Fortune is almost profaned by a Vulgar pen. The attempt, I confess, admits no Apology but this, That it was fit that Posterity, when they read His Works . . . should also be told that His Actions were as Heroick as His Writings . . . Which not being undertaken by some Noble hand . . . I was by Importunity prevailed upon to imitate those affectionate Slaves, who would gather up the scattered limbs of some great Person that had been their Lord, yet fell at the pleasure of his Enemies.[39]

Related images appear in a version published in 1681, shortly before the writing of *Oroonoko*:

these Barbarous Regicides . . . his Bloody Murtherers . . . built a Scaffold
for his Murther, before the Great Gate at *White Hall*, whereunto they fixed
several Staples of Iron, and prepared Cords, to tye him down to the Block,
had he made any resistance to that Cruel and Bloody stroke . . . And then,
most Christianly forgiving all, praying for his Enemies, he meekly submitted
to the stroke of the Axe . . . he suffered as an Heroick Champion . . . by
his patient enduring the many insolent affronts of this subtile, false, cruel,
and most implacable Generation, in their Barbarous manner of conventing,
and Condemning him to Death; and to see his most bloodthirsty Enemies
then Triumph over him. . . . they have made him *Glorious* in his Memory,
throughout the World, by a Great, Universal and most durable Fame.[40]

Charles I was a powerful presence for Behn at the writing of *Oroonoko*,
even though the story was composed only shortly before its publication
in 1688, long after Charles's death, the Restoration, and even the in-
tervening death of Charles II—the monarch with whom Behn's acquaintance was much more personal. Oroonoko's heroism is attached
to that of Charles I not just generically—in the affinity of "Great Men"
of "mighty Actions" and "large Souls" (7, 47)—but directly. Behn's slave
name for Oroonoko—Caesar—is the same she repeatedly used for the
Stuart monarchs: Charles II is Caesar in her poem "A Farewell to Cel-
ladon on His Going Into Ireland" (1684), as is James II and her "Poem
to Her Sacred Majesty Queen Mary" (1689).[41] Oroonoko, as we have
seen, is defined by his sympathy for Charles's "deplorable Death" (7).
Sentenced, like Charles in these Royalist accounts, by the decree of a
Council of "notorious Villains" (69) and irreverent swearers, and murdered by Banister, a "Fellow of absolute Barbarity, and fit to execute
any Villainy" (76), "this great Man" (78), another royal martyr, endures
his death patiently, "without a Groan, or a Reproach" (77). Even the
narrator's final apology—though it refers specifically to female authorship—reproduces the conventional humble stance of the chroniclers of
the King's death: "Thus died this great Man, worthy of a better Fate,
and a more sublime Wit than mine to write his Praise; Yet, I hope, the
Reputation of my pen is considerable enough to make his glorious Name
to survive to all Ages" (78). "The Spectacle . . . of a mangled King" (77),
at the close of the narrative,[42] when Oroonoko is quartered and his
remains distributed around the colony, evokes with surprising vividness
the tragic drama of Charles Stuart's violent death. The sense of momentous loss generated on behalf of the "royal slave" is the product of
the hidden figuration in Oroonoko's death of the culminating moment
of the English revolution.

But the tragedy is double in a larger sense. Abstractly speaking, both
Charles I and Oroonoko are victims of the same historical phenomenon—those new forces in English society loosely associated with an

antiabsolutist mercantile imperialism. The rapid rise of colonization and trade coincided with the defeat of absolutism in the seventeenth century. In a mediated sense the death of Charles I makes that of Oroonoko possible, and Oroonoko's death stands as a reminder of the massive historical shift that destroyed Charles Stuart and made England a modern imperialist power. Ironically, in this context, both King Charles and the African slave in the New World are victims of the same historical force.

We might imagine that the account of Oroonoko's death represents the moment of greatest mystification in the narrative, the proof of an absolute alterity in the confrontation between the colonialist and the native "other." What could be more divergent than the fate of Charles Stuart and that of an African slave? But the violent yoking of these two figures provides the occasion for the most brutally visceral contact that Behn's narrative makes with the historical experience of slavery in the West Indies and Guiana. Merely the information that Oroonoko is a Koromantyn (5) connects his story to eighteenth-century testimony on slavery and rebellion in the colonies. Bryan Edwards describes the character of slaves from this area:

> The circumstances which distinguish the Koromantyn, or Gold Coast, Negroes, from all others, are firmness both of body and mind; a ferociousness of disposition; but withal, activity, courage, and a stubbornness, or what an ancient Roman would have deemed an elevation, of soul, which prompts them to enterprizes of difficulty and danger; and enables them to meet death, in its most horrible shape, with fortitude or indifference. . . . It is not wonderful that such men should endeavour, even by means the most desperate, to regain the freedom of which they have been deprived; nor do I conceive that any further circumstances are necessary to prompt them to action, than that of being sold into captivity in a distant country.[43]

Edwards is obviously drawn to epic romanticization, but his historical account suggests the experience behind the romance in Behn's narrative. So common was rebellion among the Koromantyns, that Gold Coast slave imports were cut off by the late eighteenth century to reduce the risk of insurrection.

Edwards recounts one such rebellion in Jamaica in 1760, which "arose at the instigation of a Koromantyn Negro of the name of Tacky, who had been a chief in Guiney" (II, 59–60). He details the execution of the rebel leaders, who were killed, like Oroonoko, to make "an Example to all the Negroes, to fright 'em from daring to threaten their Betters" (*Oroonoko*, 70):

> The wretch that was burned was made to sit on the ground, and his body

being chained to an iron stake, the fire was applied to his feet. He uttered
not a groan, and saw his legs reduced to ashes with the utmost firmness
and composure; after which one of his arms by some means getting loose,
he snatched a brand from the fire that was consuming him, and flung it in
the face of the executioner. (II, 61)

A correspondent from Jamaica to the *London Magazine* in 1767 provides
a similar account:

Such of them [rebel Negroes] as fell into our hands, were burnt alive on a
slow fire, beginning at their feet, and burning upwards. It would have sur-
prized you to see with what resolution and firmness they bore the torture,
smiling with an air of disdain at their executioners, and those about them.[44]

And John Stedman, the period's most detailed reporter of the executions
of rebel maroons, recounts the request of a man who had been broken
on the rack: "I imagined him dead, and felt happy; till the magistrates
stirring to depart, he writhed himself from the cross . . . rested his head
on part of the timber, and asked the by-standers for a pipe of tobacco."[45]

In this context, Oroonoko's death takes on a significance entirely different from that conferred upon it through the paradigm of heroic romance or the figuration of Charles's death:

[he] assur'd them, they need not tie him, for he would stand fix'd like a
Rock, and endure Death so as should encourage them to die . . . He had
learn'd to take Tobacco; and when he was assur'd he should die, he desir'd
they should give him a Pipe in his Mouth, ready lighted; which they did:
And the executioner came, and first cut off his Members, and threw them
into the Fire; after that, with an ill-favour'd Knife, they cut off his Ears and
his Nose, and burn'd them; he still smoak'd on, as if nothing had touch'd
him; then they hack'd off one of his Arms, and still he bore up, and held
his Pipe; but at the cutting off the other Arm, his Head sunk, and his Pipe
dropt and he gave up the Ghost, without a Groan, or a Reproach. (77)

As far as this horrible fictional scene takes us from the image of Dryden's
Antony or that of Charles Stuart, those radically irrelevant figures are
the means by which this narrative finds its way to the historical experience of the Koromantyn slave—the means by which this passage offers
not merely a fascination with the brutality depicted here and in the other
historical materials I have cited, but a sympathetic memorialization of
those human beings whose sufferings these words recall.

V

In *Oroonoko* the superimposition of two modes of mystification—romantic and imperialist—crucially conjoined by the figure of the woman,
produces an historical insight and a critical sympathy that the argument

from alterity cannot explain. This is not to say that Behn herself is any more unambivalent an emancipationist that we had originally suspected. But it does suggest that even though Behn can see colonialism only in the morror of her own culture, that occluded vision has a critical dimension. As the "normalizing" figure of alterity, the romantic hero, opens up the experience of the "other," we can glimpse, in the contradictions of colonialist ideology, the workings of a radical contemporaneity.

I have tried to exemplify the notion of radical contemporaneity variously in this reading of Behn's novella. In Charles Stuart and Oroonoko we have seen two creatures who could never meet in this world joined as historical contemporaries through the contradictory logic of Behn's imperialist romance. We have used a feminist reading of colonialist ideology, which places women at the center of the structures of rationalization that justify mercantile expansion, to ground the account of the contradictions surrounding the representation of race in this work. And we have juxtaposed the figure of the woman—ideological implement of a colonialist culture—with the figure of the slave—economic implement of the same system. Though Behn never clearly sees herself in the place of the African slave, the mediation of the figure of the woman between the two contradictory paradigms upon which her narrative depends uncovers a mutuality beyond her conscious control.

These relationships of contemporaneity spring from the failures of discursive coherence in *Oroonoko*, from the interaction of the contradictory aristocratic and bourgeois paradigms that shape the novella. This interaction is the dialectical process that my reading of *Oroonoko* has aimed to define, the process by which we may "meet the Other on the same ground, in the same Time." By this means, we can position the African slave in Behn's novella not as a projection of colonialist discourse, contained or incorporated by a dominant power, but as an historical force in his own right and his own body. The notion of a relatively autonomous native position, of a site of resistance that is not produced and controlled by the ideological apparatuses of colonialist power, has crucial consequences for our conclusions about colonialist ideology, the critique of colonialism, and ideology critique in general. It suggests that we can read the literature of those in power not only for the massive and elaborate means by which power is exercised, but also as a source of leverage for those in opposition, that while sites of resistance may be produced within a dominant ideology, they are not produced by it, and they do not serve it. They are produced despite it, and they serve to locate opposition in a body and a language that even the people of the colonialist metropole can be made to understand.

3

"WHEN MEN WOMEN TURN":
Gender Reversals in Fielding's Plays

Jill Campbell

I

Having earned royal favor and the stature of a hero by preserving King Arthur's kingdom from the giants, Fielding's little Tom Thumb asks not for political power or monetary reward but for domestic bliss: "I ask but this,/To Sun my self in *Huncamunca*'s Eyes." The King grants Thumb the Princess Huncamunca, but Queen Dollalolla objects, since she is in love with Thumb herself. When Arthur remains firm, Dollalolla threatens violence, but Arthur refuses, on principle, to "truckle to her Will:"

> For when by Force
> Or Art the Wife her Husband over-reaches,
> Give him the Peticoat, and her the Breeches.[1]

For *Tom Thumb*'s original audience in 1730, King Arthur's blustering defense against "petticoat government" must have called to mind a specific scenario of female domination: England's own queen, Caroline, was widely rumored to govern the country indirectly through her control of King George.[2] At the same time, for the audience at many of the play's early performances, the dramatic scenario before them itself provided satiric commentary on this passage: the Thumb King Arthur here addresses was himself most often a "her" in breeches—a female actor typically filled Thumb's singularly heroic trousers—and in some cases the Princess Huncamunca Thumb is to wed was a "him" in Petticoats— a male actor occasionally took this role.[3] In *Tom Thumb*, Fielding burlesques political and literary notions of public heroism or "greatness" not only by mixing inflated with deflated diction and by shrinking his hero to a "Lilliputian" scale, but by casting a woman as masculine hero.

King Arthur's principled defense of patriarchy confirms that the theatrical device of cross-gender casting signifies as more than farce in this play. In the widely varied body of the twenty-six plays Fielding wrote in the first decade of his literary career, interest in problems of gender identity recurs again and again, and Fielding repeatedly links the significance of gender, particularly as revealed at the moment of gender inversion, to matters of "government," both political and literary. He often uses gender as a means of representing other issues, but also as a vexed issue with political and literary consequences itself. Of course, it is the historical meaning of "masculine" and "feminine" that he draws on when he makes a female Tom Thumb serve to comment on the nature of that hero, and much of his satiric use of gender works to protect or enforce certain historical notions of masculine authority. But his plays also explore the costs of that system. While his career as a playwright and stage manager lasted, the genre of drama and its forum, the theater, provided Fielding with a particularly powerful—though ultimately restrictive—means of imagining and representing issues of gender identity and reversal, and all they might imply.

In his plays, as elsewhere, Fielding often uses ridicule of a character's compromised masculinity to associate that character with the compromising of traditional political, cultural, or social standards. He uses familiar figures from the standard repertoire of contemporary topical satire to make the association. The figure of Lord Hervey, agent of Walpole and bisexual—Pope's "Sporus" and "Lord Fanny," Pulteney's "pretty, little *Master-Miss*,"[4] and an inexhaustible ideological crux for many Opposition satirists—serves to link political with sexual corruption in the role of Miss Stitch in *Pasquin*. Fielding repeatedly uses the ambiguous gender as well as the foreign birth of the Italian castrato singers so popular in London at this time to represent the decline of the values of native theater. That signature of Restoration comedy, the fop or beau, marks Fielding's comedies as well, but with a difference: most often, this familiar comic type is reduced by Fielding to its disruptive signification in a system of gender oppositions. "I have known a beau with everything of a woman but the sex," observes Wisemore in *Love in Several Masques*, "and nothing of a man besides it."[5]

The stock jokes about gender in Fielding's plays show not only a satiric interest in men who abdicate their masculinity and all it is imagined to entail—the corrupt courtier, the castrato singer, the beau—but an apocalyptic vision of women's appropriation of that masculine power. "And if the Breed ben't quickly mended," warns the poet's muse at the end of a passage satirizing beaus in Fielding's first published work, *The Masquerade*,

> Your Empire shortly will be ended:
> Breeches our brawny Thighs shall grace,
> (Another *Amazonian* Race.)
> For when Men Women turn—why then
> May Women not be changed to Men?[6]

Women's appropriation of male "empire," the threat of "petticoat government," is the most general and persistent topic of sexual satire in Fielding's plays. "We are all under petticoat government," Trapwit announces as the Cibberian "moral" to the second act of his comedy within *Pasquin* (II.i). In *The Grub-Street Opera*, which presents the English royal family as a Welsh family of henpecked husband, domineering wife, and "puny" son, Puzzletext the parson comforts Sir Owen with the company his misery keeps: "Petticoat-government is a very lamentable thing indeed.—But it is the fate of many an honest gentleman"(I.i). And Fielding extends the problem even into the after life and the underworld: when a critic asks the author of the rehearsal play within *Eurydice*, "Why have you made the devil hen-pecked?" the author replies, "How could hell be better represented than by supposing the people under petticoat government?" King Arthur himself is described in the Dramatis Personae of *The Tragedy of Tragedies* as "A passionate sort of King, Husband to Queen *Dollalolla*, of whom he stands a little in Fear."

Most of these scenarios of the "misrule" of female domination involve the government of a public realm as well as of a household, superimposing a domestic onto a political hierarchy of power: the henpecked husband is also the dubious ruler of the English people of King Arthur's or King George's reign, or of hell's ghostly "people." Domestic and political satire are, for Fielding, closely linked. Often, the content of his political satire might be said to *consist* of linking it with domestic material—the intrusion of the domestic realm into the realm of public action and rule, or the domination of political by domestic or sexual power, is repeatedly the source both of Fielding's humor and of his serious critique. When Fielding presents inverted masculine and feminine power relations, he often seems to be representing through them an inversion in the priority of public over private concerns assumed to be the respective domains of men and women.[7] As we can see in the conjunction

of a female Tom Thumb with Arthur's remarks on "petticoat government," gender reversals or impersonations signify analogously to express more than the disruption of sexual roles. In a period that saw itself
as fallen hopelessly below past standards of public heroism, the gender
inversion of a female hero functions as one species of mock-epic. The
diminishment or corruption of the public world of heroism and power
appears in its collapse into the female world of mere domestic squabble.

Many of Fielding's uses of gender inversion, however, do not employ
a sense of the feminine domain simply as the negation of the masculine
public world but as a domain of other kinds of values and powers that
can itself be betrayed by a collapse into its opposite. Fielding often employs the association of women with internal life—both the moral life
of virtue and the psychological one of feeling. He counts on women to
preserve that province apart from the public and commercial world of
the male, but he frequently suspects them of merely using their association with virtue and feeling to serve their own purposes of power
and acquisition. "Virtue" becomes "vartue" in Fielding's *Shamela*, a
high-blown word deflated by vulgar usage, reduced to a means for getting her man; and, once married, Shamela overreaches her husband
through an artful use of feminine feeling—feeling that is calculated and
constituted for the effect of its representation. The rupture of gender
categories involved in "petticoat government" implies for Fielding,
then, not only the intrusion of domestic concerns into political or public
ones, but the betrayal of the space of interior feeling associated with
femininity by a counterfeit or "sham" exterior version of it, fabricated
for its effects in the public world of the male.

When Fielding discusses affectation as the central problematic of character in "An Essay on the Knowledge of the Characters of Men," printed
in his *Miscellanies* in 1743, he explicitly renders the problem in the terms
of dramatic acting: "the generality of mankind mistake the affectation
for the reality; for, as Affectation always overacts her part, it fares with
her as with a farcical actor on the stage, whose monstrous overdone
grimaces are sure to catch the applause of an insensible audience."[8]
Fielding immediately identifies Affectation as both female and hyper-
theatrical, and the mixed sexuality of cross-dressing may be what evokes
the strong term "monstrous" in the description of Affectation's grimaces, for the image of "a farcical actor on the stage" raises the idea of
both the male players in female roles and female players in male roles
that were an important element of English farce tradition. The arguments of the antitheatricalists—which extended 150 years before Fielding and which contributed to the Stage Licensing Act that ended his
career—had used cross-dressing as a paradigm for the moral dangers
of the theater, making gender the ultimate preserve of natural identity

to be broached, in its most scandalous extremity, by theatrical impersonation, and setting up the theater as the forum in which the boundaries of gender might be tested.[9] Problems of gender and problems of
affectation or impersonation were historically linked, then, in the controversial institution of the English theater within which Fielding began
his literary career.

As we saw in the scene from *Tom Thumb* with which we began, Fielding explores issues of gender identity and inversion in his plays not only
by treating them thematically, or by recurring to topics of social satire
involving gender, but also by actually staging the situation of gender
impersonation. As the manager of the Haymarket Theatre, he capitalized upon the dramatic possibilities of the theatrical device of cross-
gender casting objected to by the antitheatricalists. With this device,
Fielding made the institutional and representational space of the theater
a vivid embodiment of larger cultural and ideological structures. Stephen
Orgel's work on Renaissance theater has allowed us to conceive this
function of the stage.[10] More broadly, Stephen Greenblatt has suggested
strategies of reading Renaissance literary texts in conjunction with the
documents and experiences of social life which we will bring to the
problem of gender in Fielding's dramas and to the new institutions and
cultural forces of eighteenth-century England.[11] These methods of reading, designed to tease out the complicated underpinnings of cultural
forms, will not provide us with a single feminist, political, or sociological
summary of Fielding's dramatic production, but they will open up the
constellation of interrelated problems—sexual, political, and social—
that that production repeatedly stages. Using Fielding's *Historical Register* as a touchstone and a guide through the complex and ambivalent
commentary on gender in Fielding's plays, we will focus in what follows
on Fielding's employment of cross-gender casting as a usefully bald and
explicit rendering of his interest in the abstract systems of oppositions
associated with gender, dramatically disrupted by these parts.

II

Fielding's *Historical Register for the Year 1736*, performed at the Little
Theatre in the Haymarket in May 1737, places us and a small onstage
audience of author, critic, and lord at a rehearsal of Medley's new play.
This new play consists of a series of brief satiric scenes that are to provide
an "historical register" of the events—political, social, and theatrical—
of the preceding year. Medley's first scene is spare: a thinly veiled political satire of Sir Robert Walpole and his cohorts. The second scene is
more complex. At its center is the stage enactment of an auction, which

Medley calls the best scene in the whole performance, for it is "writ in allegory."[12] The casting of Medley's auctioneer—a satiric portrait of London's popular auctioneer of the time, Mr. Christopher Cock, here called Mr. Hen—contributes to the allegory of the scene: the role of Mr. Cock/Hen was filled by the noted male impersonator and eccentric, Colley Cibber's daughter, Mrs. Charlotte Charke. Fielding's cross-gender casting of Mr. Hen creates a dramatic context for the selling of goods that interprets both that selling and sexual inversions in a particular way. But before the auction has even begun, the terms of such an interpretation have been established in a short dramatic prologue, a conversation among the ladies who will attend.

"Now you shall have a council of ladies" or "female politicians," Medley promises as his second scene opens, but the "affairs of great importance" they are discussing when the curtain is drawn replace the politics of Medley's first scene with matters of social and sexual fashion—an interchangeability characteristic of Fielding's satiric humor.

The LADIES all speak together.

ALL LADIES.	Was you at the opera, Madam, last night?
2d LADY.	Who can miss an opera while Farinello stays?
3d LADY.	Sure he is the charmingest creature!
4th LADY.	He's everything in the world one could wish!
1st LADY.	Almost everything one could wish!
2d LADY.	They say there's a lady in the city has a child by him.
ALL LADIES.	Ha, ha, ha!
1st LADY.	Well, it must be charming to have a child by him.
3d LADY.	Madam, I met a lady in a visit the other day with three. . . . All Farinellos, all in wax.
1st LADY.	O Gemini! Who makes them? I'll send and bespeak half a dozen tomorrow morning. (II.i.6–18)

The stage direction and first line open the scene with a caricature of the univocal control fashion exerts over the ladies' words: the same voice, the voice of fashionable society, speaks through all of them. They all seem to have attended the opera the night before, but they discuss not the music or performance but its lead singer. And they discuss Farinelli (that is, Carlo Broschi, the great Italian singer in Porpora's opera between 1734 and 1737)[13] not as musical performer but as an object of desire: "He's everything in the world one could wish!" When the 1st Lady qualifies this statement with an "almost," she acknowledges the irony of female society's selection of Farinelli as popular sex symbol or romantic idol: the sweet extraordinary voice of Farinelli that is said to have ravished the heart of every woman in his audience manifested precisely his inability to ravish a woman physically, his victimization and election to that strange foreign elite of castrato singers. But it is the same 1st Lady who complicates the view of Farinelli's disabled phallus as simply a qualification to his desirability when she declares, "it must be charming to have a child by him." The ladies laugh at the rumor that Farinelli has fathered a child, yet the 1st Lady's comment and their universal willingness to resume discussion of the rumor *as if* it were truth express some simultaneous wish for this contradiction.

Fielding's "female politicians" weren't alone in their titillated interest: the Italian castrato singers who began to perform in London in 1707[14] served widely as a cultural occasion through which the ambivalences and pressures of the period's sexual ideology could be played out, in the form both of a tremendous popular vogue and of a tireless satiric abuse. Even without children, the castrati presented their audiences with a contradiction in terms; and their treatment elsewhere, both by Fielding and by other satirists of the 1730s, helps us understand all that is at stake in the simple jokes of this prologue, and how it prepares us for the auction scene to follow.[15]

The satiric reactions to the disruption a castrato creates along the boundary between masculine and feminine identity reveal some of the larger systems of oppositions normally stabilized by alignment with gender terms. Because the castrato's exception to masculine identity consists ultimately in the facts about his genitals, the castrati provided an occasion to isolate, and to literalize, to make explicit, the cultural significances of the phallus itself: in considering the nature of the castrato's loss, the satirists at times assume the phallus to be the guarantor of everything from moral discourse to English currency to English-ness. And, in the real or imagined responses of women to them, the castrati provided a rare opening in the normally monolithic entity of masculinity in which to explore—whether with wishfulness, fear, or denunciation— complexities or contradictions in women's relation to the phallus. While some of the satiric material concentrated its ridicule on the castrati themselves, much of it, like this scene from *The Historical Register*, turned its satiric attention on the women interested in them, competing to articulate what it would mean for a woman to prefer a man without the use of his penis.

By the time Fielding presented the ladies' discussion of Farinelli in *The Historical Register* in 1737, two pamphlets, appearing in London in 1735 and 1736, had humorously argued for the greater desirability of a castrated man. In the first, Teresia Constantia Phillips, the notorious courtesan who appears in the shadowy background of *Shamela*,[16] had rejected the male fantasy (present in *Pamela*, *Fanny Hill*, and many other novels) that a woman's sexual desire is necessarily adjoined to dread,

pain, and awe, and with it, she at least playfully rejected the phallic
ideal of a lover in favor of Farinelli:

> Man, like his Brother Brute, the shaggy Bear,
> Where he attempts to stroke, is sure to tear. . . .
> Discord and Thunder, mingle when he speaks,
> And stunning Noise the Ears thin Membrane breaks.
>   How fit for Dalliance and for soft Embrace,
> Is Man, that carries Terror in his Face? . . .
> Can we with Pleasure, what we dread enjoy,
> That very Dread does Love itself destroy.
>   How much do those display their want of Sense,
> Who scoff at Eunuchs, and dislike a Thing,
> For being but disburthen'd of its Sting?[17]

In the first stanza, masculine "Discord" and "Noise" stand in for the
phallus, deflowering the female ear, and in the last, the sweet-voiced
and "sting"-less Eunuch emerges as the ideal object of a feminine desire
unmixed with terror or pain. Fielding had used a similar set of images
in 1733 in his epilogue to *The Intriguing Chambermaid*, where he complains
that the popularity of "Italian warblers" has brought about the decline
of native theater. He ironically approves his female audience's choice:

> —But though our angry poets rail in spite,
> Ladies, I own, I think your judgments right:
> Satire, perhaps, may wound some pretty thing;
> Those soft Italian warblers have no sting.
>   . . .
> 'Tis hard to pay them who our faults reveal,
> As boys are forced to buy the rods they feel.
> No, let 'em starve, who dare to lash the age,
> And, as you've left the pulpit, leave the stage.
> (26–29, 34–37)

Fielding, like Con Phillips, compares the uncastrated phallus to a
wounding sting and a violent rod, but his irony attempts to recuperate
the masculine discord and noise that Phillips rejects as the harsh but
moral voice of satire: phallic satire "gives the wounded hearer pain"
(33) but only in order to reveal our faults; the rod "lashes" us that we
may learn. Thus Fielding presents the rejection of phallic masculinity
as a moral "softness" or degeneracy, and at the same time he renders
a man's penis violent, alienating, an inhuman tool. Fielding associates

this degeneracy particularly with the reduction of moral discourse to a consumer transaction: satire's instruction is passed over in favor of "tuneful charms" (30) because "'Tis hard to pay them who our faults reveal."

When, in *The Author's Farce* (1730), Fielding recreated Pope's vision of the reign of Mother Dullness on the stage, he characteristically combined Pope's satire of a court's misrule and the inverted literary and social values it promotes with his own insistent satire of inverted sexual identity and nonsensical female desire. In the play within this play, not only does the Goddess of Nonsense choose Signior Opera as the dunce-laureat of her underworld realm, but she has fallen in love with him, and plans to marry him until Mrs. Novel arrives and claims him as her own. When the Goddess of Nonsense chooses the castrato singer over the other competitors for her hand, he bursts into a passionate aria— not one, however, that frames his gratitude or love, but one that sets to music his belief that "In riches is centered all human delight."[18] The Goddess repeats the last line of his tribute to riches "in an ecstasy" and cries "Bravissimo! I long to be your wife": like the ladies' choice in Fielding's epilogue, Nonsense's choice of Signior Opera, rejecting together the phallus and moral "sense," reduces both cultural value and personal desire to a highly-charged monetary worth. The enormous salaries and extravagant gifts commanded by several of the castrato singers performing in London at this time figured repeatedly in the satire against them,[19] serving to link fashion's inflation of prices and destabilizing of value with that intrusion of foreign influence and disruption of gender categories represented by the castrato. Mrs. Novel objects to Nonsense's choice, claiming Signior Opera as her own with the surprising announcement that "he knows I died for love; for I died in childbed" with his child (III.i.390). The important subjects of female desire, reproduction, and value intersect repeatedly in the figure of the castrato—who stands for trouble within each of them—and satire's variations on the simple joke of a castrato reproducing, with which we began, show that joke working through complex relations between the three subjects.

When Fielding included this joke in the scene of the "female politicians" in *The Historical Register*, it had already been spun out at some length in the second of the two pamphlets about Farinelli published in the years preceding the original performance of the play. In Fielding's *Pasquin*, performed one year before *The Historical Register*, the country mayor's daughter shows off her taste and her knowledge of London by describing what she expects to see in town: ". . . and then we shall see Faribelly, the strange man-woman that they say is with child; and the fine pictures of Merlin's cave at the play-houses; and the rope-dancing and the tumbling" (II.i). Miss Mayoress only reveals, of course, her appetite for low entertainments, and she garbles Farinelli's name, but she does so in a way coherent with her version of the miracle of a castrato parenting a child. In giving her the story that Farinelli himself is pregnant, Fielding probably refers to a pamphlet that appeared the same year as *Pasquin*: "An Epistle to *John James H—dd—g—r*, Esq.; On the Report of *Signior F-r-n-lli's* being with Child"[20] This pamphlet reiterates the theme of female sexual desire for a eunuch, but it also imagines the revelation that Farinelli's ambiguous gender actually disguises his true identity as a woman, exposed by the disgrace of his pregnancy:

> What may we think? the Doubt has made me wild;
> Is the soft Warbler then a Wench with Child?
> . . .
>
>   WHAT Words can speak the chaste CLARINDA'S Woe!
> Who now must all her hop'd-for Bliss forgoe?
> Her lovely *Eunuch* to a Woman turn'd,
> For whose secure Embrace so long she's burn'd!
> She who's refus'd a thousand filthy Men,
> Must she still hug her beastly Lap-dog then?
>
>   (pp. 3–4)

The pamphlet's exclamation, "Her lovely *Eunuch* to a woman turn'd," recalls *The Masquerade*'s apocalyptic vision of gender instability: "For when Men Women turn—why then/May Women not be changed to Men?" At the same time, the pamphlet, by turning the castrato into a woman, explicitly reveals the threat of a woman's sexual preference for another woman beneath the threatening oddity of a woman's sexual preference for a eunuch. Con Phillips's pamphlet had linked Farinelli, with his ambiguous gender, to interruptions of the class system ("Your glitt'ring Equipage the Ring shall grace,/And to no Man of Quality's give place"), to disruptions of others' gender identities ("And he that would not start at Death, or Fire,/Shall like a Girl at thy soft Trill expire"), and even to confusions of the categories of animate and inanimate beings ("Your Voice shall cast all Mortals in a Trance,/Ev'n Things inanimate to that shall Dance").[21] This second pamphlet ends by implying that the stability of currency's value rests on the stability of gender categories: as long as a castrato stays at least "half a Man," his value insures the value of his subscriber's investment, and only the proof of his possession of a phallus, even a castrated one, can provide that insurance. The pamphlet presents the abstract principle of the masculine basis of monetary value in crude and material form: the author recommends to opera subscribers that in the future they "serve your Eunuchs as they serve the

Pope/ Before they sign, let every Member grope." Each member of a
jury of "good Matrons" is to swear

> That she has seen and felt how Matters stand,
> With her own naked Eye and naked Hand.
> Unless you take this Method for the future,
> Your Silver Tickets may as well be Pewter.
>
> (pp. 6–7)

The penis here submits to examination by palpation to sustain a system of monetary values, just as it submits to use as a lashing rod to
sustain a system of moral values in Fielding's vision of satire, or as the
Pope's penis must be grasped, according to the pamphleteer, before he
can head a system of religious authority. Of course the phallus to be
witnessed by the opera subscribers is a specifically diminished one. Ironically, by focusing on the "half" of masculine identity the castrato maintains rather than the half he lacks, the pamphlet deepens the castrato's
association with instability of value; by taking a castrated penis as its
guarantor that silver will not turn to pewter, the pamphlet comments
on the already deteriorated standard of its society; and by reenacting
the replacement of the phallic man by the prized eunuch with the turning of that eunuch to a woman, it implies that once ambiguity has been
introduced, value is open always to further deterioration. In an economy
undergoing a financial revolution, newly dependent on the impalpable
worth of paper credit and the invisible transactions of "stock-jobbing"
and national debt,[22] the author warns investors to see and feel the object
of value themselves, here embodied in a penis, and figures the collapse
of value as the disastrous interruption of the opera season by the pregnancy of its supposed castrato lead singer—actually a male
impersonator.

This pamphlet imaginatively links the significance of the figure of the
castrato to the significance of the figure of a male impersonator, and I
think that this interpretation of the fertile castrato informs Medley's
scene in The Historical Register, even though the ladies go on to imagine
the miracle of a castrato's reproduction in a different way, as the miracle
of mechanical reproduction and market distribution. The children they
imagine for Farinelli are the wax figures, sold at the New Exchange,
that were the fashionable purchase of the moment.[23] When the 1st Lady
says she'll "bespeak half a dozen tomorrow morning," the 2nd outdoes
her, planning to order "as many as I can cram into a coach with me."
The women who have "all spoken together" in favor of Farinelli, sub-
stituting fashion's influence for sexual desire, blur together sexual reproduction and consumer transaction; their idol Farinelli fathers fash-

ionable commodities that present multiple, identical images of life. One lady suspects that her husband will resent her acquisition of the "children"—"I'm afraid my husband won't let me keep them, for he hates I should be fond of anything but himself"—but another asserts the autonomy from male authority that the ladies' new-found power of purchasing can give them, and treats her devotion to commodities as a replacement for her maternal role within the family: "If my husband was to make any objection to my having 'em, I'd run away from him and take the dear babies [i.e., dolls] with me" (II.i.19–36). The lady extends the refusal of phallic moral enforcement implied by women's choice of "tuneful charms" over satire to a threatened desertion of masculine authority and masculine lineage altogether.

In this scene, Fielding links the figure of the woman as a powerful consumer in a newly commodified society with the figure of the castrato performer, and he implicates the two of them in the issue of ambiguous gender and gender impersonation, the notion of inanimate objects representing or even impersonating life, the spectacle of prices being attached to what should be living things, and the spectre of value's instability in such a scene—all of which concerns will carry over into the onstage auction.

III

The public space the auction occupies is coextensive with the theatrical space of the play within *The Historical Register*. When Lord Dapper, one of the onstage viewers of Medley's work, finds himself carried away by the action and begins to bid on the lots offered (II.i.239), crossing from audience of a play to participant in an auction, we are reminded of the ways in which an auction is itself a kind of theatrical event. The fashionable pastime that Fielding chose to succeed the ladies' discussion of the opera is at once the scene of theatrical, social, and economic activity: it is a performance with material consequences, a theatrical event that sets prices and establishes values through the dramatics of the auctioneer's presentation of objects and the dynamics of audience reaction. Fielding's frequent references to auctions in his work show his interest in this process of dramatic value-setting.[24] The value finally assigned to a lot at an auction marks the strength of the mediated desire it provokes in the audience, arrived at through the interplay of imitation and competition in the crowd. This method of price-setting does not register either the labor value or the use value of an object; the auction attaches value in some sense not to the object but to its dramatic shell, to the representation of the object the auctioneer offers. The auction did not emerge in England as a method of price-setting until the end of the seventeenth century, and it was in the eighteenth century that it first became institutionalized with the founding of the earliest auction house, Sotheby's, in 1744, followed by Christie's in 1766.[25] Christopher Cock has been called "the first auctioneer,"[26] and the events he presided over provided a new form of social occasion for the fashionable set in London: Cock's auctions made *buying* a social event, and the crowds that gathered at an auction for entertainment acted out the movement of price-setting through demand that was crucial to their emerging "consumer society," as well as the spectatorship to consumption upon which that society depends.[27]

When the ladies of the introductory conversation turn their attention from the opera to the auction they will attend, the 1st Lady links Mr. Hen, the auctioneer, to Farinelli, the castrato, when she exclaims, "Oh, dear Mr. Hen! . . . I never miss him," recalling the 2nd Lady's rhetorical question, "Who can miss an opera while Farinello stays?" In the play's original productions, the auctioneer's entrance enforced and rendered more substantial this association of the two men: Charlotte Charke enters, in male dress, as *"Mr. Hen,* auctioneer, bowing," another figure of ambiguous gender. The castrato singer and the auctioneer are similarly public characters and objects of fashion's hyperbolic and platitudinous desire ("I never miss him"), and Fielding's alteration of the name of the real auctioneer he satirizes—Hen for Cock—deepens the relation between them. The simple alteration involves not only changing gender but also taking the penis out of the slang denotations of the auctioneer's name,[28] and instead evoking connotations of "hen-pecking," the term of "petticoat government" derived from henhouse politics. When the auction begins, we see that, as Medley has promised, the curiosities Hen offers are all allegorical objects, abstract personal qualities represented as pieces of clothing, cosmetics, liquid in a bottle, massive books. Hen takes bids not only on the public virtues of political honesty and patriotism but on modesty, courage, wit, a clear conscience, interest at court, the cardinal virtues, and Common Sense. Fielding here renders comically literal the externalizing of personal virtue with which Shamela makes her bid for profit. To the extent that personified inner virtues are identified as the cultural realm of the feminine, those ideally female qualities here take the form most often of outer garments, to which the public affixes a price.

Although the humor of the scene depends on this nonsensical notion of auctioning off abstract personal qualities in the form of concrete objects, in his advertisements for many of the lots Hen acknowledges that what he offers for sale are not those qualities themselves but the profitable appearance of them. When he argues to raise the bids offered for patriotism, for example, Hen emphasizes that it is something that can be taken off or put on when its appearance is advantageous: ". . . sir, I don't propose this for a town suit. This is only proper for the country. Consider, gentlemen, what a figure this will make at an election." He promises his inquiring audience that the "valuable commodity" of modesty which he offers in the form of "a beautiful powder" will "not change the color of the skin" but "serves mighty well to blush behind a fan with, or to wear under a lady's mask at a masquerade" (II.i.157–77). Thus Fielding implies that Hen's farcical reduction of political honesty to the visible, palpable cloak sold in his auction is only an extension or literalization of the way in which the impalpable virtue of political honesty, like other virtues, has been reduced by the times to the advantageous appearance of such. This reduction leads, Fielding implies, to a confusion of the feminine and masculine realms of inner life and public action, to a kind of cross-dressing of one as the other—to Shamela's (profitable and powerful) affected sufferings and affected "vartue," the "cloak" of honesty, or the impersonations of a Mr. Hen.

Fielding would satirize Christopher Cock again by supplying Cock's name in place of a general reference to auctions in his translation of Juvenal's Sixth Satire as "modernised in Burlesque Verse" (revised and published in the *Miscellanies*, 1743). The context of the reference in Juvenal's satire allows Fielding to associate Cock and his auction directly with the transgression of gender categories. The misogynist satire turns its attention for the moment from adultery and female willfulness to "fighting females,/Whom you would rather think to be males." As translated by Fielding, the poem asks, "Will they their sex entirely quit?" and warns:

> . . . should your wife by auction sell,
> (You know the modern fashion well)
> Should Cock aloft his pulpit mount,
> And all her furniture recount,
> Sure you would scarce abstain from oaths,
> To hear, among your lady's clothes,
> Of those superb fine horseman's suits,
> And those magnificent jack-boots.
>   And yet, as often as they please,
> Nothing is tenderer than these.
> A coach!—O gad! they cannot bear
> Such jolting!—John, go fetch a chair.
> Yet see through Hyde Park how they ride!
> How masculine! almost astride![29]

While Cock remains Cock in this passage, what he sells from his pulpit are the cast-offs of women dressing as men. Fielding expands Juvenal's reference to an auction into a description of the "modern fashion" and its primo auctioneer, and this description leads to his free rendering of Juvenal's complaint in the terms of "masculine" women riding in Hyde Park. But, following Juvenal, he complicates his portrait of the masculine woman by saying she, contradictorily, can at times assert the special claims of high femininity: when not riding astride, she may insist on her need for a more delicate conveyance than a coach. The woman's demand for a chair in this passage repeats an association of women with extravagant consumerism throughout the satire, and Fielding's use of Juvenal to comment on modern women makes clearer a complication in the cross-dressing of *The Historical Register*'s auction of virtues.

While in many contexts women are consigned to the idealized or at least etherealized realm of inner virtues, in the context of the classical tradition of misogynist satire, they are implicated in the material realm of the commodity more deeply than men. As Pope does in "To a Lady," Fielding uses Juvenal's satire to turn his attack on modern luxuries and commodification against women.[30] Tellingly, Fielding chooses to close his translation of the satire—he breaks off less than half way through Juvenal's poem—at the point at which Juvenal makes his denunciation of women a denunciation of luxury, consumption, and money. Juvenal goes on to consider women's crimes of lust and violence, but Fielding stops here to conclude his version of the satire:

> Whence come these prodigies? . . . I' th' mountain
> The British dames were chaste, no crimes
> The cottage stain'd in elder times;
> When the laborious wife slept little,
> Spun wool, and boil'd her husband's kettle. . . .
> Money's the source of all our woes;
> Money! whence luxury o'erflows
> And in a torrent, like the Nile,
> Bears off the virtues of this isle.
>
> (pp. 341–43)

Fielding locates the virtue of chastity in the past economy of a "laborious wife" with her cottage industry, and, in associating the luxury and expenditure of the new economy with the women Juvenal's satire abuses, he acknowledges that England's developing capitalism has made women generally consumers rather than producers, and so figures for commodification itself.[31]

If we look back to Hen's auction of virtues now, we can see how it uses the contradiction between two simultaneously maintained cultural realms of the feminine. Its reverse allegory of abstract qualities offered for sale as concrete objects ironically conjoins, in those objects, the sentimental association of women with inner life and the satiric association of them with material commodities. The auction shows one passed off as the other, and so makes women the brunt of its commentary on a society in which luxury has borne off virtues and the public world of action has been converted to a theater of goods. Mr. Hen, the cross-dressed auctioneer who calls for bids on items with names from one feminine realm and shapes from the other, stands as a figure for the way money and purchasing have entered into, and disrupted, the division of male and female roles. The influence of fashion upon women is one way both Fielding's translation of Juvenal and his auction scene in *The Historical Register* describe women's betrayal of the realm of virtues for that of commodities. Mr. Hen receives no bids on the "valuable commodity" of modesty, for his audience informs him that it is "out of fashion" (II.i.163–5).

As Neil McKendrick has demonstrated, the first half of the eighteenth century saw the emergence in England of a commercialized society that made rapidly changing fashion for the first time more influential than tradition.[32] And Fielding often locates his account in his historical moment, making it a satiric commentary on what the world has come to. At the same time, the implications of his commentary are often philosophical: he uses England's consumer revolution as a means of raising, and negotiating, the most basic questions about gender and identity.

IV

By offering virtues and other personal qualities for sale by bidding, Mr. Hen's auction caricatures the possibility that aspects of personal identity may be mere acquisitions. The last lot Hen offers receives no bids because, as Medley explains, "everyone thinks he has it" already: Lot 10 consists of "a little Common Sense." Medley's satire, however, depends on the implication that in passing over the "very valuable commodity" of Common Sense, the crowd doesn't realize its own lack, and Fielding's original audiences would be especially ready to catch this implication if they knew of Fielding's extremely popular play of the year before, *Pasquin*. Lot 10 is the first of Hen's lots that appears in capital letters as a personified entity, and the figure Common Sense had appeared, not only personified but dramatized and enthroned, as Queen Common-sense in Fustian's tragedy within *Pasquin*. Indeed, Fielding's presentation of Common Sense there had been memorialized just a month and a half before *The Historical Register*'s first performance when Chesterfield and Lyttelton named their new Opposition newspaper after her, commenting in their first leader that they took the name from "an ingenious Dramatick Author [who] has consider'd Common Sense as so extraordinary a thing, that he has lately, with great wit and humour, not only personified it, but dignified it too with the title of a Queen."[33] In *Pasquin*'s final scene Queen Common-sense, with only one follower, battles against Queen Ignorance, who lands with a "foreign force."

Fielding often imagines fashion as a force from outside native English society, responsible for its increasing decadence. And this foreign force, as we might expect, is deeply implicated in gender confusions and inversions. It includes opera singers and welcomes "Squeekaronelly" to its fold; it sponsors Lord Hervey's play *The Modish Couple* (V.i.);[34] and it extends its sponsorship of impersonation beyond gender to species when it welcomes "Two dogs that walk on their hind legs only, and personate human creatures so well, they might be mistaken for them" and "A human creature that personates a dog" (V.i.). Gender impersonation remains the central paradigm for Ignorance's inversions: played by Mr. Strensham in *Pasquin*'s original productions, the role of Queen Ignorance is one of Fielding's most obviously significant cross-gender casting choices. Common-sense is a feminine personification, and she lacks any attendant, active force in the masculine military world. Ignorance, with all her followers, is a man masquerading as a queen.

A poet who approaches Queen Common-sense in the last stages of her battle identifies Ignorance as an impersonator by nature. He threatens Common-sense:

> . . . I'll dedicate my play
> To Ignorance, and call her Common-sense:
> Yes, I will dress her in your pomp, and swear
> That Ignorance knows more than all the world. (V.i.)

The force of Ignorance has dressed itself, according to this play, in feminine pomp in order to impose upon the England it seeks to conquer. The danger Fielding sees in his equation of virtues with clothing in the auction scene of *The Historical Register* is that clothing and pomp, inherently transferable, immediately introduce the possibility of appropriation: any ways in which virtue manifests itself externally allow for its impersonation. We are left to choose between the invisible authenticity of Virtue and the dramatically visible but monstrous impersonations of Affectation.

Defeated, Common-sense is murdered at the end of *Pasquin*, though she returns as a ghost to pronounce the moral:

> My ghost, at least, they cannot banish hence.
> And all henceforth, who murder Common-sense,
> Learn from these scenes that though success you boast,
> You shall at last be haunted with her ghost. (V.i.)

The triumph of Common-sense here is equivocal at best; she loses her life but retains some form of voice, gaining the special authority of ghostly speech. Under the humor of this surprise second ending to Fielding's version of the *Dunciad*, lies, I think, some kind of serious attempt to imagine a way out of the dilemma posed in his writing by the separation of inward virtue and outward authority: Common-sense escapes the hopeless alternatives of invisible truth and visible impersonation by returning as an after-effect, a lost presence, a haunting. To ward off any possibility of impersonation, apparently, she must be deprived not only of clothing and pomp but of her body. Woman bears the representational burden for Fielding of his disappointment about the relation between internal and external selves, as, culturally, she must sustain the realm of private life, interior feeling, and personal identity apart from the public and commercial world of the male; inevitably, then, she must fail Fielding through her reliance on the "harlotry" of pomp, ostentation, or the drama of self-display if she is to be a part of this world. Becoming a ghost is her only alternative. And yet Fielding fears this alternative fate as well, though he may seem to wish it on her.

In taking on a cultural understanding of gender and identity that divorces the private, inner life from the physical and public self, and grants to women that shadowy inner realm, Fielding finds himself with a mixed legacy, which he represents with all the intelligent subtleties of his own ambivalence. Women are rendered by this system of thought both conveniently powerless in public terms and conveniently receptive to all the values men abdicate, values perhaps in conflict with the demands of public life, and yet ones which they have some stake in preserving, even as ghost-presences. Yet Fielding seems to suspect that by using gender to divorce these realms, he has rendered both sexes genderless, inhuman in some way: a ghost's spirit or a mechanically animated body. In insisting that Virtue remain invisible and not seize the raiments of outward authority or drama, Fielding exiles spirit to the underworld of ghostly abstraction—and also exiles outward authority to the lifeless materiality of puppetry or costume. Fielding's interest in puppets and other mechanical impersonations of life is as insistent as his interest in ghosts.

V

We can conclude our inspection of Fielding's exploration of gender and impersonation by moving outside the theater—though not far from Cock and Hen—and considering his account of the career of one male impersonator, who came to represent for Fielding the failure of the phallus to guarantee a masculine authority based on the possession of an inalienable natural part. The spectre of a constructed or acquired phallus—so shocking an object as to remain unnameable for Fielding—figures large in his most direct, extended, and violently defensive representation of gender impersonation, the pamphlet account of *The Female Husband* (1746).

Based very loosely on an actual case tried before Fielding's first cousin, *The Female Husband* recounts the adventures of "Mrs. Mary, alias Mr. George Hamilton," a lesbian and male impersonator who courts and actually marries several women in the guise of a man.[35] Fielding fabricates most of his account of Mary's life,[36] and one possible source for much of his fabrication seems to me revealing. The fictional life he gives Mary Hamilton shares much with the real life story of another male impersonator, Charlotte Charke, whom we have met already in the role of Mr. Hen in *The Historical Register*.[37] Fielding's treatment of her life, as conflated with Mary Hamilton's, can provide us, then, with a view into a final level of reference for the figure of Mr. Hen as he presides over the auction of virtues within the "allegory" of this scene.

Within the theater, Fielding played with and capitalized upon the dramatic possibilities gender impersonation offers, but Charlotte Charke's acting career carried over into her offstage life—she lived as a male impersonator outside the theater as well—and her life, superimposed onto Mary Hamilton's, seems to have raised for Fielding the difficulty of containing impersonation within the theater, the frightening extension of impersonation onto the whole "stage of life," where appropriation comes to stand in for identity and donning the breeches makes one as good as male. In this pamphlet Fielding tells us that, for all intents and purposes, it matters not to the female husband's wives what her penis is made of, whether it is artificial and "affected" or real. After the consummation of Mary's first marriage, "the bride expressed herself so well satisfied with her choice, that being in company with another old lady, she exulted so much in her happiness, that her friend began to envy her"(38). When Mary's second wife is questioned as to whether "she imagined [her husband] had behaved to her as a husband ought to his wife? Her modesty confounded her a little at this question; but she at last answered she did imagine so" and that she had harbored no suspicion of "being imposed upon"(50). In fact, this wife too had aroused suspicious envy in other women by "the extraordinary accounts which she had formerly given of her husband"(49).

At the same time, not everyone he meets is thoroughly impressed with "George" Hamilton's masculinity. A widow he courts early in his adventures sends him a sarcastic letter of rejection that describes her astonishment at receiving a written proposal from him: "I thought, when I took it, it might have been an Opera song, and which for certain reasons I should think, when your cold is gone, you might sing as well as *Farinelli*, from the great resemblance there is between your persons"(36). Like the dramatic satires of the 1730s, the letter Fielding writes for the widow makes explicit for us the male counterpart to the female husband, appearing beside her within the same halo of anxiety she inhabits for Fielding: the detachability of masculine identity and power implied by the castrato prepares us for the appropriation of phallic identity represented by that "something of too vile, wicked and scandalous a nature, which was found in [Hamilton's] trunk," the artificial phallus which forms the basis of her conviction and the final and unspeakable outrage in Fielding's account of her (49). Of course, this appropriated phallus has its shortcomings, its inconvenient absences, but, as Fielding himself points out, so does a natural phallus—Fielding glosses a story of George's near discovery through the unexpected amorous advances of his wife with an analogy to the failures of unimpersonated masculinity:

One of our English Poets remarks in the case of a more able husband than Mrs. *Hamilton* was, when his wife grew amorous in an unseasonable time.

> *The Doctor understood the call,*
> *But had not always wherewithal.*

So it happened to our poor bridegroom, who having not at that time *the wherewithal* about her, was obliged to remain meerly passive, under all this torrent of kindness of his wife. (39)

That phallus which was to safeguard normative masculinity from the disruptive implications of the figure of the castrato—that phallus which was to insure moral and rhetorical, financial and political order—we here find reduced to an erratic and undignified means, a *"wherewithal"* which flickers in and out of the possession even of "a more able husband than Mrs. *Hamilton*." And *"wherewithal"* in this passage serves to describe both the original and the constructed phallus: they are bracketed together here under one demeaning term, and belittled, together, in the face of the demands of female desire.

The Female Husband plays out the concerns that pervade Fielding's early plays, literalizing in an unpleasant but often revealing way one valence of those concerns. An implication of Mary's story that Fielding refers to but does not emphasize hints at other valences. As an effective female husband, she may disrupt systems of distributing not only sexual but financial power by gender. The scandalous motivation for her first marriage, Fielding tells us, is not lesbian love but "the conveniency which the old gentlewoman's fortune would produce in her present situation" (36–37)—as nominal husband Mary would legally control the fortune she wedded in her impersonated role.[38] In some sense, it is all the authority of every kind with which the masculine phallus has been entrusted in Fielding's works that makes it hard to distinguish from its "vile, wicked and scandalous" counterfeit: vested with so much authority, the phallus threatens detachment and dispossession, the possibility of appropriation. Other repositories of authority and power, other fetishized parts of sexual or political bodies, undergo a similar process. A *Champion* essay printed at the end of 1739 discusses the "strange *Lignifaction*" that spreads from the staffs of authority to the men that wield them, turning living flesh to wood and puppetry.[39]

As personal identity merges with social, political, or professional role in the exclusive masculine realm of public life, an acquired phallus comes to serve as well as a natural one. While the women who attend Hen's auction represent the collapse of the disembodied feminine realm of virtue into the alternative, negative realm of the material commodity, the male impersonator who presides over the auction reminds us of the susceptibility to impersonation of masculine identity as conceived in relation to those realms. The notorious offstage life of the woman who played Mr. Hen provided another layer to the figure of Mr. Hen onstage, deepening the audience's awareness of that susceptibility. *The Female Husband* shows Fielding at once at his most violently defensive about the scandal of female appropriation of male identity and at his most explicit about the thorough appropriability of a masculine identity constituted by clothing and the force of the phallus. When the phallus, counted on to insure so much, becomes indistinguishable from an inanimate impersonation of life, like Virtue's treacherous "pomp," it becomes transferable—then the castrato appears too typical, and the male impersonator emerges as too powerful, too capable of convincingly wearing the breeches which the man, after all, only filled with something not really his own. Fielding holds an ambivalent relation to patriarchal power: he wants to clothe phallic identity in the outward authority of political, financial, and moral power, but he is not blind to the ways in which, put to such uses, the phallus becomes a part of the impersonal trappings of power, leaving the domain of personal identity and desire void and the trappings in precarious possession of their wearer. Though in the satire of his plays he cannot seem to move beyond imagining separate domains of masculine and feminine power, Fielding anxiously observes that such a geography of gender populates its world with ghosts and puppets.

4

REPRESENTING AN UNDER CLASS: Servants and Proletarians in Fielding and Smollett

John Richetti

I

My title rehearses a long-discarded issue, for as Bruce Robbins reminds us in his provocative book, *The Servant's Hand: English Fiction From Below*, modern criticism has no illusions about the novel's social comprehensiveness. The genre, as he puts it, has always in fact avoided representing in any sustained way the common people, "occupying itself with servants rather than with proletarians" and thereby casting "its lot with rhetoric rather than realism."[1] To some extent, this state of affairs is a scandal, for in its substitution of the literary servant for the masses of men and women who have done the hard work over the centuries, novelistic realism thereby exposes itself as a silent refusal to represent historical and social difference. But in Robbins's view such a refusal provides a textual ground where the excluded can make their presence felt. His argument, in part, is that this exclusion exposes realism as a "signifying practice" rather than as a mirror held up to nature, allowing us to see in the novel a "medium or arena of political skirmishing."[2] In other words, in these rhetorical operations that rehearse the overtly conventionalized figure of the servant, the novel compromises its realistic claims and bears traces of the strains of that exclusionary process, pointing to its essential nonreferentiality and conventionality and denying the transparency of its representations.

It should come as no surprise that the eighteenth-century novel has this bias and prefers comic servants to recognizable working people. The historian W. A. Speck has recently surveyed this familiar terrain and concluded that the "lower orders" were in effect invisible, as literature in the early century presented "not the reality of life among the lower orders, but how it, and they, were perceived by those above them."[3] Such a process of reflexive representation is probably inevitable in any ruling culture's view of the dominated. A character's subordination in a master-servant relationship seems, in every novel from the period that I can think of, an ineradicable sign of comic inferiority. Such status limits characters to the repetition of stock responses and precludes the self-discovery or expansion or transformation that identifies the novel's protagonists. Readers of *Moll Flanders* will recall the intensity of her childhood aversion to the "service" that seems her fate as an orphan dependent on the parish welfare system. Defoe clearly signals by the prominence he gives this opening detail that Moll is a character worth writing about, a singular and individualized self, precisely because she can embark on a career that traverses normal social boundaries and thereby undermines the hierarchical inevitability summed up in "service." In her revulsion to that service, Moll in effect points to Defoe's implicit understanding of the dangers for the particular sort of authenticity he was after that are built into the representation of servants. Service as such excludes the singularity of personality that defines an authenticity (in fact a class privilege) we now identify as novelistic.

What makes Defoe's narratives a unique and to some extent false starting point for eighteenth-century fiction is just this dramatization of the possibility for free individual action in the face of the social necessity embodied in service. The major novelists of the mid-century who follow Defoe may be said to ground their narratives in social inevitability and class stratification undermined by characters like Moll. Richardson's correspondents in *Clarissa*, to take a glaring example, assume the existence of a world of anonymous or interchangeable workers as the sustaining backdrop for their epistolary self-elaborations. When servants appear, they are necessarily part of that processed experience, visible only through the filters of their leisured masters' perceptions. On those rare occasions when they actually appear through their own writing, their discourse is marked by grammatical and orthographic awkwardness that makes it worthless for self-definition, revealing in its clumsiness an unredeemable class location that highlights the freedom of movement their masters enjoy. Pamela, of course, signifies by her extraordinary fluency and correctness as a writer that she is destined for social elevation.

In Fielding's and Smollett's novels, the situation is somewhat different and quite a bit more pertinent to the issue of social representation. Social comprehensiveness is, after all, one of their explicit features. In their variety of action and scene, such novels seem to promise the eighteenth-century reader a social-moral wholeness otherwise unavailable. The open road along which their characters travel is crowded with a rowdy cross-section of eighteenth-century society. But what looks at first like disorderly plenitude is in fact governed by a hierarchical system of values and a linear progress toward moral and social order summed up in the career of the protagonist as he moves toward integration within society. Indeed, the implicit project of such narrative is the extraction of that order from what appears at first as a chaotic sort of plenitude. Part of the essential comedy of these novels is that beneath all these historically specific social surfaces there lies a recurrent and indeed an inevitable generalized human pattern. But these available historical materials out of which Fielding and Smollett partly construct their narratives can offer, it seems to me, a certain resistance to their appropriation by comic rhetoric, and at some points the actual may be said to leave its traces on that rhetoric. Specifically, the greatest difficulty for comic appropriation occurs in the representation of characters who are in one way or another temporarily outside stabilizing master-servant relationships and in whom we glimpse for a moment the proletarian alternative to the literary reconstruction of the lower orders. What I wish to explore in the following essay are a few interesting cases in Fielding and Smollett where one can observe the literary servant being constructed out of an actuality in which there lurk other beings, the under class from which the eighteenth-century servant class was in fact recruited.

Of late, the eighteenth-century under class, rural as well as urban, has been rediscovered or at least redefined, notably by E. P. Thompson and other historians he has influenced.[4] Briefly summarized, their revisionist view of eighteenth-century English society emphasizes that ruling-class hegemony was imperfect, and that social control was only partially ideological, depending on an increasingly bloody and repressive penal code in the face of various popular forms of resistance. Part of such resistance is manifested, say these historians, in crimes like smuggling and poaching, which were often the expression of traditional or precapitalist popular prerogatives violated by an increasingly rapacious or efficient landed oligarchy and an emerging capitalist order founded on the extension of private property and laws to protect it by a legislature dominated by what Thompson calls a "patrician banditti."[5] For Thompson, such crimes express a sort of countercultural opposition, which is visible as well in outbursts of popular rage like riots, a species of class warfare (or "class struggle without class," as Thompson calls it) that is almost explicit in the enactment of the so-called Black Act of 1723, which extended the death penalty to cover crimes against property as trivial as cutting down young trees or deerstalking in disguise. Thompson evokes a *"rebellious* traditional culture" that resisted economic innovation, often in the name of older patriarchal forms, and he defines the eighteenth-century "crowd" opposed to the ruling oligarchy as a group stretching from the small gentry and professional men down to the poor. There is, he emphasizes, no coherent under class culture as such but rather a set of gentry-pleb relationships manifest in widespread behavior such as "resistance to religious homily," a "picaresque flouting of the provident bourgeois virtues," "ironic attitudes toward the Law," and in "a ready recourse to disorder."[6]

To some extent, the attitudes Thompson extracts from historical evidence are dramatized if not always explicitly endorsed in much eighteenth-century comic fiction. And some writers, Fielding for one, sympathized with the resistance against the abuses perpetrated by the ruling oligarchy. As Thompson emphasizes, there was humane, enlightened opposition to ferocious legislation like the Black Act, and he notes the moral influence of literature when he says that "men whose sensibility had been nourished by *Joseph Andrews* were reluctant to enforce it."[7] The epigraph to *Whigs and Hunters* is a brief bit of dialogue from *Joseph Andrews*: "'Jesu!' said the Squire, 'would you commit two persons to bridewell for a twig?' 'Yes,' said the Lawyer, 'and with great lenity too; for if we had called it a young tree they would have been both hanged!'"[8] The persons in question are Joseph and Fanny, and the squire is Richardson's Mr. B— become Fielding's Squire Booby, who learns here that the justice is applying the dreadful, ludicrous letter of the law on the instructions of the jealous Lady Booby, and the squire's sister. Much of *Joseph Andrews* is a high-spirited but deeply indignant indictment of actions performed by characters whose identities and motives point in two directions: the moral-literary tradition of satire and the specific social and economic circumstances of the mid-eighteenth century.

On the one hand, *Joseph Andrews* features traditional satiric targets: self-serving, often fraudulent or incompetent professionals like doctors, lawyers, and clergymen; sexually aggressive women like Mrs. Slipslop and Lady Booby herself; and aspiring petit-bourgeois types like publicans and land managers. But on the other hand, Fielding places these characters, quite specifically at certain moments in the narrative, within that pattern of exploitation and resentment Thompson has isolated. Lady Booby, in this sequence he quotes from, attempts to exploit the letter of a repressive contemporary statute in order to satisfy a jealousy provoked within a story that deliberately echoes the biblical tale of Joseph and Potiphar's wife. The object of traditional satiric scorn for her unseemly passion for Joseph, she is also the absentee landlord whose return to the country temporarily restores a disrupted rural economic order:

> The coach and six, in which Lady Booby rode, overtook the other travellers as they entered the parish. She no sooner saw Joseph than her cheeks glowed with red, and immediately after became as totally pale. She had in her surprise almost stopt her coach; but recollected herself timely enough to prevent it. She entered the parish amidst the ringing of bells, the acclamations of the poor, who were rejoiced to see their patroness returned after so long an absence, during which time all her rents had been drafted to London, without a shilling being spent among them, which tended not a little to their utter impoverishment; for, if the court would be severely missed in such a city as London, how much more must the absence of a person of great fortune be felt in a little country village, for whose inhabitants such a family finds a constant employment and supply; and with the offals of whose table the infirm, aged, and infant poor are abundantly fed, with a generosity which hath scarce a visible effect on their benefactor's pockets! (IV.1.277)

Fielding's insistence in this passage on socio-economic particularity is balanced by his universalized moral generality. Indignation is tempered by amusement; specific economic abuse by perennial moral generality. Fielding's characters belong almost entirely to the literary traditions of satire and pastoral comedy, the Cervantic manner promised on the book's title page. They are shifted from 1742 to the timeless realm of human comedy by the tongue-in-cheek moral and biblical typology. Thanks to these perspectives, Joseph and Fanny are only playing at being plebeians threatened by repressive laws, and they are transformed by the entirely traditional turns of Fielding's pastoral comedy into members of the gentry in a timeless social order. The scene Thompson cites is ironically supplemented by this literary solution; Joseph and Fanny are rescued by literary tradition, not by any alteration of the harsh statute that threatens them. And Lady Booby, with her sustaining entourage, returns to London, abdicating again her vital role as chief consumer in the country economy to repeat (as she must as a satiric character locked into recurrent self-enactment) her passion for Joseph with a "young captain of dragoons."

With Thompson as our guide, we can easily find a clearly focused indignation and compassion in the narrator of Fielding's novels, but the social actualities behind that moral response tend to be diffused by their narrative elaborations, which direct a reader's attention away from particularity to comic generality. The energetic resistance to the dominant culture Thompson finds in a plebeian eighteenth-century counter- or subculture is in effect missing or neutralized in Fielding's fiction, the conflict implicit in its outbursts replaced by a rendition of social actuality that accommodates to a moral-literary tradition the potentially subversive energy and cultural integrity of those observed. Consider, as a typical example, the scene at the local church where Molly Seagrim, wearing a gown donated by Sophia, "with a new laced cap, and some other ornaments Tom had given her," is attacked by the envious women of the parish.[9] Fielding makes this the occasion for a broad mock-heroic battle in the church yard, but his playfulness is accompanied by a distaste implicit in the rendering of the specifically localized rural brutality of the "*Somersetshire* mob," dispersed in the end of this sequence, it is worth noting, by Tom's horsewhip:

> As a vast herd of cows in a rich farmer's yard, if, while they are milked, they hear their calves at a distance, lamenting the robbery which is then committing, roar and bellow: So roared forth the *Somersetshire* mob an hallaloo, made up of almost as many squawls, screams, and other different sounds, as there were persons, or indeed passions, among them: Some were inspired by rage, others alarmed by fear, and others had nothing in their heads but the love of fun; but chiefly envy, the sister of *Satan*, and his constant companion, rushed among the crowd, and blew up the fury of the women; who no sooner came up to Molly, than they pelted her with dirt and rubbish. (IV.8.178–79)

A historian might see this scene (and others like it in eighteenth-century novels where lower-class social pretension is punished by similar intra-class rioting) as based to some extent on the traditional custom of "rough music," which as Robert W. Malcolmson summarizes it, was the "ritualized expression of hostility towards individuals whose behavior was judged to be flagrantly unnatural, unjust or otherwise deviant."[10] Actual "rough music" was less violent and more culturally coherent than Fielding's battle in the church yard, usually as Malcolmson says a matter of "raucous noise-making, accompanied by hostile chants and other forms of derision" meant to punish deviations from the moral norms of plebeian culture, or to provoke a sense of shame in the offender and assert a communal outrage.[11] In explaining the origins of the battle, Fielding ignores the plebeian actuality it resembles; rather, he makes the scene into a confirmation of comic universalizing: "The great are deceived, if they imagine they have appropriated ambition and vanity to themselves. These noble qualities flourish as notably in a country church, and church-yard, as in the drawing-room, or in the closet. Schemes have indeed been laid in the vestry, which would hardly disgrace the conclave. Here is a ministry, and here is an opposition. Here are plots and circumventions, parties and factions, equal to those which are to be found in courts" (IV.7.177).

Tom Jones promises a richly comprehensive social representation, but Fielding undercuts that promise by these recurring moral equivalences that reduce or even nullify social distance and difference. Especially from our current historical perspective, the specific effect is to suppress or deny the existence of plebeian culture, which becomes simply a degraded or parodic mirror image of the dominant culture. When he describes at the beginning of Book IX the talents that separate the "historian" from the ignorant authors of "novels and romances," Fielding singles out as crucial what he calls "conversation," worldly experience he defines as "universal, that is, with all ranks and degrees of men":

> For the knowledge of what is called high-life, will not instruct him in low, nor *e converso*, will his being acquainted with the inferior part of mankind teach him the manners of the superior. And though it may be thought that the knowledge of either may sufficiently enable him to describe at least that in which he hath been conversant; yet he will even here fall greatly short of perfection: for the follies of either rank do in reality illustrate each other. For instance, the affectation of high-life appears more glaring and ridiculous from the simplicity of the low; and again the rudeness and barbarity of this latter, strikes with much stronger ideas of absurdity, when contrasted with, and opposed to the politeness which controuls the former. Besides, to say the truth, the manners of our historian will be improved by both these conversations: For in the one he will easily find examples of plainness, honesty, and sincerity; in the other of refinement, elegance, and a liberality of spirit; which last quality I myself have scarce ever seen in men of low birth and education. (IX.1.494)

Superficially a recognition of social difference, the social panorama offered here provides a controlling and stabilizing moral perspective, and makes these ends of the social spectrum into a static taxonomy of human possibility rather than a register of social diversity. All this is hardly surprising, for such elegant commonplaces are the stock in trade of neoclassical moralizing aesthetics. What is worth noting, though, is the polemical and specifically literary purpose of these formulations. They are part of Fielding's half-serious definition of a new genre, which is made up of the traditional narrative patterns of epic and romance imposed upon the contemporary or historical world. But that imposition, Fielding carefully and repeatedly insists, excludes both a vulgar totality, the dreary inclusiveness of "the painful and voluminous historian" (II.1.75), and the ignorant partial views of the authors of contemporary novels and romances that he ridicules. Fielding, in effect, identifies his narrative art as moving in two complementary directions: an informed omission and selectivity that resists a pressingly shapeless and temporary actuality, and a comprehensiveness that constructs a synthetic totality or universalized moral representation out of the un-informative diversity of that same actuality.

Given Fielding's practice, some theoretical remarks by Pierre Mach-erey are both applicable and illuminatingly irrelevant. "The literary work," says Macherey, "is *simultaneously* . . . a reflection and the ab-sence of a reflection." Literary expression, he continues, "does not mean a direct reproduction (or even knowledge), but an indirect figuration which arises from the deficiencies of the reproduction."[12] But Fielding's novels place their own production in the foreground, to use modern critical parlance, pointing to their own deliberate omissions and skillful transformations and rearrangements of what are implicitly the paltry actualities of direct or unmediated experience. Macherey's "deficien-cies" of reproduction, seen as such from the point of view provided by historians like Thompson, seem defiantly inherent in the literary tra-dition to which Fielding turns when he fashions plebeian characters and their world as we now choose to understand them. Promising a richly totalized social representation, Fielding retreats while advancing, mak-ing his "indirect figuration" a synthesizing abridgement of an actuality that otherwise yields no knowledge worth having. What *Tom Jones* makes clear is that to represent the lower orders so that they can be properly apprehended, made part of a moral and social order, the nov-elist must necessarily reconstruct them, extract the universality that is their truth from the temporary historical difference that merely serves to obscure them as knowable subjects. In so doing, Fielding is overtly cancelling history in favor of a recurrent "natural" order, openly pro-ducing what a modern critic might want to call ideology. What *Tom Jones* offers its readers is, to adapt one of Terry Eagleton's formulations, an object "which is inseparable from its modes of fashioning it—which is an *effect* of those modes rather than a distinct entity."[13] Eagleton's ren-dering of ideology, like Macherey's appeal to a reality that literary expression cannot reproduce or even know, insists upon an order of experience (history, a Marxist critic would want to call it) that is coherent and, potentially at least, available for reproduction in some sense (or for some sort of latter-day reconstruction). But this "distinct entity" is visible in *Tom Jones* only as a raw material now no longer present, as circumstances necessarily transformed by ordered representation. Given Fielding's obtrusive fashioning, his avoidance of representational di-rectness, history in this special Marxist sense is by no means denied, but openly and comically negated.

At the beginning of *The Political Unconscious*, Fredric Jameson quotes these stirring words from *The Communist Manifesto*—"The history of all hitherto existing society is the history of class struggle"—and defines his effort as a "restoring to the surface of the text the repressed and buried reality of this fundamental history."[14] But when Ronald Paulson looks very specifically at what he describes as the interaction of "popular and polite art" in the mid-eighteenth century in England, he finds instead a sort of class cooperation between the disorderly energies of popular entertainment (embodied in phenomena like joke books, fairs, puppet shows, bull and bear baiting, farces, prize-fighting, freak shows) and the satiric purposes of artists and writers like Hogarth and Fielding. Paulson sees them as deeply sympathetic to the subversive popular culture Thompson evokes, and he finds a number of key mid-eighteenth-century works (including *Tom Jones*) as drawing a "renewing and revivifying energy" from that culture.[15] In *Tom Jones*, it seems to me that history in the Marxist sense, the buried or repressed reality Jameson speaks of, is in fact occasionally visible, appropriated by an openly ideological representation that demonstrates its comic range and moral confidence precisely by stabilizing those turbulent energies of popular culture Paulson evokes. The simultaneous looking and turning away from the properly historical that Marxist criticism proposes as the key to literary representation is one of the recurrent turns of Fielding's narrative when it confronts social difference. And that difference is most clearly visible in *Tom Jones* precisely when Fielding moves away from servants in the households and entourages of the main characters—Sophia's Mrs. Honour or Tom's Partridge, for example—to figures who seem to inhabit another and recognizably separate realm, the plebeian world glimpsed in the Somersetshire mob in the churchyard.

Of course, there are moments when the narrator refers to that world so incidentally that there is no need to align it to his larger ideological purposes. But one of these marginal references strikes me as inadvertently significant, a fairly graphic rendition of the raw material Fielding normally transforms. In what must be the book's funniest moment, Tom visits Molly Seagrim's garret room to tell her that their love affair cannot continue, but the scene is interrupted by what Fielding calls an "accident" that leads for a moment, unexpectedly, to the urban lower orders in a somewhat unmediated form. After Tom offers to support the pregnant Molly and find her a suitable husband, she is upbraiding him eloquently, railing against the faithless male sex when this accident reveals the philosopher Square, Tom's tutor, squatting ("among other female utensils") in Molly's makeshift closet. The narrator insists with comic precision on the necessity of Square's posture ("as ridiculous as can possibly be conceived"), since Molly's garret precludes standing upright anywhere but in its middle and Square is caught hiding in her closet on the side of the room. "The posture, indeed, in which he stood, was not greatly unlike that of a soldier who is tyed neck and heels; or rather resembling the attitude in which we often see fellows in the public streets of London, who are not suffering but deserving punishment by so standing" (V.5.229).

This last seems an oddly serious comparison for so ludicrous a position. Robert Alter has suggested that Square's attitude is like "the shameless squat of the London rabble in the act of using the streets as a privy."[16] Alter backs away somewhat in a footnote to this remark, saying that the reference could also be to squatting London beggars, whom Fielding regarded as a public nuisance. Whatever the truth, we are violently transported from a Somersetshire transformed by comic invention to an actual London, from economically based reciprocal sexual exploitation and Fielding's comically symmetrical rendering of it, to urban squalor unmodified and unmediated by comic artifice, to brazen defiance or unsightly mendicancy. Eventually Tom will get to London but readers will hear little of that world of plebeian disorder and effrontery, a sort of degraded version of the subversive popular energies evoked by Thompson. As Fielding could write a few years later in one of his social pamphlets, the actual London was a place teeming with beggars: "There is not a parish in the liberty of Westminster which doth not raise thousands annually for the poor, and there is not a street in that Liberty which doth not swarm all day with beggars, and all night with thieves."[17]

In the broad terms I have outlined, *Tom Jones* is overtly ideological in its comic transformation of eighteenth-century society, but those defecating or begging fellows who intrude here seem intractable, unable to be used for anything except a satiric comparison to work out a striking incongruity. The philosopher Square, with his pseudo-geometrical claim to control experience, is caught in a posture closely related to the sexual one he has just been in, and this comparison suddenly forces him into that properly natural awkwardness he denies. Fielding seems to offer it as a direct resemblance, lacking the careful qualification and double negative of the preceding comparison to a trussed-up soldier. Unlike those fellows in the public streets, Square is suffering as he squats, exposed and placed within the moral order *Tom Jones* elaborates. The fellows in the streets escape punishment, since in this version of the world that suddenly here touches the novel disorder may prevail and moral symmetry is extremely difficult to attain. Note the coyness of Fielding's formulation, morally direct but visually uninformative, so that we at least are unsure (if Alter's inspired guess is correct) whether those fellows are begging or defecating. As usual, Fielding's narrative resists the visual or pictorial, stressing position and moral perspective, forcing those fellows down into the bottom of the frame in which Square remains frozen in his ludicrous attitude, aligning them with the soldiers tied up for disciplinary action and thereby instructing us how to understand their meaning in this pictorial but moralized arrangement. Hogarthian grotesques, at least potentially, these squatting fellows point briefly to something like an actual urban disorder the novel pointedly avoids and consistently transforms.

Can it be otherwise in eighteenth-century comic fiction? Can such narrative ever in some sense represent what is always already transformed by comic universalizing and naturalizing? Inevitably, I think the answer is no, but it is perhaps possible to make that transformation less efficient or more visible than Fielding's and to dramatize more clearly than he does the process whereby the historical (in the Marxist sense) is appropriated by fiction. Some moments in Smollett's *Humphry Clinker* illustrate that possibility well.

II

Described when he first enters the book as "a shabby country fellow" taken on by the Bramble entourage as a temporary servant on their journey from Bath to London, Humphry Clinker offends Matt's virago of a sister, Tabitha, by the sight of his bare posteriors, which show through his clothes as he rides postilion ahead of her. His initial appearance after that partial physical exposure is remarkably precise and detailed, visualized as clearly and specifically as his humiliating buttocks (although to the maid servant, Winifred Jenkins, they are a glorious sight, as white as alabaster). The ironical Jery Melford, Matt's nephew, describes Humphry thus: "He seemed to be about twenty years of age, of a middling size, with bandy legs, stooping shoulders, high forehead, sandy locks, pinking eyes, flat nose, and long chin—but his complexion was of a sickly yellow: his looks denoted famine; and the rags that he wore, could hardly conceal what decency requires to be covered."[18] Next to Fielding's visually uninformative renditions, focused as they are on motives and manners, Jery's description of the physical actuality of poverty and dispossession is striking, direct and detailed, a relatively unmediated visual evocation. For the moment at least, Humphry stands as a starving, physically deprived scarecrow, twisted by hard work, bad or meager diet, both "queer and pathetic" in Jery's unsparing view. Humphry is not in costume; his garb denotes only misery and his body real starvation, and what Jery calls "pinking [i.e. squinting] eyes" mark the appearance of fear and uncertainty rather than a bold regard or cunning glance such as a peasant in romance or satire might present. A model of deference, Humphry apologizes to Tabitha for his appearance: "I have had the fever and ague these six months, and spent all I had in the world upon doctors, and to keep soul and body together;

and saving your ladyship's good presence, I han't broke bread these four and twenty hours" (112). His story, as recounted by the landlord of the inn where they've stopped, seems equally free of literary precedent or implication, a starkly brief and uncomplicated case history: "a love begotten babe," Humphry has been raised in the work house and apprenticed by the parish to a blacksmith. When the smith dies before the apprenticeship is complete, Humphry is forced to work as a stable boy, until illness renders him unfit for even that.

Humphry's story claims documentary validity, and his plight evokes a rural proletariat for whom work was varied, seasonal, and uncertain and for whom the local welfare system in case of illness or disability was harshly inefficient. But this ragged plebeian who materializes out of nowhere (or rather is plucked out of the faceless masses available for such labor emergencies) is quickly absorbed by the satirical purposes and the magical transformations of Smollett's novel: his physical particularity provokes not just the comic stereotype of Tabitha's hypocritical prudery and callous indifference but serves as well to illustrate further the breakdown of English social-moral order that Matt excoriates as he travels. The landlord protests when Matt accuses him of having turned the sick and destitute Humphry out to die: "I pay the poors' rate . . . and I have no right to maintain idle vagrants, either in sickness or health; besides such a miserable object would have brought a discredit upon my house" (112). Humphry, in Matt's memorable summary in this scene seems more a satiric device than an individual, an opportunity for moral declamation: "Heark ye, Clinker, you are a most notorious offender— You stand convicted of sickness, hunger, wretchedness, and want" (113).

Perhaps the very alacrity with which Matt's philanthropy transforms Humphry after his introduction is a sign of Smollett's instinctive recognition that a rather too literal and therefore unusable reality has intruded for a moment:

> In the afternoon, as our aunt stept into the coach, she observed, with some marks of satisfaction, that the postilion, who rode next to her, was not a shabby wretch like the ragamuffin who had drove them into Marlborough. Indeed, the difference was very conspicuous: this was a smart fellow, with a narrow brimmed hat, with gold cording, a cut bob, a decent blue jacket, leather breaches, and a clean linen shirt, puffed above the waist-band. When we arrived at the castle on Spin-hill, where we lay, this new postilion was remarkably assiduous, in bringing in the loose parcels; and at length, displayed the individual countenance of Humphry Clinker, who had metamorphosed himself in this manner, by relieving from pawn part of his own clothes, with the money he had received from Mr. Bramble. (113–14)

But this is only the first and least significant of Humphry's transformations: he quickly becomes Matt's devoted servant, a Methodist lay preacher, and finally is discovered to be Matt's long-lost and indeed quite forgotten illegitimate son—rather than part of the faceless under class who have no history worth recording. But as the story progresses, Humphry's independence and difference from the other travelers (even the other servants) is a recurring emphasis. He is given a carefully specific historical identity and function within the novel. That is to say, he is no foundling whose biological connection to the gentry betrays itself in striking beauty or instinctive talent but an awkward Wiltshire lad inseparable from his experiences and acquired skills within a rural plebeian society. When Matt asks him why he should take him on as a servant, this is Humphry's resumé:

> 'An please your honour (answered this original) I can read and write, and do the business of the stable indifferent well—I can dress a horse, and shoe him, and bleed and rowel him; and, as for the practice of sow-gelding, I won't turn my back on e'er a he in the county of Wilts—Then I can make hog's puddings and hob-nails, mend kettles and tin sauce-pans.—' Here uncle burst out a-laughing; and inquired what other accomplishments he was master of—'I know something of single-stick, and psalmody (proceeded Clinker); I can play upon the Jew's-harp, sing Black-ey'd Susan, Arthur-o'Bradley, and divers other songs; I can dance a Welsh jig, and Nancy Dawson; wrestle a fall with any lad of my inches, when I'm in heart; and, under correction, I can find a hare when your honour wants a bit of game.' (114–15)

This casualty of social mismanagement is improbably but instantly and profoundly grateful to his benefactor. Like Shakespeare's Kent but without his self-conscious playing of the diminished role of faithful retainer, Humphry sees that in Matt's countenance which he "would fain call master." To Lear's question, "What's that?" Kent answers, resonantly, "authority" (I.iv.25–32). As Smollett works matters out, to be a part of rural plebeian culture, like this enthusiastic Humphry, is to have acquired the capacity to recognize order and authority and to be immune to the social disorder that has excited Matt's satiric passions at Bath. By seeming to refuse the transformations of comic romance and thus deriving Humphry from his exactly rendered socio-historical circumstances, Smollett's narrative is cunningly ideological as it weaves together Humphry's "natural" instincts for service and his roots in a rural actuality both grimly real and pastoral. Humphry is a rural proletarian, as we may call him, who makes himself willingly into a servant and holds together, albeit unsteadily, those two antithetical possibilities for rendering an under class. At this point in the novel, with the insertion of his titular character, Smollett begins to establish the possibility of a return to a "natural" hierarchical rural order, thereby predicting the ultimate goal of the expedition through England and Scotland and back to Brambleton Hall in Wales with a renewed sense of a social and moral order. Humphry's deference evokes a pastoral alternative to actuality, but his immediate origins in the grimmer aspects of the rural scene lend that alternative a certain authenticity. Moreover, Humphry's instinctive submission points to an order and inevitability meant to contrast with the social disorder and historical contingency Matt has furiously denounced at Bath.

But Humphry introduces this overtly ideological construction only in so far as he remains rooted in the plebeian actualities that have produced him, only in so far as he is immune to comic universalizing in what Jery calls his "originality" or what we might see as his ineradicable class experience. Smollett, we may say, thus attempts to appropriate actuality for his narrative by imagining a character for whom service is not an imposition or a literary transformation but a self-fulfilling discovery. As the novel arranges it, Humphry's desperate case history is the necessary prelude to those lucky accidents and discoveries whereby he finds his biological destiny as both son and servant to the gentry. The magic inevitability in the plot infects, as it were, his prosaic case history of a life, both justifying and redeeming it and the social order that fostered or permitted it. To return to the terms of the Marxist critics I invoked earlier, we may say that Humphry, vividly realized rural plebeian *and* therefore a servant both comic and invaluable, is Smollett's way of looking at both literary tradition and history, and represents thereby his attempt to admit and to exploit the relationships of a dominant culture to its under class.

But the strain of this ideological denial of ideology shows as the novel progresses and Humphry's energy and independence flare out, notably in his conversion to Methodism. The Methodist subplot, though, is a means of placing Humphry within a satiric frame of reference that denies him self-discovering interiority and serious psychological and moral identity by deriving them from external factors. After Humphry is caught preaching before a Methodist congregation (that subversively includes the ladies of the family), Matt reduces his servant's fervor to a pair of possibilities that make service impossible: "Heark ye, Clinker, you are either an hypocritical knave, or a wrong-headed enthusiast; and in either case, unfit for my service" (171). Humphry's reply is interesting, both a submission and an assertion of quick and ingratiating intelligence that in its wit turns Matt's reduction into another reason for service: "Your honour says, I am either a knave or a madman; now, as I'll assure your honour, I am no knave, it follows that I must be mad;

therefore, I beseech your honour, upon my knees, to take my case into consideration, that means may be used for my recovery" (171).

Humphry's singularity is, in one remarkable scene, both affirmed and denied, as he rescues the stranded Bramble party when their coach breaks down on the Yorkshire moors. "A surprising compound of genius and simplicity," as Jery calls him, Humphry repairs the coach with the tools of the recently "defunct" local blacksmith. In a scene that is for Jery "too pathetic to occasion mirth," Humphry as he works at the smith is mistaken for the blacksmith by his grieving, hysterical widow:

> Finding the tools of the defunct, together with some coals in the smithy, he unscrewed the damaged iron in a twinkling, and, kindling a fire, united the broken pieces with equal dexterity and dispatch—While he was at work upon this operation, the poor woman in the straw, struck with the well-known sound of the hammer and anvil, started up, and notwithstanding all the nurse's efforts, came running into the smithy, where, throwing her arms about Clinker's neck, "Ah, Jacob (cried she) how could you leave me in such a condition?" (220)

The powerfully competent servant of patricians who are in the practical sense helpless, Humphry has mastered these skills in the world of real work he comes from, and he is essential as a worker for enabling the expedition, with its various moral and social resolutions pending, to proceed to a successful conclusion. As the scene dramatizes, Humphry is for the moment interchangeable with other workers like the deceased blacksmith. The uncertain emotional tone of the scene as Jery records it testifies to that double embarrassment whereby Humphry is both essential and interchangeable, that is, ultimately disposable as an individual whose identity lies in his efficient and unquestioning service.

Humphry Clinker, then, shows the impossibility for Smollett of seeing a character like Humphry as anything but an ideological subject. For Humphry, as Smollett eventually resolves his identity, self-realization and emancipation from the hopelessness and anonymity of his previous life are possible only within the master-servant relationship as literary tradition represents it. Smollett presents him in a richly particularized, almost distractingly concrete manner precisely to revise him from a social fact into a comic, satiric, and sentimental subject and thereby, of course, to appropriate and "naturalize" the historical experience and identity that make Clinker unique among the book's characters. Such an effect is ideological in the classic sense, quite distinct from Fielding's comic universalizing, which attempts to negate the historical entirely. Smollett's novel thus marks a crucial step in the sophistication of fiction's ideological strategies as history looms larger and eighteenth-century society moves slowly toward open class antagonism and self-consciousness.

5

THE RESIGNATION OF MARY COLLIER: Some Problems in Feminist Literary History

Donna Landry

THO' She pretends not to the Genius of Mr. DUCK, nor hopes to be taken Notice of by the Great, yet her Friends are of Opinion that the Novelty of a *Washer-Woman*'s turning Poetess, will procure her some Readers.
Advertisement to the first edition of *The Woman's Labour* (1739)

It should be clear that *working class* women's oppression poses the key theoretical problem here; for unlike women's subordination in feudal society or within the bourgeoisie, it cannot be related to male control of property.
Johanna Brenner and Maria Ramas, "Rethinking Women's Oppression" (1984)[1]

I

In the case of Hannah More and Ann Yearsley lies a feminist parable for our time, a cautionary tale for those within the discipline of English studies engaged in writing a "properly historical" or materialist feminist literary history. Hannah More (1745–1833) was a writer of morally improving works whose essays, Cheap Repository tracts, and Sunday Schools were attempts to defuse radical social protest in England in the wake of the American and French revolutions; Ann Cromartie Yearsley (1756–1806)[2] was a milkwoman who claimed that poetry helped her

survive hard work, poverty, and near starvation. Winters were especially hard on the laboring poor, with male agricultural laborers usually
jobless. Early in 1784 the pregnant Yearsley, her husband, five children,
and her aged mother "all got together into a stable," expecting to die
of hunger. They were saved by a Mr. Vaughan's "accidentally looking
into the stable," though relief came too late to preserve old Mrs. Cromartie.[3] In the summer of 1784 Yearsley became the object of More's
philanthropy. There they are, the middle-class reformist and the working-class prodigy. The abolitionist who liked to play at life in a cottage
salubriously named Cowslip Green, and the milkwoman whose chief
delight lay in composing verses and offering them to an audience like
that of More's cook, from whom Yearsley obtained the "hogwash" with
which to feed her pig. They first come together in More's kitchen in
Bristol, mediated by this nameless cook, who shows her mistress Yearsley's poems.

How is the privileged middle-class reformist to avoid "patronizing,"
wounding, and exploiting her protegée? How is the working-class poet
to make use of the offer of feminist literary alliance without sacrificing
her dignity and independence, confronted by middle-class propertied
confidence, self-righteousness, fear of insurrection, and the authority
of "educated" speech? There is a danger, too, in reading as texts of
liberation texts that encode merely more subtle forms of subjection, fantasies of servitude that please the master (or mistress), as Julia Swindells
has argued.[4] These are questions that any study of social relations must
take into account, not least in the writing of a feminist literary history.

Reading in Yearsley's poems the "high literary" skill or sense that the
century called "genius," so sought after and here so mysteriously acquired, More recognizes a prodigious talent in these "unlettered
verses."[5] Yearsley herself will be favorably judged more sober and industrious than More might have expected. As time passes and money
does and doesn't change hands in their partnership, More appears to
Yearsley increasingly condescending, and the servility of dependence
becomes unbearable. And once Yearsley comes close to attaining an
independent, private income—the basis of More's own class privilege—
More will have nothing more to do with her. Yearsley uses her capital
to establish a circulating library, but according to Southey, dies in strai-
tened circumstances.[6] The mutual ideological tensions of class expectation and antagonism, always present, finally make continued alliance
impossible.

For More, Yearsley represents that contradiction in eighteenth-century
literary theory, the natural genius, "one who writes under every complicated disadvantage," not the least of which is being a woman. Poverty
exacerbates the ordinary female exclusions from learning and literature.[7]

Hence comes More's dwelling on Yearsley's combining of "the genuine spirit of Poetry" with what renders it "still more interesting," "a certain natural and strong expression of misery."[8] But More cannot countenance the move towards fracturing the "natural" connection between literature and middle-class privilege that Yearsley's independent pursuit of a literary career might bring about. Perhaps one should see here as well a conservative connection between literature as social propaganda, exemplified in More's depoliticizing tracts for the poor,[9] and the de-radicalizing function of literary patronage if it succeeds in providing a member of the working class with certain ameliorations and amenities while reconciling her to her "rightful place." This is the shifting limit of More's reformism, the counterrevolutionary tendency of her interest in Yearsley, and the liberal feminist dilemma writ large: "a good heart and an inadequate methodology."[10]

It is in the interest of more adequate ways of reading, critically and politically, such "marginal" literary texts as Yearsley's that the present essay is offered, in the hope that we need not replicate the theoretical and practical limits of a model like More's in order to gain for a Yearsley a new reading public. But a failure to perceive the homologies that link us to reformists like More might be to court that very replication.

II

Mary Collier represents another working-class "discovery," though one whose social trajectory was even more modest than Yearsley's. So far as we know, the publication of her poems brought her little remuneration and no escape from her labors as a laundress, housekeeper, and occasional field hand in West Sussex and Hampshire. Her most important poem, *The Woman's Labour: An Epistle To Mr. Stephen Duck* (1739), is beginning to receive some scholarly attention, but until recently she was a poet almost entirely forgotten by literary history.[11] *The Woman's Labour* is an important text for at least three reasons. First, the poem's appearance as early as 1739 suggests that English laboring- or working-class feminism has a history that predates its usual association with the nineteenth century. Second, the poem demonstrates that a plebeian poet such as Collier can take aesthetic advantage of her distance from the dominant literary culture by filling a familiar vessel—the georgic, the neoclassical epistle—with strong new content. And, in so doing, she can challenge some of the sexual and socio-political assumptions of the very culture from which she has so skillfully appropriated her aesthetic materials. Finally, the poem articulates an emergent working-class con-

sciousness with an emergent feminist critique of the misogynist tendencies embedded in that consciousness.[12]

The Woman's Labour directly redresses traditional historical silences
regarding working-class women's oppression; the triple burden of wage-
labor, housework, and childcare; and the gender ideology that places
women illusively outside both material production and language. Collier
thus subverts the georgic more radically than Stephen Duck had done
in *The Thresher's Labour* (1736); she definitively alters traditional maps of
eighteenth-century literary history. At the same time, there are significant limits to the radical potential of this and other poems by Collier
which must be addressed if we are to understand such women's histories
in a nuanced way, alert to the often limiting material and social exigencies of their situations. When the woman in question is herself a writer,
we can begin by examining the way she figures herself as a writing
subject, for the self-who-writes is socially constructed.

In *The Woman's Labour* Collier locates herself quite clearly in relation
to the act of writing as well as in relation to the social space from which
her writing emerges. At the point of departure for her speculative flight
on the prehistoric origins of sexual relations, Collier figures herself as
imagining its arguments while lying in bed at the end of a tiring and
monotonous working day:

> Oft have I thought as on my Bed I lay,
> Eas'd from the tiresome Labours of the Day.[13]

Poor women, taken collectively, may have little time to sleep or dream,
as we shall see, but the poet inscribes herself here as conceiving her
arguments for verse in repeated moments of meditation that border on
dream-work. The source of Collier's productivity as a poet is also the
source of her "purity," as well as her "peace" of mind: her relatively
exceptional status as a single woman, without children.[14] Despite the
grinding poverty that so often accompanied life as a single woman in
this period, her working life is more circumscribed, her waking hours
are less restricted than those of the married majority of her class, the
women on whose behalf she writes *The Woman's Labour*. She works only
a double (wage labor, housework), not a triple shift. That is presumably
the difference that counts for her, that separates her from other working
women: her literacy, her talent, her desire to devote her leisure time to
books and writing are in a sense supererogatory. If she had a husband
and children to tend, her literariness would be effectively cancelled in
advance. Such was not the case with Yearsley, who by the time of her
discovery in 1784, had borne six children.[15] But Yearsley appears to be
the exception here. For Collier, as for a significant number of other,

particularly lower-class, women writers, the single life was seen as crucial to the liberty of literary production.

The one form of "labor" omitted from Collier's poem is the "labor" of human reproduction as child*birth*. In place of the labor of birth, Collier gives us a textualization of women's work as social and material, but not exclusively or primarily biological, reproduction. This she can write about knowledgeably, and link with her literary endeavors. Such general social and cultural work is the compensatory prerogative of the spinster, reputedly always with time on her hands, available for child-minding or night-nursing or more public good causes.[16]

If Collier's talents might have been wasted without leisure, her leisure would certainly have been unrewarding to her without education. Not that she received much; as she writes in "Some Remarks of the Author's Life," her "poor, but honest" parents taught her to read when "very Young." But she was never sent to school; at some unspecified time she learned to write "to assist" her memory (iii, iv). Throughout her life, she claims, reading books and composing verses have been her chief, if not her only, recreation. In "An Epistolary Answer To an Exciseman, Who doubted her being the Author of the Washerwoman's Labour,"[17] Collier asserts that women's inferior education is the basis of their social subordination, and not merely an effect of it. This poem represents her example of a genre that seems to have been obligatory for working-class and many female poets of the period, the poetical self-authentication statement, and as such it serves as a welcome autobiographical moment in an otherwise self-effacing *oeuvre*. Collier closes this text with a mock admission of female idiocy, from which she hopes the exciseman can protect himself, concluding:

> Tho' if we Education had
> Which Justly is our due,
> I doubt not, many of our Sex
> Might fairly vie with you.
> (41–44)

This challenge combines confidence in her sex with a plea for inclusion in the possession of an unproblematized "education." It is a challenge that assumes education to be an unbiased equalizer between the sexes, something that women have been unjustly denied, and *can* safely possess; the question of misogyny within traditional erudition itself is not addressed.

Such an assumption marks a limit to the radical potential of Collier's writing; her utopian impulses tend to manifest themselves in an assumed faith in a higher authority that will be capable of rectifying injustices sometime in the future. Here it is education, elsewhere in her work religion or the monarchy. A certain deferral of desire for radical social transformation can read much like a reactionary resignation to the status quo, though such a reading would be neither very historically accurate nor responsive to the sexual and social nuances of Collier's texts. So also with Collier's aesthetic achievement. Her subtle innovations and breaks with convention, her skillful appropriation of stock neoclassicism and occasional verse forms, may not seem very daring to modern readers.

The Woman's Labour, like Collier's other poems, challenges our institutionalized critical and aesthetic criteria as working-class poetry is likely to do.[18] We run up against some hard questions about how we define and allocate "literary value," about the intractable importance of political criteria in our evaluative judgments, about whether or not the establishment of a female (or feminist?) counter-canon is a sufficient or even desirable project for feminist criticism to pursue.[19] If one project of a feminist literary history might be not only to rediscover women's texts that have been forgotten or devalued by the exclusionary practices of canon formation, but also to establish a critical and political feminist discourse within which to read such texts, then it is necessary continually to historicize our own discourse of feminism by learning to recognize its continuities and discontinuities with earlier instances of resistance to oppression. Collier's writing, particularly *The Woman's Labour*, powerfully represents such as instance.

To read *The Woman's Labour* is inevitably to confront what crucial determinants class and gender are in textual production.

> No Learning ever was bestow'd on me;
> My Life was always spent in Drudgery:
> And not alone; alas! with Grief I find,
> It is the Portion of poor Woman-kind.
>
> (7–10)

The weighing of class allegiance and female identity is present early in the poem in that ambiguous phrase "poor Woman-kind." Worthy of pity as a sex or remarkable for their poverty? Are only impoverished women being addressed, because other women have their marriage "portions" to insulate them from drudgery? We may begin by reading according to the code of "pity," keeping sexual difference to the fore. But without stating anything polemically, Collier manages to convey as the poem unfolds that this is a class issue rather than simply an issue of sexual difference, as a middle-class woman writer would most probably have expressed it. There is an unbridgeable gap between the women of the landowning and employing classes, "our Ladies" (159), and "ourselves." The lot of *"poor* Woman-kind" is her theme, and it is one of the themes given least literary treatment in English up to 1739 and for some time afterwards (Defoe notwithstanding). At a crucial moment slightly more than halfway through the poem, Collier's protest against the laboring man's lack of sympathy with or even comprehension of the nature and extent of "women's work" is supplemented by an equally effective critique of the hardnosed middle-class mistress for whom poor women "char"—do the laundry, polish the pewter, scour the "Pots, Kettles, Sauce-pans, Skillets . . . /Skimmers and Ladles, and such Trumpery,/Brought in to make complete our Slavery" (210–12). Like Dryden, at moments of high feeling Collier employs the emphatic triplet, which, given her subject matter, often has the added effect of a sense of labors prolonged, of the rhythms of work as regulated by the sun's movements being violated, all too regularly.

Over against the undeniable hardships and indignities of working-class men's lives, Collier repeatedly asserts the equally never-ending and futile contribution of working women's labor:

> So the industrious Bees do hourly strive
> To bring their Loads of Honey to the Hive;
> Their sordid Owners always reap the Gains,
> And poorly recompense their Toil and Pains.
>
> (243–46)

The ambiguity of "sordid Owners" here deserves comment, for it is precisely the site of the convergence of Collier's feminism with her critique of property and class power. Surely (land) "Owners" ought to spring to mind first, so solidly grounded is the text in class consciousness. But a lingering association of women's lot with thankless drudgery may carry from the poem's opening and come to rest here as well. The working-class woman is doubly (dis)possessed, her body and her labor owned, but neither acknowledged nor appreciated, by employer and father or husband. Yet it is the hold of gender oppression within the working class that Collier's text sets out to pry loose. Her poem evidences an implicit optimism about redress and improvement where relations between the sexes are concerned. In this, she may be seen to be participating in the discourses of a wider social context in which the debates about middle- and upper-class gender equality and women's fitness for "public" work seem to have been a keen focus of intellectual energy in 1739.[20] Class relations, by contrast, remain insuperably in place in Collier's text, critiqued as unjust, but not challenged as historically subject to change through political action.

Collier secures her claim to historical truth by means of an appeal to empirical facts, right down to the crucial matter of women's inadequate wages:

> And after all our Toil and Labour past,
> Six-pence or Eight-pence pays us off at last;
> For all our Pains, no Prospect can we see
> Attend us, but *Old Age* and *Poverty*.
>
> (198–201)

Subsequent research by social historians has confirmed Collier's testimony.[21] Collier does not stress the sexual differential signalized by the difference between men's and women's wages, but working men and women would be bound to recognize in her "Six-pence or Eight-pence" an allusion to the higher, though still inadequate, wage of a male laborer. How this difference may have functioned to divide the working class, thus effectively diminishing its revolutionary potential, remains a matter of debate.[22] But Collier, by quietly reminding us of the material facts of working women's exploitation, also adds a dimension to our understanding of Stephen Duck's anti-feminism in *The Thresher's Labour*, the text that most immediately provoked her into writing. For the wage differential, as a sign of women's symbolic expendability within the work force, might have varied effects in particular historical circumstances. Yet its general function, symbolically, is always to distinguish men from women as agents of material and social (re)production within a class, thus investing this distinction with those residues of power and antagonism which characterize class relations in the society as a whole.

The articulation of feminist and working-class consciousness in *The Woman's Labour* is not a matter of ostensible content alone. Collier's textual strategies open up questions of aesthetic criteria in a challenging way. Two features of the poem particularly demand an historically informed and theoretically conscious reading if they are not to be undervalued or inadequately understood: the status of *The Woman's Labour* as an epistolary reply to Duck's version of plebeian georgic, and Collier's use of what may seem like rather hackneyed "high literary" troping. Is Collier's poem in some sense a mere supplementary appendage to Duck's? Does she fail to invent a suitably oppositional discourse of plebeian female—poor woman's—georgic?

It is true that Collier stakes her text on class solidarity with Duck, despite their differences regarding women's contributions to productive labor. We know from "Some Remarks" that she admired Duck and got his poems by heart, but that she fancied "he had been too Severe on the Female Sex." Less personal pique than the desire to speak out on behalf of the women of her class, to "call," as she puts it, "an Army of Amazons to vindicate the injured sex" (iv), generated *The Woman's Labour*. In the annals of English working-class literature, Duck's trajectory as a farm laborer patronized as a poetical prodigy by royalty, given place and pension, and encouraged to enter the clerisy—a social rise that ends in suicide—represents working-class deracination in an extreme form. Duck had made his mark on the literary scene by mocking the leisured conventions of English pastoral and georgic verse, while dramatizing the experience of agricultural labor as *lived*. Scything during the hay harvest becomes an epic competition not entirely innocent of Homeric as well as Virgilian overtones:

> And now the field, design'd to try our Might,
> At length appears, and meets our longing Sight.
> The Grass and Ground we view with careful Eyes,
> To see which way the best Advantage lies;
> And, Hero-like, each claims the foremost Place.
> At first our Labour seems a sportive Race:
> With rapid Force our sharpen'd Blades we drive,
> Strain ev'ry Nerve, and Blow for Blow we give.
> All strive to vanquish, tho' the Victor gains
> No other Glory, but the greatest pains.[23]

As Raymond Williams has shown, the vigorous colloquial triumph of *The Thresher's Labour* is followed, ironically, by traditional "high literary" pastoral rhetoric: "When sooty Pease we thresh" becomes "Of blissful Groves I sing, and flow'ry Plains:/Ye Sylvan Nymphs, assist my rural strains."[24] Nevertheless, in *The Thresher's Labour* Duck puts the labor "back" into pastoral verse.[25]

In addition to celebrating the dignity of male labor, *The Thresher's Labour* vilifies greedy landlords as well as poking fun at talkative working-class women who treat their occasional labor in the fields as a form of recreation:

> Our Master comes, and at his Heels a Throng
> Of prattling Females, arm'd with Rake and Prong;
> Prepar'd, whilst he is here, to make his Hay;
> Or, if he turns his Back, prepar'd to play:
> But here, or gone, sure of this Comfort still;
> Here's Company, so they may chat their Fill.
> Ah! were their Hands so active as their Tongues,
> How nimbly then would move the Rakes and Prongs!
> (162–69)

Indeed, Duck goes so far as to imply that talking is women's chief activity, apart from cooking, child-minding, and keeping hard-working but exhausted husbands on their toes. Structurally, *The Thresher's Labour* obliges us to spot the analogy between the epic heroicism of the men's competitive scything and the bathos of the women's conversation, which Duck strains to make competitive as well as noisy and nonsensical. After dinner, the female haymakers continue to sit on the ground and "chat." The traditional tropes of women's irrational, garrulous behavior, and their inability to "talk sense" while trying to outdo one another in "meaningless" gossip, are obvious enough. But Duck takes a further step of interest to post-Lacanian feminism; he represents women as, metaphorically and temporarily at least, outside the symbolic order of language altogether.

> All talk at once; but seeming all to fear,
> That what they speak, the rest will hardly hear;
> Till by degrees so high their Notes they strain,
> A Stander by can nought distinguish plain.
> So loud's their Speech, and so confus'd their Noise,
> Scarce puzzled ECHO can return the Voice.
> Yet, spite of this, they bravely all go on;
> Each scorns to be, or seem to be, outdone.
>
> (176–83)

Echo, an Ovidian figure for the relative speechlessness with which we are confronted in the "ready-madeness" of language, our imprisonment within a language that can only operate *through* a subject but cannot be operated autonomously *by* the subject, is significantly female. Thus Duck casually evokes the longstanding classical association of femininity and exclusion from language-as-power. But these women stand outside even Echo's relation to language; so confused and confusing is their loud noise that it is incapable of recuperation even by a sympathetic female ear. The implication is that what Echo cannot reproduce is not language at all. Duck's inability to understand the haymakers is a declaration of his linguistic and cultural superiority, his belonging to a realm of "sense" and meaning that working-class men inhabit, but from which their women are excluded.

Thus Duck helps perpetuate the ideological exclusion of his fellow countrywomen from both productive labor and language, at the same time that he transforms the bourgeois pastoral prospect into a worked landscape. It is hardly surprising, then, that when the "thresher poet" is answered by the "washer-woman of Petersfield," she should take Duck's refusal to "see" women's agricultural labor as, in fact, productive, to be a violation of class loyalty rather than chivalry, good manners, or even good sense.[26] One of her characteristic strategies of refutation turns upon quoting Duck's text in the light of previous pastoral refusals to recognize the contributions of labor to the picturesqueness of the countryside. Where Duck had written of the hay harvest, thus cavalierly cancelling the female haymakers' sweat and toil,

> Next Day the Cocks appear in equal Rows,
> (202)

Collier counters with:

> [We] nimbly turn our Hay upon the Plain;
> Nay, rake and prow it in, the Case is clear;
> Or how should Cocks in equal Rows appear?
> (60–62)[27]

By scorning his female fellow workers, Duck has done violence to their shared occlusion from the bourgeois pastoral prospect. By selectively quoting from Duck's poem, Collier hurls Duck's jibes at his female fellow workers back in his face. By apostrophizing Duck in her opening lines, and using the same couplet form and narrative structure as he does, Collier poetically apprentices herself to Duck, whose plebeian verse has inspired as well as provoked her own:

> IMMORTAL Bard! thou Fav'rite of the Nine!
> Enrich'd by Peers, advanc'd by CAROLINE!
> Deign to look down on one that's poor and low,
> Remembring you yourself was lately so;
> Accept these Lines: Alas! what can you have
> From her, who ever was, and's still a Slave?
> (1–6)

Collier makes the couplet form seem flexible and accommodating, not constraining. With Duck, she helps to constitute the discourse of working-class georgic by incorporating rural idioms and grammar as well as the subject matter of work experienced, not observed.

Comparable with her use of her immediate male model is Collier's appropriation of such "high literary" tropes as the classical allusion. If Duck relies upon the myth of Sisyphus to convey the working man's ceaseless and ultimately futile round of labor, Collier, as if to fix her image as a washer-woman forever in our minds, invokes Danaus's daughters with their bottomless tubs to fill:[28]

> While you to *Sysiphus* yourselves compare,
> With *Danaus' Daughters* we may claim a Share;
> For while *he* labours hard against the Hill,
> Bottomless Tubs of Water *they* must fill.
>
>   (239–42)

For the eighteenth-century poet, classical allusions are stock-in-trade: always in stock, as it were; the very stuff of which verses are made. One proves one's competence to compose, recite, write, publish, and have read, verses by acquiring this stock of, and in, popular neoclassicism. Both Duck and Collier understandably appropriate the classical figures most easily allied with labor; it would seem that they perceived there to be a certain useful congruence between the apprehension of manual and agricultural work as lived experience in the texts of antiquity and their own. We need not dismiss the engagement with "high literary" culture merely as evidence of opportunism or of failed aesthetic invention. There is a sense in which the classical allusion itself is also being reinterpreted, as perhaps having had originally something to do with a more immediate experience of agrarian labor than most literate English people of Collier's time routinely experienced themselves. Collier appropriates the myth of Danaus's daughters in order to assert working-class women's *value*, in the only literary terms that would carry in this historical moment, within such a marginal text.

This literary procedure has been theorized by Claudine Herrmann, Hèléne Cixous, and other "new French feminists" as a distinguishing feature of *l'écriture féminine* or women's writing—the stealing of masculinist (and here, "polite") language in order to subvert its values and constitute within it an oppositional domain of feminist literary practice. "*Les voleuses de langue*," the thieves of language, also "fly"—not only in the face of convention, but in order to write their own experiences, desires, bodies.[29] In these terms, then, the intimate relation between Collier's text and Duck's is paradigmatic and strategic rather than enfeebled and parasitical. The polemical edge of Collier's text depends not so much on our previous knowledge of Duck's poem, but on the way Collier dismantles and reconstitutes Duck's antifeminist contempt through selective quotation within her own text. There is no pretense of either solitary individuality or original genius in Collier's aesthetic; she has adopted a form of dialogue in order to engage in combative persuasion, and so her work, like many women's texts, discloses what masculinist texts so often deliberately mystify, the necessary "intertextuality" of all literary enterprise.[30] Without "belaboring" the point, we should also recognize that Duck's own poem was implicitly intertextual as well, engaging the whole leisured pastoral tradition in order to subvert it: "No Fountains murmur here, no Lambkins play,/No Linnets warble, and no Fields look gay;/'Tis all a gloomy, melancholy Scene,/Fit only to provoke the Muse's Spleen" (58–61). The difference is that Collier's text addresses Duck's poem specifically and explicitly; Collier does not assume a reified "tradition" of either misogynist satire or patrician georgic. Her text is thus more *immediately* and polemically intertextual than his.

It might seem that Duck's traditional description of his fellow countrywomen as incapable of working hard or speaking sense, though more than capable of generating noise, would undermine Collier's project, despite her skillful intertextual maneuvers. But Collier engages in a strategy invaluable for any form of ideology critique; she attempts to account for Duck's prejudices as the products of an historical process that is by no means inevitable. Adapting the neoclassical commonplace of a mythical Golden Age to feminist ends, she speculates that there must have been a more just relation between the sexes at an earlier moment in history: the origin of woman, if divine, could not prove an instance of slavery. There must of necessity have been some historical degeneration from that happy state, so justly designed, in order for human society to have arrived at its present arrangement of female slavery and male arrogance and ingratitude:

> Our first Extraction from a Mass refin'd,
> Could never be for Slavery design'd;
> Till Time and Custom by degrees destroy'd
> That happy State our Sex at first enjoy'd.
> (13–16)

Historically speaking, then, familiarity bred contempt. Men ceased to honor or praise women as these erotically charged relations grew stalely "customary" over time. By degrees women were degraded to their current status as slaves and drudges. Thus men are not the enemies of women, though they may "enslave" them, but fellow subjects in the realm of physical and historical exigency, also subject to the deformations wrought by living-in-time and being bound by social custom. The forces of deformation may be the same for both sexes, but their effects are clearly asymmetrical, affecting men and women differently. Collier's project is one of radical defamiliarization.[31]

Collier's method for making Duck's assumptions about female unpro-

ductiveness and mindless garrulity seem strange is a simple one. She
speaks out against them:

> For none but *Turks*, that ever I could find,
> Have Mutes to serve them, or did e'er deny
> Their Slaves, at Work, to chat it merrily.[32]
> Since you have Liberty to speak your mind,
> And are to talk, as well as we, inclin'd,
> Why should you thus repine, because that we,
> Like you, enjoy that pleasing Liberty?
> What! would you lord it quite, and take away
> The only Privilege our Sex enjoy?
>
>   (66–74)

The politics of a simple "speaking out" may seem to us today thoroughly
problematical,[33] but for Collier Duck's dismissal of women's work and
women's "noise" warranted just such a direct contradiction. Collier
writes from the following premise: if a woman addresses the public by
writing rationally and eloquently, she *may* be read, and her audience's
consciousness altered accordingly. Collier thus sets out to refute Duck's
representation of women as outside material and linguistic production
through a powerful combination of personal testimony and reportage.

The central historical subtext of *The Woman's Labour*, and the site of
its most telling political intervention, is a theme that both feminist ac-
tivists and feminist scholars have made all too familiar, that of the triple
burden of working women—wage-labor, housekeeping, and childcare.[34] This is what gives thematic unity to Collier's narrative, whether
the central activity of a passage be haymaking, brewing beer, reaping,
gleaning, or washing, and it is also what gives nearly unbearable unity
to working-class women's experience historically. Collier's case for
women's apparently endless duties, so few of which Duck seems to
have noticed, is unforgettable:

> To get a Living we so willing are,
> Our tender Babes into the Field we bear,
> And wrap them in our Cloaths to keep them warm,
> While round about we gather up the Corn;
> And often unto them our Course do bend,
> To keep them safe, that nothing them offend.
>
>   (93–98)

This "divided care" during a day of gleaning might provide a significant portion of the family income. Following Arthur Young, Ivy Pinchbeck reports that, "In either case, whether a woman's time was spent in working for wages [including reaping, in some districts, though it remained 'men's work' in others] or in gleaning, it was generally assumed at the end of the eighteenth century, that the yearly rent of the labourer's cottage was paid by the harvest labours of his wife and children."[35] And this "divided care" during the day is compounded by the evening's cooking, housekeeping, and childcare. Collier's working women belong to cottager families, for whom housekeeping might well include keeping pigs and other livestock as well as working a small garden: "*Bacon* and *Dumpling* in the Pot we boil,/Our Beds we make, our Swine we feed the while" (79–80). As Pinchbeck notes, such female contributions to domestic economy were necessary to supplement inadequate wages, but were rapidly disappearing by the later decades of the eighteenth century.[36] Duck and his mates may dream of work at night, but their women hardly have time to sleep, it seems:

> You sup, and go to Bed without delay,
> And rest yourselves till the ensuing Day;
> While we, alas! but little Sleep can have,
> Because our froward Children cry and rave;
> Yet, without fail, soon as Day-light doth spring,
> We in the Field again our Work begin,
> And there, with all our Strength, our Toil renew
> Till *Titan's* golden Rays have dry'd the Dew;
> Then home we go unto our Children dear,
> Dress, feed, and bring them to the Field with care.
>   (111–20)

So much "care" suggests another way of understanding the female "prattling" to which Duck objects: such gatherings for gossip and other forms of exchange are an expression of community among these rural women, for whom there are so few opportunities for recreation and amusement.[37] In a sense these women have become the custodians of the oral tradition to which their relative exclusion from print culture has increasingly relegated them.

The agricultural year provides another context for Collier's insistence on historical fact. In Stephen Duck's agricultural year, winter can be dismissed with a single line. But Collier saves her best effects of physical sensation and atmosphere for winter, as if to imply that women go men one better even in this: washing, polishing, and brewing provide a seasonless round of work. The vivid simplicity of her evocation also puts certain passages of James Thomson's *Winter* in a new and rather unflattering light.[38] Rising before dawn in winter, regardless of the weather, the women leave their sleeping men and trudge to the house of local gentry:

> When to the House we come where we should go,
> How to get in, alas! we do not know:
> The Maid quite tir'd with Work the Day before,
> O'ercome with Sleep; we standing at the Door
> Oppress'd with Cold, and often call in vain,
> E're to our Work we can Admittance gain:
> But when from Wind and Weather we get in,
> Briskly with Courage we our Work begin;
> Heaps of fine Linen we before us view,
> Whereon to lay our Strength and Patience too;
> Cambricks and Muslins, which our Ladies wear,
> Laces and Edgings, costly, fine, and rare,
> Which must be wash'd with utmost Skill and Care;
> . . .
> Now we drive on, resolv'd our Strength to try,
> And what we can, we do most willingly;
> Until with Heat and Work, 'tis often known,
> Not only Sweat, but Blood runs trickling down
> Our Wrists and Fingers; still our Work demands
> The constant Action of our lab'ring Hands.
>
> (149–87)

The extremes of cold and heat, of hostile weather and frantic domestic industry, always working against time, against the sun's rise, because there is always too much to be done, are features that powerfully evoke a winter of labor. The Virgilian topos of "Now we drive on, resolv'd our Strength to try," addresses the washing as if it were an epic contest, the women's strength against the task at hand, and not, we notice, the women against each other, as in Duck's description of male competition in scything. And it is labor that requires not merely sweat, but blood.

James Thomson's winter is a season of vast and awful extremes that often mark the limit or the end of labor, mankind defeated by the elements, suffering helplessly. The reason "Why the lone widow and her orphans pined/In starving solitude" while luxury strained "her low thought/To form unreal wants" (1056–59), Thomson tells us, is that such class division within seasonality is *natural*: "The storms of wintry time will quickly pass,/And one unbounded Spring encircle all" (1068–69). Collier's valorization of domestic labor radically undermines such religio-political "consolation." The self-regarding sympathetic pastoralism of Thomson looks ludicrously "literary" next to Collier's vindication of women's collective industry.

III

As we have seen, Collier closes *The Woman's Labour* on a note of resignation, not vindication:

> So the industrious Bees do hourly strive
> To bring their Loads of Honey to the Hive;
> Their sordid Owners always reap the Gains,
> And poorly recompense their Toil and Pains.
>
> (243–46)

For the working-class woman, as for bees (another Virgilian gesture), history is already unjustly determined, at the level of class at least. *How* unjustly determined, within sexual and familial relations, Collier leaves to her audience.

But if Collier offers us no radical program for change in the poem's conclusion, she nevertheless insists on the historical and empirical acknowledgment of what her text has made painfully visible. *The Woman's Labour* is, in part, a demand for a history in which women can be seen to participate. Collier's neoclassicism should be understood as operating similarly in aesthetic terms, a compromise achieved within the literary and social status quo that grants the writer some imaginative compensation while allowing her to articulate some trenchant social criticism.

If this seems a disappointingly conservative conclusion, in keeping with Collier's failure to develop a radical alternative to a neoclassical aesthetic, we should keep in mind that Collier, like Duck and other plebeian prodigies, had reason to feel resigned to the fact that her talents were not so much rewarded as exploited by patrons and audiences, whose consciences could be soothed by promoting exceptional ability among the industrious poor. There is a conservative function to the patronage by elites of members of the poor, as examples of extraordinary genius. One might speak of this function as a version of Barthes's "inoculation," in which a small dose of ideological contradiction, in the guise of some localized injustice or form of "unpleasantness" that arouses indignation, is injected into the social body, neutralizing the threat of an epidemic of social change.[39] Thus we should read the declaration of Collier's generalized patron(s), in the "Advertisement" to the "New Edition" of her *Poems*, "that had her genius been cultivated, she would have ranked with the greatest poets of this kingdom,"[40] *against* the material conditions of patronage of *The Woman's Labour* as Collier describes them in "Some Remarks": ". . . at length I comply'd to have it done at my own charge, I lost nothing, neither did I gain much, others run away with the profit" (iv).

Collier's patrons' declaration, which simultaneously celebrates and regrets the phenomenon of uncultivated genius, evades the question of the conditions of such cultivation. There is no suggestion that in the future such prodigies will be encouraged. Nor is a revolution in aesthetics, which would acknowledge the value of working-class poetry *as such*, being proposed. Collier is of literary interest, we must assume, precisely *because* her genius "remains uncultivated"—she represents the undereducated writer as an object of pathos, not an indictment of social injustice or an enticement to social revolution. The pressure of egalitarian impulses in the discourses of revolution and abolitionism of the 1780s strains this precept of permanent pathos and inferiority to its limit in the case of More's patronage of Yearsley. For Collier, it is enough to have one's exceptional status recognized in however limited a way, to be content with "mere" unlettered prodigiousness, itself something of an emancipatory novelty in 1739 or 1762.

Thus Collier's apparent resignation to an unchanging social order, that can at best be modified in local and temporary ways to render the oppressed some compensation, stands as a figure for her own poetical production. Resigned to class oppression, if not to gender oppression within her class, she offers in *The Woman's Labour* a provisional corrective. Such a gesture eases the burden of plebeian history by subjecting its cultural effects to a certain sardonic scrutiny. Her poetry is not without critical social content, as we have seen, but her protests remain carefully circumscribed and localized rather than becoming radically programmatic. Historically, she accepts her lot, though textually she seeks to argue against the conditions of oppression. By publishing verse at all, she addresses primarily an elite readership, but she never offers to confuse their class with hers, or to become one of them through the act of writing. Her stance of uncultivated genius preserves her marginality while securing for her an audience.

We have seen, then, in *The Woman's Labour*, that though Collier asserts an account of an oppressed "poor Woman-kind," her stance in relation to political and social authority is at best problematical. This is even more true of her *oeuvre* as a whole. Whether the topic be education, marriage, royal dynasticism, or scriptural history, Collier tends to couple moral reformism with a certain amiable accommodationism, or compliance with the will of the fathers. Thus, when men become kind and virtuous husbands, though not before, women *will* prefer marriage to spinsterhood.[41] Kings should be militantly strong, if not explicitly expansionist, in the name of protestant liberty; royal couples should set the pattern of domestic virtue for their peoples.[42] And women's interests can best be served by a humble commitment to fulfilling God's will for which they will be rewarded.[43] In a sense, then, despite the fact that she speaks *on behalf of* women like herself, Collier usually writes in a way that is rhetorically "male-identified," written for a projected audience in which men predominate. This orientation is supported by the limited evidence we have of her relations with patrons. The nine Petersfield residents attesting to her authenticity in the signed statement of September 21, 1739, are all men.[44] The respective numbers of male (102) and female (61) subscribers—not counting one "Audry Budd," as a name of ambiguous gender—listed in her 1762 *Poems, on Several Occasions* also support this sense of Collier's projected audience. It is as if the fathers' law superseded and circumscribed any feminist speaking, permitting Collier access to the public on the condition that radically different female desires and recommendations not be featured too prominently in her work.

The paradigmatic text for this strategy is *The Three Wise Sentences, from the First Book of Esdras, Chap. III and IV*, published with, and conservative ballast to, *The Woman's Labour*, encoding an insistent subtext of plebeian female consolation in the Word: the displacement of self for the greater good, the displacement of Woman for the glory of the Father, keeper of Truth. Though *The Woman's Labour* may be Collier's most important poem in literary-historical as well as proto-feminist terms, *The Three Wise Sentences* is in at least one way more typical of her collected *Poems* of 1762. In this text, the discourse of "Woman," historically and philosophically conceived, is examined for its ideological contradictions only to find itself subsumed within metaphysical, and specifically religious, discourse. This textual maneuver characterizes well Collier's frequent retreats from the potentially radical implications of her subject matter. The poem begins in the court of Darius, King of Persia, where three favorite youths decide to amuse the king by competing with one another in answering the question, "What, in their Judgments, did in Strength excel/All other Things."[45] The first offers "wine," the second, "the king," and the third—Zorobabel—"women—except that God's truth is stronger." Zorobabel's is the winning answer, and as a reward, Zorobabel is granted a wish; ever selfless, the youth asks Darius to fulfill his promise to rebuild Jerusalem, which Darius promptly does. Why did Collier choose to versify this apocryphal text? At the request of a gentlewoman whom she was nursing, Collier tells us in "Some Remarks": "she and her Friends persuaded me to make Verses on the Wise Sentences, which I did on such Nights as I waited on her" (iv). A composition to please the ladies, then, Collier's poem discursively elaborates their power and importance—through the "words" of Zorobabel, a handsome young hero of Judaeo-Christian history, we might add—only to displace these topics for a sermon and a vision of a renovated Jerusalem.

This text helps to indicate the possible functions of religious discourse for Collier or her patrons. Collier (re)presents in this piece of writing a social subjectivity most immediately tailored for her employers' consumption, and it is one in which piety is central. Women's strength is no sooner celebrated—in terms of their production and reproduction, their desirability and influence—than divine knowledge/power is invoked as greater through the logics of divine causality and purity. We can see in this reworking of Esdras on the history and theory of gender relations parallels to Collier's similar resort to Golden Age commonplace and Christian myth in the much more purportedly feminist *Woman's Labour*. Zorobabel's winning answer contains the following shift from women's power in giving birth to men to the imperial sovereignty of divine "Truth":

> The greatest Heroes that the World can know,
> To *Women* their Original must owe;
> . . .
> The Glory and the Praise of Men they are,
> And make the Garments which they daily wear:
> Nay, without *Women*, Men can't be at all,
> But soon the Species would to Ruin fall.
> . . .
> In Toil and Labour hard he spends the Day,
> To gather Wealth, that so he may provide
> Treasure to bring unto his dearest Bride:
> While other boldly, with a Sword in Hand,
> Will cross the Seas, and wander on the Land;
> . . .
> How great then HE, by whose divine Command,
> All Things at first were made, Earth, Sea, and Land!
> Strong is the *Truth*, who did create all Things;
> . . .
> Not only strong, but good beyond compare;
> . . .
> Whatever Thing is virtuous, good, and great,
> In *Truth* we find it perfect and complete:
> Then prais'd be *Truth* to all Eternity,

In whom alone is Strength and Majesty!
(132–235)

This is exultant piety indeed, just the thing to brighten a sickroom, or soothe a solitary sleeper. It is also a displacement of the discourse of "Woman" as agent of both production and reproduction, indeed also as chief subject of history. Displaced first, we notice, by "Man" in his accumulative and imperialist mode, industrious at home or "wandering" armed abroad in search of "Booty" (164) to bestow upon the woman at home. "Woman" is thus transposed from material producer to consumer. This shift happens within a vaguely historical syntactic progression: woman's power to give birth and make garments within a "primitive" domestic economy is displaced by her implicitly more "modern" ability to influence the worker and the warrior to exert themselves on her behalf. According to the poem's logic, how much stronger, then, must be the divine agent who created woman! Collier's broaching of socio-sexual injustice here is tentative and highly mediated: Zorobabel as "feminist man," championing women before a male audience; Collier herself "merely" versifying a text from the fathers for a pious female patron. But even this tentative broaching is soon abandoned for conventional pieties about the "strength" of women's influence and the comfort to be had in the Father's One Truth.

E.P. Thompson has described the function of working-class religion, particularly Methodism and evangelicalism, in the latter part of the eighteenth century as "the chiliasm of despair."[46] For Collier, neither a Nonconformist nor an enthusiast, not the hope of spectacular salvation but the certainty of divine truth is invested with desire. In her *oeuvre* the radical possibilities of a discourse of "Woman" are occluded, the question of female subjectivity itself displaced in the name of piety. Her resignation here takes the form of self-displacement as well as self-denial. Rather than pitch hopes on a radical transformation of social relations, apparently unthinkable in 1739, Collier defers her expectation of a joyous Jerusalem until eternity.

For Mary Collier, then, compliance with paternalist authority is legitimated by patriarchal "Truth." Men as individuals may be queried and challenged, but the Father's Word and the fathers' laws demand submission. Religious discourse subsumes further potentially radical investigation of woman, or women, or plebeian female subjectivity. Collier's resignation of her critical tune for the harmonies of metaphysical truth may represent a form of chiliastic impulse in Thompson's sense. But hers is not the chiliasm of despair; it is, rather, the cautious displacement of utopian impulses onto a desirous metaphysics, if not quite a metaphysics of desire.

To rise socially by means of the pen, as Duck did, is to embrace deracination, with all of its ambiguous and sometimes destructive consequences. And in the absence of a working-class movement, the prospect
of education or a literary livelihood without deracination remains unthinkable. Thus Collier's texts reproduce the ideological contradictions
of her historical situation. Her discursive position on the margins of a
literary establishment that can tolerate unlettered genius as a novel commodity permits considerable textual resistance but not open rebellion.
We have seen how skillfully Collier situates her poetry within available
genres and conventions while transforming these materials in the interests of a feminist and working-class social critique: "speaking out"
in combative dialogue, making use of female ventriloquism and intertextuality, investing a religiously informed but prophetic future with
desire, insisting upon the historical and empirical details of plebeian
Englishwomen's experience as a class and as a sex. Coming to terms
with Mary Collier's achievement requires a bold reassessment of our
own conceptions of literary history and value. Unquestionably praiseworthy though it is, however, such literary resistance to oppression
should not be read as *unproblematically* liberationary. Collier's texts remain as troubling in their resignation and proud servitude as they are
potentially emancipatory.

It would not be banal or misleading to see in Collier's problematical
status a warning to feminist scholars who seek to create a new literary
canon of women's works. To incorporate *The Woman's Labour* into any
canon without questioning the hierarchical and exclusionary practices
of canon formation would be to replicate Collier's—and Yearsley's—
experience of patronage as tokenization. To praise exceptional merit in
such individualist terms, while leaving the politics of class untouched,
is to help perpetuate the very conditions of More and Yearsley's *més-
alliance* and Collier's relative conservatism. The limits of liberal "inclu-
sionism" lie in the making of "exceptions" only to prove the rule of
unchanging class hierarchies and inequities of power: these are class-
bound, depoliticizing tactics that a radical and emancipatory feminist
criticism cannot afford to endorse. Surely we should be at least as bold,
in the context of our own historical moment, as Mary Collier was in
hers.

6

ON THE USE OF CONTRADICTION: Economics and Morality in the Eighteenth-Century Long Poem

John Barrell and Harriet Guest

I

The *Night-Thoughts*, according to Johnson, exhibited "a wilderness of thought . . . in the whole there is a magnificence like that ascribed to Chinese Plantation, the magnificence of vast extent and endless diversity." "The great defect of the *Seasons*," he commented, in a judgment equally famous, "is want of method; but for this I know not that there was any remedy. Of many appearances subsisting all at once, no rule can be given why one should be mentioned before another; yet the memory wants the help of order."[1] In his essay on *The Deserted Village*, John Scott went rather further: "Modern poetry has, in general," he wrote, "one common defect, viz., the want of proper arrangement. There are many poems, whose component parts resemble a number of fine paintings, which have some connexion with each other, but are not placed in any regular series."[2] Scott's point, it seems, is directed against modern poetry in general, because modern poetry was, to him, generally concerned to be descriptive, and descriptive poetry must of necessity sacrifice the advantages available to a diachronic medium, in the attempt to annex those of a synchronic.

Like Scott, Johnson in his remarks on Thomson does not go so far as to suggest that poetry should abandon the attempt to represent "appearances subsisting all at once"; but, like Scott, he sees that attempt as inevitably inimical to method. The *Night-Thoughts*, however, was not a descriptive poem, or at least no one in the eighteenth century seems to have classified it as such. If it seemed to be a "wilderness," this was the result not of the juxtaposing of word-pictures in random order, but of the fact that, as Young explained, "the method pursued in it was rather *imposed*, by what spontaneously arose in its Author's mind . . . than meditated, or *designed*."[3] It was perhaps Young's own willingness to point out the absence of an organizing principle in his poem that led Johnson to represent its lack of unity as a magnificent "diversity" and "copiousness" (*Lives* 437), but still he registered that absence.

On this showing, then, three of the most popular long poems of the century were remarkable for their "want of method," and we will not need the authority of any contemporary reader to extend the remark to a fourth, *The Task*. But if eighteenth-century critics were quick to point out the "want of method" exhibited especially by long poems in the newly invented genres of poetry—the meditative poem, the descriptive poem, the moral essay—they did not often comment upon what has seemed in this century the inevitable consequence of that want, that such poems appear regularly to contradict themselves. There are exceptions to this general silence, of course—the most notable, perhaps, is Dennis's thorough and withering analysis of the argument of the *Essay on Criticism*.[4] In our century, however, critical discussion of *The Seasons*, for example, or of the *Essay on Man*, has been largely preoccupied, either with pointing out contradictions in those poems—say between Thomson's accounts of history as progress and as decline, or between Pope's representation of moral behavior as naturally or providentially determined and as subject to the control of the will—or with arguing that those contradictions are apparent only. Eighteenth-century critics exhibit no similar degree of concern with the consistency of the argument of either poem, and this in spite of the interest in "method" we have already observed, and in spite of the fact, too, that in common with many other long poems of the eighteenth century, both these poems seem to invite us to inspect that consistency by prefixing to every book a summary of its contents, an "argument." Obviously enough, this phenomenon begs a number of questions. Did eighteenth-century critics as a rule concern themselves with whether or not the argument of a poem was consistent? If they did not, what did they mean by "method," by "proper arrangement"? If they did, are we to assume that they judged the arguments of most contemporary long poems not to be so inconsistent as to justify adverse comment? Or that for some reason they chose, or were able to overlook contradictions which have seemed only too conspicuous to many recent scholars of eighteenth-century poetry?

We can put some of these questions into focus by offering a version of what has become a routine exercise in the criticism of Pope's poetry, the analysis of the famous instance of contradiction, real or apparent, in the account of Old Cotta the miser and his prodigal son, and the paragraphs surrounding it, in the *Epistle to Bathurst*.[5] Before we begin that analysis, however, we should say something about what we intend by the title of this essay. In his *Prison Notebooks*, Antonio Gramsci argues that "all hitherto existing . . . philosophical systems" have been "manifestations of the intimate contradictions by which society is lacerated." Such systems he describes also as "ideologies," "in the worst sense of the word"—we shall call them discourses. But, he continues, "each philosophical system taken by itself has not been the conscious expression of these contradictions," which find expression only in "the *ensemble* of systems in conflict with each other."[6] But Gramsci also describes the *ensemble* of discourses as "ideology" in the "highest sense" of the word, by which it stands for "a conception of the world that is implicitly manifest in art, in law, in economic activity, and in all manifestations of individual and collective life." Thus if the analysis of the *ensemble* of discourses enables us to uncover the "contradictions by which society is lacerated," that *ensemble* itself is also a means of masking those contradictions, for as David Lloyd has put it, the "disparate hegemonic discourses" of which it is composed are "knotted together . . . into an apparently self-reinforcing, limiting structure of thought"—nature, as delivered up to us by ideology.[7]

Our reading of the *Epistle to Bathurst* is an attempt to analyze how the different discourses of the poem can be read as contradicting each other, and of how, by being "knotted together," they were able nevertheless to mask the very contradictions that might have been disclosed by their conjunction. And if this is indeed what happens in the poem, then it may be the case, we go on to argue, that poems which enabled disparate discourses to be assembled into an aesthetic whole may have been performing the function of *enabling* contradictions to be uttered. Each individual discourse privileges some issues and marginalizes or conceals others, and no discourse therefore is capable of enunciating the contradictory components of a complex conception of the world. Only by the knotting together of disparate discourses can answers be provided to the questions raised by the very fact that a particular discourse ignores them.

II

The account of Old Cotta and his son is introduced by these lines:

> "The ruling Passion, be it what it will,
> "The ruling Passion conquers Reason still."

> Less mad the wildest whimsey we can frame,
> Than ev'n that Passion, if it has no Aim;
> For tho' such motives Folly you may call,
> The Folly's greater to have none at all.
>   Hear then the truth: "'Tis Heav'n each Passion sends,
> "And diff'rent men directs to diff'rent ends.
> "Extremes in Nature equal good produce,
> "Extremes in Man concur to gen'ral use."
> Ask we what makes one keep and one bestow?
> That POW'R who bids the Ocean ebb and flow,
> Bids seed-time, harvest, equal course maintain,
> Thro' reconcil'd extremes of drought and rain,
> Builds Life on Death, on Change Duration founds,
> And gives th' eternal wheels to know their rounds.
>   Riches, like insects, when conceal'd they lie,
> Wait but for wings, and in their season, fly.
> Who sees pale Mammon pine amidst his store,
> Sees but a backward steward for the Poor;
> This year a Reservoir, to keep and spare,
> The next a Fountain, spouting thro' his Heir,
> In lavish streams to quench a Country's thirst,
> And men and dogs shall drink him 'till they burst.
>
> (155–78)

The problem posed by the passage these lines introduce has been familiar enough since Courthope published his edition of the poem in 1881.[8] We can take a hint from Warburton's commentary as to how to approach it. "In the first part" of the epistle, he explained, "the *use* and *abuse* of Riches are *satirically* delivered in *precept*. From thence to ver. 177, the causes of the abuse are *philosophically* inquired into: And from thence to the end, the *use* and *abuse* are *historically* illustrated by *examples*."[9] We can translate this into the suggestion that the poem is characterized by a series of discursive shifts, and that between the lines we have quoted, and those that follow, there is a shift between what Warburton thinks of as the "philosophical" and the "historical," or "exemplary"—though we shall label the discourses rather differently.

The argument of these three paragraphs has been conceived within a hybrid discourse, one we often encounter in the second quarter of the eighteenth century, and one of whose constituents is that form of theodicy whose governing maxim is *concordia discors*. God's providence is evident in the harmonious reconciliation of extremes, of contraries; the harmonious duration of the universe is based on the very changeability of its constituent elements. In the moral universe, no less than the physical, extremes of behavior are the means by which God produces the general good of the whole of human society. To this end, human behavior has to be imagined as entirely determined by providence: different modes of behavior are functions of the different ruling passions that "Heaven" implants in "diff'rent men," and over which they have no control—for whatever power to restrain the passions Pope may grant to "Reason" elsewhere in his poems, in the opening couplet of this passage he categorically denies it any such capability.

According to Warburton, everywhere anxious to acquit Pope of the charge of fatalism, this couplet says that the ruling passion will conquer reason unless we employ "the greatest circumspection" to ensure that it does not (Bowles 294). But of course it says no such thing, and this is no doubt the kind of interpretation Johnson had in mind when he remarked that "Dr Warburton has endeavoured to find a train of thought" in this and the *Epistle to Burlington* which "was never in the writer's head" (*Lives* II.324–25). That Pope is nevertheless confused in his fatalism is clear enough from lines 159–60, where he seems to declare a rational or an ethical preference for mere "whimseys," mere caprice, directed to determinate ends, over aimless passions by which no such ends can be secured; the declaration seems to be predicated on the supposition that human beings are autonomous moral agents, a supposition which is painstakingly denied elsewhere in these paragraphs. But this supposition, of course, mentioned here only to be ignored, soon returns to contradict, in a more thoroughgoing fashion, the argument that is being elaborated in these lines.

On this theodicean discourse is grafted the discourse of what we shall call economic amoralism, the scandalous discourse associated most notably with Mandeville, which said what should never be said, and which produced an account of economic activity too evidently convenient to emergent capitalism to be openly acknowledged. For it proposed that virtue was not just an irrelevant consideration in the conduct of economic life, but that an insistence on the principles of virtuous conduct actually interfered with the maximization of pleasure and happiness that was the proper end of all economic activity and social life. If luxury was vicious, it was also the great agent in increasing the number of people in employment, in raising standards of living, and in ensuring continued economic progress. Because people are naturally luxurious, naturally vicious, the operations of vice, left to themselves, will guarantee a continuously expanding economy, and the maximum diffusion of happiness. Only moral regulation of economic behavior, moral intervention in the marketplace, can endanger this happy result.

The attempt of the discourse of economic amoralism to challenge conventional condemnations of luxury, avarice, and improvidence *was* scan-

dalous not simply because it represented an attempt to withdraw economic activity entirely out of the sphere of moral regulation, but because
it attempted to do this at the same time as it effectively conceded to
human agents a free will by which, perversely, they could choose not
to indulge their vices. It was thus a discourse at once too useful to be
ignored in defenses of emergent capitalism, and too direct to be allowed
unambigous utterance in the tradition of high literature, officially committed to moral instruction as well as to pleasure. Thus to those who,
writing within that tradition, were anxious to represent emergent capitalism as a morally legitimate form of social and economic organization,
but were concerned equally not to prescribe inconvenient limits to the
operation of acquisitive economic activity, the problem presented by this
amoral discourse was to find a way of modifying it, so as to reinsert
economic activity within the sphere of the good, while ensuring that
not much if any of the economic freedom the discourse offered was
sacrificed. The result was a knotting together of economic amoralism
and theodicy we have already glanced at, to compose a hybrid discourse—what we shall call the discourse of economic theodicy.

As a result of this knotting, the discourse of Mandeville acquired a
moral legitimacy, a polish that it had forfeited by blurting out its meanings in so unvarnished a form. By this means, greed could be allowed
full scope, and yet be represented not as vice, but as having a sanction
which made it *more* than merely virtuous, by seeing it as a passion im-
planted by God which no human considerations of vice and virtue could
uproot. It is God who makes misers, and God also makes spendthrifts.
Both are intended by God, are part of his purpose, are the discords by
which a concordant universe is produced. Far from being weakened by
its appropriation by theodicy, the discourse of economic amoralism was
thus considerably strengthened; for the freedom of the will was by this
means abolished, and no one could now choose to restrain their rage
either to hoard or spend.

Apparently to convince us of these truths more thoroughly, the poem
now offers to expatiate on the nature of the miser, the "reservoir," "pale
Mammon," and his spendthrift heir, the "fountain." And so it offers
us these contrasting portraits, as if to show that the behavior of neither
is reprehensible, since both are the unconscious agents of the providential plan:

> Old Cotta sham'd his fortune and his birth,
> Yet was not Cotta void of wit or worth:
> What tho' (the use of barb'rous spits forgot)
> His kitchen vy'd in coolness with his grot?
> His court with nettles, moats with cresses stor'd,

With soups unbought and sallads blest his board.
If Cotta liv'd on pulse, it was no more
Than Bramins, Saints, and Sages did before;
To cram the Rich was prodigal expence,
And who would take the Poor from Providence?
Like some lone Chartreux stands the good old Hall,
Silence without, and Fasts within the wall;
No rafter'd roofs with dance and tabor sound,
No noon-tide bell invites the country round;
Tenants with sighs the smoakless tow'rs survey,
And turn th' unwilling steeds another way:
Benighted wanderers, the forest o'er,
Curse the sav'd candle, and unop'ning door;
While the gaunt mastiff growling at the gate,
Affrights the beggar whom he longs to eat.
   Not so his Son, he mark'd this oversight,
And then mistook reverse of wrong for right.
(For what to shun will no great knowledge need,
But what to follow, is a task indeed.)
What slaughter'd hecatombs, what floods of wine,
Fill the capacious Squire, and deep Divine!
Yet no mean motive this profusion draws,
His oxen perish in his country's cause;
'Tis GEORGE and LIBERTY that crowns the cup,
And Zeal for that great House which eats him up.
The woods recede around the naked seat,
The Sylvans groan—no matter—for the Fleet:
Next goes his Wool—to clothe our valiant bands,
Last, for his Country's love, he sells his Lands.
To town he comes, completes the nation's hope,
And heads the bold Train-bands, and burns a Pope.
And shall not Britain now reward his toils,
Britain, that pays her Patriots with her Spoils?
In vain at Court the Bankrupt pleads his cause,
His thankless Country leaves him to her Laws.
(179–218)

But though these portraits of Cotta and his son seem to be introduced to reinforce the argument of the preceding paragraphs, they seem to do the very opposite. For the discursive history of these two exemplary types situates them within some other discourse than that of economic theodicy—a satirical discourse, which prescribes an entirely opposite account of economic activity to that proposed in the paragraph that introduced them. The satire of types is a moralizing discourse. It sees each type it identifies as exemplary of some kind of moral deviation; all types, insofar as they are available to satire, are deviants from the central, normative position occupied by whatever individual is adduced as evading typical classification. In this satirical discourse, extremes of behavior are not necessary to God's providential plan, but rather evidences of humankind's vicious and willful tendency to frustrate that plan. To attempt to appropriate these characters to the discourse of economic theodicy is, on the evidence of these two paragraphs, extremely difficult. They arrive carrying the discursive baggage of satire, and so tenaciously do they refuse to be parted from it, that instead of being appropriated by the discourse of economic theodicy, they appropriate the poem to their own purposes. The result (though this has, of course, been disputed) is a complete contradiction between the three paragraphs we first examined, and these two.

This new process of appropriation can be examined in the first couplet about Old Cotta. In terms of what we have read before, this couplet may seem to operate as an unproblematic exemplification of the truth of what has just been announced. That is, it can be read as saying that though, according to some merely human calculus of moral behavior, Old Cotta's miserliness made him a disgrace to his family and social position, in fact he was not stupid, and certainly not void of worth. Such judgments have nothing to do with the case, for the behavior of the miser is as much a part of the providential plan as anyone else's. Cotta's worth is not to be measured by merely human notions of virtue, but by the function God intended him to perform, and in those terms he is worth no more nor less than anyone else. But as we read on down the paragraph, this couplet seems to echo in our minds as having said something altogether different, and its second line seems to have been uttered in the voice of some other speaker than the narrator, a voice which is soon further distanced from the narrator when it attempts to make a quite new defence of Cotta: that it was he, not God, who made the decision that he should be a miser, and that he chose miserliness on grounds of principle. This voice considers the evidence of Cotta's meanness, and attempts to reinterpret it as evidence of a scrupulous moral concern, until it is silenced at line 189. And so from the first couplet, which can be read as a vindication, if not of the miser, then of the wisdom of Heaven in implanting within him the passion of avarice, the paragraph becomes, by its end, a moral and satirical attack on miserliness itself. The paternalist moral considerations dismissed by the discourse of economic theodicy as irrelevant, have reasserted their relevance to economic behavior by means of the discourse of the satire of types.

The triumph of this latter discourse is confirmed in the account of Cotta's son. Once again, the passage is divided between the satirist, and the voice of an advocate for young Cotta, who represents his prodigality as the principled behavior of a Hanoverian patriot. Once again, the authority and victory of satire is ensured when the counsel for the defence falls silent at line 213; and once again, the voice that is *not* heard is the voice of the discourse of economic theodicy. And in this paragraph, especially, our desire to find a consistent argument would lead us to expect that voice to be allowed to speak. For the whole point of the lines in which the topic of miserliness and prodigality was first introduced, was that God is vindicated in creating misers by the fact that he also creates spendthrifts. He creates the first, because they naturally, they inevitably lead to the creation of the second. The riotous expenditure of spendthrifts enables money to circulate, to percolate down to the poor, and so ensures the maximum diffusion of money and happiness. The discourse of economic theodicy insists that we should attend to the effects, rather than the motives, of misers and spendthrifts, and that in those terms we will see that their creation by providence is entirely vindicated. But the discourse of satirical types has turned out to be largely uninterested in effects: what is fought out, by the competing voices of these last two paragraphs, is an argument about whether or not the motives of Cotta and his son are selfish, or can be justified in terms of disinterested, unselfish moral principle. The passage so far can thus be seen as an exemplification of that discursive disjunction, by which throughout the first three-quarters of the eighteenth century, writings on the vulgar topic of wealth and trade invite us to understand behavior in the utilitarian terms of its effects, while writers within the polite tradition of ethical philosophy endeavour, with increasing lack of success, to contain the discussion of behavior within a discussion of intentions.

Indeed, the next paragraph makes it quite clear that beneficial effects can only be relied upon if they are the result of benevolent human intentions, and cannot be expected from what are now to be understood as the capricious operations of "Fortune" rather than the providential arrangements of Heaven:

> The Sense to value Riches, with the Art
> T' enjoy them, and the Virtue to impart,
> Not meanly, nor ambitiously pursu'd,
> Not sunk by sloth, nor rais'd by servitude;
> To balance Fortune by a just expence,
> Join with Oeconomy, Magnificence;
> With Splendour, Charity; with Plenty, Health;

> Oh teach us, BATHURST! yet unspoil'd by wealth!
> That secret rare, between th' extremes to move
> Of mad Good-nature, and of mean Self-love.
>
> (219–28)

Now Bathurst is appealed to as the model by which the rest of us may learn to regulate our economic behavior in accordance with the very moral principle that earlier had been seen as irrelevant to it, and that, in terms of the discourse of economic theodicy, could only have been represented as interference in the natural and beneficial operations of the divine economic plan. The contradiction has now become focused on the word "extremes," which in the first paragraphs of the passage were so far from being reprehensible that they were the necessary discords out of which God produced harmony. Now, however, such extremes of economic behavior as are represented by Cotta and his son are entirely reprehensible, and Bathurst must teach a prudential mode of paternalism by his exemplary observance of the golden mean. If he succeeds, of course, then in terms of the first paragraphs the economic system will collapse, for without extremes there can be no balance. But if he fails, then in the terms of this paragraph the economic system must also collapse, for it is the responsibility of moral agents to "balance Fortune," which God, apparently, does not do.

Or rather, it is suggested in the final paragraph we want to consider, God *does* mend the faults of Fortune, but it is our duty to help him do so, by attempting to pattern our economic behavior on his own exemplary economic interventionism:

> To Want or Worth well-weigh'd, be Bounty giv'n,
> And ease, or emulate, the care of Heav'n,
> Whose measure full o'erflows on human race;
> Mend Fortune's fault, and justify her grace.
> Wealth in the gross is death, but life diffus'd,
> As Poison heals, in just proportion us'd:
> In heaps, like Ambergrise, a stink it lies,
> But well-dispers'd, is Incense to the Skies.
>
> (229–36)

In these lines, God is apparently acquitted of the charge that he is responsible for the maldistribution of wealth that is the prior condition to its equitable redistribution. It is now Fortune who makes misers and prodigals, as clearly as at line 166 it was God. And now God's task, like Bathurst's, is to clear up after the accidents of Fortune. The task of human beings, as moral agents, is to regulate both the intentions and the effects of moral behavior, their own and that of others. The moralism of the discourse of the satire of types has entirely supplanted that of economic theodicy; and the next passage will be devoted to praising the Man of Ross who, precisely, eased and emulated God's care, and certainly did not wait for him to get round to balancing the extremes of wealth he, or Fortune, had created.

III

For three paragraphs, then, we seem to have encountered a discourse that functions to insulate economic activity from moral inspection, and to do so rather more firmly than Mandeville, or than other early eighteenth-century writers on wealth had managed. And then for four paragraphs, we have encountered a discourse which, if not positively hostile to the values and beliefs of emergent capitalism, is certainly concerned to propose that economic behavior should be regulated by a consideration of moral principle that earlier had been shown to have no bearing at all on the matter. But this contradiction need not be seen as an embarrassment to the discourse of economic theodicy with which the passage began. It can be seen, indeed, as immensely convenient to it, a further stage in the knotting together of discourses by which hegemony is confirmed. Both the contradictory statements made in the passage can perfectly well find their place within the ideology of laissez-faire capitalism. The first statement can be taken as an announcement that the free economic activity of individuals should not be constrained by an insistence on judging it by irrelevant moral considerations. God worries about what is good and bad, and leaves us to get on with whatever he has created us to do; "Whatever IS," at any time, "is RIGHT," so we need not bother ourselves with questions of morality, with what *ought* to be. The second statement can be taken as announcing that economic activity should be policed—indeed, that it *is* policed, by such men as Bathurst—by scrupulous standards of morality based upon a careful adherence to the golden mean; "Whatever IS," the way things are just now, "is RIGHT," so your preoccupation with how things ought to be is meddlesome and unnecessary.

The convenience of saying both these things will be evident if we reflect upon the contradictory argument by which the financial institutions of the City of London have, in recent years, successfully resisted pressure to subject them to external regulation. On the one hand, the nature of the market is such that it cannot function if it is fettered by moral regulation; on the other, it is already regulated by the principles of a scrupulous morality, and could not function if it were not. The second half of this argument is not, of course, quite the same as that elaborated by Pope, but the argument that he offers is no less convenient a justification of acquisitiveness. For while it claims that the equitable distribution of the gifts of fortune is the true end of morality in matters of economics, it represents "the rich man," as Warburton put it, "as the substitute of Providence, in this unequal distribution of things" (Bowles, 302). The inequalities of wealth produce rich men, and rich men must continue to exist, if by their benevolence inequalities of wealth are to continue to be abolished—a moral justification for acquisitiveness quite as convenient as the moral justification offered by the discourse of economic theodicy, and in some contexts no doubt more so.

It is, then, no embarrassment, but a positive advantage, to the interests of the rich and the reasonably well-off—in short, to almost all the likely readers of this poem, and of poetry in general—that both these contradictory statements should be uttered. And it will therefore also be convenient that there should be forms of literary expression available to the polite culture by which such contradictions could be enunciated. We want now to suggest that the institutions of poetry and criticism in eighteenth-century Britain invented just such forms. These may not have been invented for the *purpose* of giving utterance to contradiction. The power of ideological formations to conceal their function, even and perhaps especially from the class whose hegemony they confirm, is such that we could hardly expect to find evidence of such a purpose; and their power to conceal contradictions, again perhaps especially from those who give them voice, would make it difficult to assert that these forms could have been invented for a purpose which was not itself open to inspection. But such forms certainly *facilitated* the utterance of contradictions; and we want further to suggest that the institutions of criticism managed to train the readers of poetry in the forms thus invented to read it in such a way as ensured that they would overlook the contradictory nature of the ideologies those forms were able to express.

From the beginning of the eighteenth century, what were perceived as new forms of poetry began to be invented, and we can see their invention as a response to a pervasive sense that some of the older genres, epic and pastoral in particular, were incapable of representing the nature of the modern world, the diversity, as it was understood to be, of modern European society. The heroes of epic were now unimaginable, for the essential condition of epic heroism was that the hero should somehow represent, within himself, all the members of his society. But the proliferation of interests and occupational identities within a commercial society meant that no individual could now fulfill that representative task. The ideology inscribed within the conventions of

pastoral—more or less egalitarian and entirely precommercial—disabled
that genre too from describing the divided and ramified forms of commercial society. Satire, of course, could do just that, but satire, uncom-
pounded with any genre more hospitable to the values of commercial
society, could represent that society only in negative terms. There were,
however, classical genres which seemed to offer more potential for more
positive representations of the modern world: the epistle, for example,
which was inhospitable to the high-principled morality of satire, "suitable to every subject," and could treat "all the affairs of life and re-
searches into nature";[10] and the didactic poem, which had conventionally been interrupted by frequent digressions, as it were to sweeten the
pill of its didacticism. The branch of didactic poetry most committed to
the representation of economic activity in a positive light was the
georgic, which had also traditionally been ventilated by digressions, and
was thus hospitable to a diversity of topics which could be used, as
could the ranginess of the epistle, to represent the diversity of modern
experience. These were all forms which no critic of authority had meth-
odized, reduced to rule, or separated out; and thus they could even be
combined with each other, or with other genres, to produce the characteristic vehicle of eighteenth-century poetry, the poem of mixed genre,
variously mingling satire, the epistle, and the didactic poem whether
philosophical or georgic.

Such mixed compositions by their very nature evaded classification
by genre: thus *The Seasons*, according to an early critical account, "notwithstanding some parts of it are *didactic*," might also "with propriety"
be termed a "descriptive" poem;[11] the "epistle" to Bathurst was described at one time as an epistle, later as an essay, and was written
according to "a new Scheme of Ethic Poems."[12] Poems of mixed genre
running to no more than a few hundred lines were apparently thought
of either as epistles, hospitable to meditation, description, didacticism,
and playful ridicule, or as essays, the range of whose subject matter was
licensed by that of the prose-essay. Mixed poems which ran into a number of books were primarily modeled on the rules which Addison, Trapp,
and others established for didactic poetry, rules concerned to emphasize
the digressive nature of that genre over and above its preceptive character. Thus at the start of the century it was agreed not only by Addison
and Trapp, but by Tickell in his unpublished lecture *De Poesi Didactica*,
that the suitability of a subject for treatment in this genre was a question
less of its dignity or its usefulness to the purposes of society, than of
the degree of variety it admitted. The advantage of agriculture as a subject, Addition explained, was that it could offer "a pleasing variety of
scenes and landscapes," and "surprize and variety" were the essential
characteristics of the genre.[13] According to Tickell, moral philosophy

was "foreign to a nature that delights in the Variety of Didactic Poetry";
natural philosophy was "so far . . . from possessing Variety, that it . . .
concentrates thousands of objects into a single Concept"; and poems
which treated of the rules of criticism were bound, if they were to be
of any use, to set out those rules with the utmost conscientiousness and
the least possible variety. But if none of these subjects can "charm the
mind with Variety," there remains "the fourth sort of Theme," "compounded out of them all": "country scenes" offer so "joyous" a "Variety
of Imagery" that the greatest effort in this genre, Virgil's *Georgics*, "will
never weary its readers, since its variety is everlasting."[14] If Trapp sometimes arrives at different valuations of the suitability of subjects for didactic poetry, his principle is the same as Tickell's. Natural philosophy
is "agreeable to the variety" of the genre; agriculture, too, affords an
"agreeable Variety," and the art of painting would offer "a boundless
field of Invention," and opportunities for "novel Excursions," to the
didactic poet.[15] The same overriding concern with the variety of topics
a subject will admit characterizes mid-century accounts of the genre, by
Warton, and by the anonymous author of *The Art of Poetry*.[16]

The preoccupation with variety in didactic poetry seems to invite us
to regard the summaries prefixed to different books of poems of mixed
genre, and variously termed "The Argument," "The Design," "The
Plan," or "The Contents," in a double light. On the one hand, such
summaries are clearly intended to exhibit the coherence, the "method"
of the composition, which according to William Enfield, writing at the
end of the century, was "perfectly consistent with that variety, which
characterizes genius,"[17] but which, according to John Scott, was seldom
found coexisting with it. On the other hand, they could be used also to
exhibit the variety of topics the poem had succeeded in treating. Thus
the "argument" of the "Epistle to Bathurst" summarizes the paragraphs
we have been examining in four topics:

> *That the conduct of men, with respect to Riches, can only be accounted for by the*
> ORDER OF PROVIDENCE, *which works the general Good out of Extremes, and*
> *brings all to its great End by perpetual Revolutions, v. 161 to 178. How a* Miser
> *acts upon Principles which appear to him reasonable, v. 179. How a* Prodigal *does*
> *the same, v. 199. The due Medium, and true use of Riches, v. 219.*

That the second and third of these topics could exemplify the extremes
referred to in the first is clear enough; and that the last could take the
form of a conclusion based on the second and third is equally evident.
But how we could logically proceed from the first to the fourth is no
less mysterious in the argument than it is in the poem. The point of
these "arguments," which seem to invite a critical inspection of the

rational development of the poems they introduce, takes on a new light if we see them also as advertising the variety of the topics to be treated. An argument or summary could no doubt be read as representing a poem's process of development and its variety at the same time. Or different styles of argument could foreground either connection or variety. In the first collected edition of *The Seasons*, published in 1730, Thomson managed to summarize "Spring," which then ran to 1,205 lines, in an "Argument" of only 71 words, identifying only five or so separate topics. But this argument was itself a summary of "The Contents" prefixed to "Spring" in the second edition of that poem in 1729, which, consonant with Thomson's belief that no subject could compete with the variety of the *"Works of Nature,"* ran to little less than 400 words and listed 45 distinct topics.[18]

Our discussion of Pope's epistle has suggested that the various topics admitted into a properly various poem will each enter encased in its own discursive history; so that the critical requirement that didactic poems, and poems of mixed genre, should contain a variety of topics, is in effect a demand or a licence for them to exhibit a variety of discourses. And as the "Epistle" has also suggested, this in turn is a tacit licence, if not a demand, for them to contradict themselves. The "Contents" of "Spring" announce that the poem will treat "the Golden Age" and "the degeneracy of mankind from that state," as well as "our happy Constitution" and "the universal benevolence, the love of mankind, and nature" which the season inspires. This variety of topics obliges the poem to employ a range of incompatible discourses—pastoral and georgic, lapsarian homily and Shaftesburian "rhapsody." And this variety of discourses necessarily produces the contradictory claims that, on the one hand, "the human mind" has lost the "harmony ineffable" it enjoyed in the golden age, and, on the other, that spring still "attunes the world" to "general harmony." The claim that the history of mankind has been a decline from golden to "iron times," coexists with the claim that the history, specifically, of Britain, has been a progress from an iron age to a golden.[19] The article of faith in much twentieth-century criticism that the value of a poem is a function of the unity it exhibits, produced a considerable volume of writing about Pope and Thomson which argues that such contradictions are only apparent. We want to suggest that these efforts may be as misconceived as they have been unsuccessful, insofar as they are predicated upon the assumption that the concern with unity and consistency, was as important to Pope and Thomson as it was (for example) to Wasserman. We are arguing that the concern for method and unity in eighteenth-century poetry was accompanied by a tacit permission for long poems of mixed genre to contradict themselves.

IV

The permission could remain tacit, partly because the excellence of such poems was conceived of as residing in their variety. A criticism that legitimates the employment of a variety of discourses within a poem is one that legitimates a new notion of what makes a work coherent. It does not demand that a poem of mixed genre should be, as a whole, *consistent*; it demands that each topic, as it is elaborated, should exhibit a discursive unity, and that the separate topics should *cohere*, should be glued together in such a way that we can see the join, but are not offended by its abruptness. When the introduction of a topic is announced, the introduction of its appropriate discourse should be clearly signaled, as the evidently fictional name of the miser, and the ironized voice of the reasonable advocate who speaks on behalf of Old Cotta, announce the introduction of the discourse of the satire of types. The art of signaling a change of discourse was the art of "managing" the "transitions." And we repeat that a successful "transition" was not one which concealed discursive shifts, but which made them appear, at least, to be appropriate and "natural"—as, in the couplet that introduces Old Cotta, the continuing voice of the discourse of economic theodicy is audible at the same time as the voice of the new, satiric discourse. As Warburton remarked, the "philosophical" portion of the poem "naturally introduces" the "historical."

In *The Seasons*, descriptions of landscape, which represent the social as well as the natural world as providentially ordered and perfectly harmonious, repeatedly give way, and on one occasion within a single paragraph, to exhortations to civic virtue, which represent society as corrupt and in urgent need of reformation. These in turn continually give way to more description of landscape. Nobody in the century seems to comment upon the contradictions these transitions produce. But John Aikin was so intrigued by Thomson's capacity or willingness to switch suddenly from one of these topics to the other, that he directly posed the question of whether, and of how, Thomson got away with it. It all depended, he decided, on "the manner of their introduction. In some instances this is so easy and natural, that the mind is scarcely sensible of the deviation; in others it is more abrupt and unartful."[20]

It was by virtue of his excellence in the management of transitions, according to Addison, that Virgil was able to include topics which "are almost foreign to his subject." His digressions "are not brought in by force, but naturally arise out of the principal argument and design of the Poem."[21] Warton too praises Virgil for digressions "naturally arising from the main subject," and for "his happy address in returning again to his subject," when "he seems to have wandered far from his purpose."²² Trapp, and the author of *The Art of Poetry*, expect no more than that transitions should be so managed that they "seem to arise naturally" out of the main subject, that they should "seem of a piece with it."²³ "Darting about" is essential to the didactic poem, writes Tickell, but it must be "nimble"—the digressions in the *Georgics* are "grafted" by Virgil "into the body of the Poem with no less skill than that with which he has taught us to imbed slips in trees that are strange to them," and the poem comes to resemble a plane tree engrafted with "novas Frondes et non sua Poma," in which, though we do not mistake the plane tree for the apple branch, or the argument for the digression, we marvel at the art by which such unlikely partners have been matched.²⁴

In Young's *Night-Thoughts* the digressive branches of the poem assume a prominence and a luxuriance that almost obscures the trunk from which they "spontaneously" (and therefore "naturally") arise. The poem exploits the freedom of didactic poetry to explore a variety of "foreign" themes, and of genius to "sport with [nature's] infinite objects uncontrouled." And it succeeded in making its very diversity one of its principal attractions: Johnson praises it for "the wild diffusion of the sentiments, and the digressive sallies of the imagination."²⁵ This diffuseness allows Young to describe the ideal virtues of a "Patriot-like" concern for the "welfare of the whole," supported by "reciprocal, unselfish aid" (IX. 701–03),²⁶ but also to sell these civic virtues by describing them, in the terms of economic amoralism, as a good bargain, a square deal:

> For what is *Vice*? Self-love in a mistake;
> A poor blind merchant buying joys too dear.
> And *Virtue*, what? 'Tis Self-love in her wits,
> Quite skilful in the market of delight.
> (VIII. 930–33)

The inconsistency between the civic and the economic is most commonly bridged in Young's poem by sublimating commercial into spiritual prudence, and then stressing the opposition of the spirituality of both discourses to earthly, immoral acquisitiveness. But their incompatibility becomes more awkward when Young comes to describe the exemplary hero of his poem, the "God-like Man" (VIII. 1249).

This heroic "*Man Immortal*" possesses an aristocratic share of civic virtue: he is "Like Ships in Seas, while *in, above*, the World," and "worldly Competitions" leave him untouched. He enjoys and occupies a disinterested eminence, from which he surveys the world with "An Eye impartial, and an even Scale" (VIII. 1116–26). His greatness is, of course, spiritual rather than merely aristocratic or material, but the terms of the civic discourse in which it is described are indistinguishable from those appropriate to worldly power in all but this respect: his obligations and most of his rewards are the same, though his possessions are apparently those promised by futurity. This exchange of worldly for spiritual preeminence is certainly inadequate, however, to the task of reconciling civic virtue with the ambitions of a sublimated version of economic amoralism, concerned with spiritual profits. In the terms of this recuperated economic discourse, the "immortal" man can earn increased self-esteem by abjuring pride, and his concern for the welfare of the whole is similarly the product of his enlightened self-interest: "Too dear *He* holds his Int'rest, to neglect/Another's welfare" (VIII. 1162–63). The good man weighs the speculative profits of the spiritual futures market against the short-term gains of dealing in worldly commodities, and sees the better bargin to lie in spiritual acquisitions:

> *He* can't a Foe, tho' most malignant, hate,
> Because that Hate would prove his greater Foe.
> 'Tis hard for *Them* (yet who so loudly boast
> Good-will to Men?) to love their dearest Friend;
> For may he not invade their *Good Supreme*,
> Where the least Jealousy turns Love to Gall?
> (VIII. 1238–43)

In these lines, the distinction between vicious and virtuous self-love must be presumed to rest on the opposition between spiritual and worldly goods. The God-like man's spiritual possessions, Young implies, do not diminish the stocks available to others, and do not therefore produce competitive jealousy. But the passage cannot spell out this implication: it is not an idea the discourses that Young has been employing can easily describe, for it calls into question the public or worldly exercise of the Good Man's virtues.

In terms of the "sublimated" discourse of economic amoralism, the spiritual interests of the Good Man are best served by retirement from the world into what Young had earlier described as the "self-enamour'd" contemplation of his own virtues (VIII. 974). The wise and virtuous merchant recognizes that worldly applause is a short-lived and overpriced pleasure, and withdraws beyond the reach of its contaminating influence: "Titles and Honours (if they prove his Fate)/He lays aside to find his Dignity;/No Dignity *They* find in ought besides" (VIII. 1155–57). The implication, in these lines, that the Good Man fulfills the duties of public office *before* retiring to count his blessings, is a concession which accomplishes the transition from the rehearsal of his civic virtues. But it also raises the problem of how his spiritual goods can be put into circulation without being debased. For the public virtues of the Good Man, which are essential to his identity as a good citizen, demand that he be the champion of political causes, in a way that compromises the unworldliness of the profits he has gained by his spiritual acquisitiveness. In the longest sustained image in the passage on the Good Man, his virtue is represented as a function of the determination with which he defends possessions, which by their very nature cannot be stolen from him. The Good Man as good citizen, as civic hero, shows a fortitude in the field of conflict that is inexplicable to acquisitive self-love, and cannot be explained either as glorious, or even as necessary for the defence of the spiritual estate from the invasion of competitive jealousy (see VIII. 1184–98). Thus the recuperated and moralized economic discourse seems to recommend spiritual miserliness without suggesting any compensating distribution, while the representation of civic virtue as a spiritual possession produces an idea of public virtue that it manifested in defending an apparently exclusive right to that possession.

To describe the contradiction within the poem in this way, however, without quoting it at length, may suggest that Young's writing proceeds by melting together the different discourses it employs, rather than by a sequence of clearly announced discursive shifts. But in fact Young maintains clear distinctions, usually reinforced by paragraph breaks, between the discourses he employs. The passage on the Good Man emerges as a digression within the book in which it is inserted; and within the passage itself, the paragraphs which attempt to sell us a private spiritual bargain appear to function as digressions from those that exhort us to civic, to public virtue.[27] The staccato movement of Young's verse—its tendency to divide into discrete aphoristic units and monitory interjections—continually concentrates attention on the present moment of utterance, and distracts it from the issue of how his sentences are logically connected. The verse thus serves both to give an emphatic presence to each discourse as it appears, and to conceal the incompatibility between discourses.

V

By a concentration on the separate topics within a poem, and the art of connecting them "naturally," or of making the connections between them *seem* natural, the question of whether a poem was consistent disappeared behind the question of whether its separate topical units were pieced together by an art which concealed itself but not its operations. And this habit of regarding poems in terms of their thematically, if not aesthetically, discrete units must have been reinforced by the tradition of practical criticism, deriving in large part from Bouhours, but in England influenced also by the epistemology of Locke, by which poems could be broken down into, and evaluated in terms of, still smaller ideational units. In the most extreme versions of this style of criticism, the different "thoughts," "images," or "pictures" a poem contained could be classified into sublime, grand, noble, pretty, agreeable, fine, delicate, true, false, beautiful, soft, natural, simple, gay, and so on.[28] Or by the tradition of verbal criticism, poems could be judged in terms of their success in handling the different figures of speech that could be discovered within them, or in terms of their "expression" in the different styles they could be identified as employing. Such modes of criticism represented the "beauties" or the "faults" of a poem as things to be looked for in units of a couple of lines or so, far more than in the unity of its design or argument.[29]

Contradiction is still registered, of course, and punished by criticism, when the rules internal to a particular discourse are infringed. But contradiction among discourses, provided that their introduction is clearly signaled, is not at all reprehensible. So far, then, the evidence suggests that eighteenth-century critics were not concerned by the fact that long poems contradicted themselves, largely because, for them, the coherence of a poem was something distinct from its consistency, and because the procedures by which such poems usually did give rise to contradiction were examined in a rather different light, as the means by which they came to exhibit the variety of the world and of the poet's genius.

But there is another body of evidence which suggests that poems of mixed genre in particular were often not read in such a way as would enable either their coherence or their consistency to be an object of attention. As another French critic, the Abbé Du Bos had remarked, and as a number of English critics repeated, the subject of a didactic poem may be

> so exceedingly curious, as to induce you to read it over once with great pleasure; yet you will never peruse it a second time with the same satisfaction you taste even from an eclogue. The understanding feels no pleasure in being instructed twice in the same thing; but the heart is capable of feeling the same emotion twice, with great pleasure.[30]

If criticism was willing to acknowledge that "the mind can hardly attend a second time" to "passages that are merely instructive,"[31] this amounts to a permission to skip and dip, to leaf through the volume reading only those passages that, elsewhere, criticism regarded as ornamental digressions from the principal argument. Thus Fanny Burney records the opinion of Mr. Fairly, that Young "was an author not to read on regularly, but to dip into, and reflect upon";[32] and Pope's *Essay on Man*, according to Johnson, was valued especially for its "flowers," its "splendid amplifications and sparkling sentences," so that "many read it for a manual of practical piety" (*Lives* II.274), a repository of moral instructions and maxims. Nor was this a permission accorded to readers of didactic poetry only: it seems to have been allowed for all nonnarrative poems of mixed genre, which were probably most often read piecemeal by readers searching for the isolated "beauties" they contained.

Two developments which gathered momentum in the final third of the century, and which are connected with the expansion of the reading public, combined to make "dipping" easier, or even unnecessary. The first of these was the proliferation of literary periodicals, in which reviewers of poetry were expected to identify and quote at length the "flowers" or "beauties" of the long poems they discussed. The ideological convenience of this practice is well exemplified in contemporary reviews of *The Deserted Village*, a poem in which the condemnation of luxury was not counterbalanced by any contradictory assertion of the political and economic advantages it secured. Those reviewers who comment on Goldsmith's attack on luxury do so only to question or condemn it. But this, they assert, does nothing to destroy the beauty of the poem, which resides, for them, in its "beauties"—in a series of affecting passages which they quote at length. The political argument of the poem could either be ignored or dismissed, with the implication that political economy has now taken over the cognitive functions of poetry with respect to social and economic questions. The poem was thus boiled down in the reviews to three main passages: the descriptions of the village schoolmaster, the village clergyman, and the village alehouse.[33] In the "dedication" prefixed to the poem, Goldsmith had asked for the "unfatigued attention" of the reader, but what he got seems to have been very different: if the poem was quickly accepted as a classic, it was largely because these three "pictures" were accorded classic status.

Copies of periodicals were kept, in this period, far more assiduously than now: one of their functions was certainly to identify and to reproduce what were reckoned to be the most remarkable passages, not of poems only, but of any book reviewed at length. But only in the case of imaginative literature was it not also one of their functions to summarize and comment upon the argument (where there was one) of the works under review. So that as the cognitive function of imaginative literature *was* appropriated elsewhere, so poetry in particular came to be read for the "ardent images" and the "fine sentiments" it could offer. And that Goldsmith's classic passages may have become more familiar through excerpts, than by being turned to in copies of the poem itself, is suggested by the second development we referred to, the proliferation

of anthologies of poetry, aids in the acquisition of good morals, sentiments, or taste, or of the power to recite with appropriate expression.

With the exception of the voluminous *Elegant Extracts*, the anthologies
selected and printed only the "beauties" of long poems, and facilitated
the process by which, like Goldsmith's "Parish Priest,"[34] Pope's "Man
of Ross"[35] must have become more familiar than his *Epistle to Bathurst*,
and Young's poem best known for its paragraphs "On Procrastination,"
"On Covetousness," "On Friendship," and "On Irresolution."[36] "In
any well-used Copy of the Seasons," wrote Wordsworth, "the Book
generally opens of itself with the rhapsody on love, or with one of the
stories, (perhaps Damon and Musidora); these also are prominent in
our Collections of Extracts; and are the parts of his Works which, after
all, were probably most efficient in first recommending the Author to
general notice."[37] The anthologies of passages of verse for reading aloud
sometimes contain instructions as to the appropriate tone of voice or
gesture to be employed, even the appropriate emotion the reader should
experience in the recitation, but never concern themselves with explanations of the meaning of the passages selected. This concentration on
"sentiment" at the expense of "meaning" no doubt did much to ensure
that among even those readers who were moved to look up the poem,
the extracts from which they had particularly enjoyed, not many would
be troubled by the issues of the "method" of the poem, or its
consistency.[38]

"If a book has no index to it, or good table of contents," wrote Isaac
Watts, "it is very useful to make one as you are reading it: . . . but it is
sufficient in your index to take notice only of those parts of the book
which are new to you, or which you think well written, and well worthy
of your remembrance or review."[39] If one function of the "Contents"
of the second edition of "Spring" was to call attention to the variety of
its topics, another must certainly have been to enable the reader to locate
the topics and passages that would offer most pleasure on a rereading.
The "Contents" of *The Seasons*, then, functioned much like the alpha-
betical index that came to be appended late in the century to the *Night-
Thoughts*, the spontaneous lack of design of which could not allow Young
to prefix an argument to it. Under "O" we read:

	Night	Page
Obligations, religious and moral, all rendered void on the plan of infidelity	vii.	168
Ocean, description of the	viii.	197
Oeconomy, true, described	vi.	132

The "arguments" of long poems should perhaps always be understood as indexes or tables of contents, as well as "designs" and displays of variety: as invitations, that is, to regard the poem in one light as consistent, in another as various, and in a third simply as a repository of detached passages whose coherence with the surrounding passages was as unimportant as their logical connection. If we look at the "argument" of the *Epistle to Bathurst* in this third way, it seems to encourage the reader to search for one passage that explains that the use of riches is not an affair of moral judgment, but of God's providential design, and to search for another that argues, on the contrary, that conduct with respect to riches should be regulated by "the true Medium" of moral behavior. By this means the contradictory components of capitalist ideology can be enunciated, but can be prevented from coming into contact with each other, by being made available to be sampled separately, as different readers and different occasions demand. Each can appear, almost, as a separate maxim. The poem becomes a repository of economic wisdom, a manual of capitalist piety, which accurately represents the contradictory pieties it contains, but does not invite an inspection of the relations between them. And for those who *do* read the poem through and attempt to connect up these separate passages, the decencies of the art of transition still conceal the contradictions they conjoin, by the very openness with which they display the variety of its topics and discourses.

The enunciation of the contradictions of ideology may not be the function for which long works of mixed genre, the characteristic production of eighteenth-century poets, were invented. But it is certainly one of the functions which they performed. In this paper we have attempted to sketch out what should perhaps be regarded as one of the most impressive achievements of eighteenth-century literary culture in England. That achievement is one by which the institutions of criticism displaced inconsistency into coherence—into an aesthetic success—and trained the readers of poetry to admire most the poems which, by their very nature, were most liable to contradict themselves, and so enabled those readers to make use of contradictory meanings in the formation of their beliefs and in the conduct of their lives.

7

HETEROCLITES: The Gender of Character in the Scandalous Memoirs

Felicity Nussbaum

"I wish to show that elegance is inferior to virtue, that the first object of a laudable ambition is to obtain a character as a human being."

Mary Wollstonecraft, *Vindication of the Rights of Woman* (1792)

"A woman's REPUTATION is forfeited if she admits the other sex to privacy . . . A man may do well enough without FAME, but how will the woman go on when she has lost her REPUTATION?"

Hester Thrale Piozzi, *British Synonymy* (1794)

I

Despite their seeming marginality as women and as scandal writers, the scandalous memoirists—Teresa Constantia Phillips, Laetitia Pilkington, Charlotte Charke, Frances Anne, Viscountess Vane, George Anne Bellamy, Ann Sheldon, Elizabeth Gooch, Margaret Leeson, and others—are intimately connected with canonical eighteenth-century literature. Colley Cibber's daughter, Charlotte Charke, appeared in Fielding's plays. Laetitia Pilkington, Cibber's protegée, corresponded with Samuel Richardson and promulgated anecdotes of Jonathan Swift in her memoirs. Richardson lamented Con Phillips's seduction by Lord Chesterfield in his letters, and Fielding mentions her *Apology* in *Amelia* (1751). Horace Walpole, Thomas Gray, and Lady Mary Wortley Montagu read

Lady Vane's memoirs—inserted as the eighty-eighth chapter of Smollett's *Peregrine Pickle* (1751)—with interest, and their enormous popularity overshadowed the rest of the novel. But in spite of Wayne Shumaker's observation that "nonreligious confession seems to have begun
in the eighteenth century with the lives-and-amours of Mrs. Pilkington,
Connie Phillips, and the Lady Vane," the memoirs have received little
serious attention in studies of the eighteenth century or books on autobiography. John Morris, for example, who argues that the (male) autobiographers he discusses "were pioneers of the modern sensibility,"
unwitting agents of the new, makes no mention of the scandalous memoirists. Shumaker, on the other hand, gives credit to Charlotte Charke
for "the earliest explicit justification in English for the writing of obscure
lives." "The effect of these autobiographical romances," he continues,
"coming on the heels of *Pamela* and *Clarissa*, may have been important
to the development of a subjective emphasis . . . "; but the implications
of his observation remain unexplored.[1]

The reasons why these memoirs have been largely ignored are complex, too complex to discuss in detail here. Let it suffice to say that
criticism of eighteenth-century first-person nonfictional narrative has
been dominated by nineteenth and twentieth-century paradigms of autobiography. Such definitions urge form and closure on these texts, and
when applied to the repetitive and digressive scandalous memoirs, they
are frequently used to demonstrate the ways in which such works fail
to measure up, the ways in which they are only hesitant thrusts and
starts toward depicting a unified and coherent "self."[2]

The impetus to "write one's self," to produce a consumable interiority,
is particularly strong in mid-eighteenth-century England. Destitute
women who defied cultural expectations of the female, or were victim-
ized by them, take up the pen for the first time in the scandalous memoirs to earn money and to defend their character. I do not wish to claim
that the uncertainties of identity were a problematic peculiar to eighteenth-century women, or that women spoke themselves in more diffuse
forms in this period than men.[3] Even a cursory look at male autobiographical writing in the eighteenth century indicates that Pepys, Wesley,
Boswell, and Gibbon represented identity and experience in scattered
and serial forms. Nor do I wish to argue that there is anything inherently
or essentially female about the scandalous memoirs. "Women" like
"men" are categories produced by social, historical, political, and economic factors. The language that individuals adopt to describe their
identity and experience is largely chosen from that which is available
in a given historical moment, and individuals are less the source of their
own meaning than the place where clashes to control meanings of words
occur.

The scandalous memoirs mediate the unresolvable clashes and contradictions in eighteenth-century arguments over character, and identity, and gender. I will argue here that these autobiographical writings
function in the context of a heterosexual gender system to insist on the
coherent containable "character" of eighteenth-century woman, and, at
the same time, that they disrupt conventional paradigms of female character. The narratives are a cultural location of the energizing ideology
of sexual differentiation which both tames and disrupts definitions of
the female.

II

The crisis of "character" in mid-eighteenth-century England surfaces
as a struggle to limit the meanings of that word. There is at mid-century
a disintegration of preexistent categories of gender and character as men
and women who wrote their lives were faced with new experiences that
could not be subsumed within types and general abstractions. The attempt to conceptualize "character"—to delineate the notion of character
and articulate its boundaries—was familiar to the eighteenth century in
its many editions of Theophrastus. A "character" was understood to be
a literary genre, specifically the Theophrastan character in its seven-
teenth- and eighteenth-century modulations by Joseph Hall, Sir Thomas
Overbury, and John Earle. But even Theophrastan characters, designed
to encapsulate an identifiable type, threaten to exceed the prescribed
limitations of the generic paradigm. J. W. Smeed in his recent history
of the genre faults La Bruyère in Les Caractères (1688) for his failure to
make his characters coherent, unified, and consistent "by over-charging
his portraits with many ridiculous features that cannot exist together in
one subject."[4] Smeed is uncritically adopting the assumptions and language of eighteenth-century commentators such as Henry Gally, translator of Theophrastus in 1725 who, in a prefatory "Essay on Character-
istick Writings," says each trait and detail must derive and be expressive
of a whole and unified personality.[5] This insistence on the unity of
personality and the importance of innate characteristics sets itself in
marked contrast to the competing notions of education and experience
as most formative of "character."
Identity, like character, comes to mean both sameness and also, in
the eighteenth century, an individuation that distinguishes the ways the
individual is itself only and is a consciousness that reflects on itself.
Identity implies permanence and sameness over time, a persistence in
being throughout its narrative presence in spite of the changes that it
tolerates or excites.[6] The individual narrator is urged to identify her or

him "self" with all the moments of discursive existence. "Character" and "identity" come to "mean" both a universal human nature and an individual principle, the ways in which we are the same and unlike others in our species. The Theophrastan characters are illustrative of typical characteristics which describe the species but which are supposed to simulate real human beings. The decline of the Theophrastan character in eighteenth-century England corresponds with the moment of crisis and the desperate attempt to disentangle competing notions of identity, character, and gender.

This crisis in the understanding of character affects both men and women, and its is inextricably bound up with issues of gender, for the eighteenth century marks an historical moment of definition and maintenance of separate domains for each sex. By mid-century gender differences become increasingly clarified, and texts such as Pope's *Moral Essays* (1731–34), Fielding's "Essay on the Knowledge of the Characters of Men" (1743), and Johnson's *Dictionary* (1755) functioned to identify and contain gender difference with a special explicitness and vigor. When Samuel Johnson defines "character" in the *Dictionary*, the familiar misogynous quotations from Milton and Pope on women's character figure prominently among the eight definitions he supplies. In the first and most familiar definition, character is a "mark; a stamp; a representation." It is the distinctive aspect that separates one from another, and *Paradise Lost* provides the exemplary text: "In outward also her resembling less/His image, who made both; and less expressing/The *character* of that dominion giv'n/O'er other creatures" (VIII.542). "Character" is also, of course, a letter of the alphabet and the manuscript hand in writing, but most relevant to our purposes, it is "an account of any thing as good or bad," "the person with his assemblage of qualities," and finally "personal qualities; particular constitution of the mind," which Johnson illustrates with the first two lines of "Epistle to A Lady": "Nothing so true as what you once let fall,/Most women have no *characters at all.*" Female character is thus juxtaposed to men's character as the lesser or the negation. Here the definition moves to the universal—the way that individual members of one gender are like each other—as female character is asserted to be unified while it is also unmarked or without identity. Women, as Pope writes in the argument to the "Epistle," can be "contradistinguished from the other Sex" as "inconsistent," "incomprehensible," and yet more "uniform and confin'd."[7] In short, female character with its combining of uniformity and uncertainty poses an especially problematic crux for notions of character and identity in the period.

Women were discouraged from "knowing" their own character and intelligence in other documents published in the later eighteenth century. A neglected feminist text, *An Essay on the Learning, Genius, and Abilities of the Fair-Sex: Proving them not Inferior to Man, From a Variety of Examples, Extracted from Ancient and Modern History* (1774), concludes by noting that men often fear women's self-knowledge because "it may . . . occasion many mischiefs, as fomenting the pride and presumption of women." This work argues instead for the benefits of women's knowing their own character: "Therefore, a women's knowing what they are does not lead them to entertain any overweaning conceits of their accomplishments, it cannot puff them up with vain-glory or presumption."[8] In other words, to "know" one's character—to assert a specifically female identity—both threatens and confirms the heterosexual gender system, an assumption that seems implicit in the treatment of gender and character throughout this period.

In "An Essay on the Knowledge of the Characters of Men," Fielding excludes women as he constructs a closed masculine system in which reader, author, and subject are male. In Fielding's essay, as in the anonymous *Characterism, or the Modern Age display'd: being an Attempt to expose the pretended Virtues of both Sexes; with a Poetical Essay on each Character* (1750), true character can seldom be ascertained from external appearances: "the whole world becomes a vast masquerade . . . a very few only shewing their own faces."[9] Fielding summons his readers to place character in the public domain and make it an object of scrutiny. His essay interpellates a reader-spectator who must become a skilled observer and interpreter of "human nature" in order to begin to distinguish the external manner from the interior truth. But Fielding openly ignores "the Fair Sex, with whom, indeed, this Essay hath not any thing to do." He asserts that drawing female character requires a separate skill: "the Knowledge of the Characters of Women being foreign to my intended Purpose; as it is in Fact a Science, to which I make not the least Pretension."[10] Neither male nor female character is easily known, but by implication the disparity between exterior and interior is greater for women than for men. Even for so discerning an observer as Fielding, female character is construed to be complex and elusive.

Similarly, in *Characterism*, inner life is the indicator of character. Unlike Fielding's text, *Characterism* divides the characters evenly between the sexes: the first of two parts is on the ladies, the second on gentlemen. The male characters are defined by profession: the "Ambitious Clergyman," the "Corrupt Statesman or Complete Courtier," the "Avaritious Lawyer." The women are identified exclusively by personality or character traits—the "Inquisitive Lady," the "Jealous Lady or Dissatisfied Wife," the "Hypocritical Lady," the "Great Man's Prostitute or Actress." The "Female Pedant," for example "has only, by her much reading spoil'd a good Pudding-maker, and neglected those useful, tho' humble culinary Arts, more properly adapted to a female Genius, to make herself that prodigious uncouth kind of a Hermaphrodite, a deeply-read Lady" (13–14). Gender identification for a woman depends on not reading; that is, to be a woman, one must not read. Predictably, the women in *Characterism* are criticized for the dissimilarity between their interior and exterior: "Looking as innocent as Angels, whilst the *Devil* himself has an *Asylum* under their Petticoats." The truth of character for both sexes is internal, the exterior is a falsification or a disguise: as this split between inner and outer emerges, the importance of constructing an interiority as a code to the "real" character takes on greater significance.

The decline of the Theophrastan character, then, parallels the increasing belief that the key to real character is the construction of interiority and its revelation, and it is not surprising that at this time the formal character written in first person with its construction and disclosure of private character emerges. In this context, then, how do eighteenth-century women, taking up the public position as subject rather than object for the first time in autobiographical writing, construct a public secular character when "women" have no character at all? A woman must defend her public character when she is defined at some level as being characterless. She must make her "character" cohere when her unorthodox experience may not fit the codes available to her and to her reader. In short, she must possess herself of both generality and individuation.

Keeping oneself in character in the eighteenth century also means aligning oneself with a larger body of individuals, with a trade or class. To know oneself, then, functions to hold individuals in place and to fix one's character for the self and the world, in part by maintaining an easily recognized class position. An essay in the *Gentleman's Magazine* (July 1738) perceives the close connection between character and class. The author, "R. Freeman," argues for the importance of staying in character so that the world can judge a man's class by his exterior behavior: "In whatever *Scene* of *Life* a Man *places* himself, or is placed by *Providence*, his *Character* depends on the *Correspondence* between his *Behavior* and that which his *Situation* in the *World* requires . . . If a *Clergyman* should all of a sudden turn *Bricklayer*, whip on a *leather Apron*, stick his *Rule* on *one Side* and his Trowel on the *other*, would he not make a *whimsical Figure*?" (354). Women do not figure in this discussion of the relationship between class and character; instead it is assumed that they will take on the class of their father or husband, a precarious classless position easily revoked by separation, dispossession, or death. The gender of eighteenth-century conceptualizations of trade or class, like that of character, is in large part male.

"Character" in these mid-eighteenth-century renderings is perceived as a public construction of a private interior reality, the essence of a person. More recently however, modern theorists have begun to formulate the ways in which "character" in its narratological sense is always a construct, that it is negotiated between reader and text, and that reality cannot be simply and reliably imitated. For example, narrative theorist Mieke Bal is quick to acknowledge the ambiguous relationship of characters to reality. They seem to be like human beings we know, she writes, and to "act according to the pattern that we are familiar with from other sources"—"Or not," she wryly adds.[11] When the reader is unable to incorporate all traits within the codes and conventions s/he has constructed, the reader must shift frames of intelligibility or question the terms of the reading. This conceptualization of character extricates us from the belief that our readings of earlier periods constitute transparently accurate accounts of real people. It also allows us to reflect on both the ways our readings of eighteenth-century texts are inevitably shaped by our own historical situation, and the ways these readings actively produce new knowledge rather than reflect the "truth" of the past. Eighteenth-century autobiographical writing provides only mediated access to history and gendered experience; it is a matrix where cultural constructions of self and gender intersect with the individual subject's use of the particular discourses available at given historical moments. From our present vantage point, we can reconstitute eighteenth-century character in order to understand the ways Pope, Fielding, Johnson and the anonymous tracts on character attempt to fix gendered identity when traditional notions about it were disintegrating.

In addition, poststructuralist theories of character help account for the way in which eighteenth-century women's character slips away from conceptualization. For example, Bal calls character "a complex semantic unit," which she labels "the character-effect." For Roland Barthes the proper name becomes the gathering place of meanings, "the sum, the point of convergence" of adjectives and attributes. Yet the "character" exceeds the proper name: "The proper name enables the person to exist outside the semes, whose sum nonetheless constitutes it entirely."[12] The scandalous memoirists of the period were caught up in precisely this excess and instability that the theorists of character are contending with, and their works illustrate the seepage of character beyond our models of comprehension, its escape into the radical revision of received notions of gendered identity.

III

As women become the subject and object of their own scrutiny, they assume stances, often situated in contradiction, in the ideology of gender. The first significant public form of self-writing that women take up (other than spiritual autobiography), the scandalous memoir, is the narrative of an experience from which men are excluded. These works revived the Greek (male) form of public self-defense in the agora, but their content was a uniquely female situation—the fall from chastity that transformed "character" and all other experience. Like the earliest autobiography—the ancient Greek encomium that was delivered to the public—these memoirs seek to mend the public and rhetorical image of character.[13] Each text vindicates the apologist from blame, while, in contradiction, it attempts to escape the moral and social system which requires that very explanation. The scandalous memoirs are one site of confirmation of and contestation over the ways in which character is gendered at mid-century. Located at the convergence of sameness and individuation of character and at the distinction between male and female experience, the memoirs mark the point at which women become the producers rather than consumers of discourse and of the ideology of character.

Most scandalous memoirs take their genesis in an attack or accusation, and the text functions rhetorically to vindicate publicly the apologist from the charge. These texts are apologies in the classical sense of defense or justification without admission of guilt (a form made familiar in the nineteenth century by John Henry Cardinal Newman). The purpose is actively persuasive; the memoirist serves as an historian who compiles and relates the facts and encourages the reader to be judge and jury. To acknowledge a crime and to provide minute particulars of it—even to deny it—indicates a kind of collusion with the dominant powers who condemn the fallen women. Thus, by their very subject, the scandalous memoirs function in culture to maintain the bipolar gender system, confining women to good or bad, to virtuous or fallen, while the "masculine" is represented as clear, firm, and superior. Implicitly, these works define and perpetuate sexist assumptions about women: they reproduce heterosexual difference.[14]

But the scandalous memoirs also contradict authorized versions of "woman." In this sense, they are open to feminist as well as sexist constructions of character. These works implicitly contradict order and authority in their combination of a public defense of conduct with a stubborn resistance to reconciling the inconsistencies of character. To be an eighteenth-century woman speaking and writing is to appropriate cultural positions that may essentialize woman, but these texts also speak discontinuity as they display multiple and contradictory ideologies of character and gender. From our point of view, this fundamental ambiguity raises the question of the status of a text's intelligibility. The gender of the author may not dictate the terms of making texts intelligible, but rather it may "identify the issues at stake," as Michèle Barrett puts it. Barrett raises the crucial question in relation to gender: "So the

image itself, or the play or whatever, might not necessarily be intrinsically sexist or feminist, it may depend on who is reading or receiving
it and how they do so. The image itself may often be ambiguous, at least
partially open to the different meanings we choose to construct upon
it."[15] Thus women's autobiographical writing is not inherently expressive of the female but is subject to appropriation by readers who hold
various political stances. Text, writer, and reader can be inserted in
history, culture, and politics.

The radical dimension of these texts is also implied in their common
designation as "scandalous." Why were these memoirs scandalous or
culturally unacceptable, and what semantic codes are required to make
the female character produced within them seem offensive? A large part
of the "scandal" of these memoirs is the very fact that they are public;
woman's fall should be a matter of remorse privately confessed to one's
God. Pope defined this private woman's sphere in "Epistle to A Lady":

> But grant, in Public Men sometimes are shown,
> A Woman's seen in Private life alone:
> Our bolder Talents in full light display'd,
> Your virtue open fairest in the shade.
>
> (199–203)

But the memoirs require a reader, an audience, and they insist on a
public forum—a new and radically different sphere for women's writing. Unlike their sisters seduced maidens in fiction and drama, these
"real" women insist on the power of the published word to vindicate
their actions. In this sense, the scandalous memoirs attempt to give
public language to gendered character and subjectivity. For women to
speak, Catherine Belsey has written, is "to threaten the system of differences which gives meaning to patriarchy." She continues, "The in-
stallation of woman as subjects is the production of a space in which to
problematize the liberal-humanist alliance with patriarchy, to formulate
a sexual politics, to begin the struggle for change."[16] These women radically redefine the fall, away from the notion of an irrevocable act that
condemns women to solitude and retreat, and toward an argument for
contesting cultural universalization of the female.

A reaction to women's insistence on a public sphere is evident in "The
Heroines: or, Modern Memoirs," a poem published in the *London Magazine* that chastised Pilkington, Phillips, and Vane for boldly publishing
their shame, unlike nymphs of old:

> by youthful passions sway'd,
> From virtue's paths incontinent had stray'd;

> When banish'd reason re-assum'd her place,
> The conscious wretch bewail'd her soul's disgrace;
> Fled from the world and pass'd her joyless years
> In decent solitude and pious tears:
> Veil'd in some convent made her peace with heav'n,
> And almost hop'd—by prudes to be forgiven.[17]

In this poem woman's private consciousness, her interior, is simplified and characterized as tantalizingly evil. For example, Bonnell Thornton posing as "Roxana Termagant" calls attention to the public infamy of the memoirists in *Have-at-you-all*: "I have also had the honour to be mistaken for some one of those Female Apologists, who have admitted us into the privacy of their most secret (I might say, most scandalous) intrigues."[18] In other words, an individual woman's character is paradoxically impossible to know and yet, if known, it would be predictably consistent in its virtue or vice with other women's character.

The mid-eighteenth-century public read the scandalous memoirs as a canvas on which to construct their ideas of women, and the contradictions in the public's interpretations of them were multiple, not unlike the responses to their fictional counterparts, *Pamela* and *Clarissa*. Readers sought recognizable shapes and patterns as they attempted to codify the traits and attributes described in the memoirs and the novels. In *The Tablet, or Picture of Real Life* the author called attention to two opposing camps, "particularly among the ladies, two different parties, *pamelists* and *antipamelists*" who argued "whether the young virgin was an example for ladies to follow . . . or . . . a hypocritical crafty girl . . . who understands the art of bringing a man to her lure."[19] Attitudes toward the subjects of the memoirs were similarly divided as to whether they were examples of virtue or vice. Calling Pilkington, Phillips, and Vane a "Set of Wretches, wishing to perpetuate their Infamy," Samuel Richardson himself places the blame on male shoulders for the corruption of young women, but he employs the tales to maintain women's subjection. At the same time, he encourages reading Lady Vane's memoirs and uses the occasion to divide women into good and bad, to set the female sex against itself. He writes to Sarah Chapone, "I send to your worthy son (I could not before) that Part of a bad Book which contains the very bad Story of a wicked woman. I could be glad to see it animadverted upon by so admirable a Pen. Ladies, as I have said, should antidote the Poison shed by the vile of their Sex."[20]

In another letter Richardson asks Chapone's opinion of Lady Vane "and her too-forgiving Lord" and then responds passionately to her query about why "it should be thought improper for a woman at *any Age* to be independent": "I have enumerated upwards of Twenty Reasons to Miss Mulso, why Women, for their own Sakes, shou'd not wish to be so. Subordination, Madam, is not a Punishment but to perverse or arrogant Spirits." Richardson typically fails to note that most fallen women (unlike Clarissa) were not possessed of a fortune. In fact, scandalous memoirists usually wrote their stories while indigent, not independent. But Richardson chooses to utilize the scandalous narratives to forge his argument against independent women who, in his view, are the most vulnerable to victimization: "The Little Histories I have of her [Mulso], of several Women who had failed in common Prudence and common Modesty, were given to elucidate this Point, and to show that Women are safest when dependent." He continues, "The Designers of our Sex, make their first Enquiry after independent Women."[21] This factually inaccurate fixation on financial independence suggests the extent to which Richardson found the scandalous memoirs a threatening, if elusive and contradictory, assertion of female autonomy, of an aggressive and distinctive female identity.

Many eighteenth-century readers, angered by the memoirists' defense of their conduct, urge the women to admit their active role in their own downfall, the way in which they, like men, are driven by passion rather than chance. An anonymous letter to Lady Vane acidly remarks on this failure: "I must own, it is at present the Fashion for Ladies of your Profession, to write the History of their Lives in order to induce the good-natured Part of the World to pity their Misfortunes; which, if you will believe these Apologists, always flow from some fatal Cause or other that they could not possibly avoid, and never from their own ill Conduct."[22] Henry Fielding also treats the scandal writings as the site of the erotic and forbidden. In *Amelia* Fielding draws the narrator's curtain down over Booth and Miss Matthew's imagined love nest in prison to "lock up . . . a Scene which we do not think proper to expose to the Eyes of the Public. If any over curious Readers should be disappointed on this Occasion, we will recommend such Readers to the Apologies with which certain gay Ladies have lately been pleased to oblige the World, where they will possibly find every thing recorded, that past at this Interval."[23]

In another contradictory reading, the female apologists are also absolved of passion, their unconventional behavior excused if their own sexual desire can somehow be nullified. In a pamphlet that appeared in response to Lady Vane's story, *An Apology for the Conduct of A Lady of Quality, Lately traduc'd under the Name of Lady Frail*, the author defends Lady Frail's "irreproachable Character." While she is held accountable for loving Mr. Vane, she is acquitted of excessive sexuality: "the misconduct of this Lady had been entirely owing to Ill-usage, on the Part of her Husband, and Indiscretion on her own; and did not proceed from any Impulse of Sensuality." Nevertheless, further intimate details of the affair "never before made publick" are included.[24] Paradoxically, the memoirs both illustrate women's sexuality and assert women's lack of sexual desire, to insist that lust is male; they both confirm and deny that every woman is at heart a rake. When Virginia Woolf read Laetitia Pilkington, she sensed this contradiction in remarking that she was a "very extraordinary cross between Moll Flanders and Lady Ritchie, between a rolling and rollicking woman of the town and a lady of breeding and refinement."[25]

In the mythology of eighteenth-century sexuality, as Patricia Meyer Spacks has pointed out, women must not acknowledge their own passion: "The characteristic tactic of women writing about themselves is to deny their own sexuality while perceiving the quality in other people . . . The hidden parts of the personality comprise the 'self' one must war with."[26] These sexual feelings which make up the "self," the gendered subjectivity, are not inherent or essential but rather produced in the historical moment. Thus, at this point in the development of the definitions and contradictions of eighteenth-century character and identity, the reading of scandalous memoirs for both men and women allows access to the imagined innermost recesses of women's sexuality, but the writing of scandalous memoirs also publicly articulates feelings that had been unwritten by "woman" and make that female interiority an object of consumption. Once a "fallen woman" articulates a "self" that escapes prescribed patterns, she becomes a subject—the perceiver instead of the perceived—an individual capable of loneliness, anger, and passion rather than a generic abstraction. Though some scandalous memoirists capitalize on their woe, in others self-pity coexists with the celebration of sexuality. At this moment of describing sexuality and feeling, then, the problematic of female character surfaces in the production of a new female subjectivity which is individuated yet universal.

The memoirs also function in part to satisfy an emergent fascination with the production of secrets of private life. The voyeuristic reader, urged to adopt a position of moral reproof, is simultaneously compelled toward sexual excitement and potency. Many versions and translations of French confessional erotica make their way into England throughout the century, and most focus on women's imagined private lives.[27] In English, the New Atalantis (1709) had much in common with the French chroniques scandaleuses, and, as John Richetti has pointed out, "the scandal novel or 'chronicle' of Mrs. Manley and Mrs. Haywood was a successful popular form, a tested commercial pattern" of vicarious pleasure in the public scandals of the aristocrats.[28] Of course, Memoirs of a Woman of Pleasure, (Fanny Hill) was published in 1748. Narratives of trials for adultery that focus on women who "become the object of the scorn, pity, and derision of her relations, her former associates, and the public" were published throughout the century. These trials, accompanied by suggestive engravings, are structured as a series of depositions filled with sexually explicit details of the adulterous act. As such, they produce "characters" of women that condemn them. Like the memoirs, the trial volumes advertise themselves as moral tracts designed to prevent others from committing the crime of adultery. The preface to the second volume of *A New Collection of Trials for Adultery, 1780–1802* suggests that "to publish to the world these illicit Amours may, therefore, be found the most effectual Means at present of preserving *Religion* and *Morality* . . . and should the Evil complained of still increase, we shall still continue to expose it . . . and render Vice ashamed of its own Deformity."[29] With the proliferation of newspaper and periodical accounts of details previously considered private, a woman with a public reputation had to publish contradictory evidence in turn if she was to alter her public character which had become a commodity.[30]

Setting out a conflict between moral innocence and erotic fantasy, the seduced maiden novels of Haywood and Manley, according to John Richetti, simultaneously represent sacred religious values, which are centered in woman, and secular values centered in man. Richetti sees these texts as romantic tales of resignation and self-abnegation that appeal to a largely female readership (125). These novels are often collapsed in the same category with the autobiographical texts as displaying stock familiar characters and urging the reader to pity yet feel superior to the fallen woman. But perhaps more than in the novels, the heroines of the autobiographical memoirs defy the boundaries of archetypes familiar from earlier genres. They often refuse to reform or to display remorse; they take on male libertinism, frequently defining themselves as other than typical "woman." Many narratives bristle with energy and passion rather than anguished submission to female strictures. If many scandalous memoirists cite passages from *Jane Shore* to characterize themselves as victims, they also exhibit ways that the pattern of the seduced maiden is insufficient to contain many of these women's lives.

The scandal then, in the works of these eighteenth-century memoirists who recount the fall from *man's* grace, derives as much from the submerged power of producing an independent public character that diverges from the known as from salacious content. What also allows these texts to exceed definitions of "woman" is the persistence of Pilkington, Charke, and other secular autobiographers in assigning responsibility for their fate to "man," not God. The scandalous memoirs can be read as a corpus of antimasculinist literature in their frequent attempt to blame men and circumstances, "not so much to *justify* or *apologize* for her own Conduct, as to fix the Saddle on the right Horse."[31] Frail blames her husband's impotence, Robinson her father's desertion, Leeson her brother's tyranny, Phillips her husband's polygamy. If Lady Vane writes,

"I have been unhappy because I loved and was a woman," Charlotte Charke announces, "I THEN WAS WHAT I HAD MADE MYSELF" and Elizabeth Gooch claims, "I have a soul that will never bend under the yokes of tyranny and oppression."

IV

These gendered characters of the lascivious whore or the seduced maiden are among the models that produce women's interiority and allow readers to tame their complex individual lives into conventional and familiar forms. But as I have demonstrated, the memoirs also threaten to expose the contradictions involved in limiting text and character to these paradigms. In fact we can discover in the scandal memoirs another model for the definition of female character, one that both overlaps with and takes a different course from that of the seduced maiden or the whore. This production of female identity finds its source in the imitation of male spiritual typologies. No *female* spiritual model seems to satisfy the memoirists as a desirable exemplum in their struggle between subversion and compliance with cultural expectations. For eighteenth-century woman, "character" or selfhood was guaranteed only if the "I" could recreate itself in the images created by man and God, and women's autobiographical writing testifies in part to that kind of patriarchally authorized "selfhood." But it also testifies to the absence of the female "self" from theological and philosophical formulations of identity in the period.

For example, the male fortunate fall of the Prodigal Son—the compelling spiritual and familial myth of separation and reunion, of independence accepted and rewarded—seems largely unavailable to women in eighteenth-century English culture. The Fall, a moment of identity crisis for male figures which assumes an originary essence, leads to metamorphosis from one assumed "character" to another. In this common type of the century, the Prodigal Son parable portrays a crisis of filial rebellion that reaches resolution in the son's ability to turn a tyrannous into a caring father who respects his son's newfound right to an independent character. For the Prodigal Son, it is the separation from family and the fall into sin that enables him to achieve independence, as well as return to the father's fold.[32] In contrast, the female autobiographers in their writing, subvert the idea of permanent regret or change which follows the fall. Such individuated characters for women are written without benefit of universal models. Because women are excluded from the spiritual myth of separation and reunion, of independence accepted and rewarded, some female memoirists celebrate their fall from chastity and familial favor in an assault on those who would deny them the "character" they assert. These writing women translate the female fall into public notoriety, the fall from chastity and familial favor into the pattern of a public declaration of identity.

The parallels between the fall into knowledge of sin and the fall from chastity are familiar to eighteenth-century readers, and both kinds of falls are associated with woman's release into speech and discourse. According to the serpent in the garden, the tree of knowledge releases both speech and reason. Such a temptation to power and autonomy is especially desirable in Milton's *Paradise Lost* where man is woman's author and authority. Eve reminds Adam of her subservience: "My Author and Disposer, what thou bidd'st/Unargu'd I obey; so God ordains,/God is thy Law, thou mine: to know no more/Is woman's happiest knowledge and her praise" (IV.635–38). Sexuality is frequently associated with writing in satiric attacks on women. Women who write are lustful women who scratch their scribbling itch in such antifeminist satires as *The Great Birth of Man* (1688), *The Folly of Love* (1691), *Sylvia's Revenge* (1688), and *The Poetess* (1688). These conventional formulations make it difficult for a female memoirist to claim individuation and difference, for they are read as the universal failings of the whole sex.

But Charke, Phillips, Pilkington, Robinson, and others speak a secular gendered interiority that revises the fall of spiritual conversion narrative. Though it is structured around a literal fall from chastity, the memoirists' moment of transformation is usually also a fall away from social acceptance and culturally sanctioned discourse. The female autobiographers capture this moment of crisis as an occasion and focus for articulating a "character." In traditional spiritual autobiography, crisis brings transformation, a time when the individual becomes inevitably and incontrovertibly different from what s/he was. The crisis requires a permanent change in identity which, for the female apologists, is an attempt to convert the *reader* to a belief in a version of their character as an innocent. In a lengthy plea for her virtue to the reader, Mary Robinson writes, "GOD . . . will know how innocent I was of the smallest conjugal infidelity. . . . These pages are the page of truth, unadorned by romance, . . . and I know that I have been sufficiently the victim of events, too well, to become the tacit acquiescer where I have been grossly misrepresented. Alas! of all created beings I have been the most severely subjugated by circumstances more than by inclination."[33] Laetitia Pilkington gives lip service to Providential order at the conclusion of her narrative, but she suggests that whatever structure the Deity has designed is overwhelmed by the plenitude of competing constructions of her life and character. Both defiance and manipulation of male religious convention thus produce the female character.

V

Autobiographical texts such as those by Charke, Pilkington, and Phillips reproduce individual historical experience and human chronology to invent new tropes for women's lives, while simultaneously speaking in the language of the culture that is available to them. Eighteenth-century women writers insert the possibility of making themselves their own object into the current discourse on character, and in doing so, subvert and contest male life patterns and female stereotypes. Because no existing model fully or consistently satisfies them—not seduced maiden, remorseful convert, lusty lass, or Prodigal Son—these women and their texts are both victims and revisionists of received ideas about female character. The scandalous memoirs implicitly collude with the dominant powers to reproduce sexual difference and confirm male superiority. But they also contradict that authority by redefining the fall and the status of women, by resisting the textual production of a consistent and unified character, and by exploiting a public forum to insist on the power of the printed word.

I want to turn now to look more closely at a number of these texts to mark the multiple ways that these autobiographical works mediate the impossible contradictions of eighteenth-century female character. Charke, Pilkington, Phillips, and Vane excite the reader with the erotic and violent consequences of producing public female character. For example, in her *Apology* (1748) Phillips herself indicates the difficulty of the task of countering other versions of her character that are in circulation: "The Minions of publick Fame are generally dress'd out with accumulated Virtues, to which they have no manner of Pretension. On the other Side, let the Cry begin against any Person (especially a Woman and a fine one too) she shall instantly be loaded with Crimes that her very Thoughts are a Stranger to, and utterly abhor."[34] Seduced at the age of ten by Thomas Grimes (Lord Chesterfield), she writes to defend herself to the public, even including extracts from legal pleas and answers in Chancery. The *Apology* is testimony that "once in a *thousand Years*, a Woman should be found who has the Courage to take up Arms against her Oppressors, and prove that even *a Lord* may be—*a Villain*" (III.40). The *Apology* recounts lurid details of the seduction, which resembles Clarissa's with its woman panderer, entrapment, drugging, and exchange of letters: she is beaten, stripped, and branded with a red-hot poker because she is unwilling to sleep with her bigamous husband. The question is, which sex is to be blamed in the gender war: "It was to be taken for granted, I must be the worst of all Women, or the Tables would turn, and you must appear the vilest of all Men" (I.iii).

Biographical passages describe Phillips as an innocent persecuted maiden, but the spirited and lively autobiographical letters interspersed with these passages contradict the suffering maiden model. The male narrator congratulates her because she does not resort to the usual female responses. Both male and female narrators argue that her "character" exceeds her gender: "She is formed with a Disposition very opposite to this *Female Supineness*. Her Misfortunes have shown her the Necessity of becoming superior to them, and every new Oppression she meets with, adds fresh Vigor to her Fortitude: . . . for she has a Soul too masculine, to become an Opponent fit to answer his Lordship in the *Billingsgate Stile*" (III.33). In the letters mingled with the biography, Phillips acknowledges the futility of her effort to make her case convincingly, for a woman can never recover from her fall: "No, my Lord, these are the Disadvantages we labour under from being born Women; and they are such, that for my own Part, were Beauty as lasting as our Date of Life, to change my Sex I would be contented to be as deform'd and ugly as *Aesop*" (III.13). Her experience cannot be contained within the definition of "woman." She writes to an unknown gentleman, "My fingers are crampt, and my Mind no more at Ease than it was; nor will it be, 'till I have the Pleasure of seeing you; for in this Particular, I am no Woman" (II.117). In the *Apology* it is not possible to be held to the category of "woman" and, at the same time, defend oneself courageously from male oppressors.

The lively and popular version of the memoirs of Lady Vane that appears in *Peregrine Pickle* is filled with sexual encounters. In those memoirs, Vane's "essential" gendered character brings about her misfortune. She calls herself an innocent, but contradictorily feels she must account for woman's natural envy and pride. She is without remorse for sleeping with Mr. S. but refuses to separate from her husband "as her character was still unblemished."[35] Wondering how her own individuated character can fit, Vane is divided between self-defense and self-alienation in condemning her whole sex. She writes, "I found as many trifling among the men, as ever I observed in my own sex" (519). Her husband's character, she writes, is weak and womanlike. In fact she concludes by completely turning the tables to aim the lines from Pope's "Epistle to A Lady" ("'Tis true, no meaning puzzles more than wit") against her reprobate husband who, she says, has no human character at all (538). For both Phillips and Vane, conventional male character serves as a resource or an enabling contrast for the production of an unconventional female identity. The resulting tensions are typical of the scandalous memoirs.

Writing memoirs may set the autobiographer against "herself" as well as against other cultural norms. The female apologists acknowledge this splitting, which makes recognizing one's own "character" or "self" difficult. Laetitia Pilkington invents a dialogue between these divided parts, criticizing her own style and content. Speaking to herself she writes, "Madam, your story has nothing in it either new or entertaining; the occurrences are common, trivial, and such as happen every day; your vanity is intolerable, your style borrowed from Milton, Shakespeare, and Swift, whom you pretend to describe, though you never knew him; you tell us a story of his beef being over-roasted, and another of a mangy-dog—fine themes truly!"[36] Charlotte Charke goes further than Pilkington in distancing herself from the "self" or "character" she hails in the text. Calling herself a "nonpareil," a great curiosity, she begins with "The Author to herself" rather than the author to the traditional patron. "I . . . shall, for the Novelty-sake venture for once to call you, FRIEND; a Name I own, I never *as yet have known you by.*"[37]

Both Charke and Pilkington display their "inner" character as an index to their "real self"; but both puzzle over the contradictions made manifest in trying to explain the disparity between their unconventional actions and their conviction of worth. Pilkington repeatedly indicates that she writes, in part, to contravert her husband's public accusations and to revise the public's version of her personal history: "though I led the life of a recluse, I had every day some new story invented of me" (166). The world lies about her disobedience to her parents and about her elopement, and she writes to correct her public character (210–14). She repeatedly appeals to the reader as the judge and jury of the facts she presents to clarify that she is *not* the "Irish whore" of her public reputation. But she also describes titillating situations and the ways she avoids them, sometimes including the teasing seductive talk of the male subscribers to her poetry.

At times Pilkington, like Phillips, presents herself as passive, persecuted and helpless. Her early history calls for a pitying reader who will believe that her unfortunate marriage was to assuage her parents, not to rebel against them. "As solitary in London as the pelican in the wilderness" (210), she recalls the biblical Martha and her troubles, and the classical Niobe and her tears. At one point she plays Jane Shore to a lover's Lord Hastings (250). Resorting to the language of sentimental tragedy, she laments "one fatal folly" and claims that her alleged infidelity occurred because an admirer trapped her in a room: "but Lovers of Learning will, I am sure, pardon me, as I solemnly declare it was the attractive Charms of a new Book, which the Gentleman would not lend me, but consented to stay till I read it through, that was the Motive of my detaining him" (100). Pilkington then enacts the cultural expectation that reading leads to female downfall.

Yet, commenting within the memoirs on the public's response to the earlier volumes, Pilkington also revels in the power of the published word, "more especially as my word is passed to the public; and my word I have ever held sacred." She usurps the language of spiritual autobiography, claiming that she is the Word, but she refuses the identity between body and language that the word would imply: "I am, in short, an heteroclite, or irregular verb, which can never be declined or conjugated" (35). She is both verb and noun: "But, alas! poor I have been for many years a noun substantive, obliged to stand alone, which, praise to the eternal goodness! I have done, notwithstanding the various efforts of my enemies to destroy me, many of whom I have lived to triumph over, though they encompassed me on every side like so many bulls of Basan" (307). The achronological and disjunctive narrative, written a decade before *Tristram Shandy*, prefigures Sterne's in that the trivial is always disrupting the linear description of the past. Pilkington peppers the narrative with liberal quantities of her own poetry; her mind publicly roams from gossip to dreams, from anecdotes of Swift to opinions on conjugal bliss. Though she has obviously read Shakespeare, Milton, and Pope, her female muses are Madame Dacier and Catherine Philips, "the matchless Orinda." Her poetry insists on woman's right to distinguish herself from men, and from other women, by producing private and individual feelings in text, to reveal to the reader "the inmost recesses of my soul" (242). Pilkington unquestionably includes the poetry to fill the blank pages; but it also brings to articulation the felt experience of her loneliness—poems on memory, solitude, sorrow, adversity, and a prayer for tranquility. The original poems she includes become another convincing argument against accepting public versions of her character, male typologies for a female identity, or generalized assumptions about women's interiority.

One of her longest poems, "The STATUES or, the Trial of Constancy: A Tale for the LADIES," answers Mr. Pilkington and Swift, and accuses men of the inconstancy they level against women (69). *Man* is tested, and *man* fails, offering the lovely maid a chance to deliver an antimasculine diatribe. Within the poem, the maiden's attack paralyzes the pursuing prince, and turns him into a statue:

> She spoke. Amazed the list'ning monarch stood,
> And icy horror froze his ebbing blood;
> Thick shades of death upon his eyelids creep,
> And close them fast in everlasting sleep;
> No sense of life, no motions he retains,
> But, fixed, a dreadful monument remains;
> A statue now, and, if revived once more,
> Would prove, no doubt, as perjured as before.
>
> (69–74)

If Pilkington bemoans her fate because of her husband's supposed tricks, she also celebrates the power of her word against her accusers, the force of her vital female character against a lifeless male convention. When the character displayed in all three volumes is weighed, the memoirs seem less self-pitying, plaintive, and passive than critics have suggested. If reading, writing, and learning bring about her downfall, she also depicts these activities as the agents of her release from conventional female character. They enable financial gain, the expression of emotion, diversion for herself and her reader, the attention of those who would despise her, a means of self-defense, a mask of self-scrutiny behind which to reconceive authority, and finally, a contestatory public version of gendered character.

But whenever her character begins to resemble an autonomous and coherent whole, she fractures it by adopting the mask of anonymity or of Mrs. Meade (a pseudonym she assumed soon after leaving Dublin). She frees herself to redefine Mrs. Pilkington's public character: "for by that [Mrs. Meade] I always went in London; so that the numerous stories of Mrs. Pilkington's being in taverns, bagnios, etc, which my husband says he can prove (*Mem.* he lies) never appertained to me; but to his own Cousin Nancy Pilkington, whose father lives in Pill Lane—and who is herself as common a prostitute as ever traversed the Hundreds of Drury" (228). Or she plays at switching gender so that she will be treated less deferentially. She recounts an incident with Swift: " 'I wish, sir,' said I, 'you would put the question to the company, and accordingly to their votes, let my sex be determined.' 'I will.' said he. 'Pilkington, what say you?' 'A man, sir.' They all took his word; and, in spite of petticoats, I was made a man of after dinner: I was obliged to put a tobacco-pipe in my mouth" (411). Pilkington can explore a variety of identities that affect to care very little about the world's opinion.

Pilkington defends herself by writing her text, but she is also quite literally befriended by Colley Cibber, the poet laureate after 1730, actor and manager at Drury Lane, himself an author of an *Apology* (1740), and oddly, father of Charlotte Charke, who wrote her own autobiographical narrative as a plea to be restored to his favor. Like Laetitia Pilkington, Charke's narrative (1755) describes a disguised and fragmented character that defies universal typologies. A heteroclite like Pilkington, Charke also invents multiple and serial subjectivities which play among the available gendered characters.

An actress and author of three novels and three plays, Charke, like her father, exhibits a contrived eccentricity. Charke's work begins in the spiritual autobiographical mode. If her earthly father Cibber allows her to return to his bosom, she will enact the role of the Prodigal daughter. I am not, she declares, as sinful as the Prodigal Son, yet my father cannot forgive me (121). Because Cibber ignores the first installment of her memoirs, a reconciliation to her earthly father is thwarted and the reader, not God, will judge her: "The Reader may remember, in the First Number of my Narrative I made a publick Confession of my Faults, and, pleased with the fond Imagination of being restored to my Father's Favour, flattered myself, ere this Treatise could be ended, to ease the Hearts of every Humane Breast, with an Account of a Reconciliation" (117). The happy ending Cibber demanded of Clarissa was denied to his own daughter. Her secularized prototype is to be found in the sentimental reconciliation exemplified by Thorowgood's forgiveness of Barnwell (a role she frequently played) in Lillo's play *The London Merchant*: "If my Pardon, or my Love be of Moment to your Peace, look up secure of both" (121). Her history, like a criminal's, ought "to be properly examin'd, before it is condemn'd," and she acknowledges that she has done "a Thousand unaccountable Things" (11–12).

Charke also toys with the dramatic fiction of seduction and betrayal. Announcing that she was the tenth child of a woman of forty-five, "an unwelcome Guest," and "impertinent intruder" (15–16), she describes how her rebellious marriage to Mr. Richard Charke, a violinist, sours when he turns unfaithful. She blames her father's tyranny on the malice of her eldest sister who played Goneril to her Cordelia. The material conditions of Charlotte Charke's life were, to judge from all reports, incontrovertibly tragic. According to Mr. Samuel Whyte, an eighteenth-century witness, she presented a pitiful figure near her death, "a tall, meagre, ragged figure, with a blue apron, indicating what might else have been doubted, the feminine gender; a perfect model for the copper Captain's tattered landlady." Only "a mutilated pair of bellows" served as a substitute "for a writing desk, on which lay displayed her hopes and treasures, the manuscript of her novel." She presented a sorry vision of a woman writing with a broken tea cup for an inkstand: "the pen worn to a stump; she had but one!"[38]

But in the *Narrative* the suffering innocent oppressed by male tyranny gives way to a comically aggressive character: "There is none in the World MORE FIT THAN MYSELF TO BE LAUGH'D AT" (86). Her favorite character type, she writes, is a low comic, the one she anticipates for her daughter, for a low-comic woman, she postulates, could undergo more transformations throughout her acting life. She alternates between humor and pathos, encouraging the reader to construct her writing as comedy or tragedy. The title page of the second edition cites a passage in *The What d'ye Call It*: "*This* Tragic Story, *or this* Comic Jest,/*May make you* laugh, *or* cry—*As you like best*." She turns the tyranny of her father and her brother Theophilus into comic absurdity. When Theophilus's daughter could not act in a play with Charlotte, she turns the slight on the perpetrators: "'Tis plain the rancourous Hate to me had spread itself to so monstrous a Degree, that they rather chose to make themselves, I may say in this Case RIDICULOUSLY CRUEL, than not load me with an additional Weight of Misery" (173). Charke fills the typological void that Scriptural, epic, or allegorical models might have provided with dramatic models for her character—not the tragic female figure of Jane Shore, but comic male figures like Captain Plume in *The Recruiting Officer*, Macheath in *The Beggar's Opera*, Lord Foppington in *The Careless Husband*, and Bevil junior in *The Conscious Lovers*.

Learning traditional male activities such as shooting and hunting, being a hog merchant, pastry cook, farmer, and puppeteer, Charke describes adopting the identity of a Mr. Brown, dressing in men's clothes and taking a female companion. Several times she must reveal herself to unsuspecting heiresses who propose marriage. Becoming the gardener after her family dismissed one, she writes, "I was entirely lost in a Forgetfulness of my real Self" (42). But she worries about what her self really is, for "I was as changeable as Proteus" (203). Convinced that she possesses something called "self," Charke, like other scandalous memoirists, remains uncertain about the way to assign gender to the subjectivity produced by the culture. Her consistent resort to comedy indicates the centrality of conventional genre in her production of a female identity, but at every turn of the narrative those stable, conventional rules are tipped or skewed by her protean "changeability," her subversive undercutting of gender distinctions the culture assigns.

Charke, playing with the fixity of name to assign identity, by her own account lived as Mr. Brown with a wife and daughter. But Charke was not alone in her radical adoption and inversion of secular male patterns to invest female "character" with meaning in the mid-eighteenth century and to titillate the reader with the erotic possibilities of gender shifts. She remarks in her *Narrative* that her daily world was filled with imposters. Susannah Centlivre lived for many years dressed as a man. A woman named Sally Paul, according to the *Monthly Review* (1760), was brought before the magistrate for being married to a woman. Mary Hamilton, also known as "George," came to trial in 1746 for transvestism and marriage to another woman. The Hamilton case probably inspired Fielding's *The Female Husband*, a fictional history depicting Mary Hamilton's invented sexual exploits in masquerade and her threat to sexual difference.[39]

Hannah Snell's *The Female Soldier; or, the Surprising Life and Adventures of Hannah Snell . . . Who took upon herself the Name of James Gray; and, being deserted by her Husband, put on Mens Apparel, and travelled to Coventry in quest of him, where she enlisted in Col. Guise's Regiment of Foot . . .* (1750), recounts that woman's adventures when dressed as her brother-in-law

James Gray. Born in 1723 in Worcester, she served in 1745 as soldier and sailor during the Siege of Pondicherry while searching for the husband who deserted her and her daughter. Snell's book is addressed to female readers who are invited to admire Snell's disguise and moral strength, and to male readers who are encouraged to unleash their prurient imaginations concerning a woman's life on a ship filled with men. A comrade testifies to Snell's Amazonian courage when she is wounded in the groin: "This Wound being so extreme painful, it almost drove her to the Precipice of Despair; she often thought of discovering herself, that by that Means she might be freed from the unspeakable Pain she endured, by having the Ball taken out by one of the Surgeons." On another occasion, forced to bare her breasts during whipping, she camouflaged her breasts with a handkerchief tied around her neck.[40] The account describes one woman's aggressive response to male perfidy. Snell maintains her female virtue while usurping male prerogatives to travel, swear, and fight.

In describing their characters, these women recount their representation of themselves as something they are not: men. Female identity is here aggressively asserted, but in such a way as to undercut the ideology of the gendered subject that eighteenth-century theorists of character were attempting so desperately to preserve. The sexually ambiguous man/woman certainly supplies individuation, but only by obliterating entirely the category of sameness, of the consistency of the species of "woman."

The public narrative of women's lives continues to serve as a location where the contradictions of gender and character surface throughout the eighteenth century. A later spate of texts including Ann Sheldon's *Memoirs* (1787), Elizabeth Gooch's *Life* (1792), George Anne Bellamy's *Apology* (1785), Elizabeth Steele's *Memoirs of Sophia Baddeley* (1787), and Margaret Leeson's *Memoirs* (1797) continue to confront the problems of writing "woman's" character and experience. Some of these memoirists, adopting male typologies, find the language of the culture which constitutes "woman" sufficient and satisfying, but others draw attention to the inadequacy of the erotic, the pathetic, and the spiritual. Like the earlier autobiographies, these narratives display the tensions among various discourses on woman—the religious privatization of self-inspection, the display of the sexual, and the production of a language of inner emotional life. They speak of the coercion of the notions of "male" and "female" which pressure women to make their public characters unified and intelligible.

Autobiographical writing is an ideological ground of gendered subjectivity where some women employ the subjective to individuate themselves and to insist that they cannot be treated as an unfeeling abstraction. These scandalous memoirists, in responding to the way their "characters" were constructed in the public domain, indicate that the production of women's private subjectivities evoked disturbing discoveries which sometimes violated public perceptions. Positioned in contradiction (between excessive sexuality and lack of desire, between virtue and vice), eighteenth-century "woman" is defined as all of a kind, yet characterless. These public narratives of private character divide women from "themselves" and threaten the coded character of "woman" current in the culture. No simple code contains the contradictions; no existing paradigm of gender reproduction suffices to mold the memoirists' writing so that each distinctive detail is expressive of a unified and essential personality. The texts both refuse and adopt the substantial unified identity that the heterosexual gender system requires in order to reproduce itself.

Eighteenth-century women autobiographers recuperate and sabotage the (male) culture's signifying practices about gender and identity through their texts. They usurp the discourse that defines them while they invent disguises to mask their dissension from it. In speaking and writing publicly for the first time, the scandalous memoirists push toward defining a new typology for the "female"; they disrupt hegemonic hierarchies of value while inevitably confirming them. Women's autobiographical writing, then, becomes a crucial site for struggles over the meaning of female "character" at an historical moment of erosion and rigidification of gender boundaries.

8

PRISON REFORM AND THE SENTENCE OF NARRATION IN *THE VICAR OF WAKEFIELD*

John Bender

> Now that particular psychology, in the name of which you can very well today have your head cut off, comes straight from our traditional literature, that which one calls in bourgeois style literature of the Human Document. . . . Justice and literature have made an alliance, they have exchanged their old techniques, thus revealing their basic identity.
>
> Roland Barthes, *Mythologies*[1]

The Vicar of Wakefield is not often described as a political novel. Ordinarily it is treated as a fable, a parable, or a fairy tale without meaningful reference to the actual social realm that produced it. But in order to purchase such timeless coherence for the work, readers have tended to blink at some remarkable ruptures in fictional continuity and oddities of narrative technique. Once noticed, these discontinuities are apt to be passed off as generic conventions, read as ironic, or judged as faults arising from carelessness or ineptitude, not be be analyzed as significant. In this essay I attempt to uncover the import of one such rupture. I move from a discussion of the apparently disruptive arguments for prison reform in chapters twenty-six and twenty-seven to suggestions about the place of *The Vicar of Wakefield* in the history of the novel and about its significance in the framework of post-Enlightenment culture. Goldsmith may have sought to transcend petty faction, even to "dispel the prejudice of party," as he claimed to have attempted in his first *History of England*, but his novel's form and technique, no less than its contentiousness, are profoundly ideological.[2]

I am interested here not only in Goldsmith's articulate political stance but also in unforseen consequences—in the meaning of his textual practice. Essentially tactical government of the kind England experienced during this period tended to conceal deeper motivations, broad societal movements, and long-term innovation. I call this government "tactical" because its political programs were shaped more by the maneuvers necessary to maintain the working entities of day-to-day rule—especially ministerial coalitions—than by sustained or coherent principles or even by articulate party allegiances. Under such government, any specific issue such as prison reform could be appropriated for transient political ends that obscured its larger import. Of course tactics play a role in every government; but in England during the third quarter of the eighteenth century they were dominant. Tactical government during the period of Goldsmith's novel both represented a fundamentally contradictory social structure and established conditions under which an emergent ideology could come into focus. I associate this ideology with the illusionistic aesthetic of transparent discourse in the realist novel; with the moral idea of character governed by conscience; and with modern governmental procedures that disperse authority into depersonalized rules, systems, bureaucracies, and institutions—most especially the penitentiary. I discuss the ways in which incongruent methods of narration and exposition in *The Vicar of Wakefield* at once mask this ideology and make it accessible—ways in which the novel is poised between speaking out and acting out reformist thought. Since, as Mikhail Bakhtin maintains, the novel

is constructed in a zone of contact with the incomplete events of a particular present, [it] often crosses the boundary of what we strictly call fictional literature—making use first of a moral confession, then of a philosophical tract, then of manifestos that are openly political, then degenerating into the raw spirituality of a confession, a "cry of the soul" that has not yet found its formal contours.[3]

Novels not only reveal ideology through their registration of contradictory voices, they *must* do so in order to maintain their generic identity. They make visible the means of production of the social text. They have the dual structure that Anthony Giddens finds in other cultural formations and social institutions: they are both the medium and the outcome of the practices that constitute social systems.[4]

By "ideology" I intend not merely an articulate framework of belief, but the symbolic practices through which we manifest our social pres ence, or subjectivity. Such practices produce material institutions but also structures of domination, as well as the imagery through which emergent social and cultural formulations come into focus and gain conceptual status. A primary medium of these symbolic practices is linguistic behavior, which produces kinds of discourse ranging from everyday speech, through argumentation and exposition, to literary representation in the technically discrete language of written narrative fiction. Through the analysis of discourse we can understand how articulate belief operates and also how its disfunctions mark out the terrain of future social and institutional structures. As Raymond Williams suggests, "What matters, finally, in understanding emergent culture, as distinct from both the dominant and residual, is that it is never only a matter of immediate practice; indeed it depends crucially on finding new forms or adaptations of form."[5] Such forms anticipate forthcoming organizational principles and master narratives.

I

Certainly the reformist dimension of *The Vicar of Wakefield* occupied the press when Goldsmith's novel first appeared in 1766. London newspapers and magazines often excerpted the work during the year of its publication, and chapter twenty-seven was by far the most frequent selection.[6] In this chapter (and that just previous) Dr. Primrose is jailed under a warrant of arrest for unpaid rent because he has resisted his landlord, Squire Thornhill, the unscrupulous seducer of his eldest daughter. Primrose seeks to reform the prison in which he is held with the remnants of his family. He sums up the contemporary view of jails as licentious spawning places where debtors and petty criminals learned the arts of felony. He preaches to the common prisoners and goes among them with a series of precepts, rules, and regulations which, under his enforcement, reform the prison into a prototype that anticipates the penitentiary as later delineated by the Penitentiary Act of 1779. Chapter twenty-seven was warmly discussed in the press on the same footing with essays and letters from correspondents. Why were Dr. Primrose's thoughts on prison so timely? What were these ideas? Where do they stand in the history of reform? What have they to do with politics? Why, above all, should an essay on prison reform be lodged in a novelistic context?

Dr. Primrose's ideas about imprisonment may have struck the editors of journals as topical because Cesare Beccaria's book *On Crimes and Punishments*, which took intellectual circles in Europe by storm upon its publication in July of 1764, had gained wide currency when the French translation appeared in January of 1766. Beccaria praised the "immortal Montesquieu" as the guiding light of his treatise,[7] and more than a trace of the *Persian Letters* (1721) and the *Spirit of the Laws* (1748) also appears in Goldsmith. In fact, Goldsmith had been engaged with questions of legal reform at least since 1760–61, when he composed *The Citizen of the World*, a series of periodical pieces in imitation of the *Persian Letters*. By the early 1760's, when Goldsmith was writing these essays and *The Vicar of Wakefield*, it had become commonplace to argue, in Montesquieu's vein, that punishments ought to be proportional to crimes and that excessively severe punishments for moderate offenses inspired indiscriminate criminal behavior. For example, when robbery and murder are both capital crimes, the law encourages highwaymen to kill their victims (as Samuel Johnson maintained in *Rambler* 114, 1751). These and other ideas in chapter twenty-seven recall both the matter of the *Spirit of the Laws*, as well as its anecdotal manner, which Goldsmith declared to be more that of a "poet than a philosopher" (*Works*, I.301).[8]

The French connection was important to Goldsmith, but his ideas also figure in a line of English thought about prison discipline that dates, most memorably and consistently, from the activist years of Fielding's magistracy during mid-century. The case for reformative imprisonment involving supervised labor and reflective solitude set forth in chapter twenty-seven reads like an abstract of Fielding's plan for a Middlesex County House in *A Proposal for Making an Effectual Provision for the Poor* (1753). These ideas do not appear in works by Montesquieu or Beccaria; rather, they are presentiments of a consensus that would emerge among English intellectuals, philanthropists, and legislators of the 1770's, a consensus that eventually led to the replacement of prisons like the one in which Primrose is confined with newly designed and constructed penitentiaries.[9]

This is part of the story, but in addition Goldsmith associated with men at the center of contemporary British legal thinking. The famous jurist William Blackstone authoritatively brought together Continental and English strands of thought about legal reform and prison discipline in his *Commentaries on the Laws of England* (1765–1769), the fourth volume of which concerns criminal law and was written, explicitly, under the influence of Beccaria. The *Commentaries* were based in large part upon Blackstone's lectures as the first Vinerian Professor of Law at Oxford, a position he held from 1758 until his resignation in 1766. Robert Chambers, Blackstone's leading student and eventual successor to the Vinerian Chair, was a long-standing friend of Samuel Johnson's. Such a friend, indeed, that Johnson assisted him as a collaborator when he proved incapable of composing the lectures required of him as Vinerian Professor. When Goldsmith received the Bachelor of Medicine at Oxford in 1769, he stayed four days as a guest of Chambers, who had recently been elected a member of the Reynolds-Johnson Club.[10] Goldsmith, as a friend who shared Johnson's interest in law, had ample opportunity to know about the ideas Blackstone presented in his lectures, which were in progress during *The Vicar of Wakefield*'s composition and revision. Although any similarly acquired knowledge of *On Crimes and Punishments* probably would have come too late to affect his revision of the novel, Goldsmith could have known quite early about Beccaria.[11]

It is worth pausing to describe the kind of imprisonment under attack by the reformers of this period. The typical residents of eighteenth-century prisons were debtors and people awaiting trial, often joined by their families, as is Goldsmith's vicar. Their society might include convicts awaiting transportation or execution as well as innocent witnesses held by the court. The old prisons were not intended, in themselves, as penal instruments but as places of detention prior to judgment or disposition. Death was the common penalty, though often commuted to transportation abroad. Prisons were temporary lodgings for all but a few, and the jailer collected fees from prisoners for room, board, and services like a lord of the manor collecting rents from tenants. As Smollett observed, these prisons microcosmically condensed the society that created them.[12]

The reformers rejected these old, domestically ordered prisons, conceiving instead the penitentiaries later perfected by industrial society. This reconception occurred in several stages. As impulses to reform became intellectually focused during the 1760's, prison *exteriors* were reimagined, although their *interiors* actually remained much as before. While the old contract system based on jailor's fees sturdily resisted change, prisons during this decade outwardly assumed a fearful, awesome, sublimely intimidating aspect—imagery envisioned in the graphic arts by Piranesi and in architecture by George Dance's 1768 design for London Newgate. *The Vicar of Wakefield* went beyond this early stage of reformist reconception by presenting the old prison interiors as the sites of a new kind of regime.

Following the Penitentiary Act of 1779, newly designed English prisons displayed revolutionary changes in interior plan. Governmental authorities began to pay all expenses and to dictate every detail of penitentiary architecture along with every movement in the prisoner's carefully specified daily regime. Each structure was contrived as the physical setting implied by a narrative—or series of narratives—of criminal reformation. Often inspired by a religious fervor that proved remarkably compatible with Beccaria's utilitarian analysis of human nature, the reformers aimed to reshape the life story of each criminal by the measured application of pleasure and pain within a planned frame-

work. Upon entering one of the new penitentiaries, each convict would
be assigned to live out a program or scenario that took as its point of
departure a generic classification based upon age, sex, type of offense,
and social background. Confinement itself became the punishment, and
by the mid-nineteenth century penitentiary sentences had virtually supplanted other criminal punishments except execution for murder or
treason.

II

What did the old prisons mean to Goldsmith? And what did the issue
of prison reform have to do with politics in the narrower sense? These
questions may be condensed into another: how could a writer ordinarily
described as something of a backward-looking traditionalist find himself
on the side of reform?

In eighteenth-century England, reformist arguments concerning criminal law and prisons, at least in their earlier manifestations, are more
accurately understood as aspects of the politics of opposition than as
elements in a sharply defined program. When Goldsmith was drafting
The Vicar of Wakefield in the early 1760's, soon after George III's accession,
the old oligarchy of court Whigs that had ruled the country for most of
the century was thought, by diverse factions with very little in common
besides their opposition to those in office, to have imposed ever harsher
criminal laws—especially capital punishment—as a means of enforcing
its power. Thus Goldsmith, whose secular politics may be fairly if
broadly characterized as those of a nostalgic country conservative, could
have views on prisons and the criminal law generally consonant with
those of a man as different in other respects as Jonas Hanway. Hanway,
like a number of philanthropists of the time, came from an essentially
disenfranchised category of traders and manufacturers whose reformism
was consciously motivated by powerful, very often dissenting, religious
belief. By the same token, reformist argumentation and the introduction
of Parliamentary bills during the later 1760's and the 1770's helped the
Rockingham group define its political opposition to the king and his
ministers, even though significant members of their party had figured
in the old corps of Whigs earlier responsible for the rapid increase in
the number of crimes designated as capital offenses. Party relations in
this world were positional, not absolute. Indeed, modern ideas of party
and class were not yet sharply defined, though the forces that would
delineate them were already powerfully at work.[13]

Goldsmith's opposition to rule by "aristocratical" plutocrats is vehemently set forth in "The Revolution in Low Life" (1762; *Works* III.195–

98). His repeated references to "the Great" unmistakably place this essay in a long tradition of attacks on the Whig oligarchy reaching back through Fielding and Gay. He sees foreign commerce as enabling the accumulation of "immense property," which leads in turn to government by numerous petty tyrants. In the country, as landlords and magistrates, these magnates abrogate ancient rights and push small farmers—the virtuous "middle order of mankind"—off the land. In the city, the "Great" indulge in luxurious entertainments that set a disastrous example for shopkeepers and craftsmen of the "middling class of people."[14] This view of contemporary history, along with the theory of government that justifies it, is voiced most trenchantly in *The Traveller* (1764):

> But when contending chiefs blockade the throne
> Contracting regal power to stretch their own,
> When I behold a factious band agree
> To call it freedom, when themselves are free;
> Each wanton judge new penal statutes draw,
> Laws grind the poor, and rich men rule the law;
> The wealth of climes, where savage nations roam,
> Pillag'd from slaves, to purchase slaves at home;
> Fear, pity, justice, indignation start,
> Tear off reserve, and bare my swelling heart;
> 'Till half a patriot, half a coward grown,
> I fly from petty tyrants to the throne.
>   (IV.265–66; 11. 381–92)

Taken in historical context, these lines mark out a distinct political position. The antidote to the tyranny of "aristocratical" plutocrats whose vast wealth is founded upon commerce (especially foreign trade) is to contain them within a reinvigorated royal authority.

A more detailed exposition of the ideas behind *The Traveller* appears in chapter nineteen of *The Vicar of Wakefield*, where Dr. Primrose argues vehemently against a "very well-drest gentleman" who has asked him home to a fine supper but who is soon discovered to be a politically radical butler masquerading as the absent master. The upstart servant merely parodies his master's "aristocratical" imposture. Primrose asserts that "external commerce" not only destroys home industry, and class identity, it also undermines sovereignty because it yields accumulations of wealth so vast that they cannot be expended on "necessaries and pleasures." Instead, this wealth is spent to purchase power competitive with the king's. And in the very next chapter, when Primrose is reunited with his wandering son, George, he hears that the poverty-stricken young man's adventures in quest of patronage have included a time as servant-companion to a rake who required him to fight as his substitute in a duel. The rake is none other than that same Squire Thornhill who has just seduced George's sister and will shortly imprison his father. All three fall prey to the Squire's expression of superfluous wealth as power. The wealth actually belongs to the Squire's uncle, Sir William Thornhill, whose omniscience extends to heights that might well be envied by a king, yet whose power, though miraculously benevolent, also derives from riches gained abroad. The two Thornhills are fantasy opposites who move, respectively, beneath and above royal notice.

The 1760's in England was a period of transient ministries within the government and radical action outside it. George III aggravated both the instability of his cabinets and the radicalism of the Wilkesites even if he did not cause them. But though the king proved to be politically inept, he stood for much that men of Goldsmith's stamp admired, and his defects were far less evident during the first few years of the reign than later. Six days after the succession, he issued a proclamation "for the encouragement of piety and virtue, and for the prevention of vice, profaneness and immorality."[15] In addition, he worked successfully to force the end of an ongoing, and largely triumphant, imperial war with France in which Pitt, as Prime Minister, had been enthusiastically backed by commercial interests in the City. George, the first notably "English" king in living memory, stood for traditional values and against the grasping machinations of clever politicians. He called the counterbalancing arrangement of Britain's constitution "the most beautiful combination ever framed,"[16] and eagerly sought to maintain, even to rejuvenate, the crown's operative role in the processes of rule.

The throne to which the poet would fly in *The Traveller*, like the overarching royal authority that Dr. Primrose views as a protection against the "aristocratical" tyranny of new wealth on the one hand and the intrusion of "liberty" men on the other, unmistakably idealizes Goldsmith's aspirations for the reign of George III. Dr. Primrose exclaims in a similar vein:

> It should be the duty of honest men to assist the weaker side of our constitution, that sacred power that has for some years been every day declining, and losing its due share of influence in the state. (IV.98)

In such a context, attacks on prison conditions and arguments against capital punishment become tokens of a broad resentment against Whiggish petty tyrants who assume the forms of aristocracy but not its values:

> And thus, polluting honour in its source,
> Gave wealth to sway the mind with double force.
> (*The Traveller*, IV.267; 11. 395–96)

Squire Thornhill stands for the lot of them. By their means,

> the natural ties that bind the rich and poor together are broken, and . . .
> [the] middle order of mankind may lose all its influence. . . . In such a state,
> therefore, all that the middle order has left, is to preserve the prerogative
> and privileges of the one principal governor with the most sacred circum-
> spection. (IV.101–2)

Goldsmith's later *Life of Bolingbroke* (1770) characterizes St. John's *Idea of
the Patriot King* as "that excellent piece" which "describes a monarch
uninfluenced by party, leaning to the suggestions neither of whigs nor
tories, but equally the friend and the father of all" (*Works*, III.470). Goldsmith appears sincerely to have viewed George III in such a light. For
him, reform participates in a large wish for authoritative intervention
and supervision.

The idealization of George III has broad implications for an ideological
understanding of *The Vicar of Wakefield*. Goldsmith clearly longed for
reform of the body politic to come about through paternalist intervention
by the throne, his view of which, again, aligns with that of Bolingbroke
who wrote that "the image of a free people" living in a "genuine" polity
is "that of a patriarchal family, where the head and all the members are
united by one common interest."[17] Thus Dr. Primrose in his roles as
"priest" and "father of a family" can appropriately, if somewhat im-
plausibly, reform the microcosmic, old-style prison into which he is
thrown by Squire Thornhill. Prison serves as a condensed image of tyranny that is at once traditional and loaded with contemporary political
significance. As E. P. Thompson observes, both the Whig "jealousy" of
the Crown and Walpole's lavish financial support of the throne as a
partner sharing the spoils of government arose less from anxiety about
an absolutist takeover than from "the more realistic fear that an enlightened monarch might find means to elevate himself, as the personification of an 'impartial', rationalizing, bureaucratic State power, above
and outside the predatory game [of party and court politics]. The appeal
of such a patriot king would have been immense, not only among the
lesser gentry, but among great ranges of the populace."[18]

In the short run, reformist adaptation might well have been part of
the program of the kind of enlightened, patriot monarch whom Bolingbroke and Goldsmith envisioned, and whom George III hoped to be.
Goldsmith's advocacy of the king as the agent of change is comprehensible not only in the English context but in the larger frame of European
politics: a number of absolutist monarchs and princes on the Continent
did in fact reform their criminal laws on principles recommended by
Beccaria and other intellectuals. In the long run, however, the ration-

alization of the state—its emergence as an impersonal network of laws, rules, parties, and bureaucratic procedures that intersperse authority throughout everyday life—would in part accomplish the containment of oligarchic depredation that Goldsmith sought. To the degree that such rationalization ultimately would come to epitomize bourgeois class interests, it also would serve the "middle order of mankind" which, as Primrose argues, subsists independently "between the very rich and the very rabble" and in which "are generally to be found all the arts, wisdom, and virtues of society" (IV.101–2).

Finally, however, the procedures of the modern state could not effectively be assimilated to a royalist program like Goldsmith's because their authority could not be personified: their regulative power depends upon their impersonality. In the fully realized penitentiary, for example, impersonal authority is projected as the "principal of inspection" as Jeremy Bentham described it in his *Panopticon*.[19] Bentham's idealized plan revealed that the operational fact of the penitentiary is the *principle* of inspection itself, not the person of the inspector. The point is that the inspector-keeper is not really omniscient, or even really a person, but rather that the transparency of penitentiary architecture forces the prisoner to *imagine* him as such. Goldsmith envisioned the new penitentiary regime but misapprehended its means by attributing its power to the throne. Both the French connection and the politics of opposition enabled him to define prison conditions and abuses in the criminal law as crucial issues and brought about his advocacy of changes that had quite different implications than he could have foretold in the early 1760s. But Goldsmith's lack of foresight is not surprising. Reform found its initial representation within the existing boundaries of those political, conceptual, terminological, generic, or institutional species it eventually would alter, because it encoded emergent social practices in such mystified shapes that their significance was easily misunderstood by actors in a fundamentally tactical political context. In short, reform had a wide range of unforeseen consequences. The novel served as a laboratory where potential outcomes were enacted as textual experiments.

The novel provides a formally distinct arena where political and social contradictions become accessible to analysis. This is because works of art—perhaps the novel above all—attempt the unified representation of different social and cultural structures—the residual, the dominant, the emergent—simultaneously in a single frame of reference. In aesthetic works the very contrivance of formal coherence out of disparate materials allows us to glimpse—through what have been called eloquent silences—the process of generation and regeneration that drives all cultural formation.[20] Such works are peculiarly revealing as compared with the infinite sequences of historical process as a whole because of those breaks in tone, conflicts in representational method, and tensions among generic expectations that occur within their formal boundaries. Alterations in form, the emergence of new subject matters, or developments in technique, can enact broader cultural change. But works of art are not mere reflections. They clarify structures of feeling characteristic of a given historical moment and thereby predicate those available in the future. This is the specific sense in which they may serve as a medium of cultural emergence through which new images of society move into focus and become tangible.

III

The implicit logic of Goldsmith's reformist advocacy stands in contradiction to his politics and yields a fractured, paradoxical mode of narration. The ironies that mid-twentieth-century critics have found in *The Vicar of Wakefield* are generated not by flaws in the character of Dr. Primrose but by contradictions that mark reformist thought during the 1760's and that more generally characterize the transition to modern impersonal governance. At one level—that of political consciousness—Goldsmith undoubtedly was a monarchist with nostalgic longings for the old constitution; but the textual ideology of his novel—the import of its form—points categorically to the emergence of an all-present state order, not to the personal rule of a benevolent individual. Precisely because the king was a personification, he could not act during the 1760's as the embracing, neutral, guarding force Goldsmith so desired and so struggled to embody in a surrogate, Sir William Thornhill. Thus Sir William must make a personal appearance in order to set things right at the story's end; to do this he must unmask since, quite remarkably, he has acted in disguise as the family friend, Mr. Burchell, throughout much of the novel. Goldsmith's politics were rather old-fashioned, but both the institutional reformation advocated in chapter twenty-seven and the narrative techniques that structure the text anticipate the all-embracing rule of rules, the neutral impersonality of modern government as epitomized in the penitentiary and in the transparency upon which the illusionism of the realist novel depends. The generic shift toward reformist argumentation that occurs in chapters twenty-six and twenty-seven is a rupture that asks for investigation and alerts us to seek out meaning in the text's most fundamental procedures.

Primrose's surprise and revulsion at conditions in the old-style prison where he is taken make the reformist position seem inevitable. Although the narration is nominally personal and ostensibly reflects Primrose's personal response, the novel provides a context and point of view within which these observations take on the appearance of natural, intuitively obvious facts, not merely opinions. Primrose describes his prison in these terms:

> I expected upon my entrance to find nothing but lamentations, and various sounds of misery; but it was very different. The prisoners seemed all employed in one common design, that of forgetting thought in merriment or clamour. I was apprized of the usual perquisite required upon these occasions, and immediately complied with the demand, though the little money I had was very near being all exhausted. This was immediately sent away for liquor, and the whole prison soon filled with riot, laughter and prophaneness. (IV.141)

The "usual perquisite" is "garnish," a levy imposed upon new arrivals by the prisoners themselves in order to buy drinks all around. The vicar depicts his prison scene like a dedicated reformer and recoils at the unchecked "execrations, lewdness, and brutality" that reign in a jail where there is "no other resource for mirth, but what [can] be derived from ridicule or debauchery" (IV.144–45).

Primrose soon establishes a proto-penitentiary within his old-style jail. And in doing so he creates a social institution as yet unnamed (modern usage of the word "penitentiary" was new in the 1770's). He begins with sermons that inspire the prisoners to a consciousness of their situation and then consolidates thought into habit by establishing a disciplinary regime based on labor, fines, and rewards:

> Their time had hitherto been divided between famine and excess, tumultuous riot and bitter repining. Their only employment was quarrelling among each other, playing at cribbage, and cutting tobacco stoppers. From this last mode of idle industry I took the hint of setting such as chose to work at cutting pegs for tobacconists and shoemakers. . . . I did not stop here, but instituted fines for the punishment of immorality, and rewards for peculiar industry. Thus in less than a fortnight I had formed them into something social and humane, and had the pleasure of regarding myself as a legislator, who had brought men from their native ferocity into friendship and obedience. (IV.149)

Here are sketched the elements that would figure in various permutations and with different emphases in penitentiary schemes of the 1770's and after. The one significant omission is solitary confinement, some anticipation of which occurs when Primrose finds every prisoner in this jail to have "a separate cell, where he was locked in for the night" (IV.141). Thus, of his first night as a captive, the vicar can report: "After my usual meditations, and having praised my heavenly corrector, I laid myself down and slept with the utmost tranquility till morning" (IV.143). In solitude, the vicar displays an ideally reflective submission. In fact, separate night cells were highly unusual in prison buildings prior to the 1770's, when this solution to the riotousness of the old prisons was proposed by some of the more moderate reformers. Goldsmith's un- realistic anticipation of the "separate cell" marks the ideological content of his account of Primrose's imprisonment.

The new penitentiaries would banish Chance and Fortune—the Prov- idential order of plot so central to the events and the social structure depicted in *The Vicar of Wakefield*—in favor of the earthly planning and certitude that Primrose strives for as a "legislator" who wishes,

> that legislative power would . . . direct the law rather to reformation than severity. . . . Then instead of our present prisons, which find or make men guilty, which enclose wretches for the commission of one crime, and return them, if returned alive, fitted for the perpetration of thousands; we should see . . . places of penitence and solitude, where the accused might be at- tended by such as could give them repentance if guilty, or new motives to virtue if innocent. And this, but not the increasing punishments, is the way to mend a state: nor can I avoid even questioning the validity of that right which social combinations have assumed of capitally punishing offences of a slight nature. (IV.149)

In his small nation, the prison, the vicar first personally displaces—and then enacts laws to replace—the structures of authority that prevail else- where in the world of the novel and that have reduced him to his plight as a prisoner. He acts to retell the story by a different set of rules—those of the penitentiary.

Terminology makes the case. "Reform" assumes rationally ordered causal sequence and conceives human invention as capable of recon- structing reality. By contrast, religious rebirth proceeds from mysterious recreation. Reformative confinement in the penitentiary does not deny religion's motive power, it rather appropriates spiritual symbolism for secular ends. A process that transcends but may include religious belief shapes reformist thought and comprehends its other aspects. In this sense, *The Vicar of Wakefield* partakes of a reformist discourse, conducted in the broadly shared vocabulary of sensationalist empiricism, that will unite in common purpose figures as diverse as dissenting Christian re- ligionists like Jonas Hanway or John Howard and secular pagans like Jeremy Bentham. Certainly the unfolding of plot is understood by the vicar as a trope for the working out of Providential will. And certainly religious belief and the figurations that accompany it are central to the novel's symbolic apparatus; Martin Battestin has shown, for example, the novel's pervasive repetition of the plot, style, and thought of the

Book of Job.[21] On my account, however, the text discloses both Providence and plot as attributes of a functional omniscience more akin to that of the secular state than to Jehovah's kingdom. This effect is demonstrated in the plot itself, when Sir William Thornhill emerges, however awkwardly, not just as an *agent* of the denouement but as the *power* who will determine it.

IV

The prison episode in *The Vicar of Wakefield* is an eruption or fracture that allows us to glimpse an ideology which is at once pervasively encoded throughout the novel and contradicted by the text's political rhetoric. Virtually the whole machinery of the new penitentiary is sketched out in chapter twenty-seven, and this apparatus in turn implies a peculiarly modern way of viewing character and conscience as impersonal narrative functions. In Sir George Onesiphorus Paul's later Gloucestershire system, for example, male and female felons were confined in penitentiaries under detailed rules setting forth regimes of work and diet appropriate to different stages of the sentence, which was analyzed into segments like the stages of a classic plot.[22] To manipulate identity by restructuring the fictions on which it is founded is the exact aim of the penitentiary as an institution. Yet in the novel's prison episode the impersonal principle of inspection, which animates both the penitentiary and the rational/purposive social order it epitomizes, is enacted as the story of a personal intervention by Dr. Primrose. This personification of social power is no less incongruous than the fictional pretense that the operations of reformative confinement might be carried out within the architectural framework of an old-style prison.

The incongruous attribution of regulative omniscience to personal agents in facts occurs throughout the novel. Overdetermined personifications of authority crowd the whole text. Dr. Primrose's authoritative role is especially important in the prison episode, as in the family setting, but elsewhere he competes with the all but God-like powers of Mr. Burchell/Sir William Thornhill. Acting in the guise of Burchell, Sir William protects the family from the imposture of Squire Thornhill's dubious lady friends, who invite the Primrose girls to London in order to make them easy prey, and, when the Squire lures the eldest into elopement, Burchell tracks her and hovers about trying to warn her off. Later, he is able to foil an abduction of the younger daughter staged by the Squire. The motif of disguise itself becomes a figure for the idea that efficacious governance strives to work invisibly as a mode of control rather than through personal action. Burchell's true identity as Sir William is discovered not by himself but by accident, and the Olympian revelation inspires almost unbearable awe: "Never before had I seen any thing so truly majestic as the air he assumed upon this occasion" (IV.167). The vicar also must compete with the perverted, aggressively personal, feudal authority of Squire Thornhill, whose defeat is adumbrated by the vicar's reform of the old-style prison—at once the instrument and symbol of "aristocratical" tyranny. These overdetermined personifications manifest a frustrated struggle to find technical narrative forms both correlative to the emergent penitentiary idea set forth in chapter twenty-seven and consonant with the novel's expressed politics. A version of that struggle can also be seen in the choice of narrative mode. The text contains evidence of a reach toward the impersonal narrative procedures characteristic of later realist fiction and, analogously, of the penitentiary as idealized in Bentham's "principle of inspection." *The Vicar of Wakefield* is an intermediate socio-cultural structure whose textual operations allow us to view emergence in process.

Ronald Paulson argues that Dr. Primrose combines attributes of a simple wise man like Parson Adams in *Joseph Andrews* with the ironic perspective of Fielding's omniscient narrators. Primrose's witty character includes an ironic streak, yet his limited personality and point of view make him subject to dramatic irony.[23] The vicar also includes authoritative qualities reminiscent of Dr. Harrison in Fielding's *Amelia* (1751). Indeed, the character of Dr. Harrison in that earlier novel provides a key to an appreciation of the technical development represented by *The Vicar of Wakefield*. The narrator in *Amelia*, though at times obtrusively omniscient, all but disappears during long stretches of the fiction, and many of his authoritative attributes—including considerable management of the action—are lodged in a character in the story, Dr. Harrison. Yet Dr. Harrison also proves fallible, and his mistakes have provoked considerable commentary by critics who rightly notice inconsistencies in the character. Properly viewed as products of Fielding's experimentation with narrative technique, however, these inconsistencies in Dr. Harrison can point us toward a fuller understanding of the problematic formal status of Goldsmith's narrator. *The Vicar of Wakefield* combines similar attributes in Dr. Primrose, a character who is at once the apparent narrator, the chief actor, the possessor of considerable foresight, and a laughably erroneous good soul.

The resulting compound differs markedly from previous first-person narration because the speaker in Goldsmith's novel is framed by a coherent, controlling, putatively invisible omniscience. In *Amelia*, this omniscience had been personified as an intrusive third-person narrator, even though that narrator was often submerged and some of the attributes of authority were transferred to Dr. Harrison. In *The Vicar of Wake-*

field, although omniscience must be inferred within the body of the narrative proper, we learn on the title page that Dr. Primrose's story is "a tale, supposed to be written by himself." Who, we may ask, is doing the supposing? Some covert impersonality is at work here, some tacit collaboration between an implied third-person perspective within which Primrose's supposed narration must be staged and an implied reader who seems to require omniscience and individualism at once. The reader is licensed to imagine an individual as the figure of narrative authority, much as Bentham's prisoner is invited to imagine the keeper-inspector of the penitentiary as a representation of the principle of inspection and omniscience itself. The text attempts to contain first-person narration within a covert, impersonal omniscience. This controlling presence is manifest in the rigidly symmetrical structure of the novel and in the blatantly contrived reversals of its plot. Such features are linked in turn to the overdetermined personifications discussed above: these person-ifications may be read as outcroppings of disfunctionally manifested authority. These and other qualities of the novel cause it to seem more like a fable, parable, or fairy tale than a realist fiction. But, as Robert Rosenblum has observed of painting during this same period in Britain, some of the most striking formal developments in realist technique ap-pear in tandem with their opposites—the visionary, the romantic, the fantastic, and the gothic.[24]

I say that the novel "attempts" the containment of the first-person point of view within a coherent third-person perspective because this is a contradictory aim that cannot be fully realized in first-person nar-ration. Only later when full development of the third-person technique known as *style indirect libre* (free indirect discourse) enables the presen-tation of consciousness through seemingly untrammeled, all-seeing, im-personal narration does this become possible. Fielding has a place in the early history of free indirect discourse because of the scattered in-stances in which he employs this device "for rendering a character's thought in his own idiom while maintaining the third-person reference and the basic tense of narration."[25] It is a fundamental mechanism un-derlying the convention of transparency that distinguishes the later real-ist novel. Flaubert condensed the basic principle into a vivid formulation later echoed by Joyce: "The illusion (if there is one) comes . . . from the *impersonality* of the work. . . . The artist in his work must be like God in his creation—invisible and all-powerful: he must be everywhere felt, but never seen."[26] Free indirect discourse disperses authoritative pres-ence into the very third-person grammar and syntax through which the illusion of consciousness is created. Transparency is the convention that both author and beholder are absent from a representation, the objects of which are rendered *as if* their externals were entirely visible and their internality fully accessible. Transparency treats the one presence within which all other presences are staged as if its embrace were invisible.

The Vicar of Wakefield, though written in the first person and not self-evidently part of the pre-history of free indirect discourse, nonetheless reaches toward this technique: in fact, certain passages can be understood as third-person narration reinscribed *as if* from the first-person perspective of the vicar. Dr. Primrose may not be an extraordinarily reflective character, and he is decidedly fallible, but he does have penetrating qualities as an observer. These qualities are less functions of his character than of the encrypted person of his narration. Collaterally, because of inconsistencies and contradictions in Goldsmith's technique, the implied omniscient narratorial presence not only is displaced into the first person, it is variously projected into the actions of characters who—like Burchell, Sir William, Squire Thornhill, and, in certain episodes, Primrose himself—seem to transcend typical human capacity or even to assume all but supernatural powers.

A simple test can reveal how the novel obliquely ventures upon the representation of consciousness from the impersonal, all-penetrating perspective that free indirect discourse makes possible. Roland Barthes proposes such a test during a discussion of personal and apersonal narration as systems or codes independent of superficial linguistic markers: "there are narratives or at least narrative episodes . . . which though written in the third person nevertheless have as their true instance the first person."[27] And he proceeds to rewrite the third-person pronouns of such a text in the first person. Run in reverse, his test yields fascinating results when applied to the passage in chapter fifteen where Primrose, having intermittently assumed some attributes of a third-person narrator in describing the discovery of Mr. Burchell's letter-case, then shifts to a brief account of his own thoughts upon discovering that Burchell had written to prevent Squire Thornhill's London women from taking the Primrose daughters to town. The following translation of this passage yields a convincing episode of third-person narration ranging in technique from neutral psychological description (first sentence), to a passing instance of free indirect discourse (marked with my italics), to a summation ambiguously poised between impersonal narratorial observation and another rendering of thought (last sentence). I insert the alternate pronouns in brackets:

As for my [his] part, it appeared to me [him] one of the vilest instances of unprovoked ingratitude I [he] had met with. *Nor could I [he] account for it in any other manner than by imputing it to his [Burchell's] desire of detaining my [his] youngest daughter in the country, to have the more frequent opportunities of an interview*. In this manner we [they] all sate ruminating upon schemes of vengeance, when our [their] other little boy came running in to tell us [them] that Mr. Burchell was approaching at the other end of the field. It is easier to conceive than describe the complicated sensations which are felt from the pain of a recent injury, and the pleasure of approaching vengeance. (*Works*, IV.77–78)[28]

Primrose's private observations take on the perspective of impersonal narration, though hidden under the first-person. The novel actually alerts us to the possibility of such interchanges of person when, quite early in the text, Mr. Burchell momentarily slips from the third-person into the first during his account of Sir William Thornhill's life and works (IV.30). Goethe describes this famous slip as the point at which, according to Herder, the audience of the novel must divide between those who view the work as "a production of Art" and those who, like children, naively confuse it with the "productions of Nature."[29] Interestingly, the intermediate mode of personal/apersonal narration that I am noticing here appeared contemporaneously with Adam Smith's identification of the psychic interchange of "I" and "he" as the fundamental mechanism establishing morality and character through the introjection of social norms as individual values. Smith named this internalized representation of the third-person the "impartial spectator." *The Vicar of Wakefield* allows us to see the embodiment of the "impartial spectator" in literary culture, and to uncover the dispersed and secret assertions of omniscience and power in the private voice of the individual.[30]

Attention to *The Vicar of Wakefield*'s articulate politics, to its reformist episode in chapter twenty-seven, and to its "supposed" first-person narration shows certain ways in which it displays a new ideology. Goldsmith's individual politics brought him to idealize the personal powers of the monarch as if they represented a new system of impersonal, transparent order—an enabling anachronism that allowed him to delineate the essential character of the new penitentiary in considerable detail, without giving explicit voice to its overarching rationale. His novel, in epitomizing those details, and in producing narration with technical features that anticipate the impersonal omniscience of modern supervisory authority—whether in novelistic procedures or in governmental technology—defines a textual scene within which ideological contradictions become visible and through which we can witness the emergence of a new system of order beneath the surface evocations of divine Providence and first-person narration. These contradictions have meaning. They have cognitive force.

V

We may return, at last, to my earlier question: why should an essay on prison reform be lodged in a novelistic context? My answer has two elements. First, the novel, even more than other literary forms, is sensitive to emergent institutional orders because it incorporates the dialogic transactions at work in society at any given historical moment. Second, the penitentiary as conceived during the later eighteenth century and institutionally established following the Penitentiary Act of 1779 is itself a narrative institution structured on principles analogous to, and within the same epistemology as, the realist novel. Penitentiaries have regimes, schedules, disciplines; their inmates progress or regress, and they have stories not to be told upon release or just prior to execution (like the subjects of the *Newgate Calendar*) but to be lived out in the penitentiary itself. Much of the history of penology subsequent to the establishment of penitentiaries in England during the last quarter of the eighteenth century can be described as an attempt to order the prison story generically with divergent classifications for each age, sex, and type of convict. This idea is central: the form prisons took when they were remade in correspondence to and collaboration with the period's new systems of political and moral consciousness was *narrative* form of a distinctively novelistic kind; this form, in turn, implied a whole new way of being in a transparent world.

Finally, one may ask why it now has become possible, even necessary, to read *The Vicar of Wakefield* as a document of ideological emergence. The work's previous critical reception can offer a clue. The idea that the text maintains two fundamentally disparate points of view—that of Primrose and that of some embracing ironist—became established only during the mid-twentieth-century after nearly two hundred years in which the novel had been prized for its simple clarity of representation. Only during the past generation has Primrose been viewed primarily as a figure with comic, even ridiculous, limitations or as an object of sustained satire.[31] My analysis works to explain these critical strategies as last-ditch efforts to maintain the novel's coherence and illusionism in face of ever-increasing evidence of its contradictions. My reading accepts these contradictions as meaningful rather than trying to reintegrate them into a more complex illusionism. Such a critical move becomes possible, I believe, only once the order of transparent realism and the mechanisms of neutral, rational/purposive social institutions that it reproduces have ceased to be accepted as inevitable, unremarked conventions and have begun to take on the awkwardness of residual formulations. These conventions can and do remain powerful forces in present-day culture and society, but their operations have fallen into the line of critical vision and have become subject to ever more corrosive analysis. Their dissolution has been in progress through most of the twentieth century. Free indirect discourse, for example, was recognized, described, and named by Romance philologists around the turn of this century, about 100 years after it came into pervasive use but precisely when the mode of realism it defined was undergoing radical revision in novelistic practice and when the destructive impact of world war and revolution forever altered the European social order.[32] By the 1920's and 1930's it was an avant-garde commonplace to treat realism as an historical development, and its contradictions, once visible, became increasingly unsupportable in literary and cultural theory even though the practice of everyday life and techniques of popular fiction continued to take many aspects of the convention for granted.[33] Those who remain unperplexed by theoretical concerns may live still within the residual convention of realism—either entirely undisturbed or engaged unselfconsciously in the business of keeping it in operation (this is where I would locate most ironist critics of *The Vicar of Wakefield*).

Today, it seems to me that self-conscious criticism of the novel has to deal with two irreconcilable facts. First, everyday life still proceeds for the most part within the conventions of transparency and realism, just as the penitentiary (in however decrepit a form) remains the ordinary last resort and essential symbolic projection of state power. And second, these conventions and institutions have been subjected to critiques which, though aimed at profound deconstruction, have yet to prove fatal. What characterizes our moment—our *episteme* as Michel Foucault would have called it—is the seemingly indefinite persistence of a parallax existence in which these conditions pertain practically but do not pertain intellectually. We live in a fractured state of illusion/disillusion of which I believe the theoretical eclecticism of this essay to be a product. The contradictions that we have observed in mid-eighteenth-century society inversely parallel the fissures in our own. Both societies are transitional. What was emergent two hundred years ago now is residual— but also different. The novel is now a commodity—part of the culture industry—and penitentiaries now serve as mere holding areas primarily populated by racial and cultural aliens. Signs appear that prisons, known now as "facilities," may soon be returned to operation by private industry like the unreformed eighteenth-century jails that went before them. Even the Enlightenment zeal to abolish capital punishment, a reform closely linked to the rise of the penitentiary, has waned: in California, for example, three justices of the state Supreme Court were recently unseated because the public believed them opposed to the death penalty. In this context, then, I rationalize my own theoretical eclecticism as having, at least, the virtue of keeping fissures in the present mode of social and literary production in constant view by restaging them in multiple perspectives.

9

JOHNSON AND THE ROLE OF AUTHORITY

Fredric Bogel

1. TRIPOD. "A seat with three feet, such as that from which the priestess of Apollo delivered oracles."

Samuel Johnson, A Dictionary of the English Language

2. "They used to read to me, and, among some other things, some papers of 'The Rambler,' which I liked not at all; its tripod sentences tired my ear."

Maria Edgeworth, Helen, A Tale, chap. 7

3. "Johnson . . . took them up into a garret, which he considered as his library; where, besides his books, all covered with dust, there was an old crazy deal table, and a still worse and older elbow chair, having only three legs. In this chair Johnson seated himself, after having, with considerable dexterity and evident practice, first drawn it up against the wall, which served to support it on that side on which the leg was deficient." "Mr. Johnson never forgot its defect, but would either hold it in his hand, or place it with great composure against some support, taking no notice of its imperfection to his visitor."

Northcote's Reynolds, i. 75; Johns. Misc. ii. 259; quoted in Boswell, Life I.
328 n. 1

I

For more than two centuries, the image of Samuel Johnson has been so closely intertwined with a certain idea of mastery, and of the over-mastering, that the phrase "Johnsonian authority" is nearly a redundancy. What does "Johnsonian" mean if not "authoritative"? But what, in this context, does "authoritative" mean? Johnson himself, in his dictionary, does not offer a simple answer, for he defines "authoritative" in two ways: "1. Having due authority." "2. Having an air of authority." The first of these stresses the possession of authority; the second, the appearance of possessing it. Johnson's definition of the adverbial form, "authoritatively," is similarly divided, though here the order is reversed: "1. In an authoritative manner; with a shew of authority." "2. With due authority." In each case, the idea of the authoritative displays both an attributive and a rhetorical dimension.[1]

These dimensions are not necessarily in conflict; but the *possibility* of conflict, and especially of a conflict between an authoritative manner and an absence of due authority, is always present, because authoritativeness is both a condition or possession and the effect of a performance. That possibility of conflict, I think, is written not only into Johnson's definitions of the authoritative but into his ways of assuming authority as well. How it is, and why it is, are questions I want to explore in the present essay.

My approach combines literary criticism, rhetorical analysis, and biographical investigation, and it focuses primarily on three aspects of Johnson's relation to authority. First, I try to rethink Johnson's struggle—existential as well as analytic—with pride and vanity by inflecting this struggle in the direction of the discourse of narcissism. Second, I explore what I take to be the principal rhetorical consequence of the Johnsonian confrontation with narcissism: a deconstruction of the idea of authority, particularly literary authority. Since, at the meeting point of the psychological, the rhetorical, and the institutional, this deconstruction exerts its force on the concept of authorship, I attempt to consider afresh Johnson's relationship to anonymous publication; to literary tradition and borrowing, to plagiarism, and to the mirror image of the latter, ghost-writing; to the characteristic genres and conditions of production of Grub Street; and, consequently, to questions of "high" and "low" literature and of canonicity. Such theoretical and critical implications as the essay may have, or as I may be aware of, are spelled out a bit more fully in its concluding section. My principal aim, however, is to investigate Johnson's startlingly rich and subtle revision of the idea of authority, and thereby to alter the angle of vision from which we look at his career as a writer and thinker.

II

Let us begin on familiar ground: Johnson's intense and often paralyzing guilt about being less productive than he felt he should be—especially about writing less than he thought was required of him. Despite his occasional, vociferous assertions that no man is obliged to do all that he can do, the story told in his essays, in his prayers and meditations, and in Boswell's *Life* is one of overpowering guilt at not writing more. Walter Jackson Bate has argued convincingly that this guilt is the obverse of a massive perfectionism. Unable to live up to his own punishing standard of excellence, Johnson frequently could not write at all and felt, with Milton, that "that one Talent which is death to hide" was "lodg'd with [him] useless." His guilt was thus not mere worldly anxiety but a conviction of impious slothfulness.[2]

What is *strategically* interesting about Bate's interpretation of Johnson is that, in setting productivity against indolence, ambition against guilt, authorship against anxiety, it inevitably deflects scrutiny away from the first item in each pair; as a result, we find it difficult to wonder whether Johnson might have been guilty about assuming authorship as well as about failing to do so. And still more difficult to ask whether Bate's interpretation—which is to a great extent Johnson's, Boswell's, and our own—might not function powerfully to divert us from a more obscure and conflict-ridden area of Johnson's inner life: the struggle with his own assumption of authority.

How might Johnson have conceived of authority—authorial, conversational, personal—so as to discern in it a threat capable of inducing guilt and requiring to be resisted? The central question is where authority comes from—whether from a source beyond our solitary selves and wills or from them alone. This is what worries Milton at the opening of the ninth book of *Paradise Lost*, and it is one of the things that worry Johnson about Milton. Johnson alludes to the problem in *Rambler* 158, where he contends that many critical rules are merely "the arbitrary edicts of legislators, authorized only by themselves."[3] Whether it is the edicts or the legislators who are "authorized only by themselves" (Johnson's syntax allows for both possibilities), the danger is one of self-authorization, of an authority founded on nothing external to the self and its constructions.

It is easy to imagine the threat that Johnson discerned in such self-authorization if we remember the powerful links that Milton's Satan forges (in all senses) between rebellion against God the Father and the rebels' own radical autonomy. "Remember'st thou/Thy making, while the Maker gave thee being?" he asks Abdiel:

> We know no time when we were not as now,
> Know none before us, self-begot, self-raised
> By our own quick'ning power. . . .
>
> (*PL* V.857–61)

Seen against the background of this archetypal act of defiance, self-authorization might readily appear proud, Satanic, parricidal, despairing, and sinful. And the remarkable extent to which the Miltonic analysis of rebellion penetrated Johnson's moral sensibility might lead us to regard with particular seriousness those of his remarks that seem to endorse, or to identify himself with, rebelliousness, singularity, and defiance of external authorities—remarks such as his explanation of his apparent gaiety at Pembroke College: "Ah, Sir," he tells Boswell, "I was mad and violent. It was bitterness which they mistook for frolick. I was miserably poor, and I thought to fight my way by my literature and my wit; so I disregarded all power and all authority."[4] In his *Life of Milton*, he had written: "Milton's republicanism was, I am afraid, founded in an envious hatred of greatness, and a sullen desire of independence; in petulance impatient of control, and pride disdainful of superiority. He hated monarchs in the state and prelates in the church; for he hated all whom he was required to obey. It is to be suspected that his predominant desire was to destroy rather than establish, and that he felt not so much the love of liberty as repugnance to authority."[5] Against this background, one hears with a special and disquieting resonance another of his remarks in Boswell's *Life*. "It was observed to Dr. Johnson," Boswell writes, "that it seemed strange that he, who has so often delighted his company by his lively and brilliant conversation, should say he was miserable." Johnson's reply provides much more than the occasion requires: "Alas! it is all outside; I may be cracking my joke, and cursing the sun. *Sun, how I hate thy beams!*" Boswell can hardly be alone when he confesses, "I knew not well what to think of this declaration."[6]

The claiming of authority may also involve an act of revenge—at least, of reappropriation—rather than of simple rebellion: revenge against an authority-figure who has somehow powerfully compromised one's own authority, rendered it illegitimate, and thereby inflicted the sort of shaming psychic wound that is sometimes called a narcissistic injury. Taking the incident as symptomatic rather than causative, as a "representative anecdote," in Kenneth Burke's terms, we might see the traces of such illegitimation in the story of Michael Johnson's attempt to pass off his own verse epitaph for the dead duckling on young Sam (*Life* I.40). Johnson assured Boswell that his father had made the verses and "wished to pass them for his child's." "My father," Johnson added, "was a foolish old man; that is to say, foolish in talking of his children."

Bate writes sensitively of this incident, arguing that Johnson's "self-demand" was already so strong that he resented the claims of others—in this case, the doting effort of his father to "exhibit" his son's abilities (18–20). But it is possible to see Johnson's annoyance in somewhat different terms: as a response to having his power of self-representation snatched away from him, his identity appropriated by his father, and his own authority thereby nullified or illegitimated. In its extreme form, such a response might verge on what Heinz Kohut has termed "narcissistic rage," which derives its energy from an insistence on "the limitlessness of the power and knowledge of a grandiose self."[7] To reclaim that true authority—or, more to the point, powerfully to *wish* to reclaim it—would be to negate both the false authority that his father ascribed to the boy and the father who falsely ascribed it, and thus to engage in a kind of parricidal revenge, denying the paternity of the father and claiming instead to father oneself. And this, of course, would be to act like Satan when he denies the priority of the Father and claims, however despairingly and suicidally, to have created himself.

The suicidal implications would themselves be functional, of course, insofar as they expressed not just a logical consequence of denying one's father-creator but intense guilt at wishing to do so. John Berryman, in one of the *Dream Songs*, catches this little knot of overdetermined behavior in a pun, describing himself as "suisired"—that is, at once self-fathering and self-destroying. I want to suggest that the guilt which at times clung to Johnson's assumption of authority is the source not just of behavior like his remarkable penance at Uttoxeter, where he stood bareheaded in the rain in guilty remembrance of refusing his father years before, but also of a massive resistance to writing—to assuming the authority of the writer—that "perfectionism" cannot adequately explain.

III

If Milton displays "a lofty and steady confidence in himself," a robust authoritativeness that threatens to slide into satanic self-authorization, Richard Savage—as a man chronically dispossessed and always almost annihilate—seems to represent a threat diametrically opposed. It is not too hard to picture Johnson poised uneasily between the Miltonic Satan and the disowned Savage, between defiant self-authorization and incurable illegitimation. But the symbolic relationship of Milton to Savage, and of Johnson to both, is not quite so simple as this crisply antithetical scheme suggests. For if Savage, in Johnson's *Life*, is repeatedly denied the solidities of birthright, gainful employment, secure residence, and almost identity itself—"while *legally* the Son of one Earl," he writes in a preface, "and *naturally* of another, I am, *nominally*, No-body's Son at all"—he is nevertheless resolutely, obsessively self-authorizing as well.[8]

Of Savage's pride, his high estimation of his own abilities, and his tendency to regard the world as a source of undeserved afflictions or a supplier of merited support few readers of Johnson's *Life* will need to be reminded. "When he loved any Man," says Johnson, "he suppress'd all his Faults, and when he had been offended by him, concealed all his Virtues."[9] The obsessive and self-regarding character of Savage's stance toward the world appears in what Johnson calls "the most innocent species of Pride," Savage's vanity:

> He could not easily leave off when he had once begun to mention himself or his Works, nor ever read his Verses without stealing his Eyes from the Page, to discover in the Faces of his Audience, how they were affected with any favourite Passage.
>
> (*Savage* 138)

And although he "paid due Deference to the Suffrages of Mankind when they were given in his Favour," says Johnson, when they were not, "he contented himself with the Applause of Men of Judgment; and was somewhat disposed to exclude all those from the Character of Men of Judgment, who did not applaud him" (73).

This tidy definitional circularity, which denies the claims of the world in order to meet the narcissistic needs of the self, has its counterpart in another of Savage's curious projects. Some time after the place of Poet Laureate, on the death of Eusden in 1730, was awarded to Colley Cibber rather than to Savage, despite the latter's vigorous campaigning for himself, Savage wrote what was to become an annual poem to the queen on her birthday, a poem with "the odd Title," as Johnson terms it, of *The Volunteer Laureat* (*Savage* 75–76). The title is odd because it treats what can only be conferred by another as though it were assignable by the self. To term oneself "Volunteer Laureat" is a striking appropriation, a kind of infelicitous speech act, like saying "You're pleased to meet me" when encountering someone for the first time. Cibber saw the difficulty clearly, informing Savage "that the Title of *Laureat* was a Mark of Honour conferred by the King, from whom all Honour is derived, and which therefore no Man has a Right to bestow upon himself; and added, that he might with equal Propriety stile himself a Volunteer Lord, or Volunteer Baronet" (*Savage* 79). While one can imagine Savage, or even Johnson in a particularly anarchic mood, responding "Just so" to this objection, it is not surprising to find Savage's proposal, however canny or humorous it may have been, taking the linguistic form of fantasied omnipotence.

Such fantasies can be sustained only by casting out what conflicts with them. Savage's career is marked by a powerful habit of projection to which Johnson is extremely alert:

> By imputing none of his Miseries to himself, he continued to act upon the

same Principles, and follow the same Path; was never made wiser by his Sufferings, nor preserved by one Misfortune from falling into another. He proceeded throughout his Life to tread the same Steps on the same Circle; always applauding his past Conduct, or at least forgetting it, to amuse himself with Phantoms of Happiness, which were dancing before him; and willingly turned his Eyes from the Light of Reason, when it would have discovered the Illusion, and shewn him, what he never wished to see, his real State.

(74)

This sounds like many Johnsonian paragraphs about the snares of fantasy and the flight from self-knowledge, so it is particularly important to recall that the entire passage depends on its opening phrase, "By imputing none of his Miseries to himself," and that it directly follows the account of projection I have quoted above. Whatever authority Savage might have won by allowing his real abilities to engage with the real world, in Johnson's *Life* he largely devotes his energies to nurturing a fantasy-identity—only one component of which is his claim to be the son of the Earl Rivers—and to disposing, often through projection, of whatever will not harmonize with that identity. It is clear that what is from one perspective a tale of illegitimation, abandonment, and victimization is also, from another perspective, a drama of progressive narcissistic estrangement.

The latter portions of Johnson's *Life* show Savage turning in on himself in a number of ways. They reveal, for one thing, an increasing oddity and fantasy-energy in his dealings with others. A lengthy letter to "one of the Gentlemen with whom he had supped" on the night of his arrest for debt is marked by two surprising features. First, Savage is filled with angelic forgiveness for everyone concerned in the arrest, and urges his correspondent neither to utter nor harbor any resentment. Second, he never seems to consider that the cause of his being arrested is ultimately the debts he has himself contracted. In an act of anger-free projection that at once ascribes agency elsewhere and converts disapproval into acceptance, he sweetly forgives Mrs. Read, who has had him arrested, commends the civility of the arresting officers, and gives thanks to "the Almighty" (122–23). A few weeks later, he can "thank the Almighty, *I am now all collected in myself*" (125, my emphasis).

The energies required to construct such forgiveness, tranquility, and enclosure can be gauged from a letter in which the once-forgiven Mrs. Read appears in her scapegoated form as "Madam Wolf Bitch, the African monster," (133n). And in another letter, Savage displays, perhaps more overtly than anywhere else in Johnson's *Life*, a willingness to act and to judge as though he were accountable only to himself. He is answering several questions, among them, why he added "delineated" to the title of his poem on London and Bristol. Here is part of his answer:

> Why did Mr *Woolaston* add the same Word to his Religion of Nature? I suppose that it was his Will and Pleasure to add it in his Case; and it is mine to do so in my Own. You are pleased to tell me, that you understand not, why Secrecy is injoin'd, and yet I intend to set my Name to it [the poem on London and Bristol]. My Answer is—I have my private Reasons; which I am not obliged to explain to any One.
>
> (131–32)

This insistence on controlling the boundaries of the self recalls Savage's "superstitious regard to the Correction of his Sheets":

> the Intrusion or Omission of a Comma was sufficient to discompose him, and he would lament an Error of a single Letter as a heavy Calamity. . . . [H]e remarks, that he had with regard to the Correction of the Proof *a Spell upon him*, and indeed the Anxiety, with which he dwelt upon the minutest and most trifling Niceties, deserved no other Name than that of Fascination.
>
> (58)

The vocabulary of demonic agency in this passage—"superstitious," "*a Spell*," "Fascination"—is more than sufficient to indicate Savage's obsessive investment in controlling every detail of the mode in which he was to present himself to the world. Of course, the narcissistic component in correcting proof, especially the tendency to regard typographical errors as mutilations that a more alert megalomania might have averted, is a relatively innocent and relatively well-known phenomenon. At two other points, however, Savage's anxiety about where his own text ends and another's begins takes more troubling forms. In a letter that Johnson does not quote, Savage writes to a friend concerning one Saunders: "I cannot but smile at Saunders—he calls you 'poor creature!' he stole that very expression out of my letter to him, where, with great propriety, it was applied to himself" (122n). It is striking, and disturbing, that Savage should consider so common a phrase to be his own possession and thus capable of being stolen. His concern clearly has to do not with the intrinsic value of the expression but with anxiety about the permeability or uncertainty of the boundaries of the self. Whether a phrase is good or bad, striking or unmemorable, the important question is whether it is *your own* or not. Somewhat later, Johnson generously (or naively) treats as a mode of moral integrity what is clearly another of Savage's efforts to keep the self inviolate:

A kinder Name than that of Vanity ought to be given to the Delicacy with which he was always careful to separate his own Merit from every other Man's; and to reject that Praise to which he had no Claim. He did not forget, in mentioning his Performances, to mark every Line that had been suggested or amended, and was so accurate as to relate that he owed *three Words* in THE WANDERER, to the Advice of his Friends.

(138)

Like projection, such hyperscrupulous assigning of words to their proper author has self-aggrandizement as its ultimate end. The first strategy seizes what is unacceptable and casts it out, assigns it to another, in order to ensure the perfection of the self; the second seizes what—*because* it is another's—is unacceptable and casts it out in order to ensure the inviolateness of the self. Both strategies depend not only on habitually thinking in unexamined polar oppositions (self or other, friend or foe), but also, in particular, on overestimating the efficacy of the border between self and other. One might say that if Savage were writing his own biography, its narrative stance toward the subject would be wholly sympathetic or wholly critical and its account of his distresses would assign them—whether individually or collectively—unambiguously either to external or internal causes, to his "condition" or his character. And it would have only one conclusion.

But Johnson's *Life of Savage* concludes twice, and in opposed ways, its last paragraph emphasizing the role of Savage's own character in his sufferings while the two preceding paragraphs insist on his "Fortune," his "perpetual Hardships," his "Condition"; throughout, it supplies abundant evidence both that Savage is the victim of others and that he is principally his own victim; and its narrator at once sympathizes deeply with Savage and sharply criticizes his character and behavior.[10] In the penultimate paragraph, for example, Johnson warns against declaring oneself superior to Savage, but he embeds in that warning just such a declaration and, by casting it into the first person and into direct quotation, he requires every reader of the *Life* in some sense to repeat the declaration even while registering the warning: "nor will a wise Man easily presume to say, 'Had I been in *Savage*'s condition, I should have lived, or written, better than *Savage*'" (140). The mere reciting of Johnson's sentence does not, of course, seduce us into proud superiority, but it does acquaint us with what it might feel like to assume that posture—and to resist assuming it—and it does so far more powerfully than would an alternative phrasing that avoided both the first person and the direct quotation, a phrasing like: "nor will a wise Man easily presume to say that, had he been in *Savage*'s condition, he should have lived, or written, better than *Savage*."

Johnson was alert to the ways in which the act of quotation may compromise the quoter (especially in eighteenth-century usage, which did not always sharply distinguish direct from indirect quotation), to the possibility that quotation marks may only imperfectly inhibit leakage between categories such as utterance and quotation, use and mention. In the *Life of Milton*, discussing the impiety of some of Satan's speeches in *Paradise Lost*, he notes that "there are thoughts . . . which no observation of character can justify, because no good man would willingly permit them to pass, however transiently, through his own mind."[11] In thus remaining attentive to the permeability of categorical barriers even while insisting on the separateness of categories, Johnson does what Savage could not do. Yet the warmth, the energy of identification, with which he champions Savage, celebrates him, and laments his fate, keeps critical difference from becoming biographical scapegoating, or narcissistic projection in the style of Savage himself. The subject of the *Life* is not only Savage but, through that identification, Johnson himself as a figure who once deserved, or who always might deserve, to be the object of the criticism he directs at Savage. The complexity of Johnson's relation to Savage, the narrator's refusal to distinguish himself categorically from his subject, is what keeps this biography from being a simple cautionary tale unwittingly reenacting the behavior it confidently condemns.

The *Life of Savage* thus bears significantly on Johnson's relation to authority. The figure of Savage himself demonstrates that social disenfranchisement, powerlessness, and illegitimation are no protection against the dangerous self-authorization so clear in Johnson's *Life of Milton*. If anything, the mournful narrative of Richard Savage reveals a broad path leading from social dispossession to the tenacity of narcissistic fantasy, a path that can perhaps be traveled in both directions. Johnson does not simply criticize Savage for traversing that path, but neither does he wish to follow him along its entire length, and his narrator's relation to Savage suggests an alternative. By dividing or fracturing his own narrative posture, identifying himself with the figure he also criticizes, resisting rather than scorning and therefore repeating his subject's behavior, countering the difference between narrator and subject by means of a difference within the voice of the narrator himself, Johnson refuses the stance of univocal authority that would have condemned at once his subject and himself.[12]

IV

The problem is how to assume authority without simply doing so, how to both claim and disclaim authority so as to exert its power without being crushed by its guilt. For one thing, Johnson frequently ascribes authority elsewhere, displacing it from the self. Here we might think of the anonymous writing that he began producing for Edward Cave's *Gentleman's Magazine* in 1738; the role-playing that generated the Parliamentary Debates a few years later; the personae of Rambler, Idler, and Adventurer; and the constant recourse to those forms of authorship that, whatever the passions of their prefaces indicate, traditionally require something other than Pindaric originality and dangerously individual authority: editing, biography, lexicography, translation, critical prefaces, and so on. Johnson also parcels out authority among various voices within a single work. If the narrators of *Rasselas* and *The Vanity of Human Wishes*, for example, are figures of authority, they also compete for that authority with various narrator- (or author-) surrogates: "Observation, with extensive view," Democritus, "Hist'ry," Imlac, and others.

A more radical disclaiming of authority appears in the remarkable amount of ghost-writing that Johnson produced for others and which it is one of the aims of this essay to restore, in its generic and rhetorical importance, to the center of Johnson's canon, even though—or rather, precisely because—it is by its nature marginal and authorially decentered. I suspect that much of this writing was motivated by a wish to resist just such a narcissistic concern with the boundaries of oneself and one's productions as led Savage, in a passage I have already quoted, to distinguish compulsively between his own and others' literary property. In contrast to such "accuracy" of attribution, Johnson's ghost-writing and lendings enact a fraying or dissolving into the texts of others that precisely undoes the ability to assign property or authorship with certainty. As J. D. Fleeman notes of Johnson's contributions to other writers' work, "it can never be conclusively known exactly how much of such work remains undiscovered."[13] It would be naive, though, to assume that the satisfactions of ghost-writing are so simple or so innocent. If it permits the writer to evade full authority in his text, it also allows him to escape full responsibility for it. And, as the productive component of a quasi-plagiaristic activity, it also permits a certain flirting with lawlessness. Three incidents can suggest something of its moral complexity, complicated satisfactions, and at times dizzying character.

In the last weeks of 1749, William Lauder published his *Essay on Milton's Use and Imitation of the Moderns in His Paradise Lost*, a work claiming to demonstrate that *Paradise Lost*, despite its promise of "Things unattempted yet in prose or rhyme" (a line which Lauder took as his own sarcastic epigraph), had been shamefully plagiarized from a host of neo-Latin writers, that it was, as he put it a few years later, "a Poem entirely compiled from the Writings of others."[14] Johnson, who was at first impressed by Lauder's project, wrote a short essay to accompany his *Pro-*

posals (1747), an essay "which Lauder then used as a Preface to his full book on the subject."[15] But Lauder's attack was soon shown to be a fraud—more exactly, an elaborate and malign drama of projection, in which, having extracted numerous quotations from a Latin translation of *Paradise Lost* by William Hog (or Hogg), he then pretended that these quotations were from Latin poems by modern authors whom Milton had plagiarized.

When Johnson learned the truth, he wished to have Lauder's fraud publicly known as soon as possible. The method he chose, however, is curious in the extreme. He went to Lauder and either wrote or dictated a confession which he had Lauder sign, a confession uttered in the first person as though by Lauder himself. Insofar as Johnson's aim was to supply the public with a satisfactory statement of Lauder's guilt, this course of action was reasonable enough; for one thing, it ensured that Lauder would not produce a false or weaseling statement such as that which he later added in a postscript, and in a subsequent pamphlet.[16] But insofar as Johnson sought to dissociate himself crisply and unambiguously from the man whose devious practices he had unwittingly endorsed, he could not have chosen a less happy method. The writing of another man's confession is a tricky matter in the best of circumstances, but when what is to be confessed is that the man has falsely accused one poet of plagiarism and falsely ascribed texts to the poets allegedly plagiarized, to write his confession for him is to come dangerously close to reenacting the original crime.

Several things might be said about Johnson's action. First, the shadowy complicity with Lauder that it suggests is structurally analogous to the narrator's relation to his subject in the *Life of Savage*, much as Lauder's penchant for scenarios based on the mechanism of projection recalls Savage's own characteristic procedure. This pattern—a half-critical, half-identificatory relation to a figure staging narcissistic dramas of projection—will recur in Johnson's career.[17] Second, while this pattern may offer one sort of "explanation" for Johnson's dictating Lauder's confession, other, more particular, motives also suggest themselves. To the extent that Johnson's initially favorable response to Lauder's revelations was colored by his own ambivalent response to Milton's magisterial self-confidence and surly republicanism, dictating Lauder's apology may have given him the opportunity to utter a kind of penitential discourse at one remove.[18] Third, it is important that Lauder's crime specifically concerned writing, and particularly the manipulation of textual authority (involving, in this case, questions of both literary property and literary greatness), as is clear from the fact that (fourth) the Lauder affair was not an isolated instance.

A quarter of a century later, Johnson tried unsuccessfully to get the death sentence of the fashionable preacher, William Dodd, reduced by appealing to various noblemen and directly to the king. What is especially interesting is that Dodd's crime was forgery (he had forged the signature of the Earl of Chesterfield on a bond of 4200 pounds), and that Johnson tried to assist him by writing letters—to the king, to Lord Chancellor Bathurst, to others—not only in Dodd's behalf but in his voice. It is particularly unsettling to read letters written by Johnson, in the voice of Dodd, confessing the crime of forgery, as in this excerpt from Dodd's *Last Solemn Declaration*:

> I am brought hither to suffer death for an act of Fraud of which I confess myself guilty. . . . For this Fraud I am to die; and I die declaring that however I have deviated from my own precepts, I have taught others to the best of my knowledge the true way to eternal happiness. My life has been hypocritical, but my ministry has been sincere.[19]

What must it have been like to write this declaration? Who was Johnson as he was writing it? Situationally, structurally, he was undeniably both Dodd and himself, but I am contending that the structural coalescence of the two voices—more accurately, their contention—answered to deep needs in Johnson's conception of himself and powerful constraints on the ways in which he allowed himself to assume authority.

A final instance can enlarge our sense of the satisfactions offered by ghost-writing while illustrating some of the special constraints—and curious liberties—with which it surrounds literary authority. Between 1766 and 1769 or 1770, Johnson assisted Robert Chambers in preparing the fifty-six law lectures that he was to give under the terms of the Vinerian Professorship at Oxford.[20] Chambers seems to have needed assistance of several kinds: encouragement, suggestions, outlines, and—on internal evidence at least—even the dictation or composition of a significant number of passages. Certainly, as Bate says, Johnson's "own frustration at not entering the law led him to identify himself with [young men such as Chambers], and to take a generous, vicarious pleasure in their careers" (418). But while a collaboration like Johnson's with Chambers may be an occasion for generous assistance, it may also call forth other motives, such as that peculiar combination of ostensible self-effacement, muted competitiveness, and secret triumph that often characterizes the ghost-writing relationship. (When one of the addresses he had anonymously produced for the Parliamentary Debates was praised as an especially fine speech of the elder Pitt, Johnson announced: "That speech I wrote in a garret in Exeter Street.") Chambers also had to contend with the fact that his predecessor in the Vinerian Professorship had been the eminent Sir William Blackstone. By assisting Chambers, therefore, Johnson entered into a complicated drama of identification and authority.

Consider the opening paragraphs of the introductory lecture, which take up what Johnson's first *Rambler* terms "the difficulty of the first address":

> If I commence with Diffidence and Timidity the Employment to which I am now advanced, it is not merely because I consider the Law, which I am to profess, as by its Extent difficult to be comprehended or by its Variety difficult to be methodized; for Obstacles like these must be encounter'd in all Studies, must be encounter'd with Vigour and surmounted by Diligence.
>
> My Fears proceed from Discouragements peculiar to myself. Professors like princes are exposed to Censure not only by their own Defects, but by the Virtues of their Predecessors.[21]

The passage goes on to enact an interesting double drama of authority. If we take the writer to be Chambers alone, we read a fairly conventional "Introduction" of homage, diffidence, and aspiration that nevertheless manages to stage several canny reversals of priority. Chambers acknowledges Blackstone chief in both matter and manner, "equally eminent for *Extent of Knowledge* and *Elegance of Diction*, for *Strength of Comprehension* and *Clearness of Explanation*" (my emphasis). This seems to give the contest away entirely, for what is left to Chambers? At such a point, the rhetoric of deference usually insists on the predecessor's originality and power of mind, his having constructed a sublime edifice to which those who follow can only add stylistic elegance and decorative beauty (one might call this the Homer-Virgil topos). But that is not at all what Chambers does. By virtue of "Fidelity and Industry," he hopes "to erect such a *Fabrick* of Juridical Knowledge as may stand *firm* by its *Solidity*, though it should not please by its Elegance, and shall think it sufficient to *mould those Materials into Strength*, which only the Genius of a Blackstone could polish into a Lustre." Though he retains the syntax of deference ("though it should not please . . . shall think it sufficient"), he assigns to himself those qualities traditionally reserved for the predecessor or founder—solidity, firmness, constructive and shaping power, strength, the supplying of knowledge—and leaves to Blackstone only "Elegance"—a matter of pleasing—and the ability to "polish into Lustre." By the end of the passage, Chambers is the (logically prior) builder and Blackstone the (logically secondary) refiner and polisher.

This striking bit of rhetorical reversal becomes even more interesting if we consider the author of the passage to be Johnson.[22] On this hypothesis, Chambers stands to Blackstone as Johnson stands to Chambers, and we can imagine Johnson writing into this reversal his own complex relationship, at once secondary and superior, to the young man whom he was aiding. And perhaps, beyond him, to Blackstone himself. (It was in 1765, shortly before his collaboration with Chambers, that Johnson thought seriously of studying the law, and in 1778 that Sir William Scott, lamenting his not having done so, made Johnson "much agitated" and roused him to exclaim angrily: "Why will you vex me by suggesting this, when it is too late?"; *Life*, I.489, III.310.) As a mode of authorship formally disclaimed and therefore derealized or parenthesized, ghost-writing inhabits a territory bordering on that of fantasy, a territory in which ambition may be at once expressed and suppressed, satisifed and punished, and in which the authority of authorship, precisely because it is compromised, may be more readily assumed.

V

Within the voice of the Johnsonian narrator itself, one can also discern self-contestatory impulses: between the announced concern with timeless wisdom and the adoption of a singularly idiosyncratic style, for example, or between the voice of the sage "played straight" and the role of the sage that Johnson often self-consciously assumes, in writing and in conversation, to question the very authority he is assuming. This questioning sometimes teeters on the verge of self-parody, what Martin Price has called Johnson's "self-mocking formal sententiousness," in part because Johnson's style depends so powerfully on the *sententia*.[23] The possibility of such self-mockery is in some sense written into an intensely sententious style. "The paradox of the maxim," as Philip E. Lewis has noted, "lies in the supreme confidence with which it states a relative truth, in the stamp of certitude it confers upon the problematical."[24] At other times, Johnson generates a polemical manner that reveals, by exaggerating and thus purifying, the agonistic character of discussion and the role of personal authority—and not merely "experience"—as the "test of truth." One episode in the *Life of Johnson* can serve to illustrate this manner, since its tone will resonate with dozens of others. The topic of conversation is "a very respectable author" who married a printer's "devil":

> "And she did not disgrace him [says Johnson]; the woman had a bottom of good sense." The word *bottom* thus introduced, was so ludicrous when contrasted with his gravity, that most of us could not forbear tittering and laughing. . . . His pride could not bear that any expression of his should excite ridicule, when he did not intend it; he therefore resolved to assume and exercise despotick power, glanced sternly around, and called out in a

strong tone, "Where's the merriment?" Then collecting himself, and looking aweful, to make us feel how he could impose restraint, and as it were searching his mind for a still more ludicrous word, he slowly pronounced, "I say the *woman* was *fundamentally* sensible"; as if he had said, hear this now, and laugh if you dare. We all sat composed as at a funeral.

(*Life*, IV.99)

The real subject of this episode, as Boswell's inferences and attributions of motive insist, is a certain drama of power that allows Johnson to play the role of authority, to acknowledge that he is playing a role, and still to keep anyone from saying so. It is the copresence of genuine authority and the histrionic affectation of authority, of Johnson and "Dr. Johnson," of the imposition of restraint and the parading of the power to impose restraint—above all, of the demystification of authority and the continuing potency of that authority—that makes this episode so revealing.

This is to say that one of Johnson's principal strategies for simultaneously claiming and disclaiming authority is to adopt the role of sage, and to do so in ways that call attention to its status as a role. This strategy involves a double construction: the construction of a world of great intelligibility, and of a knower of that intelligibility. These are not, however, to be simply identified with Johnson's world and Johnson himself. Speaking of those who, like Johnson, rearrange the world "into more agreeable antitheses," Richard Lanham notes that "Clarity . . . always means daring simplification and much trickery. . . . To rhetorical man at least, the world *is* not clear, it is *made* clear."[25] This making clear is a dramatic and histrionic effort, and whether he is ostentatiously simplifying a complex problem or correcting an admirer's effort to get the Johnsonian style right, Johnson's manner frequently reminds us of that element of the dramatic.

Thus if Johnson is a combatant, he is so not only in Bertrand Bronson's sense but in Roland Barthes's as well. Comparing the theatre with professional wrestling, Barthes remarks: "In both, what is expected is the intelligible representation of moral situations which are usually private."[26] And in words that might describe Johnson Agonistes as well as Armand Mazaud the wrestler, he writes: "[he gives] to his manner of fighting the kind of vehemence and precision found in a great scholastic disputation, in which *what is at stake is at once the triumph of pride and the formal concern with truth.*" The grandiloquence of gesture in wrestling, continues Barthes, is "the popular and age-old image of the perfect intelligibility of reality. What is portrayed by wrestling is . . . an ideal understanding of things; it is the euphoria of men raised for a while above the constitutive ambiguity of everyday situations."[27] If we fail to recognize the artifice employed in efforts like these, it is the fault not of the wrestler but of our nostalgia for perfect intelligibility and for univocal authority. The same is true, I think, of our response to Johnson.

I have been suggesting that for Johnson the assumption of authority was both necessary and necessarily guilt-ridden, and that he sought ways to assume and disclaim that authority in a single gesture, evident and unmistakable role-playing being a principal one of those ways. If we see Johnson's strategy as enacting a certain relation to narcissistic patterns, his own and those of some of his intimates, we might term it a rhetoric of the ego-ideal as administered by the canny ego (this could serve as a rough psychoanalytic definition of aphoristic writing), the expression, and necessarily partial resolution, of powerful conflicts. I think it was, beyond that, a redefinition of authority itself as a matter not of personal unity and univocal authoritativeness but of energies intrinsically divided by internal conflict and self-questioning. In one sense, this means that Johnson discloses the *inherently* dramatic or histrionic character of authority, the space between its attributive and rhetorical aspects as these appear in the *Dictionary* definitions I began by quoting. In the final number of the *Rambler*, he quotes Castiglione to help him explain "the privilege which every nameless writer has been hitherto allowed: 'A mask,' says Castiglione, 'confers a right of acting and speaking with less restraint, *even when the wearer happens to be known.'*"[28]

Beyond this dramatic understanding of the discipline of self-estrangement, Johnson's career suggests that internal dividedness and self-contestation may be not just a challenge to authority but its very form. It is difficult to surrender our nostalgia for at least the possibility of a masterly and unself-questioning authority; in working on his *Dictionary*, however, Johnson noted that while the authority of a given word cannot be absolute, since it rests on simpler terms, the simplest term itself rests, in a sense, on nothing: its authority is both unquestioned and arbitrary, in the manner of an axiom.[29] This is like what Kenneth Burke calls a paradox of substance, for the authority of words is caught between dependency and empty absoluteness. The less dependent a word is on other words, the more it seems to be self-authorizing and thus both curiously powerful and fragile—the explanation as Almanzor, so to speak, or as "Johnson" in the "bottom of good sense" episode. As authority approaches absoluteness, then, it unwittingly reveals its own frailty, whereas a stabler authority will disclose, paradoxically, its internal division and imperfection. We might say that the Delphic tripod on which Johnson rested his own bottom of good sense was the remains of a four-legged chair, and that if he took "no notice of it to his visitor" (he didn't need to) he also "never forgot its defect."

The ending of Conrad's *The Secret Sharer* catches in its management of point of view (and its relation to doubling) a conception of authority somewhat like the one I am trying to describe. The ship's crew, standing outside the captain's consciousness, hears only the decisive commands of a daring and confident leader. The reader, however, hears the captain's internal voices expressing fear, confusion, and desperate riskiness. In some way, Conrad seems to argue, the former depends on the latter, the apparently seamless and univocal authority on the internal self-division. Johnson's own diaries supply a homely version of the story Conrad tells, recounting a moment when the young boy, anxious at having to conjugate verbs at school, nevertheless performs with credit and reports the triumph to his mother: "'We often,' said she, dear mother! 'come off best when we are most afraid.'"[30] I am suggesting that Johnson is always shadowed by one or another figure of radically illegitimated authority, whether Richard Savage, William Lauder, the disgraced and dead brother (possibly both a forger and a suicide) of whom he once dreamed only to note cryptically in his journal, "The dream of my Brother I shall remember," or himself.[31] These and others are his secret sharers. It is by keeping them within him—rather than once more exiling them as others had done, as he himself may well have done—that Johnson redefines the role of authority so as to be able to assume it.

VI

Johnson's habitual demonstration of those "maneuvers . . . by which an author becomes an *auctor*," as John Guillory puts it, is from one perspective a deconstructive effort, an insistence on the constructedness of his characteristic mode of authority and on the work required to construct it.[32] This work might always be ignored in favor of the illusion of a free-standing discourse, authorized by its fidelity to experience, its self-circumscribing formal coherence, and—precisely—its effortless issuing from a personal source that at once grounds that discourse and is unproblematically expressed by it. In refusing that illusion, Johnson does not surrender authority, but he redefines and demystifies it. He shows that the magisterial absoluteness which often functions as the very image of authority—that "state of solemn elevated abstraction" which Boswell had inferred from Johnson's writings and which had grown in his fancy "into a kind of mysterious veneration"[33]—depends on, is produced from, is often but a special case of all that it is taken to transcend: labor, rhetoric, artifice, textuality, self-division, histrionic energy, and the ambition to display magisterial absoluteness. From another, and congruent, perspective, Johnson's management of the role of authority can be understood as part of a continuing effort to register, and resist, narcissistic overestimation of the self and the principal mechanisms of that overestimation, projection and scapegoating. There is always someone or something that Johnson wishes to cast out, to repudiate connection with, and always something which opposes to that casting out the compensatory energies of identification. It is as if the "Brother" in Johnson's dream were less a particular individual than a psychic place or position that might be occupied by numerous figures, a place that is repeatedly the site at once of a temptation and a penance.

Pat Rogers has contended that in several respects Johnson's *Life of Savage* "is not only the story of an archetypal Grub Street figure" but, like the anonymous *Life of Mr. Richard Savage* (1727) on which Johnson drew extensively, "itself a Grub Street product."[34] In one sense, a Grub Street product is nothing more than a work that has not (yet) been canonized, and "Grub Street" performs its principal work by ensuring the continuing existence of the complementary category whose unity and reality it insulates from overenergetic scrutiny: the category of "literature." In another sense, however, "Grub Street" names a certain collection of genres, certain conditions of literary production, a certain relation to immediately contemporary life, and a good deal more, and if Rogers's claim is not fully argued, it can nevertheless alert us to the remarkable extent to which Johnson's writings and career are formed in part within the cultural space of "Grub Street" in this second sense. Renegade productions like the Parliamentary Debates, with their anonymity, contemporary journalistic interest, and uncertain status as fact or fiction (all of which applies to Johnson's *Life of Savage* as well); periodical essays such as the *Rambler*, *Idler*, and *Adventurer*; the innumerable prefaces, dedications, sermons, compilations, dictionary and encyclopedia entries, minor biographies, translations, and political pamphlets, many of them anonymous; *Rasselas*, a version of the "Oriental Tale" such as Johnson had already produced in the *Ramblers* devoted to Seged; and the ghost-writing, traceable and untraceable—all of these display recognizable connections with the forms of discourse that were typically produced in "the ramshackle mansions of Grub Street"[35] by the kind of writer whose condition Johnson had shared and who might, therefore, count as another "Brother" appearing in dreams that Johnson would not forget.

Johnson's career can also show us something about the institution of authorship and the procedures of interpretation. Having noted, for example, the place of "Grub Street" in Johnson's career, in what ways shall we permit that knowledge to function? If we keep the political pamphlets or the Parliamentary Debates or the writing for Chambers's

law lectures in the corpus but out of the canon, so to speak, interpreting
them in the light of resolutely central and canonical works like *The Vanity
of Human Wishes* or *Rasselas*, we will arrive at different conclusions than
we would if we reversed the procedure, and conclusions not simply
about "high" and "low" literature. To read works traditionally termed
"major" in the light of those taken to be "minor", rather than simply
the reverse, is to find persisting in the former patterns that appear in
the latter with great clarity, and to take that clarity as indicating the
centrality of those patterns rather than the author's limited success in
muting or inflecting them. One's interpretation of the minor works, in
short, is if not decisive—as of course it cannot be, any more than our
understanding of major works can decisively determine our understanding of minor—at least highly influential in one's reading of the major
works. (This strategy is especially cogent in the case of a writer like
Johnson, the chronology of whose career does not allow us to equate
"earlier" with "minor" and "later" with "major" in the secure way that
traditional literary history has often sanctioned.)

It would be relatively simple, for example (chronology aside), to treat
the voice of the narrator in the *Rambler*, or *Rasselas*, or *The Vanity of Human
Wishes* as a Johnsonian norm, emphasizing its power and authority and
supporting this emphasis by developing a contrast with such ghost-
written texts as we have been considering in this essay. The latter could
be understood as simply extra-canonical; or as displaying an uncertainty
of voice that Johnson was to outgrow; or even as a series of literary
experiments from which the magisterial voice of the major works was
to emerge. To take the ghost-written texts as in some sense normative,
however, is to develop a different sort of argument about the characteristic Johnsonian voice, seeing it as derived or constructed from frag-
mentariness and self-division, and seeing something of that self-division
even in the oracular tones of the major works: in the apportionings of
voice, the theatrics of emphasis, the stylistic habit of maxim-ization, the
wry, last-minute inclusions of the Sage in the human community he had
at first seemed to scorn, and so on. From this perspective, ghost-writing
is neither peripheral nor aberrant, but one of the principal conditions
of Johnsonian authorship.

That condition can tell us something about the idea of originality, in
Johnson's work and elsewhere. The *Life of Milton* argues the importance
of originality to great writing, but also suggests its dangers: inventions
merely singular, authority peremptorily claimed, a style at once new
and deformed, and an imagination raised to sublimity by studies whose
range is repeatedly tinged with the self-indulgence that terms like "curiosity" and "luxury" carry for Johnson. In contrast to the poet of *Paradise
Lost* is a figure like Newton who, says Johnson in an *Adventurer*, "stood

alone, merely because he had left the rest of mankind behind him, not because he deviated from the beaten track."[36] In Johnson's own practice, we are made conscious—despite the singularities of his own poetic and prose styles—not only of the role of previous writers, or the obligation to illuminate a common rather than singular humanity, but of a rich tradition of meditation on human problems, a tradition to which Johnson repeatedly directs us, often by ascribing general statements, as Isobel Grundy remarks, "to the general voice of humanity, which he cites in just the same way as a published source."[37]

To approach this practice from a concern with ghost-writing is to become aware of the embeddedness of any writing in previous texts, written and unwritten, and of its dependence on innumerable intertextual materials (texts, genres, conventions, cultural assumptions) that give to originality itself the capacity to be read and received. This is not to deny that terms like "ghost-writing" and "plagiarism" frequently designate what Johnson calls "literary crimes," only to recall that they may also serve as part of a mechanism of scapegoating that allows us to overestimate the originality of other kinds of authorship and authority. I seem to recall, in fact, that Walter Jackson Bate has made a similar point about Coleridge's plagiarisms. And that act of recollection leads me to observe that my earlier argument about projection and resistance, scapegoating and identification, in some sense rewrites Bate's account of "satire manqué," that generic hybrid, central to Johnson, in which the energetic rejections and tense self-definitions of satire fade into a more inclusive and communal vision of human experience.[38] The curious mixture of pleasure and alarm that accompanies these observations has, I suspect, a close connection with the problems of literary authority that have been my theme.

10

SENTIMENTALITY AS PERFORMANCE: Shaftesbury, Sterne, and the Theatrics of Virtue

Robert Markley

At the beginning of the second volume of *A Sentimental Journey*, Sterne's narrator encounters a chambermaid in a Parisian bookstore. While flirting with her, Yorick slips a crown into her purse with this advice: "be but as good as thou art handsome, and heaven will fill it."[1] In this line, Sterne articulates concisely the ideological values of his sentimental narrative; the woman's goodness, beauty, and piety merit a reward that literally puts a price on her virtue. Yorick's demonstrative generosity to the chambermaid is cast in a language that is explicitly mercantile—and ideological—rather than pristinely moral or poetic. The crown he gives her, as he recognizes, is not an innocent token of his admiration but a talisman, a symbol of the values that define their relationship hierarchically: he is the freeborn English gentleman who may flatter, bribe—or even command—the French chambermaid. Money becomes the sentimentalist's medium of exchange, a palpable, materialist manifestation of good nature as a commodity.

Yorick's scene with the chambermaid is characteristic of a self-confessedly sentimental narrative that implicitly assumes and explicitly asserts the values of a middle-class culture intent on demonstrating the naturalness and benevolence of its moral authority. Instances of Yorick's charity and generosity abound in the novel; whenever Sterne wants to dramatize his hero's benevolence he has him give away his money—to chambermaids, beggars, and wandering monks. Sterne's foregrounding of the equation of money and virtue, however, seems a deceptively simple solution to a complex ideological problem: as a sentimental novelist, he attempts both to assert the "timeless" nature of a specific historical and cultural construction of virtue and to suppress his reader's recognition of the social and economic inequalities upon which this discourse of seemingly transcendent virtue is based. Like most eighteenth-century sentimental narratives, *A Sentimental Journey* suppresses questions about how one acquires the wealth to be able to afford one charitable act after another. The poverty and social inequality that Yorick encounters on the Continent are not described as the result of any specific economic or political conditions, any authoritarian strategies of repression, or any conscious malevolence abroad in the world; they are simply presented as opportunities for him to demonstrate his "natural," innate virtue. Paradoxically, however, the novel's commodification of "good nature" reveals the strategies it employs to ascribe an absolute and ahistorical value to particular cultural forms of self-congratulation and mystification. By emphasizing the theatrics of Yorick's generosity and by highlighting the equation of money and virtue, Sterne testifies to—and dramatizes—both his own difficulties as a half-hearted apologist for sentimentality and the tensions that inhere in a genre that is both assertive and self-consciously defensive about its claims to moral authority. In this respect, Sterne the Christian moralist coexists uneasily with Sterne the propagandist for bourgeois sensibility. Although, as many of the novel's admirers note, *A Sentimental Journey* comically questions naive forms of sentimental benevolence, it ultimately neither subverts nor transcends the ideology that upholds them. Unlike *Tristram Shandy*, it comes close to sentimentalizing the conditions of its own performance; it does not mock its generic history and narrative strategies, nor does it demythologize the genealogy of sentiment. Instead it remains caught within the ideological contradictions of sensibility—at once alert to the excesses of the genre yet seemingly powerless to offer a sustained critique of them.

I

Sentimentality—the affective spectacle of benign generosity— emerges early in the eighteenth century less as a purely "literary" phenomenon than as a series of discursive formations that describe what amounts to an aesthetics of moral sensitivity, the ways in which middle- and upper-class men can act upon their "natural," benevolent feelings for their fellow creatures. It is, as G. S. Rousseau and John Mullan have demonstrated, at least in part a masculinist complex of strategies designed to relegate women to the status of perpetual victims, biologically constrained by their hypersensitivity and emotionalism to passive suffering and sociopolitical docility. Yet at the same time sensibility valorizes masculine sensitivity as a virtue, as an indication of a "natural" sympathy possessed by men of feeling.[2] The ideology of sentiment also explicitly promotes narrowly conservative and essentialist views of class relations, implicitly identifying the victims of social inequality—men, women, and children—with "feminine" powerlessness. This strategy of rendering the victims of sentimental ideology as politically and symbolically impotent becomes a crucial means of mystifying the class prejudices and ideological imperatives that underlie the workings of sensibility. Yet this subtly coercive strategy of defusing class conflict by sentimentalizing its victims offers us a way to investigate how and why sentimentality developed as it did during the eighteenth century and to explore its myths of "natural" benevolence and class-specific virtue.

The strategies which, taken together, might be described as constitutive of sentimentality have a complex genealogy. Donald Greene's long-needed attack on R. S. Crane's "The Genealogy of 'The Man of Feeling'" has left critics of eighteenth-century sentimentality in a bind; no longer able to allude to a vaguely-defined latitudinarian tradition in the seventeenth century as the definitive origin of sensibility, we have been put in the position of having to account anew for the rise of the phenomenon we study.[3] The genealogy Greene invokes as an alternative to Crane's is, for students of eighteenth-century moral philosophy, a familiar one—he argues that sentimentality gets it start in the deistical idea of a self-sufficient virtue advocated by Anthony Ashley Cooper, Third Earl of Shaftesbury, and later by Francis Hutcheson.[4] Yet neither Greene nor other historians of sensibility have explained how Shaftesbury, a deist who mocked Christian pieties and a tireless defender of aristocratic privilege, became a seminal figure in the development of an affective, bourgeois sensibility that often explicitly invokes Christian verbal formulae, if not latitudinarian theology. Shaftesbury is no doubt a crucial influence on the development of sentimentality as both a rhetoric and a "system" of values. However, those critics who read him as a dispassionate "moral philosopher," a proponent of republican (read Whiggish) principles, or a protoromantic ignore or obscure the ideological origins of sentimentality, its genesis in the complex and uncertain relationships between aristocratic and bourgeois characterizations of virtue, power, social privilege, and moral worth. These competing reconstructions of idealized values figure prominently in the adaptation of Shaftesbury's discursive strategies by writers less interested in defending upper-class privilege than in pressing their own claims to the social status of gentlemen.

Despite the overtly polemical intentions of his work, Shaftesbury, the aristocrat and ideologue, is usually ignored by modern critics or transformed into a disinterested observer of a transhistorical human nature. Many of the twentieth-century readings of Shaftesbury one encounters are relentlessly ahistorical; they succeed in salvaging him as a "thinker" or "philosopher" only by removing him from his historical context, ignoring the two-thirds of his work given to snobbish defenses of aristocratic privilege, downplaying the warmed-over truisms of his literary criticism, and avoiding any discussion of his political and social biases.[5] By obscuring the fundamentally conservative bias of Shaftesbury's thought (or for that matter of many of the seventeenth-century latitudinarians), critics of his work and of the "men of feeling" who populate a number of eighteenth-century novels distort what Shaftesbury calls the "Sentiment of MORALS."[6] As an aristocrat, idealist, and Whig, Shaftesbury is an historically important figure because he shifts discussions of morality and virtue away from the traditional rhetoric of religious orthodoxy to secular discourses of ideological power and privilege. In effect, he depoliticizes the seventeenth-century languages of religious conflict and helps to convert the rhetoric of goodness, tolerance, and generosity into the languages of political and moral authority, into defenses of an innate—literally, for Shaftesbury, inborn—and demonstrable virtue.

In his *Inquiry Concerning Virtue*, Shaftesbury celebrates what he perceives as the cultural and ideological bases of moral behavior. He begins by defining "virtue" in ahistorical, universal, and absolute terms; it is not a "personal" attribute of individuals but, in effect, an essential, informing principle of creation. There is, Shaftesbury asserts, "no such thing as real ILL in the Universe, nothing ILL with respect to the Whole" (II.9). Man therefore is naturally, instinctively good; social and civil order are maintained by his "natural Esteem of *Virtue*, and Detestation of *Villainy*" (II.65) rather than by the Christian fear of punishment, a belief that Shaftesbury frequently attacks. Having established the beneficence of man as a social creature, he goes on to declare that it is "the *private Interest* and *Good* of everyone, to work towards the *general Good*" (II.175). However, Shaftesbury's ideas of "everyone" and "the *general Good*" are determined, as the author acknowledges, by his aristocratic biases. Far from being disinterested ruminations on innate virtue and proper political governance, the *Inquiry*, like his other works, delimits carefully the responsibilities and privileges of "the better sort." The audience Shaftesbury envisions for his writings is, he states, "the grown *Youth* of our polite World . . . whose *Taste* may yet be form'd in *Morals*; as it seems to be, already, *in exteriour Manners and Behaviour*" (III.179). His comparison of *"Morals"* to *"Manners"* is a revealing one that echoes throughout his published and unpublished works. In *The Moralists*, for example, he characteristically equates the timeless virtues of theistic enthusiasm and his own social and political values: "To *philosophize*, in a just Signification, is but To carry *Good-Breeding* a step higher. For the Accomplishment of Breeding is, To learn whatever is *decent* in Company, or *beautiful* in Arts: and the Sum of Philosophy is, To learn what is *just* in Society, and *beautiful* in Nature, and the Order of the World" (III.161). Polished language, "*Good Breeding*," "*Manners*," social grace, aesthetic perfection, natural harmony, innate virtue, and universal order form a natural circuit in Shaftesbury's mind. The vocabulary that he uses to define his conception of innate goodness—the civilized man living in a just society—is frankly idealistic and insular: "The real *Honest Man . . .* is struck with that *inward* Character, the Harmony and Numbers of the Heart, and Beauty of the Affections, which form the Manners and Conduct of a truly *social* Life" (III.34). Virtue, for Shaftesbury, becomes the inward manifestation of an "aesthetic" response to life that celebrates stability and harmony within a closed, paternalistic society.

Even as he invokes an idealized realm of a society bonded by "natural Affections," then, Shaftesbury defines personal virtue and social justice as the natural prerogatives of aristocratic existence. He argues that moral authority inheres in a social structure that elevates the well-bred above "the common World of mix'd and undistinguish'd Company" (II.224). Whatever unconventional views one might want to attribute to Shaftesbury—particularly his deriding of Christianity—are ultimately a function of his unshakeable faith in an irrevocable, "natural," and transhistorical system of social stratification that has, in effect, preemptively decided questions of individual value, virtue, and responsibility, of political, economic, and cultural power. The *Characteristicks* attempt without apology to inscribe an aristocratic system of values—based on the equation of birth and worth—in the "natural" order of the universe. In this respect, the rhetoric of "republican" principles in Shaftesbury's work (frequently taken out of context and duly celebrated by his modern critics) emerges only against a backdrop of his defenses of upper-class interests and prejudices.

Consequently, Shaftesbury's statements of idealistic principle scattered throughout his works must be read contextually as part of his ideological project. In his essay on wit, for example, he describes "common sense," rather stirringly, as the "*Sense of Publick Weal*, and of the *Common Interest*; Love of the *Community* or *Society*, Natural Affection, Humanity, Obligingness, or that sort of *Civility* which rises from a just *Sense of the common Rights* of Mankind, and the *natural Equality* there is amongst those of the same Species" (I.104). But this rhetoric is hedged by its very contingency: "*Society*," "*Civility*," "*Equality*," and his other high-sounding terms are not ahistorical ideals but culturally-specific concepts. To my mind, the more concretely Shaftesbury defines "republican" concepts like *"common Rights"* and *"Equality,"* the more they seem extensions of old-line aristocratic values. Shaftesbury's talk of liberty, for example, did not prevent him from supporting the Qualifying Bill of 1696 restricting the franchise.[7] His characteristic attitude toward his social inferiors is at best condescending, at worst frankly manipulative: "The Publick is not, on any account, to be laugh'd at, to its face; or so reprehended for its Follys, as to make it think it-self contemn'd. And what is contrary to good Breeding, is in this respect as contrary to Liberty. It belongs to Men of slavish Principles, to affect a Superiority over *the Vulgar*, and to despise *the Multitude"* (I.75–76). His argument here with ill-bred oligarchs is not over definitions of "Liberty" but over strategies to placate and control *"the Vulgar."* The "natural Affections" that he frequently invokes to justify man's capacity for goodness are, in this regard, a generic redaction of what is best in human nature, typified by the gentlemen who gather on a country estate in *The Moralists* "to talk Philosophy in . . . a Circle of good Company" (II.182); men such as these constitute "the Standard of good Company, and People of the better sort" by which writers must learn to "regulate [their] Stile" (II.165). The setting is idyllic, the exclusive nature of the company assured, and the style and substance of the dialogue correspondingly decorous. For Shaftesbury, civility, humanity, and common rights can be realized only in a harmonious, benevolent—that is, hierarchical—society. His concepts of "Liberty" and "freedom" depend on a strong aristocracy capable of checking the threats posed, on the one hand, by power-hungry monarchs, high Church clergymen, high Tory Jacobins, and Catholics; and, on the other, by the leveling tendencies of those descendants of seventeenth-century radicals for whom challenges to religious and political orthodoxies also mean challenges to hereditary privilege and the established structures of political and economic power.

Shaftesbury's rhetoric—his defense of aristocratic political and cultural authority—aspires to what Mikhail Bakhtin terms a monologic, single-voiced language. It seeks to suppress the sociopolitical differences that structure historical utterances, to restrict the dialogic nature of language to an authoritative voicing of absolute principles.[8] As one might expect, then, the ideology that Shaftesbury promotes and defends is similarly holistic, ahistorical, and—from his point of view—unproblematic. Although it is relatively simple for us to demystify the ideological strategies that he promotes, we should be wary of imposing upon Shaftesbury our own sophisticated, postmodern notions of ideology—or of attributing to him any particular insight into the complex processes by which an oligarchic society sustains both its political power and the fictive constructions that support it. Unlike the radicals of the late seventeenth century (like Henry Stubbe) or the late eighteenth century (like Blake),[9] Shaftesbury champions rather than resists the fictions of univocal authority. His appeal to his contemporaries lies in his single-voiced and even simplistic defenses of privilege, his contention that power is "naturally" held by those who by birth are worthy to hold it. In this sense, his philosophical project is to educate the up-and-coming rulers of the "polite" world, to facilitate the operations of hegemonic power. Paradoxically, however, it is precisely his emphasis on educating the ruling classes that makes him an appealing figure to his bourgeois successors.

II

Shaftesbury's championing of the hegemonic cultural and political authority exercised by "the better sort" poses both ideational and rhetorical problems for his contemporaries of less exalted social standing, particularly those figures like Addison and Steele whom we associate with the "rise" of bourgeois literature in the eighteenth century. His Whiggish sentiments, his vigorous defenses of English liberty and the "ancient Constitution" provide a convenient, indeed at times seminal, vocabulary for writers as different as Hutcheson and Steele precisely because they are manifestations of a profound conservatism, a belief in the status quo as a self-generating and self-regulating ideal.[10] It is easy enough to make Shaftesbury seem a reactionary dolt by isolating snippets of his snobbish, self-congratulatory rhetoric. But, paradoxically, his equation of morals and manners holds open the possibility of enlarging the ranks of "the better sort" by tacitly offering to admit those of demonstrated "virtue." At one point Shaftesbury asserts "that the Perfection of Grace and Comeliness in Action and Behaviour, can be found only among the People of a liberal Education" (II.190). It would probably be a mistake to read the last phrase as a retreat from his customary class prejudice, as anything other than a rephrasing of "the better sort" or "our polite World." But coming from a former student and patron of Locke's, the notion that "Grace" can be acquired by "People of a liberal Education" encourages a selective misreading of Shaftesbury's political intentions by those writers eager to advance their claims morally and socially to the status of "the better sort." Throughout the eighteenth century, Shaftesbury is read by Thomson, Shenstone, Cowper, and others as the proponent of a virtue that mediates and, to use the word in a very narrow sense, deconstructs the differences between the mercantile and upper classes.[11]

If Shaftesbury assumes that generosity and sentiment are hallmarks of aristocratic privilege, his rhetoric nonetheless allows Steele and Addison, for example, to appropriate, redefine, and reapply his vocabulary for their own ideological purposes—expanding the social parameters of politeness, virtue, and moral leadership. As Terry Eagleton has argued, the *Spectator* and the *Tatler* are the "catalysts in the creation of a new ruling bloc in English society, cultivating the mercantile class and uplifting the profligate aristocracy"; they attempt to promote an "historical alliance" between the middle and upper classes that is at once political, economic, and cultural.[12] In cultural terms, sentimentality stakes the claim of the middle class to playing the role of England's moral conscience. Sentiment thus represents the bourgeois usurpation of and accommodation to what formerly had been considered aristocratic prerogatives; in the plays of Steele, for example, it becomes a literary manifestation of an ongoing attempt to reconcile aristocratic systems of value based on innate worth and patrilinear inheritance to middle-class conceptions of value based on notions of individual merit and worthy deeds. In *The Conscious Lovers*, for example, Bevil Junior, Steele's exemplary hero, is described by his father in terms that disclose both his status, as a member of the landed gentry, as the heir to a large estate and his "bourgeois" desire to make his own way in the world: "my Son has never in the least Action, the most distant Hint or Word, valued himself upon that great estate of his Mother's, which, according to our Marriage Settlement, he has had ever since he came to Age" (I.i.34–37).[13] Sentimentality, however, has no particular claim to being the only register of this accommodation between classes. Throughout the seventeenth and eighteenth centuries, aristocratic and mercantile classes fought, intermarried, blurred, and redefined the always unstable demarcations between old wealth and new, country landholders and urban mercantilists.[14] In this respect, sentimentality is not a simple indication of the "rise" of a monolithic bourgeois ideology but a register of the literary complexities arising from the need to come to terms with class relations seemingly perpetually in turmoil. Sentimentality manifests the anxiety of a class-stratified society trying both to assert "traditional" values and to accommodate as "gentlemen" increasing numbers of economically—if not always politically—aggressive merchants, professionals, small landowners, and moneymen. In the case of Sterne's *Sentimental Journey*, Eagleton's "historical alliance" is effected only by the middle class's trying to outrefine the aristocracy by embracing the conservative biases of a hierarchical social system, and by actively demonstrating their claims to the same kind of innate, ahistorical moral authority that had been, for Shaftesbury, the exclusive preserve of the upper classes.

Eighteenth-century sentimentalists, in this regard, must negotiate the distance between the aristocratic equation of birth and worth and the middle class's celebration of upward social and economic mobility. The similar strategies of writers otherwise as different as Steele, Sterne, and Mackenzie attempt to universalize Shaftesbury's "natural Affections," to expand the ranks of the innately virtuous and good-natured to include merchants, minor clergymen, the minor gentry, technocrats, and writers. These strategies do not subvert, radically undermine, or fundamentally realign the hereditary bases of wealth and power but seek to expand them. The class struggle between the aristocracy and the mercantile classes blurs into an accommodation that reformulates the problematic of birth and worth as a celebration of qualities that both can share. For many middle-class authors, sentimentality—the generosity of feeling—becomes their claim to a cultural power-sharing based on a liberal interpretation of "Breeding" that equates hereditary power and moral sensitivity. Steele, for example, frequently engages in rhetorical juggling acts to balance hereditary and bourgeois claims to virtue:

> I think a Man of Merit, who is derived from an Illustrious Line, is very justly to be regarded more than a Man of equal Merit who has no Claim to Hereditary Honours. Nay, I think those who are indifferent in themselves, and have nothing else to distinguish them but the Virtues of their Forefathers, are to be looked upon with a degree of Veneration even upon that account, and to be more respected than the common Run of Men who are of low and vulgar Extraction.
>
> After having thus ascribed due Honours to Birth and Parentage, I must however take Notice of those who arrogate to themselves more Honours than are due to them on this Account. The first are such who are not enough sensible that Vice and Ignorance taint the Blood, and that an unworthy Behaviour degrades, and disennobles a Man, in the Eye of the World, as much as Birth and Family aggrandize and exalt him.
>
> The second are those who believe a *new* Man of an elevated Merit is not more to be honoured than an insignificant and worthless Man who is descended from a long Line of Patriots and Heroes.[15]

Steele's rhetoric suggests something of the ideological complexity of his argument. Images of innate and acquired worth interpenetrate: the "*new* Man" is "elevated" and "honoured"; the degenerate aristocrat "degraded" and "disennobled," effectively stripped of the honor with which he was born. The rigid class structure of Shaftesbury's thought is thus complicated, contorted, and opened to new kinds of misreadings by writers who acknowledge hereditary privilege but, in the course of defending its prerogatives, assert their own claims to "elevated Merit." In this regard, if a writer cannot lay an hereditary claim to an innate,

Shaftesburian virtue, he must demonstrate that he indeed possesses it; he must, as Steele implies, dramatize his worthiness. Yet, trapped in the mystifications of a rhetoric that celebrates innate virtue, he cannot allow his performance to seem—even to himself—to be a calculated act, a put-on role; instead it must sustain the fiction that it is a "natural" expression of his "true" self as it is manifest in the seemingly irrepressible eloquence of his feelings and physiology.

Sentimentality, then, is neither solely a literary nor philosophical phenomenon, but a form of moral self-promotion that manifests itself in the discursive practices of a variety of literary and nonliterary genres: the novel, moral conduct books, philosophical discourse, and, as Rousseau and Mullan argue, medical literature.[16] What unites these disparate forms is their authors' ideological preoccupation with emerging middle-class virtues of sensitivity, generosity, natural sympathy, health, and physical beauty. As Mullan has demonstrated, eighteenth-century medical writers and novelists share a common vocabulary that virtually equates hypochondria and moral sensitivity. Nervous, even debilitating, psychosomatic symptoms paradoxically become a natural, praiseworthy demonstration of the middle- or upper-class male's moral fitness. As a cultural phenomenon, hypochondria translates moral polemic into an affective semiology that makes palpable the mind's sensitivity to the body's "natural Affections." In this respect, hypochondria becomes a half-willed performance, a theatrics of the bourgeois soul. For a number of writers, including Steele, Richardson, and, in a different way, Sterne, sentimental distress and affection become the outward signs—the body's performances—of its inner virtues. Sentimentality, therefore, cannot be reified as an abstract system of values or disembodied as passive sympathy; it is manifest only in the concrete particularity of a noble or generous action or in physical symptoms: tears, blushes, and palpitating hearts.

The problem that the theatrics of sentimentality raises, however, is obvious: how consciously does the sentimental actor perform his role? how voluntary (or involuntary) are his sighs, tears, and flutterings of the heart? G. A. Starr notes that the sentimental hero is a "natural" innocent, "subjected to ordeals and stresses of various kinds, but not to the pressure of having his character made dependent on training, habit, and . . . other contingencies of experience."[17] But the problematic of acting, of displaying one's "true" nature, can never be simple or pristine. Tears and sighs, as Fielding comically demonstrates in *Shamela*, can also be read as strategies of manipulation, as challenges by the supposedly powerless to the aristocratic structures of power that—as in Richardson's first two novels—allow the predatory Mr. B— and Lovelace to terrorize their innocent victims. Richardson, though, must face ideological problems that never trouble Shaftesbury. For the latter, style *is* nature: good breeding, manners, morals, aesthetic grace, and political authority are of a worldview compact, validated by an aristocratic ideology that verges on a metaphysic. But bourgeois sentimentality represents a deformation of this holistic ideology into an attempt to equate natural virtue with a rejection of worldly, political power. In its own terms, it cannot answer the question "Pamela or Shamela?" because its affective semiotics, its assumption that the body and soul always work in unison, cannot account for the inequalities—the discrepancies between merit and reward—of the society in which it flourishes. Richardson, for example, may try to reproduce Shaftesburian assumptions about innate virtue—Pamela is a "natural" aristocrat raised to her "rightful" place as a lady of demonstrated virtue—but without advocating an explicit form of socioeconomic validation (worth equals birth) he has no way of assuring the Fieldings among his readers that his heroine is what she seems. Like Steele, he ends up trying to straddle the claims of hereditary privilege and natural goodness; the result is that he ends by celebrating the class distinctions that the novel, at first, had seemed either to disavow or conceal.

In *A Sentimental Journey* Sterne attempts to resolve the problems of championing bourgeois virtue in a hierarchically structured society by using money as a way of assigning and confirming value. For Yorick and more problematically for his creator, cash becomes a way of suggesting a one-to-one correspondence between sentimental and monetary values, between moral worth and its outward, demonstrable, material signs: the crowns that the hero passes out to those who stir his "natural Affections." This equation of money and benevolence marks a sophisticated deployment of the ideology of class privilege, but it also complicates and extends that ideology in ways not anticipated by Steele and Richardson. Yoking money and sentimental good nature, for Sterne, is less a strategy to celebrate privilege or deceive *"the Vulgar"* than a means to dramatize and paradoxically mystify the complicity of the sentimental actor in social injustice and inequality. In one respect *A Sentimental Journey* marks the passage of sensibility from self-conscious and self-interested celebrations of hereditary privilege to the comic questioning of these biases; in Sterne's wry, satiric deflating of Yorick's pretensions to goodness we are at least part way to Blake's "mind forg'd manacles," to a recognition of the self-policing and self-repressing strategies of ideology as described by Michel Foucault.[18] But this "questioning" is hardly clearcut or self-evident. If Shaftesbury is a straightforward defender of the aristocratic faith, Sterne seems both a propagandist for bourgeois good nature and its critic; if Shaftesbury's philosophical mouthpieces are simple propagandists, Yorick seems both a virtuous innocent and a naive butt. How we define the relationship between author and narrator in *A Sentimental Journey* ultimately determines how we view its display of sentimental attributes—as straightforward, satiric, or, as I shall argue, as a complex interweaving of both.

III

Virtually all critics of *A Sentimental Journey* explicitly or implicitly describe their tasks as finding a vocabulary suitable to explaining what is going on in the novel or to justifying its status as a canonical text. In general, critics have tried one of three basic strategies: comparing the novel to *Tristram Shandy* and attacking its excesses of sentimental self-interest, as Virginia Woolf does; defending it as a satire of sentimentality, as Arthur Cash, Melvyn New, and John K. Sheriff do; or celebrating its narrative sophistication, a tactic favored (in different ways) by Jeffrey Smitten, Joseph Chadwick, and Michael Seidel.[19] None of these views, however, demystifies the coercive aspects of sentimental ideology, although Woolf's reading of the novel comes closest when she calls attention to the self-dramatizing aspects of Sterne's narrative. "His mind," she argues, "is partly on us [the readers], to see that we appreciate his goodness," and she adds that the "chief fault" of the novel "comes from Sterne's concern for our good opinion of his heart" (xiv). As Woolf recognizes, the act of writing a sentimental narrative is a kind of self-advertisement, a manipulation of the reader's response. Sentimentality, as it is culturally deployed, is paradoxically a collusive and impersonal response to the display of exemplary virtue. Our appreciation of the author's goodness makes us his collaborators: if we respond as he does, then we can appreciate not only his goodness but our own; if we applaud Yorick's generosity to the chambermaid, we also must applaud our sensitivity to his virtue. Woolf, for one, remains skeptical of this self-congratulatory aspect of *A Sentimental Journey*: "instead of being convinced of the tenderness of Sterne's heart—which in *Tristram Shandy* was never in question—we begin to doubt it. For we feel that Sterne is thinking of himself" (xiii). For Chadwick, Lamb, and Seidel, the discourses of sentimentality frequently elicit a similarly ambiguous response; all three argue, albeit in different ways, that *A Sentimental Journey* suspends the reader between recognizing the hero's innocent virtue and the novelist's skillful manipulation, between passion and theater. As they suggest, the problems of interpretation are crucial in the novel, but these difficulties are less the result of narrative technique than of the ethical and ideological quandaries that define the sentimental novel.

In his sermons, Sterne frequently calls attention to the disparities between the injunctions of Christian religion and the ways of an imperfect world. As Cash and Sheriff argue, Sterne preaches a traditional brand of ethics:

> Could Christianity . . . engage us, as its doctrine requires, to go on and exalt our natures, and, after the subduction of the most unfriendly of our passions, to plant, in the room of them, all those (more natural to the soil) humane and benevolent inclinations, which, in imitation of the perfections of God, should dispose us to extend our love and goodness to our fellow-creatures, according to the extent of our abilities;—in like manner, as the goodness of God extends itself over all the works of creation:—Could this be accomplished,—the world would be worth living in.[20]

Henry Mackenzie, the author of the often misunderstood and disparaged novel, *The Man of Feeling*, makes explicit the practical problems that arise from trying to live according to both the dictates of Christian ethics and the demands of social existence. This "war of duties," he argues, produces the unrealistic and potentially dangerous "species [of the novel] called sentimental" that subordinates socially-constructed "truth and reason" to idealistic visions of sensibility: "The virtues of justice, of prudence, of economy, are put in competition with the exertions of generosity, of benevolence, and of compassion."[21] Significantly, this "competition," as Mackenzie's phrasing implies, must elevate the bourgeois, capitalist virtues of "justice," "prudence," and "economy" over sentimental virtues that in themselves are admirable but that, as he demonstrates in *The Man of Feeling*, are naive and impractical in a post-lapsarian world.

For Sterne, the discrepancies between Christian and capitalist values in *A Sentimental Journey* are not easy to reconcile. In some respects, his dilemma is characteristic of the competing reconstructions of Christianity that emerge in seventeenth and eighteenth-century England; religious debate from the reformation through the nineteenth century is the site of often overt ideological battles among the upper, middle, and lower classes. Christian doctrines are invoked, depending on the speaker's or writer's political leanings, to justify conservative defenses of the status quo, liberal apologies for gradual socioeconomic "progress," and calls to radical social action. Anglican theology in the late seventeenth and eighteenth centuries is used to justify both the fictions that equate birth and worth and those that assert that virtue is acquired rather than inborn.[22] In the context of Sterne's theological concerns, the problems of interpretation posed by *A Sentimental Journey* reflect the ideological ambiguities that result from the internal divisiveness of the ideology of sentiment, its attempt to hold on to Christian ethics and to promote the kind of materialist virtues that Mackenzie celebrates. The fact that both Christian ethics and capitalist virtue are themselves the sites of ideological conflict between notions of aristocratic prerogative and bourgeois merit only complicates Sterne's narrative problems in *A Sentimental Journey* further. The very ambiguity that the novel engenders encourages the author to try to "resolve" these conflicts by repeating his litanies of the hero's sentimental acts. For Sterne, the accumulation of Yorick's gestures of sympathy and generosity becomes a deliberate strategy to reassure those of us who, like Woolf, begin to doubt the sincerity of a character who keeps telling us how sincere he is. But this strategy is itself double-edged: it calls attention to both the hero's generosity and to the inequalities of a fallen world that renders acts of charity as marginal or ineffective attempts to embody a radically idealized Christian ethics. Sterne's theatrics of bourgeois virtue, then, are devoted paradoxically to demonstrating the sensitivity of a culture that shies away from acknowledging its responsibility for inflicting upon its victims the very injuries that it mourns and pities but does little to alleviate. The novelist cannot resolve the contradictory bases of sentimental ideology but only restage and restate them. Therefore, the more uncomfortable the reader feels about the tendentious display of sentimental affection, the more necessary it becomes for the reader to witness additional demonstrations of sentimental morality in operation.

I would read *A Sentimental Journey*, then, as a series of strategies designed to mystify the contradictory impulses of sentimentality, to celebrate and mock Yorick's faith in human nature, and to attempt to reconcile ideas of innate virtue with demonstrations of moral worth. One of the primary means that Sterne employs to effect this reconstruction is to recast traditonal forms of discourse, turning, for example, the rhetoric of courtly address to the task of dramatizing his hero's good nature. In his encounter with the chambermaid, Yorick describes their relationship in the outmoded forms of feudal rhetoric: she pays him "submissive attention" and offers him "more a humble courtesy [curtsy] than a low one" (188, 189).[23] Yorick's use of this language of courtly submission emphasizes the self-centered and exaggerated aspects of his sentimental affection; his rhetoric blinds him to her "true," sexually-experienced nature. He turns his "feelings" into a form of discourse incapable of registering departures from a simple-minded benevolence. His apostrophe to the peasants of Savoy near the end of the novel indicates that the only way he can describe social inequality and suffering is to invoke a warmed-over Shaftesburian rhetoric that trivializes what it describes: "Poor, patient, quiet, honest people! fear not; your poverty, the treasury of your simple virtues, will not be envied you by the world, nor will your vallies be invaded by it" (285). These "simple virtues" are, in effect, the rationalization of a middle-class culture that cannot reconcile its vir-tuous self-image with its dependence on economic inequality. Yorick's moral intentions are perhaps laudable, but Sterne, like Mackenzie, im-plies that moral idealism does not translate into the active, bourgeois virtues of justice, prudence, and economy.

The self-absorption implicit in the hero's narrative voice limits the responses—both individual and cultural—that his brand of sentimen-tality calls forth. On his way to Paris, Yorick is accosted by a group of beggars. One by one, he describes the beggars and gives some of them a sous each in what he describes as "the first publick act of my charity in France" (132). When he thinks he has finished, however, he finds that he

> had overlook'd a *pauvre honteux*, who had no one to ask a sous for him, and who, I believe, would have perish'd, ere he could have ask'd one for himself: he stood by the chaise a little without the circle, and wiped a tear from a face which I thought had seen better days—Good God! said I—and I have not one single sous left to give him—But you have a thousand! cried all the powers of nature, stirring within me—so I gave him—no matter what—I am ashamed to say *how much*, now—and was ashamed to think, how little, then: so if the reader can form any conjecture of my disposition, as these two fixed points are given him, he may judge within a livre or two what was the precise sum.
>
> (133–34)

Our attention in this passage, as throughout the scene, is focused on the mind and "nature" of the sentimental hero, not on the objects of his generosity. Significantly, Yorick leaves the exact amount he gives to this *"pauvre honteux"* up to the reader. By judging correctly the sum that Yorick gives, we are implicated in his act of charity and implicitly asked to judge our own moral goodness by the amount of our estimate. We are subtly but effectively coerced into sharing in the hero's demonstra-tive triumph over the forces of miserly ill nature.

The object of Yorick's charity, though, seems carefully selected. He has no name, no independent existence other than as the recipient of the hero's generosity, and, unlike the other beggars, he remains silent and suitably embarrassed by his poverty (note that *"honteux"* may carry the double meaning of ashamed and disgraced). In this regard, he is the perfect sentimental victim—inarticulate, passive, and anonymous—less an individual than an idealized object of pity. Yet he touches Yorick's heart precisely because he seems once to have "seen better days"; he is the victim of an unnamed bad fortune that, significantly, Sterne chooses to leave unexplored. As a man without a history, this figure becomes an embodiment of the disgrace of poverty: he is not simply an outsider but a projection of the narrator's unstated fears, a nightmare image of the sensitive, generous individual stripped of his only means—money— of demonstrating his goodness in a mercantile society. Left penniless, this apparently good individual becomes pathetic rather than noble, his good nature imprisoned by his poverty.

The gift of money, then, assumes a complex double function: it provides a seemingly straightforward economy of sentiment, the value of the charitable act serving as an indication of the sentimentalist's nature, and it ensures that the transaction, the exchange of currency, allows both giver and receiver to retain their anonymity. In Sterne's sentimental economy, money replaces the reciprocal obligations (at least in theory) of feudal, aristocratic society that to some extent are still resonant in Shaftesbury's kid-gloves treatment of *"the Vulgar."* The anonymity of his cash transactions serves to distance Yorick from the objects of his charity, like the *"pauvre honteux,"* even as he proclaims his sympathy for them. In one sense, his sentimental generosity allows him to assent tacitly to the bourgeois fiction that one's comparative wealth is a valid indication of both one's moral worth and social value. Yet neither Yorick nor the reader can persist in this daydream for long; paradoxically the ideological function of sentimental charity must be seen to be imperfect to justify its existence: if possessing money were an unambiguous indication of each individual's intrinsic worth, there would be no moral obligation for the sentimentalist to give away anything. Sterne's narrative, in this regard, works to disclose as well as to conceal the ideological workings of charity, leaving Yorick open, as in his encounter with the chambermaid, to the reader's suspicions that he is acting out of self-interest or hopes for sexual profit. His acts of charity at once construct and demystify the middle-class sentimentalists's fictions of depoliticized virtue in a society still ruled, to a large extent, by hereditary privilege.[24]

There is, then, in Sterne's depiction of his hero's encounters with the beggars a necessary suppression of political consciousness, a generic lack of interest in the causes of poverty. Yet we must again be careful to distinguish between the author and narrator. Sterne allows his readers to see that his hero's responses, however good-natured, are inadequate to the task of correcting the misfortunes he encounters; yet the novelist can provide no vocabulary to redress the social and economic injustices that he depicts. Sterne the Christian moralist can offer only a naive sentimentality that he implies is insufficient, yet that can never transcend limited and limiting acts of isolated, individual charity. Yorick, when he fears that his lack of a passport may land him in the Bastille, admits his inability to imagine the suffering of the poor as anything but an individual misfortune:

> I was going to begin with millions of my fellow creatures born to no
> inheritance but slavery; but finding, however affecting the picture was, that
> I could not bring it near me, and that the multiple of sad groups in it did
> but distract me.—
> —I took a single captive, and having first shut him up in his dungeon,
> I then look'd through the twilight of his grated door to take his picture.
>
> (201)

The description that follows portrays the prisoner in gothic dejection,
although the tone of the passage wryly undercuts the narrator's stance
by making him too moved to continue with his imaginative rendering:
"But here my heart began to bleed—and I was forced to go on with
another part of the portrait" (202). The prisoner's plight, however,
makes sense to Yorick only as it affects him emotionally. The portrait,
like the description of the beggars, generates sympathy in direct pro-
portion to the helplessness and passivity of the victim. Sentimentality
here operates by a straightforward calculus: the more pathetic the victim,
the greater the hero's generosity, and the more affecting the scene.

The hero's imaginary prisoner is an apt image of the isolation and
powerlessness of suffering in *A Sentimental Journey*. Yorick cannot bring
the sufferings of "millions of [his] fellow creatures" close to home because he—and Sterne—are ideologically constrained by a culture which
refuses to acknowledge the legitimacy of a vocabulary to describe large-
scale political oppression. The prisoner must be romanticized and isolated from his "millions" of fellow creatures because otherwise he would
lose his status as a helpless victim: one unfortunate individual engenders
sympathetic tears; "millions" pose a threat to the class-based ideologies
of the mid-eighteenth century that seek to identify privilege with both
hereditary nobility and demonstrated bourgeois virtue. As the representative of "the multiple of sad groups" excluded from political and
economic power, Yorick's "single captive" presents a more complex
image—and more of a potential threat to social stability—than the faceless multitude that Shaftesbury assumes it is his birthright to outwit.
That this individualized victim is imprisoned not only makes him a pit-
iable victim but also effectively isolates him from his fellow "millions,"
from any possibility of concerted and collective political action. His isolation, therefore, testifies to the radical potential of the bourgeois ideology of individual merit: if no individual is innately superior to another,
then the unpropertied and unfortunate classes of Europe have as good
a claim as their "betters" to a share of wealth and political power. Yorick's "millions" can no longer be consigned to servitude solely because
they are low-born; and, in an important sense, the ideology of sentiment
may be seen as a complex network of relationships designed to guard

against the revolutionary implications of middle-class justifications for social climbing. To move, then, from Shaftesbury's condescension to *"the Vulgar"* to Sterne's sympathy for an individual captive is implicitly to reject aristocratic arguments for the "natural" hierarchy of class relations; but what the latter cannot do is to transform his imaginary prisoner into "millions." To do so would be to move from sentiment to social injustice, from pity to either outrage or fear, and from passive sympathy to the spectres of outright repression and revolutionary action.

In this sense, sentimentality can exist, in whatever narrative forms it assumes, only in societies in which money and power are unequally distributed, only where persons of potential moral "worth" suffer "unjustly," that is without regard to their (potential) intrinsic merit. Yorick feels most pity for those who have fallen from a state of bourgeois grace: "to see so many miserables, by force of accidents driven out of their own proper class into the very verge of another, which it gives me pain to write down" (174–75). If sentiment does not have a victim to pity it must, in effect, create one hyperbolically. In a passage which seems comically to recall Shaftesbury's effusions Yorick offers an apostrophe to hypersensitivity:

—Dear sensibility! source inexhausted of all that's precious in our joys, or costly in our sorrows! thou chainest thy martyr down upon his bed of straw—and 'tis thou who lifts him up to HEAVEN—eternal fountain of our feelings!—'tis here I trace thee—and this is thy divinity which stirs within me—not that, in some sad and sickening moments, *"my soul shrinks back upon herself, and startles at destruction"*—mere pomp of words!—but that I feel some generous joys and generous cares beyond myself—All comes from thee, great, great SENSORIUM of the world! which vibrates, if a hair of our heads but falls upon the ground, in the remotest desert of thy creation.

(277–78)

The ambiguity, the problems of interpretation that Chadwick locates at the center of our experience of reading Sterne's novel seem, in this passage, to spring from ironies of disproportion and exaggeration. The metaphors which undergird this passage are economic—"precious" and "costly"—and they subtly belie the narrator's attempt to elevate sensibility to a divine hypersensitivity to falling hairs. The trivial nature of the final image brings us back to the problem of value: "sensibility" can only affix value by hyperbole, the debts and credits of small acts that carry the narrator "beyond" himself but that ironically confirm his role in a hierarchical society. The theatrics of sentimental virtue preclude any action to alleviate the suffering of the poor beyond doling out money and self-consciously recording the amount to keep one's accounts in order in the "divine" ledger book of bourgeois morality.

IV

Given the divided and divisive ideological structure of sentimentality noted by Mackenzie, it is hardly surprising that the narrative structure of *A Sentimental Journey* is, as Seidel argues, itself problematic. The class biases of sentiment—evident in Hume's bald-faced assurance that the "skin, pores, muscles, and nerves of a day-labourer are different from those of a man of quality: So are his sentiments, actions, and manners"[25]—has a profound effect on the artistic forms in which sensibility is couched. In the drama sentimentality reflexively validates its claims to moral authority, often by yoking bourgeois sensitivity to the ideology of patrilinear privilege. In *The Conscious Lovers*, to take only one example, the action onstage is designed to confirm Bevil Junior's intrinsic worth, his ability to transcend the social clichés of dissolute idleness and sexual irresponsibility that had defined his rakish ancestors on the late seventeenth-century stage. In the Prologue (written by Steele's friend, the poet Leonard Welsted) the audience is told "'*Tis yours* [that is, your responsibility], *with Breeding to refine the Age/ To Chasten Wit, and Moralize the Stage,*" and later that the sentimental hero is "*the Champion of your Virtues*" (27–28, 30). Like most sentimental comedies in the early eighteenth century, *The Conscious Lovers* works hard to flatter its audience by reassuring them of their virtues and, in effect, telling them what they already know. It does not interrogate the bases of Bevil Junior's heroism; it simply offers him as an exemplar of virtue, a model for the audience to emulate.[26]

In the novel, however, repetitive demonstrations of the man of feeling's good nature quickly grow wearisome; as Mackenzie notes, sentimentality is interesting not primarily in and of itself but in its effects and contexts, in the clash between the values of idealistic self-absorption and capitalist self-interest.[27] In *A Sentimental Journey*, Sterne's device of the journey works against the generic clichés of the private spaces of the sentimental novel by thrusting his hero into the world, a tactic Mackenzie also employs in *The Man of Feeling*.[28] Yorick is, at least part of the time, a picaresque hero, who delights in the unexpected and the comic: "I count little of the many things I see pass at broad noon day, in large and open streets.—Nature is shy, and hates to act before spectators; but in such an unobserved corner, you sometimes see a single short scene of her's worth all the sentiments of a dozen French plays compounded together" (257). The result in *A Sentimental Journey* is a marriage of con-

venience between picaresque imitations of nature and sentimental displays akin to the kind of Christian idealism that Sterne preached on
Sunday mornings. The theory underlying Sterne's experiment is articulated by the old French Officer whom Yorick meets at the opera: "there
is a balance . . . of good and bad every where; and nothing but the
knowing it is so can emancipate one half of the world from the pre-
possessions which it holds against the other—that the advantage of
travel, as it regarded the *scavoir vivre*, was by seeing a great deal both
of men and manners; it taught us mutual toleration; and mutual toleration . . . taught us mutual love" (181). But this ideal, which the narrator enthusiastically embraces, inverts the picaresque tradition that
Sterne had found and admired in Cervantes. The notion of the sentimental traveler transforms the cunning of the picaresque hero into something approaching the innocence of Candide. But Sterne, unlike Voltaire, cannot bring himself to play innocence strictly for laughs. In his
novel sympathetic observation displaces satiric critique; a self-centered
moral sensitivity apparently implies a kind of epistemological lethargy
on the narrator's part. It is tempting to say that *A Sentimental Journey*
ends where Yorick had first "ended" at the beginning of *Tristram
Shandy*—at the black page. If sentimentality is not a dead end, it is a
discrete moment that can provide the impetus only for reflection, not
action. Like Yorick, whose death in *Tristram Shandy* marks a temporary
exit, the sentimental moment is always waiting in the wings for Sterne
to bring it back onstage. Sentimental theatrics verge on idylls of benevolence; precisely because they seek to suppress the contingencies on
which their values depend, they have no history, no means of inves-
tigating the interstices of character and ideology. They provide only the
kind of repetitive tableaux we find presented in both *A Sentimental Journey* and *The Man of Feeling*.

Sterne's decision to inscribe the sentimental novel in a parody of the
picaresque mode is an ideologically revealing one; it suggests strongly
that sensibility lends itself only to paratactic structures that undermine
the fictions of socioeconomic and technological progress promoted by
the Whiggish ideology of Addison, Steele, and Locke. Because Yorick's
travels provide neither a satiric anatomy of society's foibles nor an epistemological quest for self-knowledge, his narrative can reach no conclusion; it can only stop. Had Sterne lived to write another two or ten
volumes of *A Sentimental Journey*, the narrative "end" would likely have
been the same. Generically, the only conclusions that sentimental novels
can reach are either the hero's death (*The Man of Feeling*) or the im-
probable conversions of bourgeois "prudence" and "economy" into the
millenarian Christian ethics that Sterne envisions when he imagines his
parishioners acting "in imitation of the perfections of God" (Dickens's

A Christmas Carol, for example). Ideologically, there is no other option. This may sound as though I have junked a dialogic, Bakhtinian notion of "ideology" for a more deterministic reading of the relations between eighteenth-century socioeconomic conditions and literary products. I do not think I have. The ideological constraints upon the sentimental novel in general and upon *A Sentimental Journey* in particular limit what can be done in the genre. Committed to defending the ideological structures of class prejudice, Sterne and Mackenzie can dramatize their heroes' benevolence but cannot convince either themselves or their readers that good nature is sufficient to correct the ways of a corrupt and unjust world.

Sentimentality may at times seem to represent the cry for a soul in a mechanistic age, but it also demonstrates, as Mackenzie maintains, the powerlessness and impracticality of the very benevolence it attempts to valorize. Sterne is less vocal than Steele, for example, in proclaiming that virtue is a function of social class, but the implications of *A Sentimental Journey* are that the radical ethicizing of Sunday morning sermons does not lead to selfless charity but to self-absorbed and self-congratulatory mystifications of inequality. In this respect, sentimentality represents the displacement of Christian ethics into Shaftesburian class prejudices, into myths that the world is as it should be and that individual actions, however nobly intended, matter very little when it comes to the "millions" of victims of poverty and injustice. Both Sterne and Yorick are confronted by the paradoxical impasse of sentimental morality: the more you give, the more virtuous you become, although your actions leave you with less and therefore limit your capacity to keep on demonstrating your virtue. His generosity dramatizes the sentimentalist's dilemma: his gifts do more to ennoble him than to assist those who receive his money. The tragic, rather than pathetic, undercurrents in *A Sentimental Journey* may lie in Sterne's implicit recognition that however much he would like to distance himself from his hero's naive benevolence, he can suggest no alternative to an ideology that can neither interrogate nor change the socioeconomic injustices that its "virtues" promote.

11

THE SPECTRALIZATION OF THE OTHER IN *THE MYSTERIES OF UDOLPHO*

Terry Castle

> Friends came to be possessed like objects, while inanimate objects were desired like living beings.
>
> Philippe Ariès, *The Hour of Our Death* (606)[1]

I

When it is not treated as a joke, Ann Radcliffe's *The Mysteries of Udolpho* (1794) is primarily remembered today for its most striking formal device—the much-maligned "explained supernatural." Scott, we may recall, was one of the first to blame Radcliffe for supplying anticlimatic "rational" explanations for the various eerie and uncanny events in her novels, and in *Lives of Eminent Novelists* (1824) chastized her for not "boldly avowing the use of supernatural machinery" in her greatest fiction.[2] Jane Austen's satiric depredations in *Northanger Abbey* are even better known.[3] But modern critics have been similarly put out—that is, when they have bothered to write about Radcliffe at all. "A stupid convention," says Montague Summers of her admittedly intrusive rationalizations. "The vice of her method," writes another. A few hapless defenders merely compound the damage: "the poor lady's romances,"

wrote Andrew Lang, "would have been excluded from families, if she
had not provided normal explanations of her groans, moans, voices,
lights, and wandering figures."[4] *Requiescat in pace.*

It has always been easy, of course, to patronize Ann Radcliffe. No
English writer of such historic importance and diverse influence has
been so often trivialized by her critics. Granted, we have the occasional
arch excurses on selected Radcliffean topoi—the Villain, the Fainting
Heroine (with her much-vaunted Sensibility), the Scenery. But the point
of such commentary is usually to demonstrate the superiority of the
critic to this notoriously "silly" writer and to have done with Radcliffe
as quickly as possible. Even among admirers of Gothic fiction, the
clumsy device of the "explained supernatural" is often taken as the final
proof of Radcliffe's irretrievable ineptitude and bathos. By way of a
formula, the author herself is explained away.

Which is not to say that the formula is entirely misleading. Blatantly
supernatural-seeming events *are* "explained" in *Udolpho*, and sometimes
most awkwardly. Mysterious musical sounds, groans emanating from
walls, the sudden movement of a supposedly dead body: however
strained, rational explanations for such phenomena are inevitably forthcoming. At numerous points in the fiction, moreover, Radcliffe self-
consciously condemns what she calls "superstition." Not for her those
primitive ancestral spirits described by Nietzsche in *The Genealogy of
Morals*, who come back to earth to terrify, cajole, or exact various pious
sacrifices from the living. Nor, despite occasional hesitations, has she
any residual faith in the more benign ghosts of popular Christianity. St.
Aubert, the father of the heroine in *Udolpho*, admits at one point to a
hope that "disembodied spirits watch over the friends they have loved"
(67), but later in the novel, when the enlightened Count de Villefort
argues against the reality of specters, Radcliffe resolutely endorses his
position, noting that "the Count had much the superiority of the Baron
in point of argument" (549).[5] In this denial of the traditional spirit-world,
The Mysteries of Udolpho, like the Gothic in general, anticipates the thoroughly God-abandoned forms of modern literature.

Yet already we oversimplify perhaps, for the very concept of the "explained supernatural" depends upon a highly selective—indeed schematic—vision of the novel. We "read," it seems, only part of *The Mysteries of Udolpho*: the famous part. As any survey of *Udolpho* scholarship
will show, modern critics devote themselves almost without exception
solely to those episodes in the novel involving the villainous Montoni
and the castle of Udolpho—even though these make up barely a third
of the narrative. Of the dreamlike wanderings of Emily St. Aubert and
her father through the Pyrenees (which alone take up nearly one
hundred pages at the outset of the work), of St. Aubert's drawn-out

death scene and Emily's sojourn in a convent, of Emily's bizarre relationship with her lover Valancourt, of the episodes with Madame
Cheron at Tholouse and Venice, of the lengthy post-Udolpho sections
involving Du Pont, Blanche, the Marchioness de Villeroi and the Count
de Villefort, we have heard little or nothing.

The crude focus on the so-called Gothic core of *The Mysteries of Udolpho*
has been achieved by repressing, so to speak, the bulk of Radcliffe's
narrative. Many modern critics implicitly treat the fictional world as
though it were composed of two ontologically distinct realms—one
extra-ordinary, irrational, irruptive, and charismatic (that of Montoni
and Udolpho), the other ordinary, domestic, and uninteresting (the supposedly more "familiar" frame-world of La Vallée and the St. Aubert
family). Emily, it is often argued, is temporarily caught up in the irrational Udolpho-world, and there subjected to much emotional dislo-
cation, but returns safely to ordinary life in the end. Commentators
differ, to be sure, over what exactly the irrationalism of Udolpho consists
in, some claiming that the castle is in fact a violent realm of moral and
political chaos, while others, more psychologically inclined, argue that
its terrors are merely notional, the result of the heroine's supercharged
sensibility. The assertion that Emily develops and learns to control her
"hysteria" in the course of her ordeal is a common didactic embellish-
ment in the latter sort of reading. Seldom at issue in any of these accounts, however, is the two-world distinction itself (with its normal/
abnormal, rational/irrational, ordinary/extra-ordinary oppositions) or
the implicit assumption that certain parts of *Udolpho* are intrinsically
more interesting and worthy of discussion than others. This tendency
toward bifurcation, it is worth noting, has reappeared even in the otherwise revisionist readings of the novel recently offered by feminist critics.[6]

But what happens if we reject such reductive impulses and try to read
all of the fiction before us? For one thing, the supposedly ordinary parts
of *Udolpho* may begin to look increasingly peculiar. Take, for example,
the ostensibly normalizing ending. Montoni is dead, the putative terrors
of Udolpho past, and Emily St. Aubert has been joyfully reunited with
her lost lover Valancourt. Yet Radcliffe's language here, as elsewhere,
remains oddly preternatural. Emily and Valancourt marry in an "en-
chanted palace," the Count de Villefort's castle at Chateau-le-Blanc,
under sumptuous banners "which had long slept in dust." So exquisite
is the ceremony Annette the servant is moved to exclaim that "the fairies
themselves, at their nightly revels in this old hall, could display nothing
finer," while Dorothée, the old housekeeper, observes wistfully that
"the castle looked as it was wont to do in the time of her youth." The
newlyweds proceed, as though entranced, to Emily's beloved childhood
home at La Vallée. There, in the picturesque spot "so long inhabited"

by her deceased parents, Monsieur and Madame St. Aubert, "the pleasant shades welcomed them with a thousand tender and affecting remembrances." Emily wanders through her parents' "favourite haunts" in pensive slow motion, her happiness heightened "by considering, that it would have been worthy of their approbation, could they have witnessed it." Bemused by souvenirs of the past, she and her lover seat themselves beneath a plane tree on the terrace, in a spot "sacred to the memory of St. Aubert," and vow to imitate his benevolence (671).

The mood of hypnotic, sweetish melancholy carries over into the last sentence of the novel, where Radcliffe addresses an ideal reader, likewise haunted by personal history:

> And, if the weak hand, that has recorded this tale, has, by its scenes beguiled the mourner of one hour of sorrow, or, by its moral, taught him to sustain it—the effort, however humble, has not been vain, nor is the writer unrewarded.
>
> (672)

Enchantments, shades, haunts, sacred spots, the revivification (through memory) of a dead father, a perpetually mourning reader: the scene is tremulous with hidden presences. Not, again, the vulgar apparitions of folk superstition—the ghosts entertained here are subjective, delicately emotional in origin, the subtle protrusions of a yearning heart. No egregiously Gothic scenery obtrudes; we are still ostensibly in the ordinary world. But the scene is haunted nonetheless, as Radcliffe's oddly hinting figures of speech suggest. Home itself has become uncanny, a realm of *apophrades*. To be "at home" is to be possessed by memory, to dwell with spirits of the dead.

These passages epitomize a phenomenon in Radcliffe we might call the supernaturalization of everyday life. Old-fashioned ghosts, it is true, have disappeared from the fictional world, but a new kind of apparition takes their place. To be a Radcliffean hero or heroine in one sense means just this: to be "haunted," to find oneself obsessed by spectral images of those one loves. One sees in the mind's eye those who are absent; one if befriended and consoled by phantoms of the beloved. Radcliffe makes it clear how such phantasmata arise. They are the products of refined sentiment, the characteristic projections of a feeling heart. To be haunted, according to the novel's romantic myth, is to display one's powers of sympathetic imagination; the cruel and the dull have no such hallucinations. Those who love, by definition, are open to the spirit of the other.

The "ghost" may be of someone living or dead. Mourners, not surprisingly, are particularly prone to such mental visions. Early in the novel, for instance, Emily's father, St. Aubert, is reluctant to leave his estate, even for his health, because the continuing "presence" of his dead wife has "sanctified every surrounding scene" (22). The old peasant La Voisin, likewise bereaved, can "sometimes almost fancy" he sees his dead wife "of a still moonlight, walking among these shades she loved so well" (67). After St. Aubert dies and Emily has held a vigil over his corpse, her fancy is "haunted" by his living image: "She thought she saw her father approaching her with a benign countenance; then, smiling mournfully and pointing upwards, his lips moved, but instead of words, she heard sweet music borne on the distant air, and presently saw his features glow with the mild rapture of a superior being" (83). Entering his room when she returns to La Vallée, "the idea of him rose so distinctly to her mind, that she almost fancied she saw him before her" (95). When she and Valancourt sit in the garden, she finds her father's image "in every landscape" (106).

But lovers—those who mourn, as it were, for the living—are subject to similar experiences. The orphaned Emily, about to be carried off by her aunt to Tholouse, having bid a sad farewell to Valancourt in the garden at La Vallée, senses a mysterious presence at large in the shades around her:

> As her eyes wandered over the landscape she thought she perceived a person emerge from the groves, and pass slowly along a moon-light alley that led between them; but the distance and the imperfect light would not suffer her to judge with any degree of certainty whether this was fancy or reality. (115)

A haunted lover can do nothing, it seems, but haunt the haunts of the other. To love in the novel is to become ghostly oneself. When Valancourt, defying Madame Montoni's prohibition against meeting Emily, finds his way back to her, he exclaims, "I do then see you once again, and hear again, the sound of that voice! I have haunted this place—these gardens, for many—many nights, with a faint, very faint hope of seeing you" (152). Near the end of the novel, after Emily rejects him for supposed debaucheries, he makes obsessive "mournful wanderings" around her fateful garden: "the vision he had seen [of Emily] haunted his mind; he became more wretched than before, and the only solace of his sorrow was to return in the silence of the night; to follow the paths which he believed her steps had pressed, during the day; and, to watch round the habitation where she reposed" (627).

Such porous lovers, to be sure, may sometimes be mistaken for the cruder, traditional kind of specter. But the lover's ghostliness is somehow more febrile and insistent. Emotionally speaking, it is not susceptible to exorcism. When Emily's gallant suitor Du Pont, the Valancourt-surrogate who appears in the midsection of the novel, traverses the battlements at Udolpho in the hope of seeing her, he is immediately mistaken by the castle guards (who seem to have read *Hamlet*) for an authentic apparition. He obliges by making eerie sounds, and creates enough apprehension to continue his lovesick "hauntings" indefinitely (459). Similarly, at the end of the fiction, when Emily is brooding once again over the absent Valancourt, her servant Annette suddenly bursts in crying, "I have seen his ghost, madam, I have seen his ghost!" Hearing her garbled story about the arrival of a stranger, Emily, in an acute access of yearning, assumes the "ghost" must be Valancourt (629). It is in fact Ludovico, Annette's own lover, who disappeared earlier from a supposedly haunted room at Chateau-le-Blanc and is presumed dead. Annette's own joy at seeing him, we note, "could not have been more extravagant, had he arisen from the grave" (630). Whoever he is, wherever he is, the lover is always a *revenant*.

Already, given what we might call Radcliffe's persistently spectralized language, one cannot merely say with aplomb that the supernatural is "explained" in *The Mysteries of Udolpho*. To speak only of the rationalization of the Gothic mode is to miss one of Radcliffe's most provocative rhetorical gestures. The supernatural is not so much explained in *Udolpho* as it is displaced. It is diverted—rerouted, so to speak, into the realm of the everyday. Even as the old-time spirit world is demystified, the supposedly ordinary secular world is metaphorically suffused with a new spiritual aura.

II

Why this pattern of displacement? And why have modern readers so often been impervious to it? The questions are deceptively simple, yet they bear profoundly both on the reception of the novel and the history of Western consciousness. *The Mysteries of Udolpho* became one of the charismatic texts of late eighteenth-century European culture (a fact all too easily forgotten) not merely because it gratified a passing taste for things Gothic—many contemporary works did this—but because it articulated a new and momentous perception of human experience. Like Rousseau's *Julie ou la Nouvelle Héloïse* or Goethe's *Werther*, which shared a similar shaping influence on contemporary psychic life, the novel owed its vast popularity across Europe to its encompassing emotional power—its paradigmatic role in what one writer has called "the fabrication of romantic sensitivity."[7] *Udolpho* was more than simply fashionable; it encapsulated new structures of feeling, a new model of human relations, a new phenomenology of self and other.

We often sum up such developments, of course, with the phrase romantic individualism. In what follows I will argue that a crucial feature of the new sensibility of the late eighteenth century was, quite literally, a growing sense of the ghostliness of other people. In the moment of romantic self-absorption, the other was indeed reduced to a phantom—a purely mental effect, an image, as it were, on the screen of consciousness itself. The corporeality of the other—his or her actual life in the world—became strangely insubstantial and indistinct: what mattered was the mental picture, the ghost, the haunting image.

The twentieth century, I hope to show, has completely naturalized this historic shift toward the phantasmatic. We are used to the metaphor of the haunted consciousness—indeed hardly recognize it as metaphoric. Often enough, we speak colloquially of being haunted by memories or pursued by images of people inside our heads. In moments of solitude or distress, we may even seek out such "phantoms" for companionship and solace. Not coincidentally, the most influential of modern theories of the mind—psychoanalysis—has internalized the ghost-seeing metaphor: the Freudian account of psychic events, as I will suggest in my conclusion, is as suffused with crypto-supernaturalism as Radcliffe's. Yet this concern with so-called mental apparitions, and the sense we have come to share, thanks to Sigmund Freud, of their potentially *daemonic* hold over us, is itself the historic product of late eighteenth-century romantic sensibility. Radcliffe's novel remains one of the first and greatest evocations of this new cognitive dispensation—of a new collective absorption in the increasingly vivid, if also hallucinatory, contents of the mind itself. We feel at home in Radcliffe's spectralized landscape, for its ghosts are our own—the symptomatic projections of modern psychic life.

How to recognize that which has become too much a part of us? A series of vignettes, extracted, again, from the supposedly banal parts of the novel, will help to focus our attention on the historical phenomenon I am calling the spectralization of the other: this new obsession with the internalized images of other people. I present these Radcliffean "souvenirs of the other" in a somewhat paradoxical form in order to bring out both the uncanniness of the fictional world and its oddly familiar emotional logic:

1.   *To think of the other is to see him.* Whenever Emily St. Aubert thinks about her lover, Valancourt, he suddenly appears. This is especially likely to occur even when she (and the reader) have been led to assume he is far away. After Emily's first engagement to Valancourt is broken off by Madame Cheron (later Madame Montoni), Emily is beset by a

painful "remembrance of her lover" and fantasies a clandestine reunion: "As she repeated the words—'should we ever meet again!'—she shrunk as if this was a circumstance, which had never before occurred to her, and tears came to her eyes, which she hastily dried, for she heard footsteps approaching, and the door of the pavilion open, and, on turning, she saw—Valancourt" (127). Later, after escaping from Udolpho, Emily walks in the woods at Chateau-le-Blanc and broods about the time when her father was alive and she had just met Valancourt. Then: "She thought she heard Valancourt speak! It was, indeed, he!" (501).

2. *The other is always present—especially when absent.* The familiar "objects of former times," pressing upon one's notice, writes Radcliffe, make departed loved ones "present" again in memory (92). Hats, books, chairs, rooms, pets, miniatures, gardens, mountains, graves—all possess this affecting metonymic power. Pieces of furniture in the study of the dead St. Aubert bring his "image" forcibly into his daughter's mind (94–98). Elsewhere at La Vallée, Emily finds that her parents seem "to live again" in the various objects in their rooms (591). Picturesque landscapes (La Vallée, the Pyrenees, Languedoc, Chateau-le-Blanc) provoke visions of the person with whom one first saw them (92, 97, 116, 163, 490). Valancourt, as he is about to leave Emily at one point, says to her that they will "meet . . . in thought" by gazing at the sunset at the same time of day (163). Similarly, by retracing a page in one of Valancourt's books, and "dwelling on the passages, which he had admired," Emily is able to summon her absent lover "to her presence" again (58). His "vacant chair" prompts an image of him sitting beside her (521), while the garden, with "the very plants, which Valancourt so carefully reared," supplies further remembrances (583). Graves and grave monuments are obviously the most fascinating and paradoxical relics of the other, for even as they officially confirm absence (and indeed take on all the displaced pathos of the corpse), they also evoke powerful "living" images of the person they memorialize. Forcing herself after an "hour of melancholy indulgence" to leave the site of St. Aubert's grave, Emily remains "attached" to the place in her thoughts, "and for the sacred spot, where her father's remains were interred, she seemed to feel all those tender affections which we conceive for home" (91).

3. *Every other looks like every other other.* Characters in *Udolpho* mirror, or blur into one another. Following the death of her father, Emily is comforted by a friar "whose mild benevolence of manners bore some resemblance to those of St. Aubert" (82). The Count de Villefort's benign presence recalls "most powerfully to her mind the idea of her late father" (492). Emily and Annette repeatedly confuse Du Pont with Valancourt (439–40); Valancourt and Montoni also get mixed up. In Italy Emily gazes at someone she believes to be Montoni who turns out, on second glance,

to be her lover (145). But even Emily herself looks like Valancourt. His countenance is the "mirror" in which she sees "her own emotions reflected" (127). She, in turn, also looks like the deceased Marchioness of Villeroi. Dorothée comments on Emily's resemblance to "the late Marchioness" (491). The dying nun Agnes is maddened by it: "it is her very self! Oh! there is all that fascination in her look, which proved my destruction!" (644). This persistent deindividuation of other people produces numerous dreamlike effects throughout the novel. Characters seem uncannily to resemble or to replace previous characters, sometimes in pairs. Even as they assume quasi-parental control over the heroine, M. and Mme. Montoni become, in the mind of the reader, strangely "like" a new and demonic version of M. and Mme. St. Aubert. The Count and Countess de Villefort are a later transformation of the Montoni pair—and of M. and Mme. St. Aubert. Du Pont, of course, is virtually indistinguishable from Valancourt for several chapters. Blanche de Villefort is a kind of replacement-Emily, and her relations with her father replicate those of the heroine and St. Aubert, just as the Chateau-le-Blanc episodes recombine elements from the La Vallée and Udolpho episodes, and so on. The principle of *déjà vu* dominates both the structure of human relations in *Udolpho* and the phenomenology of reading.

One is always free, of course, to describe such peculiarly overdetermined effects in purely formal terms. Tzvetan Todorov, for example, would undoubtedly treat this mass of anecdotal material as a series of generic cues—evidence of the fantastic nature of Radcliffe's text. The defining principle of the fantastic work, he posits in *The Fantastic*, is that *"the transition from mind to matter has become possible."*[8] Ordinary distinctions between fantasy and reality, mind and matter, subject and object, break down. The boundary between psychic experience and the physical world collapses, and "the idea becomes a matter of perception." "The rational schema," he writes,

> represents the human being as a subject entering into relations with other persons or with things that remain external to him, and which have the status of objects. The literature of the fantastic disturbs this abrupt separation. We hear music, but there is no longer an instrument external to the hearer and producing sounds, on the one hand, and on the other the listener himself. . . . We look at an object—but there is no longer any frontier between the object, with its shapes and colors, and the observer. . . . For two people to understand one another, it is no longer necessary that they speak: each can become the other and know what the other is thinking.[9]

The fantastic universe, he concludes—with a nod to Jean Piaget—is like that of the newborn infant or psychotic. Self and other are not properly distinguished; everything merges—inside and outside, cause and effect, mind and universe—in a vertiginous scene of "cosmic fusion."[10]

Radcliffe's fictional world might be described as fantastic in this sense. The mysterious power of loved ones to arrive at the very moment one thinks of them, or else to "appear" when one contemplates the objects with which they are associated—such events blur the line between objective and subjective experience. Magical reunion is possible. Thoughts shape reality. In such instances Radcliffe indeed creates a narrative simulacrum of that sense of omnipotence briefly experienced, according to D. W. Winnicott, in our infancy: wishes seem to come true; the hidden desires of the subject appear to take precedence over logic or natural probability.[11]

But the fantastic nature of Radcliffe's ontology is also manifest, one might argue, in the peculiar resemblances that obtain between characters in her novel. When everyone looks like everyone else, the limit between mind and world is again profoundly undermined, for such obsessive replication can only occur, we assume, in a universe dominated by phantasmatic imperatives. Mirroring occurs in a world already stylized, so to speak, by the unconscious. Freud makes this point in his famous essay "The Uncanny" in which he takes the proliferation of doubles in E. T. A. Hoffmann's "The Sandman" as proof that the reader is in fact experiencing events from the perspective of the deranged and hallucinating hero.[12] And once more, infantile psychic life provides the appropriate analogy. For we can indeed imagine, if not recollect, a stage in our early development at which we did not fully distinguish individuals from one another, or recognize other people as wholly separate beings. Our powers of physiognomic comparison must have once been quite crude, and our sense of the difference between the faces we observed somewhat precarious. Everybody *did* look like everybody else at one period in our lives. That various forms of literature, and the Gothic and romance in particular, atavistically dramatize this primal stage in human awareness, is an idea implicit, though not fully articulated, in the recent work of Eve Kosofsky Sedgwick.[13]

The formalist description, however, can only go so far. As the psychoanalytic gloss already intimates, the Todorovian notion of ontological transgression—this breakdown of limits between mind and matter—invites historicization. By invoking Freud or Piaget, we add one kind of diachronic dimension: fantastic works like *Udolpho*, we imply, return us symbolically to an earlier stage of consciousness, a prior moment in the history of the individual psyche. But we still do not contend with larger shifts in human consciousness itself. Todorov himself makes only a few comments on the place of fantastic themes in the changing psychic history of the West.

For this kind of analysis we must turn elsewhere, though one of Todorov's own remarks will again prove suggestive. He cites the following
passage from Freud—

> A young woman who was in love with her brother-in-law, and whose sister
> was dying, was horrified by the thought: "Now he is free and we can be
> married!" The instantaneous forgetting of this thought permitted the ini-
> tiation of the process of repression which led to hysterical disturbances.
> Nonetheless it is interesting to see, in just such a case, how neurosis tends
> to resolve the conflict. It takes into account the change in reality by re-
> pressing the satisfaction of the impulse, in this case, the love for the brother-
> in-law. A psychotic reaction would have denied the fact that the sister was
> dying.

And in the last sentence he uncovers one of the central themes of the
fantastic: "To think that someone is not dead—to desire it on one hand,
and to perceive this same fact in reality on the other—are two phases
of one and the same movement, and the transition between them is
achieved without difficulty."[14] Only the thinnest line separates the experience of wishing for (or fearing) the return of the dead and actually
seeing them return. Fantastic works, he argues, repeatedly cross it. Here
indeed is the ultimate fantasy of mind over matter.

Just such a fantasy—of a breakdown of the limit between life and
death—lies at the heart of Radcliffe's novel and underwrites her vision
of experience. To put it quite simply, there is an impinging confusion
in *Udolpho* over who is dead and who is alive. The ambiguity is conveyed
by the very language of the novel: in the moment of Radcliffean reverie,
as we have seen, the dead seem to "live" again, while conversely, the
living "haunt" the mind's eye in the manner of ghosts. Life and death—
at least in the realm of the psyche—have become peculiarly indistinguishable. Yet it is precisely this essentially fantastic ambiguity that is
most in need of historical analysis. Why should it be in a work of the
late eighteenth century, especially, that the imaginative boundary between life and death should suddenly become so obscure?

III

The work of the French historian Philippe Ariès provides, to my mind,
the most useful insight into this problem, for he, more than any other
recent writer, has speculated on the complex symbolic relationship between life and death in the popular consciousness of recent centuries.
Ariès's magisterial *L'Homme devant la mort*, published in 1977 and trans-

lated into English as *The Hour of Our Death* in 1981, is a study of changing attitudes toward death and dying in European culture since the Middle Ages. I cannot do justice here, obviously, to the grand scale of Ariès's project, or to his richly idiosyncratic, even lyrical response to this profound intellectual theme. Let me focus instead merely on one thread of his argument—his assertion that new and increasingly repressive emotional attitudes toward death in the late eighteenth century constituted a major "revolution in feeling" with far-reaching social and philosophic consequences (471). If Ariès is correct, Radcliffe's spectralized sense of the other may be understood as an aspect of a much larger cognitive revolution in Western culture.

In brief, Ariès's hypothesis is this—that in contrast with earlier periods such as the Middle Ages, when physical mortality was generally accepted as an organic, integral and centrally meaningful facet of human existence, late eighteenth-century Western culture was characterized by growing dissociation from corporeal reality, and a new and unprecedented antipathy toward death in all its aspects. Changing affectional patterns, the breakdown of communal social life, and the increasingly individualistic and secular nature of modern experience played an important role, Ariès argues, in engendering this new spirit of alienation. The twentieth century, he claims, has inherited the post-Enlightenment attitude. Through a complex process of displacement, he claims, Western civilization has repressed the body and its exigencies; in the face of death, it retreats into anxious mystification and denial.

Ariès finds, in essence, a new spiritualization of human experience beginning in the late eighteenth century. His evidence for such a shift is twofold. A break with traditional patterns was first apparent, he suggests, in the practical sphere, in the period's obsession with what he calls the "beautiful death"—its concern with hiding or denying the physical signs of mortality and decay. Where death was once a public spectacle of considerable magnitude, it now became primarily a private event, witnessed only by one's closest relations. The cosmetic preservation of the corpse took on a new emotional urgency: the arts of embalming and even mummification (one thinks of Bentham's corpse) became common practices among all but the very lowest classes. Funerals were carried out more and more discreetly. And in contrast with the relaxed practice of earlier centuries, the dead were increasingly segregated from the living. Cemeteries were removed from their once-central locations in cities and towns to outlying areas, and their necrological functions obscured. The romantic "garden of remembrance," with its idealizing statuary, landscaped walks and prospects, was a quintessentially eighteenth-century invention.[15]

Just such an urge toward mystification, we note, may be allegorized at various points in *Udolpho*. It is interesting to find, for example, how many moments in the novel traditionally adduced by critics as classically "Radcliffean" have to do with supposed deaths that have not really taken place, or with corpses that turn out not to be corpses after all. Radcliffe often flirts with an image of physical dissolution, then undoes it. Thus Emily at Udolpho, thinking she has found the dead body of her aunt, follows a trail of blood toward a horrible "something" that turns out to be a pile of old clothes (323). An open grave in the castle crypt is empty (345). A body suddenly jerking under a pall on a bed in the abandoned apartments of the dead Marchioness of Villeroi is found to be a pirate who has hidden there and frightens off intruders in this manner (634). And most strikingly of course, the famous terrifying object under the black veil that Emily thinks is the "murdered body of the lady Laurentini" (248) is a piece of *trompe l'oeil*: an old wax effigy of a de-composing body "dressed in the habiliments of the grave," formerly used as a *memento mori* (662). While such moments provide an undeniable *frisson*, they also hint at new taboos. Uneasy fascination gives way before the comforting final illusion that there is no such thing as a real corpse. (Radcliffe delicately refers to the *memento mori* as an example of that "fierce severity, which monkish superstition has sometimes inflicted on mankind" [662]). If we are now inclined to recoil from Radcliffe's ambiguous thanatological artifacts, or indulge in nervous laughter over the "morbid" or "macabre" nature of Gothic literature in general, our responses, if Ariès is correct, merely indicate how much further the process of repression has advanced in our own day.[16]

But the most important sign of shifting sensibilities in the period, according to Ariès, is the emergence of a "romantic cult of the dead"—a growing subjective fascination with idealized images of the deceased. Older ideas of the afterlife—those of the Middle Ages, for example—had not typically emphasized the possibility of meeting one's family and friends after death. Death meant rupture, a falling asleep, or a falling away into "the peace that passeth understanding." In the era of romantic individualism, however, the theme of sentimental reunion became paramount. The coming together of husbands and wives, brothers and sisters, or parents and children after death, the blissful renewal of domestic life in a new "home" in the hereafter became staple images in late eighteenth and early nineteenth-century popular belief. Consolatory literature, grave inscriptions and monuments, and the keeping of mementos of the dead all bespoke the new fantasy of continuity, while a host of theories, not necessarily theological in origin, regarding the eternal life of disembodied spirits reinforced popular emotion. Death was no longer ugly or frightening, supposedly, because its physical separations were only temporary. Much of nineteenth-century spiritualism,

Ariès argues, was simply an extenuation of the notion that the familiar souls of the dead continued to dwell in a nearby invisible realm, invited communication with the living, and awaited a happy future meeting with those who had mourned them in this life (432–60).

He attributes this new and fantastical mode of belief to changing patterns in family structure and the historic transformation of affectional relationships:

> The various beliefs in a future life or in the life of memory are in fact so many responses to the impossibility of accepting the death of a loved one. . . .
>
> In our former, traditional societies affectivity was distributed among a greater number of individuals rather than limited to the members of the conjugal family. It was extended to ever-widening circles, and diluted. Moreover, it was not wholly invested; people retained a residue of affectivity, which was released according to the accidents of life, either as affection or as its opposite, aggression.
>
> Beginning in the eighteenth century, however, affectivity was, from childhood, entirely concentrated on a few individuals, who became exceptional, irreplaceable, and inseparable.
>
> (472)

The underlying dream, of course, was that the precious dead were not really dead. He calls this hope the "great religious fact of the whole contemporary era" and notes its continued survival in the late twentieth century, despite all the incursions of "industrial rationalism." Even in the secular societies of the modern West, interviews with the dying and the recently bereaved reveal the same vestigial hope of an afterlife, "which is not so much the heavenly home as the earthly home saved from the menace of time, a home in which the expectations of eschatology are mingled with the realities of memory" (471). There, all shall be united "with those whom they have never ceased to love" (661).[17]

A poignant fantasy indeed—but what is perhaps most interesting here is not so much the emotional content per se, but the connection between this affective content and a new kind of introspection. What Ariès's work suggests, it seems to me, is not just a new response to death, but a new mode of thought altogether—a kind of thinking dominated by nostalgic mental images. The fear of death in the modern era prompts an obsessional return to the world of memory—where the dead continue to "live." But so gratifying are the mind's consoling inner pictures, one becomes more and more transfixed by them—lost, as it were, in contemplation itself. One enters a world of romantic reverie.

Certainly, returning to Radcliffe, we sense both a new anxiety about death, and a new reactive absorption in mental pictures. Radcliffe is fixated, first of all, on the idea of reunion, and dramatizes the romantic fantasy of futurity more explicitly than any previous novelist. Of course dreams of posthumous intimacy had appeared before in eighteenth-century fiction: in Richardson's *Clarissa*, Anna Howe's affirmation, while grieving over Clarissa's coffin, that they will "meet and rejoice together where no villainous *Lovelaces*, no hard-hearted *relations*, will ever shock our innocence, or ruffle our felicity!" anticipates the new sentimental model.[18]

What is new in Radcliffe, however, is the fervor with which the finality of death is denied. Continuity is all. Thus the dying St. Aubert discoursing on the afterlife with the noble peasant La Voisin:

> 'But you believe, sir [says La Voisin], that we shall meet in another world the relations we have loved in this; I must believe this.' 'Then do believe it,' replied St. Aubert, 'severe, indeed, would be the pangs of separation, if we believed it to be eternal. Look up, my dear Emily, we shall meet again!' He lifted his eyes toward heaven, and a gleam of moonlight which fell upon his countenance, discovered peace and resignation, stealing on the lines of sorrow.
>
> (68)

Later, after her father dies, Emily is comforted by the thought that he indeed "lives" still, invisible yet otherwise unchanged, in a nearby spiritual realm: "'In the sight of God,' said Emily, 'my dear father now exists, as truly as he yesterday existed to me; it is to me only that he is dead; to God and to himself he yet lives!'" (82) Gazing on his corpse ("never till now seen otherwise than animated"), she fantasizes for a dizzying moment that she sees "the beloved countenance still susceptible," and soon after has the first of those uncanny mental images of her father's living form (83). His convent tomb rapidly becomes the inviting "home" to which she is repeatedly drawn, and La Vallée—the counter-Udolpho—the privileged site around which his presence seems palpably to linger.[19]

Nature itself becomes a mere screen—the sublime backdrop against which the potent fancies of mourning are played out. The vast peaks of the Pyrenees, the picturesque valleys of Gascony and Languedoc, even the rocky scenes around Udolpho—all become part of the same elegiac landscape: the zone of reverie itself. Nature in *Udolpho* sets the stage for phantasmagoric dramas of memory ("'There, too, is Gascony . . . O my father,—my mother!'" [580]) or falls away against a fantastic mental picture of the blissful life to come: "She . . . fixed her eyes on the heaven, whose blue unclouded concave was studded thick with stars, the worlds, perhaps, of spirits, unsphered of mortal mould. As her eyes wandered along the boundless aether, her thoughts rose, as before, toward the sublimity of the Deity, and to the contemplation of futurity" (72). In either case, the emptiness of the world is filled: "How often did she wish to express to him the new emotions which this astonishing scenery awakened, and that he could partake of them! Sometimes too she endeavoured to anticipate his remarks, and almost imagined him present" (163). One is put in mind here of that patient of Freud's, mentioned in the case history of Schreber, who having "lost his father at a very early age, was always seeking to rediscover him in what was grand and sublime in nature."[20]

IV

What Radcliffe articulates so powerfully, as our detour through Ariès helps us to see, is not just the late eighteenth century's growing fear of death, but the way in which this fear was bound up with a new, all-consuming and increasingly irrational cognitive practice. In the Radcliffean thanatopia, immediate sensory experience gives way, necessarily, to an absorption in illusion—an obsessional concentration on nostalgic images of the dead. Yet these recollected "presences," it turns out, are paradoxically more real, more palpable-seeming, than any object of sense. No external scene, not even the most horrid or riotous, can undermine this absorbing faith in the phantasmatic. Even the castle of Udolpho, where every hallway is plunged in gore, is but the deceptive "vision of a necromancer" and yields before the mind's "fairy scenes of unfading happiness" (444). Unpleasant realities cannot compete with the marvelous projections of memory, love, and desire.

Which is not to say that people in previous epochs had been unaware of, or uninterested in, the mysterious "images" and "pictures" of the mind. Aristotle spoke of *phantasmata*, and Aquinas of the "corporeal similitudes" present to the memory.[21] In the Middle Ages and Renaissance, mental imagery played an important part in the devotional practices of Christianity. Employing the traditional mnemonic techniques known as the "arts of memory," for example, one might contemplate a certain complex mental image—a house, say, with many adjoining rooms—as a way of remembering an associated sequence of spiritual disciplines or sacred themes.[22] And needless to say, though in a somewhat different register, poets and mythographers had invoked the "shapes of fancy" for centuries before *The Mysteries of Udolpho*.

What emerges so distinctively with Radcliffe in the late eighteenth century, however, is an unprecedented sense of the subjective importance—the ontological weight, if you will—of these phantasmatic inner "pictures." In earlier times, mental simulacra, especially images of other people, had been clearly distinguished as such—as fanciful, nostalgic, or unreal. (An exception, of course, were the ambiguous visionary phenomena known as ghosts or specters. These uncanny entities were felt to exist outside the self, as real—if not material—objects of sense.)[23] At the end of the eighteenth century, however, through a complex process of historical change, phantasmatic objects had come to seem increasingly real: even more real at times than the material world from which they presumably derived. Powerful new fears prompted this valorization of illusion. Above all, as Ariès suggests, a growing cultural anxiety regarding the fate of the body after death conditioned an unprecedented collective flight into fantastic ideation.

Early eighteenth-century popular epistemology, to be sure, had prepared the ground for this conceptual shift. John Locke, interestingly enough, had hinted at the uncanny "life" of mental images in the *Essay Concerning Human Understanding*. In the section "Of Retention" (II.x), we may recall, he set out to describe in mechanistic terms the mind's curious ability to bring back into view those sensory impressions "which, after imprinting, have disappeared, or have been, as it were, laid out of sight." Locke's would-be scientific description of the memory is everywhere confused, however, by an imagery of supernatural reanimation. The mind, he asserts several times, has the power to "revive" its old impressions—i.e., to give back life to the dead. Revived ideas reappear in the mind like *revenants*:

> This further it is to be observed, concerning ideas lodged in the memory, and upon occasion revived by the mind, that they are not only (as the word *revive* imports) none of them new ones, but also that the mind takes notice of them as of a former impression, and renews its acquaintance with them, as with ideas it had known before.

These strangely "lively" images are in turn bound up with the life of the mind itself. A sad contingency, Locke is forced to admit, is that our ideas can "decay" in times of illness, and crumble like forgotten monuments: "the flames of a fever in a few days calcine all those images to dust and confusion, which seemed to be as lasting as if graved in marble." But elsewhere he celebrates the mind as a kind of magical *daemon* or demiurge—one that infuses life, brings back the dead, paints "anew on itself" things that are "actually nowhere."[24]

Writers on the imagination—Burke, Hartley, Baillie, and Blair (and after them Wordsworth, Blake, and Coleridge)—took up the transcendental implications of Lockean theory in various programmatic ways throughout the century.[25] But it was Radcliffe, without question, who gave the supernaturalized model of mental experience its most charismatic popular brief. She injected the Lockean metaphor of mental reanimation with a rapturous emotional reality. In the ardent, delirious world of *Udolpho*, the "soaring mind" indeed makes dead things live again, including dead people. Like a new and potent deity, it turns absence into presence, rupture into reunion, sorrow into bliss—aspiring in the end to "that Great First Cause, which pervades and governs all being" (114).

One can speculate, of course, on the wishful content in this new-style devotionalism: to undo the death of another by meditating on his visionary form is also a compelling way of negating one's own death. Romantic mourning gave pleasure, one suspects, precisely because it entailed a magical sense of the continuity and stability of the "I" that mourned. To "see" the dead live again is to know that one too will live forever. Thus at times Radcliffe hints at a peculiar satisfaction to be found in grief. The vision of life-in-death is so beautiful one wants to grieve forever. In the final paragraph of *Udolpho*, for example, when she hopes that her fiction will help the mourner to "sustain" his sorrow, the subtle ambiguity of the verb suggests the underlying appeal of the new immortalizing habit of thought. *Lugeo ergo sum*: I mourn, therefore, I am.[26]

That this supernaturalization of the mind should occur precisely when the traditional supernatural realm was elsewhere being explained away should not surprise us. According to the Freudian principle, what the mind rejects in one form may return to haunt it in another. A predictable inversion has taken place in *The Mysteries of Udolpho*: what once was real (the supernatural) has become unreal; what once was unreal (the imagery of the mind) has become real. In the very process of reversal, however, the two realms are confused; the archaic language of the supernatural contaminates the new language of mental experience. Ghosts and specters retain their ambiguous grip on the human imagination; they simply migrate into the space of the mind.

The Radcliffean model of mourning nonetheless presents certain problems. The constant denial of physical death results, paradoxically, in an indifference toward life itself. Common sense suggests as much: if one engages in the kind of obsessional reflection that Radcliffe seems to advocate—a thinking dominated by a preoccupation with the notion that the dead are not really dead (because, after all, one can still "see" them)—the real distinction between life and death will ultimately become irrelevant. If the dead appear to be alive in the mind, how does one distinguish between them and one's mental images of the living? Is such a distinction necessary? For, if seeing the dead in visionary form is more comforting than seeing them in the flesh, doesn't it pay to think of the living in this way too? The emotional conviction that the dead "live" in the mind can easily grow into a sense that the living "live" there too—i.e., that one's mental images of other people are more real in some sense, and far more satisfying, than any unmediated confrontation with them could ever be. One can control one's images of other people; their very stability and changelessness seem to offer a powerful antidote to fear. In the end one begins to mourn the living as well as the dead—to "see" them too—but only in this spectral and immutable form. Life and death merge in the static landscape of the mind.

I spoke at the outset of a new sense of the ghostliness of other people emerging in the late eighteenth century. I meant this in two senses. First, as we have seen, the "ghost" of the dead or absent person, conceived as a kind of visionary image or presence in the mind, takes on a new and compelling subjective reality. In the moment of romantic absorption, one is conscious of the other as a kind of mental phantom, an *idée fixe*, a source of sublime and life-sustaining emotion. But this subjective valorization of the phantasmatic has a profound effect on actual human relations. Real human beings become ghostly too—but in an antithetical sense, in the sense that they suddenly seem insubstantial and unreal.[27] The terrible irony—indeed the pathology—of the romantic vision is that even as other people come to hold a new and fascinating eminence in the mind, they cease to matter as individuals in the flesh. One no longer desires to experience flesh at all, for this is precisely what has become so problematic. The direct corporeal experience of other people, what Locke called "bare naked perception"—seeing, touching, smelling, tasting, hearing the other—has become emotionally intolerable, thanks to the new and overwhelming fear of loss and separation. Real people, needless to say, change, decay, and ultimately die before our eyes. The successful denial of mortality thus requires a new spectralized mode of perception, in which one sees through the real person, as it were, towards a perfect and unchanging spiritual essence. Safely subsumed in this ghostly form, the other can be appropriated, held close, and cherished forever in the ecstatic confines of the imagination.

We have seen certain consequences of this cognitive reorientation in the mummified emotional world of *Udolpho*. Absence is preferable to presence. (An absent loved one, after all, can be present in the mind. One is not distracted by his actual presence.) The dead are more interesting than the living. (If the dead are alive in *Udolpho*, the living might as well be dead.) Objects are more compelling than people. (Objects evoke memories; people disturb them.) But most unsettlingly perhaps, living individuals—as opposed to the visionary forms of the mind—are curiously inconsequential. A new indeterminacy enters into human relationships. Is so and so who he claims to be? He looks like St. Aubert. He makes me see the ghost of St. Aubert; I must really be with St. Aubert.

Other people seem bizarrely amorphous—lacking in specificity. Anyone can summon up the image of another. Everyone reminds us of someone else.

It's an interesting question, of course, whether the habit of seeing those who aren't there, once firmly established, can ever be broken. No one, certainly, seems able to give it up in *Udolpho*. For Radcliffe's heroes and heroines, visionary experience of this kind has become indistinguishable from consciousness itself. The issue persists, however, as a historical problem. For once mental images have been linked with powerful subjective fantasies, such as the wish for immortality, can their strange hold on us ever be weakened? Put most bluntly, do we not continue to exhibit the fantastic, nostalgic, and deeply alienating absorption in phantasmatic objects dramatized in Radcliffe's novel?

That we take for granted the uncanny Radcliffean metaphor of the haunted consciousness is one proof, it seems to me, that the romantic habit of thought has not gone away. Indeed the preference for the phantasmatic may have strengthened its grip on Western consciousness over the past two centuries. Even more than Radcliffe and her contemporaries, we seek to deny our own corporeality and the corporeality of others; even more deeply than they, we have come to cherish the life of the mind over life itself. What *The Mysteries of Udolpho* shows so plainly—could we begin to acknowledge it—is the denatured state of our own awareness: our antipathy toward the body and its contingencies, our rejection of the present, our fixation on the past (or yearnings for an idealized future), our longing for simulacra and nostalgic fantasy. We are all in love with what isn't there.

The reader may object that the kind of illusionism that Radcliffe advocates is clearly an aberration: we all know that our mental fabrications are not "real," and have a name for what happens when we lose this knowledge: psychosis. Yet, as the history of attitudes toward death suggests, it is precisely the distinction between so-called normal and psychotic patterns of belief that has become increasingly confused since the eighteenth century. The everyday has come to seem fantastic; and the fantastic more and more real.

In a much longer study, it would be possible to document the growth of this psychic confusion in more detail. Nineteenth-century romanticism, for example, undoubtedly owes much to the new belief in the reality of mental objects. Indeed, the celebrated romantic concept of the creative imagination is itself a displaced affirmation of faith in "life" of one's mental perceptions. Certain tendencies in nineteenth- and twentieth-century philosophical thought may likewise arise out of a similar emotional shift toward the phantasmatic. In particular the rise of modern skepticism—and the fact that we have come to speculate about the nature of reality with an urgency and insistence unknown to our fore-bears—may paradoxically have resulted from a subliminal faith in the reality of thoughts: for only when mental phenomena assume a powerful and disorienting emotional presence does the boundary between mind and world in turn become a pressing philosophical problem. Finally, any study of the spectralizing habit in modern times would have to take into consideration what might be called its technological embodiment: our compulsive need, since the mid-nineteenth century, to invent ma-chines that mimic and reinforce the image-producing powers of con-sciousness. Only out of a deep preference for the phantoms of the mind, perhaps, have we felt impelled to find mechanical techniques for re-making the world itself in spectral form. Photography was the first great breakthrough—a way of possessing material objects in a strangely de-corporealized yet also supernaturally vivid form. But still more bizarre forms of spectral representation have appeared in the twentieth cen-tury—the moving pictures of cinematography and television, and re-cently, the eerie, three-dimensional phantasmata of holography.[28]

V

In lieu of any such extended investigation, however, let me conclude with some remarks that may point up in a more suggestive way the preeminence of the spectralizing habit in modern Western conscious-ness. Apart from that of Ann Radcliffe, the most important ghost haunt-ing this essay has perhaps been that of Sigmund Freud, whose descrip-tion of psychic experience and the uncanny offers an interesting perspective on the theme of the supernatural in *The Mysteries of Udolpho*. And yet to think of Freud and the invention of psychoanalysis is to see what one might call the Radcliffean paradox inscribed in a new form. Freud, of course, like Radcliffe, often felt compelled to explain the su-pernatural. The following passage from *The Interpretation of Dreams* is as complacent (and amusing) a rationalization as anything to be found in *Udolpho*:

> Robbers, burglars, and ghosts, of whom some people feel frightened be-fore going to bed, and who sometimes pursue their victims after they are asleep, all originate from one and the same class of infantile reminiscence. They are the nocturnal visitors who rouse children and take them up to prevent their wetting the bed, or lift the bedclothes to make sure where they have put their hands in their sleep. Analyses of some of these anxiety-dreams have made it possible for me to identify these nocturnal visitors more precisely. In every case the robbers stood for the sleeper's father, whereas the ghosts corresponded to female figures in white nightgowns.[29]

Ghosts, for Freud, have ceased to exist anywhere but in the mind: they are representatives (in white nightgowns) of "infantile reminiscence"— visitants from the realm of unconscious memory and fantasy. The psychoanalyst supposedly has the power to raise these troubling specters— yet in a controlled fashion—and exorcise them. In the course of the therapeutic process, Freud observed, the analyst "conjures into existence a piece of real life," calling up those shapes from the "psychical underworld" that have begun to obsess or disturb the patient.[30] These figures carry with them all the frightening "power of hallucination," but can ultimately be laid to rest by the skillful clinician.[31]

Or can they? The crucial stage in Freudian analysis is the moment of transference—when the analyst himself suddenly appears before the patient as a ghost: "the return, the reincarnation, of some important figure out of his childhood or past."[32] At this stage the patient experiences a near-total "recoil from reality" and responds to the analyst as a "re-animated" form of the "infantile image."[33] It is up to the analyst to draw the patient out of his "menacing illusion" and show him that "what he takes to be real new life is a reflection of the past."[34]

There is a tremendous paradox, however, in the central Freudian notion that by calling up ghosts one will learn, so to speak, to let go of them. Psychoanalysis proposes that we dwell upon what isn't there, the life of fantasy, precisely as a way of freeing ourselves from it. Yet can such a liberation ever really take place? Freud himself, it turns out, was often strangely uncertain whether the process of transference could ever be completely resolved, and sometimes hinted that for certain patients the spectral forms of the past might continue to haunt them indefinitely.[35] In his most pessimistic statement on the matter, the essay "Analysis Terminable and Interminable," written late in his career, he even began to entertain the notion that the idea of a "natural end" to analysis might itself be an illusion and "the permanent settlement of an instinctual demand" an impossible task.[36]

The problem, of course, is that even as it tries to undo it, psychoanalysis recreates the habit of romantic spectralization in a new and intensified form. Freud's goal was to help his patients escape the sense of being "possessed" by the past—yet his very method involves an almost Radcliffean absorption in the phantasmatic. One denies ghosts by raising them up, frees oneself of one's memories by remembering, escapes the feeling of neurotic derealization by plunging into an unreal reverie. That such a paradoxical process should inspire mixed results should not surprise us. Seen in historical terms, as an offshoot of the radically introspective habit of mind initiated in the late eighteenth century, psychoanalysis seems both the most poignant critique of romantic consciousness to date, and its richest and most perverse elaboration.

It may be that any attempt to domesticate the *daemonic* element in human life will inevitably result in its recurrence in a more intense and chronic form. Ann Radcliffe, as we have seen, dismissed at a blow the age-old vagaries of Western superstition, and sought, in *The Mysteries of Udolpho*, to create a new human landscape: one in which no primitive spirits harassed the unwary, and no horror—even that of death itself—could disrupt the rational pleasures of the soul. Yet, as would be the case with Freud later, this urge toward exorcism created its own recoil effect, a return of irrationality where it was least expected—in the midst of ordinary life itself. This effect, even now, is difficult to acknowledge. No wonder we prefer to reduce Radcliffe to banalities; to see the full depth of illusion in her work would be to acknowledge our own predicament. Ann Radcliffe explained many things, but she also saw ghosts, and in these we too, perhaps, continue to believe.

12

THE LITERATURE OF DOMESTIC TOURISM AND THE PUBLIC CONSUMPTION OF PRIVATE PROPERTY

Carole Fabricant

I

In *Mansfield Park*, when Fanny accompanies the Crawfords and the Bertrams on a visit to Sotherton, the Rushworth estate, she reveals yet one more aspect of her exemplary character. Though remaining respectfully silent for the most part, she expresses her admiration for the house and grounds, respects its territorial boundaries and restraints— unlike Maria Bertram and Henry Crawford, she would never climb over a locked gate without waiting for the key, which as Crawford sarcastically observes symbolizes the "authority and protection" of the owner—and, though she herself is an outsider vis-à-vis the gentry with whom she has been raised, she psychologically and emotionally identifies with the traditional, symbolic values associated with the land. Confronted with Sotherton's landscape, "her eye . . . eagerly [took] in every thing within her reach" without making any material claims upon it, the acquisitiveness suggested by the description taking place on an aesthetic and metaphorical level only.[1] This chapter from Jane Austen's novel reminds us that, included among the exemplary figures presented by the eighteenth- and early-nineteenth-century English novel is that of the model

I would like to thank the editors of this volume and David Collings for their helpful suggestions during the final revisionary stage of this essay.

tourist: s/he who knows how to behave on someone else's property—who identifies with the values of the landowner without actually coveting his possessions.

We see another view of the proper tourist in *Pride and Prejudice*, when Elizabeth and the Gardiners visit Pemberley House as part of their Northern tour "in pursuit of novelty and amusement." Here, not only are the visitors revealed to be respectful, well-behaved, and properly admiring guests on another's property, but Pemberley's owner, Mr. Darcy, is revealed to be the model landlord and master. The disposition of his house and grounds, and the enthusiastic testimonial of his fiercely loyal housekeeper, constitute an extremely effective advertisement for the values and way of life of its owner. In addition, Elizabeth's alternating reactions both to the prospect of visiting Pemberley and to the spectacle it offers upon her arrival reflect the psychological poles of the tourist mentality: on the one hand, the fear of being an interloper, a violator of someone else's privacy and possessions, and on the other hand, the desire to be more than a mere spectator—to be mistress oneself of the things that so charm the eye and inspire admiration in the discerning viewer: "And of this place . . . I might have been mistress! With these rooms I might now have been familiarly acquainted! Instead of viewing them as a stranger, I might have rejoiced in them as my own, and welcomed to them as visitors my uncle and aunt."[2] Elizabeth's situation and her relationship to Darcy render these thoughts "safe," and allow her to entertain them with propriety. Elizabeth is not the coveter of another's property or the potential upstart, but one more of the less than privileged heroines of the eighteenth-century novel whose exemplary qualities of mind and heart permit their entrance into a more elevated social class which they will neither dilute nor subvert but, on the contrary, strengthen and reaffirm.

The passages from Austen's novels gain additional meaning within the larger context of eighteenth-century domestic tourist literature: the large number of travel journals, guidebooks, recorded tours, estate poems, and the like that appeared throughout the period. These documents indirectly illuminate some of the ideological underpinnings of Austen's novels and those of her predecessors by crystallizing the rituals and assumptions central to the period's great drama of (limited) social mobility within a framework of social stability, inevitably revolving around the question of who has access to land and on what terms. The literature most relevant to my concerns here is that which deals with country-house touring in England. It was the popularity of this activity and the widespread dissemination of the literature recording it that allowed Austen to refer to "the celebrated beauties of Matlock, Chatsworth, Dovedale, or the Peak" and to note it was unnecessary to pro-

vide a description of Derbyshire or of "the remarkable places" along the
route of the Gardiners's Northern tour, since "Oxford, Blenheim, War-
wick, Kenelworth, Birmingham, &c. are sufficiently known."[3]

The few critics who have treated the subject in the past have tended
to view it as a rather minor—if entertaining—footnote to the social history of the upper classes. But despite Esther Moir's contention that "the
Tour of Britain remain[ed], during this period, the prerogative of the
governing classes" and that its activities were restricted to the nobility
and gentry,[4] eighteenth-century domestic tourism was a phenomenon
of far wider scope, functioning on multiple socioeconomic and ideological levels and implicating a range of different social classes, including
tradesmen (booksellers, innkeepers, etc.) who profited from the tourist
business and members of the lower orders who were (as we shall see)
allowed to visit places like Stowe and The Leasowes along with their
"betters." Indeed, we can see in eighteenth-century tourism the distinct
beginnings of what it has developed into today: a collective, institutional
force, a profoundly social and socializing ritual—what Dean Mac-
Cannell, referring to modern-day tourism, calls "the ceremonial ratifi-
cation of authentic attractions as objects of ultimate value" and on the
basis of which he concludes that "souvenirs are collected by individuals,
by tourists, while *sights* are collected by entire societies."[5] When Elizabeth and the Gardiners go off to view "the celebrated beauties of Matlock, Chatsworth, Dovedale, [and] the Peak" they are, on the most
obvious level, traveling as individuals through the English countryside
to "see the sights," for their own personal amusement and pleasure.
Yet there is a larger social context and resonance to their activities—
forces that have already determined for them exactly which sights
"must" be seen, hence included on their itinerary. The very act of visiting these "authentic attractions" functions as a confirmation of an entire body of social, economic, and aesthetic values that reinforce the
dominant assumptions and the existing structure of the society—a confirmation made even more explicit and official, if also more seemingly
personal, by Elizabeth's admiring inspection of Pemberley.

There were, of course, other forms of English tourism in the eighteenth century—the Grand Tour to the Continent, for example, as well
as various other types of travel to foreign, often remote and exotic,
places. I am excluding these from my discussion, not only because,
unlike the domestic forms, they have received a good deal of scholarly
attention, but also, and even more to the point, because foreign tourism
served very different ideological ends: ones which, however significant,
have little direct relevance to the issues with which I am here concerned.
Foreign travel, along with the literature (both fictional and nonfictional)
that recorded it, allowed the English to indulge their appetite for the

bizarre and the primitive in a "safe" manner, without its having any necessary effect upon the internal workings of English government and society; it encouraged the illusion of cultural diversity while permitting—indeed, reinforcing—the continued ethnocentricity of English culture.[6] Exotic travel and the literature of foreign tourism were also closely allied to the growing colonialist projects of imperial England, as we can see from the example of Defoe, whose enthusiasm for foreign cultures was often directly proportional to his excitement over their potential as English colonies or as future enhancers of England's balance of trade.

Domestic tourism, however, was an activity that carefully orchestrated the movement of people through private sectors of the English countryside by defining the terms of their admittance onto the grounds of the wealthy, and by seducing them into an identification with the tastes and interests of the landed rich through the manipulation of voyeuristic delights and vicarious pleasures—through the illusion of shared participation in a world not in any meaningful sense their own. In this sense domestic tourism served the interests of the ruling classes, and reinforced their hegemony, by enlisting the complicity of the ruled in the fiction of their *in*clusion in an increasingly *ex*clusionary society. Domestic tourism was thus a perpetuator of false consciousness: it fostered attitudes that blocked true historical perception by masking societal contradictions and encouraging people to think and act in ways that went against their own (material and class) interests. At the same time, however, and paradoxically, tourism by its very nature set up a situation that could throw into bold relief prevailing social and economic disparities—the division of society into those who owned property and those limited to visiting the property of others—and which could thereby militate *against* false consciousness, exposing the very contradictions it was meant to conceal.

A study of domestic tourism can thus yield an insight into the way eighteenth-century hegemony functioned—more specifically, into the role played by eighteenth-century England's budding "culture industry" in creating a socially stabilizing consensus among different classes in society, via an amalgam of traditional and nontraditional values, and at the same time in providing opportunities for a new and potentially more revolutionary form of consciousness to emerge.[7] Such a study can tell us a good deal about the period's dominant culture and ideology while at the same time it reveals how what Raymond Williams terms "residual" and "emergent" elements—those incorporating values from the past and those constituting new alternative or oppositional forces— actively functioned to influence and qualify the dominant.[8] An examination of eighteenth-century tourism can thus help us to appreciate the complexity of both ideological and cultural formations—their resistance

to simple, univalent definitions and to clearcut base/superstructure explanatory models. No ruling-class ideology is simply a static, monolithic
outlook expressing the interests of a single group in society—as Williams
puts it, "a lived hegemony is always a process . . . [I]t does not just
passively exist as a form of dominance. It has continually to be renewed,
recreated, defended, and modified. It is also continually resisted, limited, altered, challenged by pressures not at all its own" (112). Perhaps
nowhere was this truer than in eighteenth-century England, where an
initial struggle for dominance between aristocratic and bourgeois ideology eventually culminated, by the end of the century, in an economic
and ideological alliance between the two classes.

The *inclusion* of more and more layers of the *nouveaux riches* into the
English ruling class was accompanied by the *exclusion* of increasing
numbers of other groups from rights and privileges they had previously
enjoyed under more feudal and precapitalist arrangements. This increasingly exclusionary society was symbolized by the new shapes and
organization of the landscape: by the high-walled deer parks, off limits
to poachers and other trespassers; by the architectural innovations in
country houses, which reflected a growing emphasis on privacy and a
desire on the part of estate owners to withdraw from the world of servants and farmers; and by the ornamental features of landscape gardening, which helped mark off the grounds of the gentry.[9] Underlying
these developments was the radically changing conception of property
during this period, largely as a result of the enclosure movement. From
its traditional, time-honored meaning as a right *in* something—often,
merely one right among many—property was now coming to be understood as the thing itself. In C. B. Macpherson's words, "limited and not
always saleable rights *in* things were being replaced by virtually unlim-
ited and saleable rights *to* things."[10]

There was, however, a countervailing force to this new zeal for privacy
and for fencing off one's property from others. In order to be ideologically effective as architectural tributes to their owners' exalted position
in the world, these houses had to be *seen*. Their value was dependent
on their aspects of display and conspicuous consumption: on their ability
to outshine rival estates and project an appropriate visual symbol of
status—hence social and economic power—and taste, which translated
into a special kind of cultural power during this period. This visual
demonstration of multiple levels of power was not only a part of the
gentry's display rituals amongst themselves and of their performances
for admiring or envious peers, connoisseurs, and (perhaps) prospective
buyers, it also played a role in their showmanship and theatrical pre-
sentations vis-à-vis the poor.

Of course, the degree to which these houses were actually "opened up" to the rest of society differed according to class, although even those on the lower socioeconomic levels were permitted carefully orchestrated glimpses into the secret realms. This is evident from Richard Wilson's painting of Tabley House in Cheshire, for example, which shows an imposing manorial structure at once clearly visible and tucked away in a distant corner of the prospect, capable of being viewed by the peasants pictured nearest us who are, however, emphatically separated from it by a large lake which dominates the foreground.[11] Once we move up a little on the socioeconomic scale, we come to the groups constituting the tourist class, who could actually be permitted entrance into the great houses (often at stipulated hours of the day, on specific days of the week, and frequently for a fee), while yet being kept in the role of outsiders, temporary visitors on someone else's property. The tourists' ocular and ambulatory penetration of the private pleasure grounds of the rich, and the vicarious entrance of their readers on the strength of their written tours and descriptions, were an important factor in enlisting a wide range of social and economic groups in the interests of the wealthy by fostering the illusion of shared property and ownership. Contemporary tourist guides and travelers' accounts, like landscape painting in the latter half of the century, rendered pieces of privately owned land accessible—and in a vicarious sense possessable—by their often middle-class audience.[12] In this respect such literature helped reinforce the paradoxical situation in which the accumulation of more and more land in the hands of fewer and fewer was accompanied by the dispersion of ownership, as psychological and aesthetic (or more precisely tourist) experience, throughout widening areas of society.

The effectiveness of tourist literature in this regard was ascribable largely to its deft promotional techniques which, far more than simply appealing to the traveler's imagination and psychology, went a long way toward actually *creating* the being called a tourist. They thus resembled the techniques of other forms of promotional—what we more usually term "didactic"—literature during the period, which in an analogous way created specific social roles for their audience to emulate and become. The tourist was defined above all as a creature on the move: a traverser of as much territory, and a collector of as many sights, as could be crammed into a limited span of time. John Byng, in many ways the eighteenth-century domestic traveler *par excellence*, reveals an ironic self-consciousness of this newly conceived role when he wryly observes during one of his tours, "After dinner I drag'd forth the reluctant Colonel; (for we must move about as tourists)."[13] The tourist was encouraged to rely on appearances and fleeting surfaces, on sights that could be apprehended in a single glance rather than ones that required intensive scrutiny or reflection, thereby threatening to become tedious and burdensome, or to slow down the progress of one's crowded itinerary, by engrossing the attention for too long. R. J. Sullivan's diplomatic protest against the amount of effort and concentration demanded by Wilton's art treasures, magnificent though he concedes them to be, must be understood in light of this creation and assimilation of a tourist consciousness:

> Wearied not a little with the survey of these curiosities, many of which are exquisitely beautiful, we at length dragged ourselves into the gardens, in the hopes that more rural subjects would dispel that heaviness which a close investigation of every bust and picture had unavoidably impressed us with; and there, having refreshed ourselves, we proceeded on to Longford, the seat of Lord Radnor.[14]

This attitude on the tourist's part fits in very well with the landowner's own agenda, for visitors on his property were rendered less threatening if their intrusions were brief—if the visitors' scrutiny of his possessions was only a fleeting glance rather than a lengthy, devouring glare, which might be interpreted as making a perceptual claim on his riches.

From various comments made by Byng in his travel diaries we can get some idea of the influence exerted by tourist publications of all sorts in shaping their readers' values and movements. After dismissing the reputed beauties of Hagley and The Leasowes, he remarks, "I must think that it is from writing they are become so celebrated: for penmanship has the power of puffing inferiour places and rendering them visitable by the curious, and admired by the ignorant" (I.47). In other words, if the tourist helped create a market for travelers' aids like topographical prints and country-house guides, the latter in their turn did much to create the tourist, whetting his appetite for the visual attractions of the English countryside, helping to shape his aesthetic judgments, and artificially (in both eighteenth- and twentieth-century senses of the word) stimulating hitherto nonexistent needs and desires: in this case, the wish to go forth into unfamiliar areas in order to see with one's own eyes how the wealthy and fashionable of society lived.

Note that the effectiveness of these promotional materials was in no way undermined by individual instances (like the above) in which the tourist was disappointed with what he saw. On the contrary, tourist publications were themselves part of, and actively promoted, a system of competition in which travelers were encouraged to make comparisons among the various houses they visited (as well as among the various guidebooks and printed tours available for purchase)—to praise some and denigrate others, as well as to outdo fellow travelers in their written descriptions. In this way tourist literature in effect duplicated the kind of competition and display that occurred on a higher level among the gentry, and drew the middle class into a complicity with their "betters" by converting potential class conflict into forms of aesthetic and literary rivalry.

Generating the kinds of competition, display, and promotional appeals I have been discussing, and providing the necessary context in which they could thrive, was what Neil McKendrick has termed the "consumer revolution in eighteenth-century England." As he describes it:

> Objects which were once acquired as the result of inheritance at best, came to be the legitimate pursuit of a whole new class of consumers. . . . In imitation of the rich the middle ranks spent more frenziedly than ever before, and in imitation of them the rest of society joined as best they might. . . .Spurred on by social emulation and class competition, men and women surrendered eagerly to the pursuit of novelty, the hypnotic effects of fashion, and the enticements of persuasive commercial propaganda.[15]

McKendrick interprets the objects of consumerism in a very literal and material way, but it seems to me what he is describing has a much broader application, one that permits us to consider the whole tourist enterprise—as well as literature that grew out of it and spurred it on—as a very central part of this consumer revolution. The period we are dealing with, moreover, was no less an age of advertising than of burgeoning consumerism, as is apparent from the growing interest in the arts of "puffing" (to use the contemporary term) evident from mid-century onward, and the popularity of periodicals such as *The Daily Advertiser*, *The London Advertiser*, *The Public Advertiser*, and *The Morning Advertiser*.[16] The conjunction of all these factors resulted in the "packaging" and "selling" of the English countryside as a privately owned but nonetheless publicly consumable product—the embodiment of a way of life one could buy *into* (on the psychological and ideological levels) if not actually buy.

II

An examination of specific eighteenth-century tourist texts reveals the marketing techniques, the dynamics and contradictions, involved in turning travelers and curiosity seekers into consumers of other people's property. An interesting case in point was the metamorphosis of Alexander Pope's villa at Twickenham into a major tourist attraction and an object of vicarious consumerism in a mere matter of months after his death. Despite Pope's injunction in the *Epistle to Dr. Arbuthnot*—"Shut, shut the door, good *John*"—intended among other things to dramatize his villa's status as an ideal realm wholly apart from, and embodying a heroic alternative to, the corrupt, middle-class, commercial society of contemporary London, "good John"—Pope's gardener, John Serle— wasted no time after his employer's demise in *opening up* Pope's gardens to all members of this society; travelers' progress along the Thames to the celebrated grotto was now not obstructed but on the contrary actively encouraged by the guidebook Serle published in 1745, *A Plan of Mr. Pope's Garden*, which included "An Account of all the Gems, Minerals, Spars, and Ores" of which the garden was composed. Although Pope's verses of the 1730s and 1740s depict his grotto in idealized political terms allied to exalted aesthetic principles that privilege nature over artifice (albeit a nature artfully arranged), the picture we get from Serle's *Plan* is of a place that is neither more nor less than a fossilary of rare minerals—a carefully contrived construct of priceless gems designed to dazzle the eye and stimulate the consumer appetites of all those who flocked to see it: in short, a perfect tourist attraction.

The seemingly endless lists of treasures obtained from all over England and from around the world give a new—rather less philosophical, decidedly more material—meaning to the celebrated Popeian principle of *concordia discors*. Along with such native products as Plymouth marble and Cornish diamonds, we are treated to a seductive array of exotic minerals from distant shores, including "Gold Ore from the *Peruvian* Mines; Silver Ore from the Mines of *Mexico*; several pieces of Silver Ore from *Old Spain*; . . . Different Kinds of *Italian* Marble," and on and on.[17] However much Pope may have been satirizing the aspect of materialism and conspicuous display at Belinda's toilet in *The Rape of the Lock* (I. 129– 34), the rare gem collection in his own grotto was soon to take on a similar aspect for the flood of tourists who came to ogle it for themselves after his death, and whose continuous incursions prompted Baroness Howe to destroy the gardens after she had purchased them in the first decade of the nineteenth century.

Serle's *Plan* was rather basic and simple in its approach and appeal; other guidebooks operated on more complex ideological levels and made use of more calculated and sophisticated advertising techniques. In this regard we might consider the fierce competition between Benton Seeley and George Bickham to corner one piece of the tourist market by producing the most popular guidebook to Stowe, another garden associated with Pope both through his poetic praise and his friendship and shared landscaping interests with its owner, Lord Cobham. The history of this decade-long competition reminds us that Stowe, along with being the gardening "wonder" and "paradise" exalted by Pope, enjoyed a more material and mundane existence at the center of the eighteenth-century tourist boom and the trade wars that it generated. Seeley got the jump on the market with his thirty-two page pamphlet, *A Description of the Gardens of Ld. Viscount Cobham of Stow*, published in 1744, which met with such great success that it was followed by an expanded edition in the next year, and by further editions, "corrected and enlarge'd," in each of the following four years.[18] The demand for information about Stowe having been stimulated by this popular pamphlet, Seeley was able to expand his trade by publishing prints of Cobham's temples and ornamental buildings, as well as William Gilpin's *Dialogue upon the Gardens at Stow* in 1748, the three Stowe publications being bound and sold together in 1750. It was in this same year that another enterprising bookseller with a nose for the tourist market, George Bickham, came out with an alternative guidebook called *The Beauties of Stow*, which streamlined and unified (as well as pirated) the material from Seeley's somewhat unwieldy volume, and promptly won over the market from his predecessor. Bickham too capitalized on the tourist boom surrounding Stowe to expand his own trade, subsequently publishing a set of topographical prints of Stowe, in both a plain and a more expensive colored version, and putting out a revised edition of the *Beauties*. The year 1756 saw an intensification of the struggle between the two publishers, with Seeley producing a new guidebook with an extensive map of the gardens, and Bickham putting out a revised edition of his own guidebook claiming to be "much improved." What George C. Clarke calls "the battle of the guidebooks" (x) was eventually resolved in Seeley's favor, with his publication of yet another *Description* that featured new and more detailed tourist information, including a tour of the principal rooms in the house. On the basis of this success Seeley was able to expand his business into a prosperous publishing trade.

If we look for a moment at the content of the 1750 edition of *The Beauties of Stow*, we can get some sense of the deft promotional techniques Bickham relied on to (temporarily) triumph over his competitor. The "selling" that takes place in the guidebook occurs on a number of different but related levels. There is the selling of the guidebook itself (i.e., of Bickham's version over Seeley's), the "selling" of Stowe (over other tourist attractions, in particular the nearby Blenheim), and the "selling" of the whole tourist experience as an activity conferring a wide range of moral, psychological, and aesthetic benefits on the individual tourist, as well as producing political and economic advantages for the country as a whole (thereby making it a patriotic enterprise, if not indeed a patriotic duty). The reader is given Bickham's personal testimony as to the miraculous benefits accruing to one's psyche and soul from a visit to Stowe:

When I . . . enjoy myself in these happy Walks, I can feel my Mind expand

itself, my notions inlarge, and my Heart better disposed either for a religious
Thought, or a benevolent Action. In a word, I cannot help imagining a Taste
for these exalted Pleasures contributes toward making me a better Man.

(61)

The claim here is that visitors' lives will be vastly improved by a visit
to Stowe's gardens. For some, the positive transformation will be registered primarily as a cultivation of taste: "I would have our Country
'Squires flock hither two or three times a Year, by way of Improvement;
and, after they have looked about them a little, return home with new
Notions, & begin to see the Absurdity of their clipped Yews, their Box-
wood Borders, their flourished Parterres, and their lofty Brick-walls."
For others, the benefits will be more emotional and psychological:

> A Sunday Evening spent here, adds a new Relish to the Day of Rest, and
> makes the Sabbath appear more chearful to the Labourer, after a toilsome
> Week . . . All Care and Uneasiness seem to be left behind at the Garden-
> Door, and People enter here fully resolved to enjoy themselves, and the
> several beautiful Objects around them.

(60–61, 62)

This statement not only indicates that tourism encompassed a broad
spectrum of social groups, including members of the laboring class, it
also suggests the ideological importance of this inclusion. By raising the
laborer's spirits "after a toilsome Week" and by creating an environment
in which "All Care and Uneasiness seem to be left behind at the Garden-
Door," the act of tourism served a conservative social function by defusing discontent with one's lot in life and by promoting the idea that
happiness could be achieved via temporary entrance into the carefree
world of a rich man's pleasure gardens.

Aside from being a boon to the individual visitor, tourism is presented
as bringing incomparable advantages to the inhabitants of the entire
area surrounding the tourist attraction. Bickham talks of "the Money
spent in the Neighbourhood, to satisfy [tourists'] Curiosity" and avers,
"There is a kind of continual Fair; and I have heard several of the Inhabitants say, that it is one of the best Trades they have: Their Inns,
their Shops, their Farms, and Shambles, all find their Account in it"
(61). According to this eighteenth-century expression of the "trickle-
down" theory, the accumulation of land and wealth in the hands of a
few is to be welcomed even by those who have neither, since all will
indirectly benefit from the revenues generated by the grand estates and
the curiosity seekers they attract.

Tourism is, moreover, identified with the older (by now largely anachronistic) social rituals of rural hospitality: "A Place like [Stowe], is a kind of keeping open House: There is a Repast at all Times ready for the Entertainment of Strangers. And sure, if there is any Degree of Benevolence, you must think an useful End answered in thus affording an innocent Gratification to so many Fellow-Creatures" (62). In this way the moral authority of tradition is combined with the emotional power of nostalgia and put to the service of promoting a very new commercial enterprise, one that in fact violated a host of traditional mores and sensibilities vis-à-vis property arrangements. What we see here is an example of tradition—or more precisely, the use of tradition—in the sense described by Williams, as "an aspect of *contemporary* social and cultural organization, in the interest of the dominance of a specific class. It is a version of the past which is intended to connect with and ratify the present. What it offers in practice is a sense of *predisposed continuity*" (116).

Finally, tourism is presented as a national asset, hence an activity deserving the support of all good Britons: "elegant Products of Art" such as Stowe have the "Tendency to raise us in the opinion of Foreigners. If our Nation had nothing of this Kind to boast of, all our Neighbours would look upon us as a stupid tasteless Set of People, and not worth visiting: So that, for the Credit of the Country, I think, something of this Kind ought to be exhibited amongst us" (62–63). Bickham's pitch here to his readers' patriotic sentiments is in fact rather restrained compared to the appeals made by other pieces of contemporary tourist literature, which were often directed to a much more aggressive assertion of nationalist superiority. Characteristic in this respect is Defoe's comment in his *Tour*:

> I think, any traveller from abroad, who would desire to see how the English gentry live, & what pleasures they enjoy, should come into Suffolk and Cambridgeshire, & take but a light circuit among the country seats of the gentlemen . . . and they would be soon convinc'd, that not France, no not Italy itself, can out-do them.[19]

Bickham, however, is content to downplay the aspect of rivalry between England and other nations, reserving his competitive zeal for the promotion of Stowe over other contemporary gardens and for the promotion of his own guidebook as the indispensable companion for all visitors to Cobham's estate. Calling the latter "The Wonder of our Days, and the most Charming Place in all England," and invoking lines from *Windsor-Forest* to describe its "unparallel'd Chain of artificial and natural Beauty," he sets up a rivalry between Stowe and Blenheim, one from which Stowe (not surprisingly) emerges the victor: while acknowledging "the Majesty of *Blenheim* House," he concludes that "all falls short of Stowe" (66).

Blenheim, in its turn, was also well served by the guidebooks put out to "sell" it as a tourist attraction, even though it wasn't until over forty years after the appearance of Seeley's initial *Description* that William F. Mavor's *Blenheim, A Poem, To Which is Added, A Blenheim Guide* was published. Two years later, in 1789, "a new, and much improved edition," under the title of *A New Description of Blenheim*, came out, with Mavor immediately impressing upon his readers the success of both his earlier guidebook and of Blenheim as a tourist treasure:

> The favourable reception with which the Public had honoured this Performance having rendered a new edition necessary, the Author has thrown the whole into another form; and by a revision of the Poem, and a very considerable enlargement of the Description, has adapted it for the general convenience and information of the numerous and respectable visitors of Blenheim, which includes almost every person of condition in these kingdoms, and all the foreigners of quality who travel into England.[20]

There is more snob appeal being exerted here than in Seeley's or Bickham's guides; Mavor's readers are invited to identify with the crème-de-la-crème of both English and European society—with persons of "condition" and "quality"—all of whom presumably share an admiration for Blenheim's architecture and landscape. Not only Blenheim itself but its environs as well are in effect packaged and sold as the embodiment of a terrestrial paradise reserved for the well-born and well-to-do but accessible to visitors and available to everyone as an ideal way of life to aspire to:

> The Palace or Castle of Blenheim, one of the most magnificent piles of architecture in this kingdom, and perhaps in the whole world, stands in the finest part of one of the finest counties in England . . . The surrounding country is fertile and irriguous, adorned with woods, and abounding with seats of the nobility and gentry; the air is pure, mild, and salubrious; and all the necessities and many of the elegancies of life are plentiful and choice.
>
> (2nd ed. 31–32)

As befit a place of such combined edenic and elitist status, Blenheim could be entered and viewed by outsiders only at certain prescribed times ("every afternoon, from 3 till 5 o'Clock, except Sundays and public Days," although visitors who arrived early were allowed to "take the ride of the Park before dinner," and portions of Blenheim could be shown at other times "on proper application"). Hence the flow of human traffic into the house and park was carefully controlled and monitored at the same time that it was actively (indeed, aggressively) promoted.

In the next decade and a half Mavor came out with several further revisions of his guide, the fourth edition of 1797 being, among other things, "embellished with an elegant Plan of the Park." That the tourist trade connected with Blenheim had significantly expanded since the appearance of the first guidebook is attested to by the announcements that the guide was now being "sold by all booksellers in town and country" and that "a few plans of Blenheim Park on grand Eagle French paper, plain or coloured, for framing, may be had where the Description is sold." There is also a specific plug for Woodstock's two major inns, the Bear and the Marlborough Arms, which, we are assured, "furnish the best entertainment and accommodation to travellers."[21] The fourth edition includes a "Preliminary Essay on Landscape Gardening" which, along with the predictable aesthetic observations, contains little ideological messages that appeal to the tourist not only as someone of refined aesthetic sensibilities but also as a person of high moral character and as a lover of his country: "To the picturesque landscape which pleases the sight, [Blenheim] adds the moral landscape that delights the mind . . . It is peopled with happy labourers—it is stocked with cattle—it waves with corn" (4th ed. 21). There are also subtler messages: "No kind of property is less the object of envy, or more grateful to the eye, than to take possession of a country in an extensive view: it contributes to the general beauty, and is equally enjoyed by all, without offense to any" (4th ed. 20). Mavor here extols extensive views on what seem to be aesthetic grounds, but they are also implicitly political since the real virtue of these views lies in their being at once "democratic"—enjoyable by all in an equal measure—*and* supportive of the status quo, the unequal distribution of land, in that they encourage people to enjoy another's property without wanting to appropriate it as their own. The act of aesthetically and psychologically "tak[ing] possession of a country" is put forward as a mutually satisfying alternative to—indeed, a politically safe substitute for—the act of materially possessing it.

The guidebooks of Seeley and Mavor were competitors—in the business of selling rival products, so to speak—yet viewed overall they seem very similar in that they share the same discourse and convey the same set of messages to their readers. Ultimately even their products appear indistinguishable, or at least mutually reinforcing and sustaining rather than opposed to one another. It is therefore not surprising that, appended to subsequent editions of Mavor's guide, were several suggested tourist itineraries which included *both* Blenheim and Stowe (along with other country houses in the area): which in effect advertised the two together as indispensable parts or stages of a single activity and experience. In this sense the promotion of country houses as tourist attractions had much in common with modern-day forms of advertising, in which rival campaigns for ostensibly competing commodities cloak a deeper collaboration among them, an ideological and rhetorical complicity: the "selling" of the same basic idea and the holding out of the same seductive promise of personal gain and transformation. As John Berger observes, "It is true that in publicity one brand of manufacture, one firm, competes with another; but it is also true that every publicity image confirms and enhances every other. Publicity is not merely an assembly of competing messages: it is a language in itself which is always being used to make the same general proposal."[22] The "competing messages" of Bickham's, Seeley's, and Mavor's respective guidebooks were all communicated via the same language of aesthetic and cultural commodification: all proposed to their readers that, by becoming tourists, they would be initiated into an elite but diversified society whose members could look forward to an increase in personal happiness, prosperity, and status.

III

As a form of advertising and propagandizing in the broadest sense, tourist literature was involved with shaping attitudes, defining needs and aspirations, and modifying human behavior. As such, it was closely allied to the didactic impulse underlying so much of eighteenth-century writing. Going along with the spate of works dealing with the correct relationship between master and servant, husband and wife, parent and offspring, tourist literature at least implicitly (and often more overtly) explored the newly emergent relationship between the landowner and the visitor to his demesne, suggesting the (extra-legal) obligations and the type of behavior expected of each. Since *property* relations were at the heart of all *proper* relations during this period, the exchange of civilities and incivilities, permissions and denials, obligations and privileges that characterized the transaction between estate owner and tourist came to mirror a whole panoply of values and social interactions.

Thus parts of *The Eaton Tourists; or, A "Colloquial Description" of the Hall, Grounds, Gardens, &c. at Eaton* read like an early nineteenth-century Richardsonian middle-class courtesy book on how to act appropriately, and show proper respect, on someone else's private property. In a series of discourses between a tourist and a bookseller we are presented with various guidelines to help us avoid overstepping our bounds when on territory belonging to another. As they prepare to visit Eaton, the wise bookseller patiently explains to the tourist, "As the first step to our progress we should enquire at the Royal Hotel on what days the Hall is to be seen; as the privacy of a nobleman should be respected."[23] Because one can view the house only at certain prescribed hours and because one shouldn't impose upon a nobleman's private space, precise timing becomes a crucial consideration. Discourse IV opens as the tourist and the bookseller meet according to prearranged plan on the Chester Bridge leading to Eaton; the tourist immediately exclaims, "By my watch to the minute—punctuality cheers the traveller on his onset," and is seconded by the bookseller, "Under such impressions, I wished not to be beyond my time, and here at six a.m. to the moment, on Chester Bridge" (23). When the tourist and bookseller begin touring the interior of the house, we are again reminded of the need to tread warily to avoid social, in the broadest sense *political*, improprieties. Descending the staircase after viewing apartments on the upper floor, the tourist—who by now has thoroughly learned his ideological lessons from his tutor—remarks: "—the private apartments to the west are occupied by the Earl and Countess, which renders public inspection of [them], impossible, or at least might be deemed an intrusion" (52).

Just as the unruliness and threats of insubordination on the part of London apprentices gave impetus to works like Richardson's *Vade Mecum*, the threat of unruly tourists stimulated the publication of works that on one level or another attempted to inculcate a healthy respect for the territorial possessions of another. A particularly interesting example of such work—interesting because it was written by a member of the laboring class—is the poetry celebrating The Leasowes written by James Woodhouse, a journeyman shoemaker from Rowley, about two miles from Shenstone's seat, who later rose to the rank of estate manager. From the Advertisement to his *Poems on Sundry Occasions*, published in 1764, we learn that

[Shenstone's] benevolence was such, that he permitted the lowest of his neighbours the benefit of these delightful scenes; . . . [but] the liberty Mr. Shenstone's good-nature granted was soon turned into licentiousness[. T]he people destroying the shrubs, picking the flowers, breaking down the hedges, and doing him other damage, produced a prohibition to every one without application to himself or principal servants.[24]

We have here a situation that embodied a perfect object lesson in the uses and abuses of private property, and that provided the raw materials for an extended reflection on the way *not* to behave when one is privileged enough to gain entrance onto someone else's grounds.

In his "Elegy to William Shenstone," Woodhouse castigates the "ruthless crowds, disdaining bounds,/[Who] Climb'd o'er thy gates, [and]

leap'd all thy mounds" and who with outrageous temerity "pathless lawns and meadows crost,/And through the crashing fences burst" (12). It would seem that the lower classes, with their shocking disregard for things like fences and carefully delineated pathways—things so crucial to the organization of the English landscape during and after the enclosures and during the growth of the great estates—made hopeless tourists. In their inability or refusal to understand private property in the way that the landowners did, they represented the ultimate threat to the existing system, so that it is perhaps not surprising that Woodhouse, writing with a consciousness that identified itself with Shenstone's interests, should depict his unruly countrymen as "Belial's sons (of gratitude the bane)/[who] With cursed riot dar'd thy groves profane" and who in effect reenacted the fall of man and the exile from paradise, thereby justifying Shenstone's anger which, "like Heaven's flaming guard,/With frowning bolts all entrance has debarr'd" (7, 8)—justifying, in other words, the whole institution of private property as it came to be conceived of in the eighteenth century, as well as the right of the landlord, taking his cue and his sanction from the "landlord" of eden, to evict undesirables from his realm. Once the gardens have been shut off to the public, the key that unlocks the gate assumes an enormous importance, becoming part of a kind of mythic ritual that separates the insiders from the outsiders, the socially redeemed from the socially damned: once granted to the decorously "supplicant" tourist, its "magic touch gives free access,/Nor leaves occasion to transgress" (8, 10).

We might think of Woodhouse's verse as one that gives explicit articulation to the implied "contract" underlying the landowner-tourist relationship. In exchange for the magic key that will provide "free access," the would-be tourist in effect agrees to certain conditions: he will not trample on the grass, pick the flowers, or enter fenced-off areas. He will respect all "bounds," accept the restrictions on his mobility and behavior imposed by the landowner, and will, moreover, show his gratitude for the privilege accorded him, perhaps even by celebrating the beauties of his host's estate—and the benevolence of its owner—in print, thereby helping to enhance the reputation of both, not to mention to augment future tourist revenues, by providing free publicity.

Woodhouse's poems throw into bold relief the kind of false consciousness most often engendered by the experience and psychology of tourism. However, there is a rather remarkable passage in Woodhouse's poem "The Leasowes"—for the most part a typical tourist exercise extolling the features of Shenstone's garden—which forces us to qualify this judgment. The passage constitutes a kind of epiphanic moment in which Woodhouse ceases to be our enthusiastic tourist guide and becomes suddenly conscious of his own state of disinheritance: of the yawning gap between Shenstone's way of life and his own. The moment takes place in Horace's grove, where Woodhouse contemplates the fortunate circumstances of the Roman poet and wishes that, like Horace, he could somehow realize his utmost desire:

> No longer, then, I'd pine a landless boor,
> Nor trudge, through sloughs around a rented door,
> In russet garb, whose ragged rent-holes grin,
> And ill conceal the skeleton within:
> . . .
> Nor wish I sceptre, diadem, and throne,
> But, Horace-like, a vill and farm my own;
> To range among my lawns, my streams, my trees,
> Such as he wish'd; or, rather, such as these.[25]

This moment of revelation, in which the deferential, admiring tourist suddenly realizes himself to be "a landless boor" whose wretched lot in life is in no way changed by his necessarily conditional access to Shenstone's grounds, passes quickly, as a perception too disruptive to dwell upon, and the passage ends with Woodhouse passively accepting his lot in life ("I'll live resign'd to my depress'd fate,/And wing my wishes to a future state"). But although these dangerous perceptions are squelched in his poems about The Leasowes, they later reassert themselves with a vengeance in Woodhouse's seemingly interminable and largely unreadable but intermittently fascinating verse autobiography, *The Life and Lucubrations of Crispinus Scriblerus*, in the passages like the following:

> Whence grew the titles of the Rich, and Great?
> To their vain treasures, and their vast Estate?
> Were loads of gold, and leagues of grassy sod,
> Mines, Woods, and Wilds—exclusive gifts of God?
> And have not brother Men, of meaner Birth,
> Some right and title to small specks of Earth?
> . . .
> They dress Your meadows—fertilize Your field;
> And ought not You some small inclosure yield,
> Where each may range, or rest, when Sundays shine,
> Look round their little spot, and cry—'tis Mine?[26]

Woodhouse's poetry in its entirety alternately highlights the two faces of eighteenth-century tourism: the basically conservative role it played as a quasi-institution designed to elicit admiration and approval for the creations of the wealthy, along with an imaginative (and imaginary) identification with its creators; and the subversive potential it possessed by virtue of exposing these creations to the hungry, perhaps covetous or resentful gaze of others, thereby possibly fostering, in spite of its official agenda, feelings of dispossession and alienation.

A different kind of subversive potential is evident in Byng's disdainful account of his visit to Chatsworth, where he complains about the sum of money extracted by overly obliging servants for a view of a "disa-greeable" and "dirty" cascade, along with "fountains [that] were made to squirt aloft for us; and a lead tree (worthy only of a tea garden in London) [made] to sport about us" (II.37). Byng's description of the Disneyland effects at Chatsworth comes close to revealing the basic hype at the bottom of all tourist experience, but it stops well short of a social critique. For something more nearly approximating the latter we might turn to Daniel C. Webb's description of his visit to Blenheim in his *Observations and Remarks* on a tour through Great Britain. Webb, although properly taken with his surroundings and even referring to Blenheim's grounds as a "terrestrial paradise," was moved by the mercenary aspect of the whole experience to expostulate:

> I shall not take leave without remarking the paltry imposition practiced by the servants in waiting, for shewing [Blenheim's] beauties to strangers. The view with which I had been gratified, cost me upwards of eight shillings; and when we advert to the immense sum that was originally taken, even from the hard earnings of the industrious poor, for the purpose of rewarding the great Duke of Marlborough, I regret that the people should be denied the satisfaction of seeing what they have so dearly paid for.[27]

IV

I would like to conclude by drawing out several of the most important implications of the preceding discussion. For one thing, it points to the need to treat the period's literature as the eighteenth century itself understood the term: not as a limited body of specifically "imaginative" or "creative" texts, but as "the whole body of valued writing in society: philosophy, history, essays and letters as well as poems"—writing which, more than merely reflecting certain social values, "was a vital instrument for their deeper entrenchment and wider dissemination."[28] Our study suggests that works as diverse as the poems of James Wood-house, the novels of Jane Austen, and the guidebooks of Benton Seeley can most fully be understood as cultural texts which, despite significant formal and generic differences, participate in the same ideological debates and share the same code of opposing discourses. Our study additionally suggests the importance of an interdisciplinary approach to the literature of the eighteenth century (and, by analogy and extension, to that of other periods as well), for it is only through such an approach that we can appreciate the profoundly relational character of all cultural institutions and artifacts, and of the classes that create and "consume" them. The study underscores the inadequacy (indeed, the fallacy) of reading a didactic essay or interpreting a poem or analyzing a painting in isolation, without dealing with their various levels of interplay within the context of a totality none of whose elements can genuinely be understood as static or separate: a totality ("history") which is not simply an inert background but an arena of active and conflicting, in the final analysis dialectical, forces.

By the same token, our study of tourism reveals the impossibility of identifying the ideology of the period, or its texts, in any simple or unitary way. The contradictions inherent in the class conflicts and the differing concepts of land ownership during the eighteenth century were expressed in the alternating struggle and fusion of different ideological values in the period's tourist literature. Aristocratic notions of leisure and privacy merged with the bourgeois ideals of industry and profit and with feudal conceptions of an agrarian community to produce a seemingly classless vision exalting patriotism, national prosperity with its concomitant, individual happiness, and a world of aesthetic improvements—all symbolized by the great estate opened to the public, at once assimilating and excluding large groups in society and reflecting a hegemony which depended on the *rapprochement* between certain classes and the widening gap between others, and which attempted to legitimize a particular definition of property against other oppositional views. To use Fredric Jameson's analytic categories, as individual texts the works we have been examining may be understood as "symbolic acts," as "resolutions of determinate contradictions"; viewed as parts of a larger social order, these works may be understood as "ideologemes," the smallest units of "the essentially antagonistic collective discourses of social classes." Considered from the first perspective they may well appear to be seamless wholes, univocal statements communicating a single, straightforward "message." But when these works are viewed within the second context, each emerges "as a *parole*, or individual utterance, of the vaster system, or *langue*, of class discourse."[29] It is in this latter context that we can, among other things, discern what J. G. A. Pocock calls the "bitter, conscious, and ambivalent dialogue" in the eighteenth century over the interrelated questions of property, authority, and the idea of virtue.[30]

An awareness of the essentially dialogic structure of literary and cultural texts, rooted in the class antagonisms of the social order, allows us to understand how given works—eighteenth-century novels, for example—can incorporate subversive viewpoints and insights into their generally conservative overall perspective: the degree to which the novels function through disjunctions and inconsistencies that lay bare, and challenge, the very ideologies they seem most obviously to affirm. I began this essay by characterizing Fanny as a model tourist and a believer in the values traditionally associated with the land, but this was an oversimplification; for these dual roles are not necessarily compatible, and in this case place Fanny in an inherently contradictory position: as model tourist, she must show proper deference for Rushworth's possessions and status, as well as, more generally, for his way of life, while as an adherent of "the traditional forms" she must necessarily disapprove of his aesthetic tastes and priorities (his plans to cut down the avenue of trees and reshape the landscape according to the newest fashion) as well as his preoccupation with material rather than moral values. Fanny's situation reveals the dilemma of the principled tourist, who is apt to have to choose between traditional landed values on the one hand, and the class who owns the land (and on whose "generosity" one depends for right of access) on the other. Mythically, *Mansfield Park* functions on the assumption of an exact correspondence between the two, but the novel shows us that the two can easily be separated, and ultimately it depicts a situation in which the preservation of traditional conservative values is left to a member of the dispossessed, landless class while many of those officially entrusted to uphold and perpetuate these values are in fact hastening their demise.[31]

These kinds of ideological tensions and contradictions grew out of an age whose great moral conflicts were frequently, on one level or another, battles over real estate, and out of a body of literature that regularly strove to establish an equation between private property and public virtue. Although this equation remains basically intact in much of contemporary tourist literature, we can detect occasional notes of qualification, occasional instances where the equation threatens to break down. And indeed, it is possible that if we follow Pierre Macherey's suggestion and pay attention to what is happening at the "margins" of eighteenth-century texts, to what they "cannot say" but nevertheless "manifest" and "uncover," we would be able to discern many more voices of questioning and protest (and certainly many more strands of contradiction) than other, more traditional forms of reading would lead us to expect.[32]

Today the tourist industry has grown to proportions unimaginable in the eighteenth century, implicating all segments of society and profoundly influencing the way we view and move through our world. Indeed, John Barrell may well be right when he claims that "we are all tourists now" as a consequence of changes in land ownership and organization beginning in the later eighteenth century.[33] This means that modern-day tourism has the ability, especially with advanced technology at its disposal, to exert enormous institutional and validating power, to exercise all forms of control over people's perceptions and behavior. Yet, precisely because tourism *is* so pervasive and all-encompassing, it has created unprecedented opportunities for social criticism and protest. We might think, for example, of Alice Walker's comment after touring ante-bellum mansions in the South, where her ancestors worked as slaves: "[I]t all comes back to houses. To how people live. There are rich people who own houses to live in and poor people who do not. And this is wrong . . . I think: I would level this country with the sweep of my hand, if I could."[34] In other words, even if we can't escape being tourists, we can at least become our own dissenting and iconoclastic kind of tourist. If tourist activity constitutes a secularized form of religious pilgrimage, as Erving Goffman suggests, we can set forth as agnostics rather than believers, and refuse to participate in such "long strings of obligatory rites" as guided tours."[35] By the same token, if the organizational and behavioral aspects of tourism are "functionally equivalent to the sacred text that still serves as the moral base of traditional society," as MacCannell contends,[36] we can "read" this "sacred text" subversively and deconstructively rather than passively accepting it at face value—much as Macherey argues we should read specific literary texts. The whole thrust of the preceding discussion strongly suggests that this mode of reading, along with the perspective it engenders, is not only desirable but imperative: not as a matter of theoretical sophistication or trendiness, but as a political act no less liberating for our existence in the present as it is revolutionary in its implications for our understanding of the past.

NOTES

REVISING CRITICAL PRACTICES: An Introductory Essay/Felicity Nussbaum and Laura Brown

1.   Howard D. Weinbrot, "Recent Studies in the Restoration and Eighteenth Century," *Studies in English Literature 1500–1900* 25 (1985): 709. All subsequent references to *SEL* reviews will be cited in the text by year of publication.

2.   See, for example, R. S. Crane, *Critics and Criticism: Essays in Method* (Chicago: University of Chicago Press, 1957); William K. Wimsatt and Cleanth Brooks, *Literary Criticism: A Short History* (New York: Knopf, 1957); Earl Wasserman, *The Subtler Language: Critical Readings of Neoclassic and Romantic Poems* (Baltimore: Johns Hopkins University Press, 1958); and Reuben Brower, *Alexander Pope: The Poetry of Allusion* (London: Oxford University Press, 1968).

3.   See J. H. Plumb, *The Growth of Political Stability in England 1675–1725* (London: Macmillan, 1967); or Paul Fussell, *The Rhetorical World of Augustan Humanism: Ethics and Imagery from Swift to Burke* (Oxford: Clarendon Press, 1965).

4.   The essays appear in Wolfgang Iser, *The Implied Reader: Patterns of Communication in Prose Fiction from Bunyan to Beckett* (Baltimore: Johns Hopkins University Press, 1974); and Edward Said, *The World, the Text and the Critic* (Cambridge: Harvard University Press, 1983).

5.   Donald Greene, "The Study of Eighteenth-Century Literature," in Philip Harth, ed., *New Approaches to Eighteenth-Century Literature* (New York: Columbia University Press, 1974), p. 19.

6.   Lawrence K. Lipking, "The History of the Future," in Harth, ed., *New Approaches to Eighteenth-Century Literature*, p. 166.

7.   "New historicism" or "cultural poetics" has been formulated in large part by Renaissance scholars. See especially Stephen Greenblatt, *Renaissance Self-Fashioning: From More to Shakespeare* (Chicago: University of Chicago Press, 1980); and more recently Jonathan Goldberg, "The Politics of Renaissance Literature: A Review Essay," *ELH* 49 (1982): 514–42; and, in a special issue of *English Literary Renaissance* (1986), Louis Montrose, "Renaissance Literary Studies and the Subject of History," pp. 5–12, and Jean Howard, "The New Historicism in Renaissance Studies," pp. 13–43.

8.   William H. Epstein, "Professing the Eighteenth Century," *ADE Bulletin* 81 (1985): 20–25, p. 22.

9.   *Studies in Burke and His Time* 19 (1978): 195.

10.   Murray Cohen, "Eighteenth-Century English Literature and Modern Critical Methodologies," *ECTI* 20 (1979): 5–23, p. 5

11. *Eighteenth-Century Life* 7 (1982): 111.

12. White's views are detailed in *Tropics of Discourse: Essays in Cultural Criticism* (Baltimore: Johns Hopkins University Press, 1978).

13. This absence of interest in theory is particularly remarkable when we compare, for example, Jonathan Goldberg, "Recent Studies in the English Renaissance," *SEL* 24 (1984): 157–99.

14. For recent related discussions of ideology, see, for example, Ellen Meiksins Wood, *The Retreat From Class* (London: Verso, 1986); Goran Therborn, *The Ideology of Power and the Power of Ideology* (London: Verso, 1980); and Ernesto Laclau and Chantal Mouffe, *Hegemony and Socialist Strategy: Towards a Radical Democratic Politics* (London: Verso, 1985).

15. On the theory of disciplines, see especially Edward Said, "Opponents, Audiences, Constituencies, and Community," *Critical Inquiry* 9 (1982): 1–25.

16. Among recent efforts to challenge disciplinary methodologies are *The Anti-Aesthetic: Essays on Postmodern Culture*, ed. Hal Foster (Port Townsend, Washington: Bay, 1983) on the fine arts; *Anthropology as Cultural Critique: An Experimental Moment in the Human Sciences*, ed. George E. Marcus and Michael M. J. Fischer (Chicago: University of Chicago Press, 1986); *Not in Our Genes: Biology, Ideology and Human Nature*, ed. R. C. Lewontin, Steven Rose, and Leon J. Kamin (New York: Pantheon, 1984); and *Changing the Subject: Psychology, Social Regulation and Subjectivity*, ed. Julian Henriques, Wendy Hollway, Cathy Urwin, Couze Venn, and Valerie Walkerdine (London: Methuen, 1984).

1. HISTORICIZING *ABSALOM AND ACHITOPHEL*/Michael McKeon

1. See *A Discourse Concerning the Original and Progress of Satire* (1693), in *John Dryden, Of Dramatic Poesy and Other Critical Essays*, ed. George Watson (London: J. M. Dent, 1962), II.115.

2. For the influential classification of *Absalom and Achitophel* as an "*epyllion*, or epic in miniature," see A. W. Verrall, *Lectures on Dryden*, ed. Margaret De G. Verrall (New York: Russell and Russell, [1914] 1963), p. 59.

3. See Morris Freedman, "Dryden's Miniature Epic," *Journal of English and Germanic Philology* 57 (April 1958): 211–19; Anne Ferry, *Milton and the Miltonic Dryden* (Cambridge: Harvard University Press, 1968); Bruce King, "*Absalom and Achitophel*: A Revaluation," in *Dryden's Mind and Art*, ed. Bruce King (Edinburgh: Oliver and Boyd, 1969), pp. 65–83; H. T. Swedenberg, Jr., ed., "Commentary," in *The Works of John Dryden*, II: *Poems 1681–1684* (Berkeley and Los Angeles: University of California Press, 1972), pp. 234–35; Thomas E. Maresca, *Epic To Novel* (Columbus: Ohio State University Press, 1974), Chap. 1. All citations of *Absalom and Achitophel* are to the "California" edition; page numbers will be cited in the text.

4. See Christopher Ricks, "Allusion: The Poet as Heir," in R. F. Brissenden and J. C. Eade, eds., *Studies in the Eighteenth Century*, III (Toronto: University of Toronto Press, 1976), pp. 231–33.

5. See Leonora L. Brodwin, "Miltonic Allusion in *Absalom and Achitophel*: Its Function in the Political Satire," *Journal of English and Germanic Philology* 68 (1969): 24–44; Irvin Ehrenpreis, *Literary Meaning and Augustan Values* (Charlottesville: University of Virginia Press, 1974), p. 20; Sanford Budick, *Poetry of Civilization: Mythopoeic Displacement in the Verse of Milton, Dryden, Pope, and Johnson* (New Haven: Yale University Press, 1974), pp. 100, 103.

6. E.g., see Ian Jack, *Augustan Satire: Intention and Idiom in English Poetry, 1660–1750* (Oxford: Clarendon Press, 1966), pp. 45, 78.

7. See Albert Ball, "Charles II: Dryden's Christian Hero," *Modern Philology* 59 (1961): 25–35.

8. See John M. Steadman, *Milton and the Renaissance Hero* (Oxford: Clarendon Press, 1967), passim; Michael Wilding, "The Last of the Epics: The Rejection of the Heroic in *Paradise Lost* and *Hudibras*," in Harold Love, ed., *Restoration Literature: Critical Approaches* (London: Methuen, 1972), pp. 91–120.

9. See William G. Riggs, *The Christian Poet in Paradise Lost* (Berkeley and Los Angeles: University of California Press, 1972), passim; Patricia A. Parker, *Inescapable Romance: Studies in the Poetics of a Mode* (Princeton: Princeton University Press, 1979), p. 135.

10. See "Preface" to the *Aeneis* (1697), in Dryden, *Of Dramatic Poesy*, II.233.

11. See Michael West, "Dryden's Ambivalence as a Translator of Heroic Themes," *Huntington Library Quarterly* 26 (1973): 347 and passim.

12. See Barbara K. Lewalski, *Protestant Poetics and the Seventeenth-Century Religious Lyric* (Princeton: Princeton University Press, 1979), Chap. 4; Steven N. Zwicker, *Dryden's Political Poetry: The Typology of King and Nation* (Providence: Brown University Press, 1972), pp. 16–23; Ira Clark, *Christ Revealed: The History of the Neotypological Lyric in the English Renaissance* (Gainesville: University of Florida Press, 1982), passim.

13. See Victor Harris, "Allegory to Analogy in the Interpretation of Scriptures," *Philological Quarterly* 45 (1966): 1–23; Hans Frei, *The Eclipse of Biblical Narrative: A Study in Eighteenth- and Nineteenth- Century Hermeneutics* (New Haven: Yale University Press, 1974), pp. 6–8 and passim; Paul J. Korshin, "The Development of Abstracted Typology in England, 1650–1820," in *Literary Uses of Typology from the Late Middle Ages to the Present*, ed. Earl Miner (Princeton: Princeton University Press, 1977), pp. 147–203, and *Typologies in England, 1650–1820* (Princeton: Princeton University Press, 1982), Chaps. 3 and 4; Joseph Wittreich, *Interpreting Samson Agonistes* (Princeton: Princeton University Press, 1986), Chaps. 4 and 5. See also Steven N. Zwicker, "Politics and Panegyric: The Figural Mode from Marvell to Pope," in Miner, ed., *Literary Uses of Typology*, p. 129.

14. Alan Roper, *Dryden's Poetic Kingdoms* (New York: Barnes and Noble, 1965), p. 191. Compare Arthur W. Hoffman, *John Dryden's Imagery* (Gainesville: University of Florida Press, 1962), p. 73; Earl Miner, *Dryden's Poetry* (Bloomington: Indiana University Press, 1967), pp. 114–15. See also Laura Brown, "The Ideology of Restoration Poetic Form: John Dryden," *PMLA* 97 (1982): 402. Roper assimilates typology to one of Dryden's "poetic kingdoms"; Miner treats it as a mode of "metaphorical history."

15. Barbara K. Lewalski, "The Scope and Function of Biblical Allusion in *Absalom and Achitophel*," *English Language Notes*, 3 (1965): 30.

16. See A. B. Chambers, "*Absalom and Achitophel*: Christ and Satan," *Modern Language Notes* 74 (1959): 592–96; Hoffman, *John Dryden's Imagery*, p. 84; Miner, *Dryden's Poetry*, p. 132; Zwicker, *Dryden's Political Poetry*, p. 91.

17. Sanford Budick's suggestive argument, in *Poetry of Civilization*, Chap. 4, that Dryden and Achitophel are rival "artists" and "plotters" accepts too easily, I think, the notion that Dryden's typology is nonetheless free of the abuses so evident in Achitophel's.

18. See Leon M. Guilhamet, "Dryden's Debasement of Scripture in *Absalom and Achitophel*," *Studies in English Literature* 9 (Summer 1969): 395–413.

19. Anthony Collins, *A Discourse of the Grounds and Reasons of the Christian Religion* (1724), pp. 238–39, quoted in Korshin, *Typologies in England*, p. 117.

20. E.g., see Maresca, *Epic to Novel*, pp. 12–14; J. Douglas Canfield, "Anarchy and Style: What Dryden 'Grants' in *Absalom and Achitophel*," *Papers on Language and Literature* 14 (1978): 83–87; Michael J. Conlon, "The Passage on Government in Dryden's *Absalom and Achitophel*," *Journal of English and Germanic Philology* 78 (1979): 17–32. See also King, "*Absalom and Achitophel*," passim.

21. See Louis I. Bredvold, *The Intellectual Milieu of John Dryden: Studies in Some Aspects of Seventeenth-Century Thought* (Ann Arbor: University of Michigan Press, 1934), pp. 147–48; Swedenberg, "Commentary," *Works of John Dryden*, II.271; Dustin Griffin, "Dryden's Charles: The Ending of *Absalom and Achitophel*," *Philological Quarterly* 57 (1978): 360, 372.

22. See Bernard N. Schilling, *Dryden and the Conservative Myth: A Reading of Absalom and Achitophel* (New Haven: Yale University Press, 1961), p. 238; compare George deF. Lord, "*Absalom and Achitophel* and Dryden's Political Cosmos," in *Writers and their Background: John Dryden*, ed. Earl Miner (Athens: Ohio University Press, 1972), pp. 156–90. Schilling associates "the conservative myth" with a belief in the "divinity of order" (see Chap. 1).

23. William Sherlock, Dean of St. Paul's, *The Case of the Allegiance due to Soveraign Powers* (1691), quoted in Gerald M. Straka, *Anglican Reaction to the Revolution of 1688*, State Historical Society of Wisconsin (Madison: University of Wisconsin Press, 1962), p. 71. For a fuller version and documentation of the argument of this paragraph, see Michael McKeon, *The Origins of the English Novel, 1600–1740* (Baltimore: Johns Hopkins University Press, 1987), pp. 42, 178–82.

24. See Michael Seidel, *Satiric Inheritance: Rabelais to Sterne* (Princeton: Princeton University Press, 1979), p. 148.

25. See Canfield's persuasive reading of 1. 795 as a politically significant instance of "grammatical anarchy": "Anarchy and Style," p. 85.

26. On David's tone see the intelligent discussion in Griffin, "Dryden's Charles," p. 363. The fruitful sensitivity of Steven N. Zwicker and Derek Hirst to the task of disclosing the buried *realpolitik* of *Absalom and Achitophel* sometimes desensitizes them to the presence of pragmatic politics very near the surface of the poem: see Zwicker and Hirst, "Rhetoric and Disguise: Political Language and Political Argument in *Absalom and Achitophel*," *Journal of British Studies* 21 (1981): 54 and passim; Zwicker, *Politics and Language in Dryden's Poetry: The Arts of Disguise* (Princeton: Princeton University Press, 1984), pp. 102 and 85–103 passim. Griffin, too, associates the poem with *realpolitik* (371).

27. See especially Seidel, *Satiric Inheritance*, Chap. 5; and Jerome Donnelley, "Fathers and Sons: The Normative Basis of *Absalom and Achitophel*," *Papers on Language and Literature* 17 (1981): 363–80.

28. For a fuller account of these matters, see McKeon, *Origins of the English Novel*, pp. 150–59. For a recognition of the relevance of the laws of estate settlement to Dryden's concerns with "poetic inheritance," see Ricks, "Allusion," p. 221.

29. [John Dryden], *His Majesties Declaration Defended* (1681), p. 13, ed. Godfrey Davies,

Augustan Reprint Society No. 23 (Los Angeles: William Andrews Clark Memorial Library, 1950).

30. For a fuller discussion of this subject, see Michael McKeon, "Politics of Discourses and the Rise of the Aesthetic in Seventeenth-Century England," in *Politics of Discourse: The Literature and History of Seventeenth-Century England*, ed. Kevin Sharpe and Steven N. Zwicker (Berkeley and Los Angeles: University of California Press, 1987), pp. 35–51.

2. THE ROMANCE OF EMPIRE: *Oroonoko* and the Trade in Slaves/ Laura Brown

1. Jean-Paul Sartre, Preface to *The Wretched of the Earth*, by Frantz Fanon, trans. Constance Farrington (New York: Grove Press, 1968), p. 13.

2. For the date of composition, see George Guffey, "Aphra Behn's *Oroonoko*: Occasion and Accomplishment," in *Two English Novelists: Aphra Behn and Anthony Trollope*, by Guffey and Andrew Wright (Los Angeles: William Andrews Clark Memorial Library, UCLA, 1975), pp. 15–16.

3. *The Rover*, ed. Frederick M. Link (Lincoln: University of Nebraska Press, 1967); *Oroonoko; or, The Royal Slave*, introduction by Lore Metzger (New York: Norton, 1973). Subsequent references to *Oroonoko* will be to this edition; page numbers are inserted parenthetically in the text.

4. Maureen Duffy, *The Passionate Shepherdess: Aphra Behn, 1640–89* (London: Cap, 1977); Angeline Goreau, *Reconstructing Aphra: A Social Biography of Aphra Behn* (New York: Dial Press, 1980); George Woodcock, *The Incomparable Aphra* (London: T. V. Boardman, 1948). In addition to these works, booklength treatment of Behn in this century includes a brief biography by Victoria Sackville-West, *Aphra Behn: The Incomparable Astrea* (New York: Viking, 1928); an historical monograph by William J. Cameron, *New Light on Aphra Behn: An Investigation into the Facts and Fictions Surrounding Her Journey to Surinam in 1663 and Her Activities as a Spy in Flanders in 1666* (Auckland: University of Auckland, 1961); and a Twayne study by Frederick M. Link, *Aphra Behn* (New York: Twayne, 1968).

5. Ernest Bernbaum, "Mrs. Behn's Biography, a Fiction," *PMLA* 28 (1913): 432–53, and "Mrs. Behn's *Oroonoko*," *Anniversary Papers by Colleagues and Pupils of George Lyman Kittredge* (Boston: Ginn, 1913). For the refutations of Bernbaum's claim that Behn owes her account of Guiana entirely to George Warren's *Impartial Description of Surinam* (1667), see Harrison Grau Platt, "Astrea and Celadon: An Untouched Portrait of Aphra Behn," *PMLA* 49 (1934): 544–59; and especially Goreau, *Reconstructing Aphra*, pp. 41–69.

6. Judith Gardiner, "Aphra Behn: Sexuality and Self-Respect," *Women's Studies* 7 (1980): 67–78; William Spengemann, "The Earliest American Novel: Aphra Behn's *Oroonoko*," *Nineteenth-Century Fiction* 38 (1984): 384–414; Larry Carver, "Aphra Behn: The Poet's Heart in a Woman's Body," *Papers on Language and Literature* 14 (1978): 414–24.

7. *The Gentleman's Magazine* 19 (Thursday, 16 February 1749): 89–90. See also *The London Magazine* 18 (February 1749): 94. This event is described by David Brion Davis, *The Problem of Slavery in Western Culture* (Ithaca: Cornell University Press, 1966), p. 477; and Wylie Sypher, "The African Prince in London," *Journal of the History of Ideas* 2 (1941), 242, among others. Page numbers for subsequent references to Davis's book and to Sypher's article are inserted parenthetically in the text.

8. Wylie Sypher, *Guinea's Captive Kings: British Anti-Slavery Literature of the XVIIIth Century* (Chapel Hill: University of North Carolina Press, 1942). Page numbers for subsequent references are inserted parenthetically in the text.

9.   E.g. Richard B. Sheridan, *Sugar and Slavery: An Economic History of the British West Indies 1623–1775* (Baltimore: Johns Hopkins University Press, 1974), esp. pp. 249–53.

10.   See Gayatri Chakravorty Spivak, "French Feminism in an International Frame," *Yale French Studies* 62 (1981): 73–87; " 'Draupadi' by Mahasweta Devi," in *Writing and Sexual Difference*, ed. Elizabeth Abel (Chicago: University of Chicago Press, 1982); and "Three Women's Texts and a Critique of Imperialism," *Critical Inquiry* 12 (1985): 243–61.

11.   Edward W. Said, *Orientalism* (New York: Random House, 1979), p. 13.

12.   See Frantz Fanon, *The Wretched of the Earth*, trans. Constance Farrington (New York: Grove Press, 1968).

13.   Abdul JanMohamed, *Manichean Aesthetics: The Politics of Literature in Colonial Africa* (Amherst: University of Massachusetts Press, 1983), and "The Economy of Manichean Allegory: The Function of Racial Difference in Colonialist Literature," *Critical Inquiry* 12 (1985): 59–87; the quoted passage is on p. 63. Page numbers for subsequent references are inserted parenthetically in the text.

14.   Tzvetan Todorov, *The Conquest of America: The Question of the Other* (*La conquête de l'Amérique: La question de l'autre*, Seuil 1982), trans. Richard Howard (New York: Harper and Row, 1984), p. 4. Page numbers for subsequent references are inserted parenthetically in the text.

15.   Homi K. Bhabha, "Signs Taken for Wonders: Questions of Ambivalence and Authority under a Tree Outside Delhi, May 1817," *Critical Inquiry* 12 (1985): 144–65; the quoted passage is on p. 156. Page numbers for subsequent citations are inserted parenthetically in the text. See also Bhabha's "The Other Question—The Stereotype and Colonial Discourse," *Screen* 24 (1983): 18–36.

16.   Stephen Greenblatt, "Invisible Bullets: Renaissance Authority and Its Subversion, *Henry IV* and *Henry V*," in *Political Shakespeare: New Essays in Cultural Materialism*, ed. Jonathan Dollimore and Alan Sinfield (Ithaca: Cornell University Press, 1985), pp. 18–47; the quoted passage is on p. 24.

17.   Johannes Fabian, *Time and the Other: How Anthropology Makes Its Object* (New York: Columbia University Press, 1983). Page numbers for subsequent references are inserted parenthetically in the text.

18.   Eugene M. Waith, *The Herculean Hero in Marlowe, Chapman, Shakespeare and Dryden* (New York: Columbia University Press, 1962).

19.   John Dryden, *All for Love*, ed. David Vieth (Lincoln: University of Nebraska Press, 1972), II.442–46.

20.   Mary Louise Pratt, "Scratches on the Face of the Country; or, What Mr. Barrow Saw in the Land of the Bushmen," *Critical Inquiry* 12 (1985): 119–43; the quoted passage is on p. 121. Page numbers for subsequent references are inserted parenthetically in the text.

21.   In the earlier period, Richard Hakluyt's *Principall Navigations* (1589) and Samuel Purchas's *Purchas his Pilgrimes* (1625); in the later period Sir Hans Sloane, *A Voyage To the Islands Madera, Barbados, Nieves, S. Christophers and Jamaica . . .*, 2 vols. (London, 1707); Churchill's *A Collection of Voyages and Travels* (London, 1732).

22.   See my *Alexander Pope* (Oxford: Basil Blackwell, 1985), Chapter 1.

23.   J. H. Plumb, "The Acceptance of Modernity," in *The Birth of a Consumer Society: The Commercialization of Eighteenth-Century England*, ed. Neil McKendrick, John Brewer, and Plumb (Bloomington: Indiana University Press, 1982), pp. 316–34; the reference to exotic birds appears on pp. 321–22.

24.   Neil McKendrick, "The Commercialization of Fashion," in *The Birth of a Consumer Society*, pp. 34–99, esp. p. 51.

25.   Joseph Addison, *Spectator* 69, 19 May 1711, in *The Spectator Papers*, ed. Donald F. Bond (Oxford: Oxford University Press, 1965), I. 295.

26.   See Goreau, *Reconstructing Aphra*, p. 56.

27.   "Letters to Sir Robert Harley from the Stewards of His Plantations in Surinam. (1663–4)," reprinted in *Colonising Expeditions to the West Indies and Guiana, 1623–1667*, ed. V. T. Harlow (London: Hakluyt Society, 1925), p. 90.

28.   Koromantyn or Coromantijn is a name derived from the Dutch fort at Koromantyn on the Gold Coast; in Suriname it designated slaves from the Fanti, Ashanti, and other interior Gold Coast tribes. For background and statistics on the tribal origins of the Bush Negroes of Guiana, see Richard Price, *The Guiana Maroons: A Historical and Bibliographical Introduction* (Baltimore: Johns Hopkins University Press, 1976), pp. 12–16.

29.   Orlando Patterson, "Slavery and Slave Revolts: A Sociohistorical Analysis of the First Maroon War, 1665–1740," in *Maroon Societies: Rebel Slave Communities in the Americas*, ed. Richard Price, 1973; 2nd ed. (Baltimore: Johns Hopkins University Press, 1979), pp. 246–92, esp. pp. 256–70.

30.   Price, *Guiana Maroons*, p. 23.

31.   Sypher, "The African Prince in London," *Journal of the History of Ideas* 2 (1941): 237–47.

32.   Myra Jehlen, "Archimedes and the Paradox of Feminist Criticism," in *The "Signs" Reader: Women, Gender and Scholarship*, ed. Elizabeth Abel and Emily K. Abel (Chicago: University of Chicago Press, 1983), pp. 69–95.

33.   See the documents under "Guiana" in the Hakluyt Society's *Colonizing Expeditions to the West Indies and Guiana, 1623–1667*, esp. "The Discription of Guyana," "To ye Right Honourable ye Lords of His Majesties most Honorable Privy Councel, The Case of ye Proscripts from Surinam wth all Humility is briefely but most truely stated. 1662," and "Letters to Sir Robert Harley from the Stewards of his Plantations in Surinam. 1663–1664"; V. T. Harlow's detailed introduction to this reprint collection, esp. pp. xxvii–lv and lxvi–xcv; Goreau, *Reconstructing Aphra*, pp. 66–69; and Cyril Hamshere, *The British in the Caribbean* (Cambridge: Harvard University Press, 1972), pp. 64–65.

34.   Goreau, *Reconstructing Aphra*, pp. 66–69.

35.   Richard Baxter, *A Christian Directory, or, a Summ of Practical Theologie, and Cases of Conscience* (London, 1673), pp. 557–60. Cited in Thomas E. Drake, *Quakers and Slavery in America* (New Haven: Yale University Press, 1950), p. 3. Drake dates the section on slavery to 1664–65. Also sympathetic, though less explicitly antislavery, is George Fox, "To Friends Beyond the Sea That Have Blacks and Indian Slaves" (1657), in *A Collection of Many Select and Christian Epistles, Letters and Testimonies* (London, 1698), Epistle No. 153; cited in Drake, *Quakers and Slavery*, p. 5. On Quakers see also Davis, *The Problem of Slavery*, pp. 304–26; Carl and Roberta Bridenbaugh, *No Peace Beyond the Line: The English in the Caribbean 1624–1690* (New York: Oxford University Press, 1972), pp. 357–59; and Herbert Aptheker, "The Quakers and Negro Slavery," *Journal of Negro History* 26 (1940): 331–62. An even earlier, unambiguous antislavery statement from the radical Puritans appears in the Digger pamphlet *Tyranipocrit Discovered* (1649), quoted in *The World Turned Upside Down: Radical Ideas during the English Revolution*, by Christopher Hill (Harmondsworth, Middlesex: Penquin, 1975), p. 337.

36.   See Drake, *Quakers and Slavery*, p. 6 for an account of Fox's recorded sermons at this time. See also Bridenbaugh, *No Peace Beyond the Line*, p. 357.

37. Cited in Drake, *Quakers and Slavery*, pp. 9–10: copy of a letter of William Edmundson, dated at Newport, the 19th 7th Mo 1676, in Records of New England Yearly Meeting, vol. 400, a ms. volume entitled "Antient Epistles, Minutes and Advices, or Discipline." See Drake for other examples of early Quaker statements.

38. Cited in Drake, *Quakers and Slavery*, p. 8; see also Bridenbaugh, *No Peace Beyond the Line*, p. 358.

39. Richard Perrinchiefe, *The Life of Charles I* in *The Workes of King Charles The Martyr* (London, 1662), pp. 92–93, 118.

40. William Dugdale, *A Short View of the Late Troubles in England* (Oxford, 1681), pp. 371–75.

41. Spengemann, "The Earliest American Novel," p. 401.

42. I am indebted to Adela Pinch (Department of English, Cornell University) for my reading of these lines.

43. Bryan Edwards, *The History, Civil and Commercial, of the British Colonies in the West Indies*, 2 vols. (Dublin, 1793), rpt. (New York: Arno Press, 1972), II.59. Most of the detailed accounts of slavery in the West Indies and Guiana date from the later eighteenth century. But there is ample evidence of marronage, rebellion, and judicial torture throughout the West Indies and including Suriname from Behn's period on. Suriname passed out of British hands in 1667, and thus the fullest documentation of the treatment of rebel slaves in that country describes conditions under the Dutch. There is every reason to believe, however, in a continuity from British to Dutch practices historically in Suriname, just as there is every evidence of the same continuity throughout the West Indies and Guiana—British or Dutch—at any given moment in the long century and a half of active slave trade. For further documentation, in addition to the works cited in subsequent notes, see George Warren, *An Impartial Description of Surinam upon the Continent of Guiana in America* (London, 1667); *Historical Essay on the Colony of Surinam*, 1788, trans. Simon Cohen, ed. Jacob R. Marcus and Stanley F. Chyet (New York: Ktav Publishing House, 1974); Price, *Guiana Maroons*; Price, ed., *Maroon Societies*.

44. *London Magazine* 36 (May 1767): 94. Also cited in Davis, *The Problem of Slavery*, p. 477.

45. John Stedman, *Narrative of a Five Years' Expedition Against the Revolted Negroes of Surinam* (1796; rpt. Amherst: University of Massachusetts Press, 1972), p. 382. Stedman's book contains the fullest account available in this period of the punishments for maroons in the West Indies and Guiana. Price finds Stedman's descriptions "to have a solid grounding in fact," and he also shows that Suriname was the most brutal of the major plantation colonies of the New World (*Guiana Maroons*, pp. 25, 9).

3. "WHEN MEN WOMEN TURN": Gender Reversals in Fielding's Plays/ Jill Campbell

1. Henry Fielding, *The Tragedy of Tragedies*, ed. by James T. Hillhouse (New Haven: Yale University Press, 1918), I.iii; pp. 98–100.

2. See Peter Quennell, *Caroline of England* (New York: Viking Press, 1940), pp. 124–28.

3. See the casting information for original productions of both *Tom Thumb* and *The Tragedy of Tragedies* in *The London Stage 1660–1800*, Part III. Vol. 1 *1729–1747*, ed. Arthur H. Scouten (Carbondale, Ill.: Southern Illinois University Press, 1961). The 1730 edition

of *Tom Thumb* lists Miss Jones as the hero, and she seems to have appeared in this role from the play's opening night on 24 April 1730 at the Haymarket through its long run into March 1731. When the play reopened as *The Tragedy of Tragedies* on 24 March 1731, the role of Tom Thumb seems to have been taken for a while by a young male actor, billed as "Young Verhuyck," but the role reverted to female actors such as "Miss S. Rogers, the Lilliputian Lucy," Miss Jones Jr., Miss Brett, and Mrs. Turner in subsequent productions in the early 1730s. Princess Huncamunca was played by the comic actor Harper at Drury Lane in 1732 and 1733, and by Pearce at Goodman's Fields in 1731. Though some cross-gender casting was part of the English farce tradition, *Tom Thumb* is highly atypical of eighteenth-century plays in the amount of cross-gender casting its productions included, particularly in the role of the hero. See Allardyce Nicoll, *A History of Early Eighteenth-Century Drama* (Cambridge: Cambridge University Press, 1925), pp. 49–50; Peter Ackroyd, *Dressing Up—Transvestism and Drag: The History of an Obsession* (New York: Simon and Schuster, 1979), pp. 90–98; and Pat Rogers, "The Breeches Part," in *Sexuality in Eighteenth-Century Britain*, ed. Paul-Gabriel Boucé (Totowa, N.J.: Manchester University Press, 1982), pp. 244–58.

4.   Fielding, *A Proper Reply to a late Scurrilous Libel; intitled, Sedition and Defamation display'd*, published under the pseudonym of Caleb D'Anvers (London: R. Francklin, 1731), p. 6.

5.   Fielding, *Love in Several Masques*, I.ii. Unless otherwise indicated, I quote throughout from the Henley edition of Fielding's works (New York: Croscup & Sterling Co., 1902). I will give citations for the plays by act and scene numbers parenthetically in the text.

6.   Fielding, *The Masquerade*, "by Lemuel Gulliver, Poet Laureat to the King of Lilliput" (London: J. Roberts, 1728), pp. 5–6; copy in Yale's Beinecke Library. I am indebted to Terry Castle, "Eros and Liberty at the English Masquerade, 1710–90," *Eighteenth-Century Studies* 17 (Winter 1983–84): 156–76.

7.   On masculine and feminine domains and the disruption of those distinctions, I am indebted to John Guillory, "Dalila's House: *Samson Agonistes* and the Sexual Division of Labor," in *Rewriting the Renaissance: The Discourses of Sexual Difference in Early Modern Europe*, ed. Margaret W. Ferguson, Maureen Quilligan, and Nancy J. Vickers (Chicago: University of Chicago Press, 1986), pp. 106–22.

8.   In *The Works of Henry Fielding*, ed. James P. Browne, 11 vols. (London: Bickers and Son, 1903), IX.414.

9.   See Jonas Barish, *The Antitheatrical Prejudice* (Berkeley: University of California Press, 1981); and Ackroyd, *Dressing Up*, pp. 92–94.

10.   See Stephen Orgel, *The Illusion of Power: Political Theater in the English Renaissance* (Berkeley: University of California Press, 1975).

11.   See, for example, Stephen Greenblatt, "Murdering Peasants: Status, Genre, and the Representation of Rebellion," *Representations* 1 (1983): 1–29; or "Shakespeare and the Exorcists," in *Shakespeare and the Question of Theory*, ed. Patricia Parker and Geoffrey Hartman (New York: Methuen, 1985), pp. 163–87.

12.   Fielding, *The Historical Register*, ed. William Appleton, Regents Restoration Drama Series (Lincoln: University of Nebraska Press, 1967), II.i.70 and 80. All references to *The Historical Register* cite this edition.

13.   For a brief account of Farinelli's career in London, see the entry under his name in *A Biographical Dictionary of Actors, Actresses, [Etc.] in London, 1660–1800*, Vol. V. By Philip H. Highfill, Jr., Kalman A. Burnim, and Edward A. Langhans (Carbondale: Southern Illinois University Press, 1982), pp. 145–52. Hogarth records Farinelli's wild popularity in

fashionable London society at this time in plate two of "The Rake's Progress," where he incorporates the famous expression of one lady's hyperbolic devotion to him: she cried out from the audience at one performance, "One God, one Farinelli!"

14. See Eric Walter White, *A History of English Opera* (London: Faber & Faber, 1983), pp. 142–45.

15. Fielding includes satire of the castrati in *The Author's Farce, Pasquin, Eurydice,* and *Miss Lucy in Town,* as well as in *The Historical Register.* When I treat the castrato as representative, for Fielding and other satirists, of the absence of phallic power, I refer not to the absence of the penis—for castration removes the testicles, leaving the penis impotent and developmentally infantile—but to the absence of the phallus as a sexually potent penis, with all its figurative implications. Recent research confirms that satires from this period concerning individual castrato singers actually impregnating women are unfounded. See Enid Rhodes Peschel and Richard Peschel, M.D., "Medicine and Music: the Castrati in Opera," *Opera Quarterly* 4 (1986): 21–38.

16. See Eric Rothstein, "The Framework of *Shamela,*" *ELH* 35 (1968): 396.

17. Teresia Constantia Phillips, *The Happy Courtezan: Or, the Prude demolish'd. AN EPISTLE From the Celebrated Mrs. C—P—. TO THE Angelick Signior* Far—n—LL (London: J. Roberts, 1735), pp. 3 and 7. I have used a copy of this pamphlet held by Yale's Beinecke Library.

18. Fielding, *The Author's Farce,* ed. Charles B. Woods (Lincoln: University of Nebraska Press, 1966), Act III, Air VIII, p. 56.

19. See James Ralph (Fielding's partner in *The Champion*), *The Touch-Stone* (1728). Photofacsimile edition, with a preface by Arthur Freeman (New York: Garland Publishing Inc., 1973), p. 12. And see *The Biographical Dictionary of Actors, Actresses, [Etc.],* V.148–50.

20. I have used the copy of this anonymous pamphlet (London: E. Hill, 1736) held at Yale's Beinecke Library.

21. Phillips, *The Happy Courtezan,* p. 13.

22. See P.G.M. Dickson, *The Financial Revolution in England: A Study in the Development of Paper Credit 1688–1756* (New York: St. Martin's Press, 1967).

23. As noted by Appleton in his footnote to these lines (no. 16, p. 25). See also D.R. Reilly, *Portrait Waxes: An Introduction for Collectors* (London: B.T. Batsford Ltd., 1953), pp. 71–80; and Alice K. Early, *English Dolls, Effigies, and Puppets* (London: B.T. Batsford Ltd., 1955).

24. The references to auctions occur in Fielding's *The Temple Beau* (II.xiii), *The Coffee-House Politician* (II.iii), *The Modern Husband* (II.x), *The Universal Gallant* (I.i), *Joseph Andrews* (III.iii), and *Amelia* (VIII.ix). See Jean-Christophe Agnew, *Worlds Apart: The Market and the Theater in Anglo-American Thought, 1550–1750* (New York: Cambridge University Press, 1986), for an extended discussion of the relations between the market and the theater in this period.

25. Ralph Cassady, Jr., *Auctions and Auctioneering* (Berkeley: University of California Press, 1967), pp. 29–30.

26. Peter Ash, "The First Auctioneer: Origin of Sales by Auction of Real Property," *Estates Gazette* (Centenary Supplement), 1958, pp. 33–37. Quoted in Cassady, *Auctions,* pp. 29–33.

27. See Neil McKendrick, John Brewer, and J.H. Plumb, *The Birth of a Consumer Society: The Commercialization of 18th Century England* (Bloomington: Indiana University Press, 1982).

28. Eric Partridge's *Dictionary of Slang and Unconventional English* (New York: The Mac-

millan Co., 1961) confirms that "cock" was used to mean penis in slang long before 1737 (p. 164).

29. Henley edition of Fielding's works (New York: Croscup & Sterling Co., 1902), XII.337–39.

30. See Laura Brown, *Alexander Pope* (New York: Basil Blackwell, 1985), p. 103.

31. See Brown, *Alexander Pope*, p. 104. As early as Ian Watt's groundbreaking *The Rise of the Novel* (Berkeley: University of California Press, 1957), critics have recognized the importance of the new exclusion of women from the means of production for the treatment of women in eighteenth-century literature. Ellen Pollak has explored this subject in depth in her *The Poetics of Sexual Myth: Gender and Ideology in the Verse of Swift and Pope* (Chicago: University of Chicago Press, 1985). See also McKendrick et al., *The Birth of a Consumer Society*, on the special association of women with the period's new consumerism.

32. See Chapter 2, "The Commercialization of Fashion," pp. 34–99, in *The Birth of a Consumer Society*.

33. Quoted in Wilbur L. Cross, *The History of Henry Fielding* (New Haven: Yale University Press, 1918), I.218–19.

34. On Hervey's authorship, see Charles B. Wood's "Captain B—'s Play," *Harvard Studies and Notes in Philology and Literature* 15 (1933): 243–55.

35. This pamphlet is available as reprinted in Fielding, *The Female Husband and Other Writings*, ed. Claude E. Jones, English Reprints Series, No. 17 (Liverpool: Liverpool University Press, 1960). I will give further citations of *The Female Husband* by page number in this edition, parenthetically in the text.

36. See Sheridan Baker, "Henry Fielding's *The Female Husband*: Fact and Fiction," *PMLA* 74 (1959): 213–24; and Terry Castle, "Matters Not Fit to be Mentioned: Fielding's *The Female Husband*," *ELH* 49 (1982): 602–22.

37. For example, Fielding invents escapades in the assumed identity of a male doctor for Mary Hamilton which seem to have no basis in her life but which do appear among the early adventures of Charlotte Charke. Fielding may have known of Charke's adventures even before the publication of her memoirs from his acquaintance with her at the Haymarket. See *A Narrative of the Life of Mrs. Charlotte Charke* (2d ed.), introduction by Leonard R.N. Ashley (Gainesville, Fla.: Scholars' Facsimiles & Reprints, 1969).

38. See Lawrence Stone, *The Family, Sex, and Marriage in England 1500–1800*, abridged paperback edition (New York: Harper & Row, 1979), pp. 221–22; and Ian Watt, *The Rise of the Novel*, pp. 141–42.

39. 12-20-39, collected in *The Champion* (London: H. Chapelle, 1743), I:113. This essay may be Ralph's rather than Fielding's.

4. REPRESENTING AN UNDER CLASS: Servants and Proletarians in Fielding and Smollett/John Richetti

1. Bruce Robbins, *The Servant's Hand: English Fiction From Below* (New York: Columbia University Press, 1986), p. 6.

2. Robbins, *The Servant's Hand*, p. 8.

3. W.A. Speck, *Society and Literature in England, 1700–60* (Atlantic Highlands, N.J.: Humanities Press, 1984), p. 76.

4. See, especially, Douglas Hay, Peter Linebaugh, John G. Rule, E. P. Thompson, and

Cal Winslow, *Albion's Fatal Tree: Crime and Society in Eighteenth-Century England* (New York: Pantheon Books, 1975); and E. P. Thompson, *Whigs and Hunters: The Origins of the Black Act* (New York: Pantheon Books, 1975).

5.   E. P. Thompson, "Eighteenth-Century English Society: Class Struggle Without Class?" *Social History* 3 (May 1978): 139.

6.   Thompson, "Eighteenth-Century English Society," pp. 144, 151. On this issue, see also Thompson's "Patrician Society, Plebian Culture," *Journal of Social History* 7 (1974): 382–405.

7.   Thompson, *Whigs and Hunters*, pp. 254–55.

8.   Henry Fielding, *Joseph Andrews*, ed. Martin Battestin (Middletown, Conn.: Wesleyan University Press, 1976), IV.v.290. Subsequent references are to this edition; page numbers will be cited in the text.

9.   Henry Fielding, *The History of Tom Jones*, ed. Martin Battestin (Middletown, Conn.: Wesleyan University Press, 1975), IV.7.176–77. All subsequent references in the text are to this edition.

10.   Robert W. Malcolmson, *Life and Labour in England 1700–1780* (New York: St. Martin's Press, 1981), p. 105.

11.   Malcolmson, *Life and Labour in England*, p. 105.

12.   Pierre Macherey, *A Theory of Literary Production*, trans. Geoffrey Wall (London: Routledge & Kegan Paul, 1978), p. 128.

13.   Terry Eagleton, *Criticism and Ideology: A Study in Marxist Literary Theory* (London: New Left Books, 1976), p. 73.

14.   Fredric Jameson, *The Political Unconscious: Narrative as a Socially Symbolic Act* (Ithaca: Cornell University Press, 1981), p. 20.

15.   Ronald Paulson, *Popular and Polite Art in the Age of Fielding and Hogarth* (Notre Dame: University of Notre Dame Press, 1979), p. 186.

16.   Robert Alter, *Fielding and the Nature of the Novel* (Cambridge: Harvard University Press, 1968), p. 33.

17.   *Proposal for Making an Effective Provision for the Poor*, in *The Complete Works of Henry Fielding*, ed. William E. Henley (New York: Barnes and Noble, 1967), XIII.141–42.

18.   Tobias Smollett, *The Expedition of Humphry Clinker* (Harmondsworth: Penguin Books, 1967), p. 112. Subsequent references will be cited in the text.

5.   THE RESIGNATION OF MARY COLLIER: Some Problems in Feminist Literary History/Donna Landry

1.   Johanna Brenner and Maria Ramas, "Rethinking Women's Oppression," *New Left Review* 144 (March/April 1984): 47, n. 37. This distinction holds so far as landed property or capital is concerned. But there remains a sense in which male control of property *in women* links the working class with the feudal and bourgeois social formations from which it can otherwise be distinguished. As Keith Thomas puts it, "Fundamentally, female chastity has been seen as a matter of property; not, however, the property of legitimate heirs, but the property of men in women," "The Double Standard," *Journal of the History of Ideas* 20 (1959): 209–10.

2.   These are the dates in the *Dictionary of National Biography*, LXIII, pp. 310–11 and followed by most scholars since. J.M.S. Tompkins, however, in *The Polite Marriage, etc.*:

Eighteenth-century Essays (Cambridge: Cambridge University Press, 1938), p. 60, gives 1752 as Yearsley's birthdate, based on parish records. My correspondence with the Bristol Record Office has unearthed yet another birthdate: 1753, based on a baptismal entry in the Clifton Parish Register.

3.   Letter from More to Elizabeth Robinson Montagu, August 27, 1784; Huntington Library manuscript MO 3986, 2. Letters from this correspondence in which Yearsley figures, MO 3986-3992, have been published in *The Female Spectator: English Women Writers Before 1800*, ed. Mary R. Mahl and Helene Koon (Bloomington and Old Westbury, L.I.: Indiana University Press and The Feminist Press, 1977), pp. 277–86. For a good recent study of Yearsley see Moira Ferguson, "Resistance and Power in the Life and Writings of Ann Yearsley," *The Eighteenth Century: Theory and Interpretation* 27:3 (Fall 1986): 247–68.

4.   In "Liberating the subject? Autobiography and 'women's history': a reading of *The Diaries of Hannah Cullwick*," a paper presented at the conference on "Autobiographies, Biographies, and Life Histories of Women: Interdisciplinary Perspectives" at the University of Minnesota, March, 1986, Julia Swindells writes, "I presuppose in my paper that we see our study of the life stories of women as part of a project to liberate ourselves as socialist feminist subjects. I show, however that this cannot be done simply by liberating our sisters from history—either by finding 'authentic' voices where these cannot exist, or by deciding, in our eagerness to liberate their texts from silence, that these sisters led liberated lives," Abstract. I wish to thank Winnie Woodhull for this reference. See also Swindell's *Victorian Writing and Working Women: The Other Side of Silence* (Minneapolis: University of Minnesota Press, 1986).

5.   See More's "A Prefatory Letter to Mrs. Montagu. By a Friend," in Yearsley's *Poems, On Several Occasions* (London: T. Cadell, 1785), pp. iii–xii. More also writes to Montagu, "All I see of her, raises my opinion of her genius. . . . Confess, dear Madam, that you and I know many a head competently stored with Greek and Latin which cou'd not have produced better Verses. I never met with an Ear more nicely tuned" (Huntington Library manuscript MO 3988, 1,4).

6.   See Robert Southey, *Attempts In Verse, By John Jones, An Old Servant: With Some Account of the Writer, Written by Himself: And An Introductory Essay on the Lives of Our Uneducated Poets* (London: John Murray, 1831), p. 134.

7.   Through the eighteenth century, women remained less literate than men. See Margaret Spufford, *Small Books and Pleasant Histories: Popular Fiction and Its Readership in Seventeenth-Century England* (Athens: University of Georgia Press, 1981), p. 34; and David Cressy, *Literacy and the Social Order: Reading and Writing in Tudor and Stuart England* (Cambridge: Cambridge University Press, 1980), pp. 128, 145–46. Since more people could read than write, women may well have figured significantly in a reading public, "the true size of which we shall never be able to assess," Spufford, *Small Books*, p. 36.

8.   More, "Prefatory Letter," pp. iv, viii.

9.   As E.P. Thompson argues, "The remedies proposed might differ; but the impulse behind Colquhoun, with his advocacy of more effective police, Hannah More, with her halfpenny tracts and Sunday Schools, the Methodists with their renewed emphasis upon order and submissiveness, Bishop Barrington's more humane Society for Bettering the Conditions of the Poor, and William Wilberforce and Dr. John Bowdler, with their Society for the Suppression of Vice and Encouragement of Religion, was much the same. The message to be given to the labouring poor was simple, and was summarized by Burke in the famine year of 1795: 'Patience, labour, sobriety, frugality, and religion, should be recommended to them; all the rest is downright fraud'," *The Making of the English Working Class* (London: Gollancz, 1980), pp. 60–61.

10.   So Angela Carter describes the "liberal lie in action" in *The Sadeian Woman: An Exercise in Cultural History* (London: Virago, 1979), p. 55.

11.   See Roger Lonsdale's *The New Oxford Book of Eighteenth-Century Verse* (Oxford and New York: Oxford University Press, 1984), pp. 325–26; and Moira Ferguson's Augustan Reprint 230, *The Thresher's Labour (Stephen Duck) and The Woman's Labour (Mary Collier)* (Los Angeles: William Andrews Clark Memorial Library, 1985), and her *First Feminists: British Women Writers 1578–1799* (Bloomington and Old Westbury, L.I.: Indiana University Press and The Feminist Press, 1985), pp. 257–65. Sheila Rowbotham includes short excerpts from *The Woman's Labour* in *Hidden From History: Rediscovering Women in History From the 17th Century to the Present* (New York: Pantheon, 1974), pp. 25–26.

12.   For working class here read those historical continuities between the experience of the eighteenth-century laboring poor, working for wages, and the experience of their descendants during industrialization, as explored by E. P. Thompson and other social historians. The category of class in recent social history has increasingly become a discursive construct, moving on from Thompson to account for the subject in history as a site of ideological conflict. This maneuver opens up possibilities of analyzing class in relation to gender, race, and other categories of cultural difference understood as discursive and social practices. See particularly the ground-breaking work of Gareth Stedman Jones, *Languages of Class: Studies in English Working Class History 1832–1982* (Cambridge: Cambridge University Press, 1983); and Sally Alexander, "Women, Class and Sexual Differences in the 1830's and 1840's: Some Reflections on the Writing of a Feminist History," *History Workshop Journal* 17 (Spring 1984): 125–49.

13.   Collier, *The Woman's Labour: An Epistle To Mr. Stephen Duck: In Answer to his late Poem, called The Thresher's Labour. To which are added, The Three Wise Sentences, Taken From The First Book of Esdras, Ch. III. and IV* (London: Printed for the Author; and Sold by J. Roberts, 1739), lines 11–12. I have quoted throughout from the British Library copy (shelf-mark 1346.f.17). Subsequent references will appear in the text.

14.   "Piety, Purity, Peace, and an old Maid" are the concluding words of Collier's brief autobiography; see "Some Remarks of the Author's Life drawn by herself," in *Poems, on Several Occasions* (Title-page missing; spine reads: Winchester, 1762), p. v. (British Library shelfmark 11632.f.12.) Hereafter abbreviated as *Poems*. Subsequent references to "Some Remarks" will appear in the text. On the ten percent of the population who remained single, see Keith Wrightson, *English Society 1580–1680* (London: Hutchinson, 1982), pp. 67–68; and Lawrence Stone, *The Family, Sex, and Marriage in England 1500–1800* (London: Weidenfeld and Nicolson, 1977), p. 652. Single women and widows were the groups most likely to require relief from their parishes. According to Ivy Pinchbeck, "The anxiety shown in some districts [including Sussex, where Collier lived for a number of years] to get single women employed, actually led to the pauperizing of domestic service," *Women Workers and the Industrial Revolution 1750–1850* (first pub. 1930; new ed. London: Virago, 1981), p. 80. See also Pinchbeck, pp. 79–86, and Bridget Hill, ed., *Eighteenth-Century Women: An Anthology* (London: Allen and Unwin, 1984), pp. 123–34, 156–72.

15.   Huntington Library manuscript MO 3986, 2.

16.   In "The Sexual Division of Labour in Feudal England," *New Left Review* 113–114 (January/April 1979): 147–68, Christopher Middleton has argued, persuasively, that the subordination of women in social formations like that of feudal England did not depend on their biological capacity to reproduce; it was "rather the direct, personal servicing of men by women that was the fulcrum of domestic labour—both in and out of marriage," p. 164. More recently, he has tried to link these insights with evidence from the early modern period in "Women's Labour and the Transition to Pre-Industrial Capitalism," in

Women and Work in Pre-Industrial England, ed. Lindsey Charles and Lorna Duffin (London: Croom Helm, 1985), pp. 181–206.

17.   Collier, *Poems*, pp. 30–32. Subsequent references, by line number, will appear in the text.

18.   See Martha Vicinus, *The Industrial Muse: A Study of Nineteenth-Century British Working-Class Literature* (New York: Barnes and Noble, 1974), for a discussion of how working-class literature is excluded from scholarly "canons of taste," pp. 1–2, 140–84.

19.   For these and related debates, see Michèle Barrett, "Feminism and the Definition of Cultural Politics," in *Feminism, Culture and Politics*, ed. Rosalind Brunt and Caroline Rowan (London: Lawrence and Wishart, 1982), pp. 37–58; Lillian S. Robinson, "Treason Our Text: Feminist Challenges to the Literary Canon," pp. 105–21, and Rosalind Coward, "Are Women's Novels Feminist Novels?" pp. 225–39, in *The New Feminist Criticism*, ed. Elaine Showalter (New York: Pantheon, 1985); and Toril Moi, *Sexual/Textual Politics: Feminist Literary Theory* (London and New York: Methuen, 1985).

20.   Relevant texts include: *Common Sense: Or, The Englishman's Journal* 135 (September 1 1739); "A new Method for making Women as useful and as capable of maintaining themselves, as the Men are; and consequently preventing their becoming Old Maids, or taking ill Courses. By a Lady," in *The Gentleman's Magazine* 9 (October 1739): 525–26; and the "Sophia" pamphlets, of disputed authorship, esp. *Woman Not Inferior to Man: Or, A short and modest Vindication of the natural Right of the Fair-Sex to a perfect Equality of Power, Dignity, and Esteem, with the Men* (1739), collected and republished with two others under the title *Beauty's Triumph: Or, The Superiority of the Fair Sex invincibly proved* in 1751. Ferguson provides excerpts from the first and third pamphlets in *First Feminists*, pp. 266–83. See G.M. MacLean's introduction to *The Woman As Good as the Man* (1677), an edition of the English translation of Poullain de la Barre's *De L'égalité des deux sexes* (Detroit: Wayne State University Press, forthcoming), for a useful discussion of the "Sophia" controversy. If we go back some months to January 24, 1738, we can include in this debate Lady Mary Wortley Montagu's *The Nonsense of Common Sense* 6, reprinted in her *Essays and Poems and Simplicity, a Comedy*, ed. Robert Halsband and Isobel Grundy (Oxford: Clarendon Press, 1977), pp. 130–34.

21.   What is most remarkable is how little rural women's wages seem to have changed between 1739 and the nineteenth century, given the rise in prices; see Pinchbeck, *Women Workers*, pp. 16, 19, 24, 53–66, 94–99. As late as 1843, in Wiltshire, Dorset, Devon, and Somerset, the average women's wage remained "six-pence or eight-pence" a day in winter, p. 95.

22.   Pinchbeck describes this differential in some detail, especially in relation to amendments in the Poor Laws, without pronouncing on its psychological or political effects, in *Women Workers*, pp. 84–102. More recent feminist accounts, making use of twentieth- as well as nineteenth-century data, admit certain social, political, and psychosexual effects of this gender-based competition into their analyses, but do not necessarily agree about their specificity. See, for example, Michèle Barrett, *Women's Oppression Today: Problems in Marxist Feminist Analysis* (London: Verso, 1980), pp. 152–86; Brenner and Ramas, "Rethinking Women's Oppression," p. 47; Barrett's reply in *New Left Review* 146 (July/August 1984): 123–28; Angela Weir and Elizabeth Wilson, "The British Women's Movement," *New Left Review* 148 (November/December 1984): 95.

23.   Stephen Duck, *The Thresher's Labour*, in the first authorized edition of *Poems On Several Occasions* (London: Printed for the Author, 1736), lines 110–19. Subsequent references will appear in the text. On the sexual division of labor in agricultural work (and the symbolically masculine significance of the scythe), see Michael Roberts, "Sickles and

Scythes: Women's Work and Men's Work at Harvest Time," *History Workshop Journal* 7 (Spring 1979): 3–28; and his " 'Words They Are Women, And Deeds They Are Men': Images of Work and Gender in Early Modern England," in Charles and Duffin, *Women and Work in Pre-Industrial England*, pp. 122–80.

24.   See Raymond Williams, *The Country and the City* (New York: Oxford University Press, 1973), pp. 88–89.

25.   Not that it had ever really "been" there in the first place, as James Turner has amply demonstrated in *The Politics of Landscape: Rural Scenery and Society in English Poetry 1630–1660* (Oxford: Basil Blackwell, 1979); see esp. his chapter on "The Vanishing Swain," pp. 173–85.

26.   In *The Literature of Labour: Two Hundred Years of Working-Class Writing* (New York: St. Martin's Press, 1985), H. Gustav Klaus suggests that in addressing Duck, "who quite obviously did not include the female agricultural workers in his 'we', Collier tentatively approaches another form of solidarity: a sisterhood of the poor, of working women," p. 15. In "Stephen Duck and Mary Collier: Plebejische Kontro-Verse bei Frauenarbeit vor 250 Jahren," *Gulliver* 10 (1981): 121, Klaus claims that Collier's use of "we" is inconsistent, but it seems to me that in every case she uses it to refer quite precisely to working-class women; I am indebted to Jerold C. Frakes for help with translation here.

27.   The mocking intensity with which Duck is quoted here is emphasized through italics in the 1762 version of *The Woman's Labour* in Collier's *Poems*: "Or how should *Cocks in equal Rows appear?*"

28.   Similarly, Yearsley closes the "Prologue" to *Earl Goodwin, An Historical Play* (London: G.G.J. and J. Robinson, 1791) with a reminder of her former, nonliterary source of income, to which she can return if the play fails: "That voice, ye patrons of the Muse, is yours/But if e'en there, her airy visions fail,/Her last best refuge is her—milking pail."

29.   See, for example, the selections from Claudine Herrmann's *Les voleuses de langue* (Paris: des femmes, 1976); and Hélène Cixous's "The Laugh of the Medusa," in *New French Feminisms: An Anthology*, ed. Elaine Marks and Isabelle de Courtivron (New York: Schocken, 1981), pp. 87–89, 168–73, 245–64. The interest in *l'écriture féminine* represents, of course, only one strand of a diverse movement. Materialist feminism in France, from Simone de Beauvoir and the now defunct journal *Questions féministes* to Christine Delphy, though not so well known in America, may prove a more durable project than the psychoanalytical/literary critical focus of *l'écriture féminine*. I thank Marie-Florine Bruneau for helping me to clarify this point.

30.   See Julia Kristeva's *Desire in Language: A Semiotic Approach to Literature and Art*, ed. Leon S. Roudiez (New York: Columbia University Press, 1980), p. 15 and *passim*. The radically subversive possibilities of the "dialogic" mode have entered critical discourse primarily by way of Mikhail Bakhtin's *The Dialogic Imagination*, trans. Caryl Emerson and Michael Holquist (Austin: University of Texas Press, 1981).

31.   This concept of "defamiliarization" or *ostraneniye* ("making strange") is elaborated by the Russian formalist Victor Shklovsky in "Art as Technique," in *Russian Formalist Criticism: Four Essays*, trans. Lee T. Lemon and Marion J. Reis (Lincoln and London: University of Nebraska Press, 1965), pp. 3–24.

32.   Collier's reliance here upon the racist trope of the oppressive "Otherness" of the Turks marks another limit to the radical potential of her text. This "Turkish prejudice" may be read as an instance of chauvinism common to both polite and plebeian English culture in the period, a chauvinism that relies heavily upon making invidious comparisons with a caricature "Ottoman" or "Mahometan" Other.

33. The feminist critique of the politics of "the authentic voice" is indebted to the work of Michel Foucault, especially the first volume of *The History of Sexuality*, trans. Robert Hurley (New York: Pantheon, 1978). The most useful examples of this critique to date include Mary Lydon, "Foucault and Feminism: A Romance of Many Dimensions," in *Humanities in Society* 5 (1982): 245–56; and Winifred Woodhull, "Michel Foucault and the Women's Movement: The Politics of 'Speaking Out' and the Dangers of Giving In," paper presented at the Modern Language Association in Los Angeles, 1982 (forthcoming). In a culture in which sexuality, far from being silenced, has been enjoined to speak, to speak "as a woman" is to risk playing into the very same oppressive forces of power one wishes to challenge.

34. A point made by Klaus, *The Literature of Labour*, p. 14. See, for example, Louise A. Tilly and Joan W. Scott, *Women, Work, and Family* (New York: Holt, Rinehart, Winston, 1978).

35. See Pinchbeck, *Women Workers*, pp. 56–57. Interestingly, regarding the "divided care" necessitated by bringing infants to the fields, Pinchbeck cites a Sussex example: According to a Poor Law Commissioners' report of 1835, "the custom of the mother of a family carrying her infant with her in its cradle into the field, rather than lose the opportunity of adding her earnings to the general stock, though partially practiced before, is becoming very much more general now," p. 85.

36. See Pinchbeck, *Women Workers*, pp. 19–26.

37. As Barry Reay argues, "Much of women's labour was domestic, and collective, so presumably the entry points for this almost invisible cultural world are the places where, or the times when, women gathered," "Introduction" to *Popular Culture in Seventeenth-Century England* (New York: St. Martin's Press, 1985), p. 12. See also Peter Burke, *Popular Culture*, p. 50; and Alice Clark, *Working Life of Women in the Seventeenth Century* (first pub. 1919; new ed. London: Routledge & Kegan Paul, 1982), pp. xxxiv ("Introduction" by Miranda Chaytor and Jane Lewis), p. 51.

38. The contrast with Thomson seems obligatory; Klaus contrasts Duck and Thomson in *The Literature of Labour*, p. 13. Quotations from Thomson's *The Seasons* are taken from J. Logie Robertson's edition (London: Oxford University Press, 1908). Subsequent references appear in the text.

39. See Roland Barthes, "Operation Margarine," in *Mythologies*, trans. Annette Lavers (New York: Hill and Wang, 1972), pp. 41–42.

40. Collier, *The Poems of Mary Collier, the Washer-woman of Petersfield; To which is prefixed her Life, Drawn By Herself. A New Edition* (Petersfield: W. Minchin, n.d.), "Advertisement," p. iii. (British Library shelfmark 11658.de.53.)

41. As in Collier, *Poems, The Happy Husband, and the Old Batchelor. A Dialogue*, pp. 33–40; "A Gentleman's Request to the Author on Reading The Happy Husband and the Old Batchelor," p. 41; and *Spectator Vol. the Fifth. Numb. 375. Versified*, pp. 54–59.

42. As in Collier, *Poems*, "On The Marriage of George the Third, Wrote in the Seventy-Second year of her Age," pp. 60–62.

43. As in Collier, *Poems, The First and Second Chapters of the First Book of Samuel Versified*, pp. 42–49.

44. Appended to the third edition of Collier, *The Woman's Labour and The Three Wise Sentences* (London: Printed for the Author; and Sold by J. Roberts, 1740), as the final page—p. 32. (British Library shelfmark 1509/4592.) Also reprinted, as an appendage to the "Advertisement To The First Edition" in *The Poems of Mary Collier. . . . A New Edition*, p. vi.

45. Collier, *The Woman's Labour and The Three Wise Sentences*, pp. 18–32, lines 17–18. Subsequent references by line number appear in the text.

46. Thompson, *The Making of the English Working Class*, pp. 419–27.

6. ON THE USE OF CONTRADICTION: Economics and Morality in the Eighteenth-Century Long Poem/John Barrell and Harriet Guest

1. Samuel Johnson, *The Lives of the Poets* (London: Oxford University Press, 1964), II.437, 359. Subsequent references will be cited parenthetically in the text as *Lives*.

2. John Scott, *Critical Essays on Some of the Poems by Several English Poets* (London, 1785), p. 251.

3. Edward Young, *Night-Thoughts*, Preface. The paragraph from which this quotation is taken was originally part of the preface to the fourth "Night"; it became the preface to the poem as a whole at the suggestion of Samuel Richardson: see *The Correspondence of Edward Young*, ed. Henry Pettit (Oxford: Oxford University Press, 1971), p. 346.

4. *The Critical Works of John Dennis*, ed. Edward Niles Hooker (Baltimore: Johns Hopkins University Press, 1939–43), I (1939), 396–419.

5. *Of the Use of Riches, an Epistle to the Right Honourable Allen Lord Bathurst* (1732/33). Quotation is from the text in Alexander Pope, *Epistles to Several Persons (Moral Essays)*, ed. F. W. Bateson, 2nd ed. (London: Methuen, 1961).

6. Antonio Gramsci, *Selections from the Prison Notebooks*, ed. and trans. Quintin Hoare and Geoffrey Nowell Smith (London: Lawrence and Wishart, 1971), pp. 404–07.

7. David Lloyd, " 'Pap for the Dispossessed': Seamus Heaney and the Poetics of Identity," *boundary 2*, 13 (1985) p. 341 n. 10. See Gramsci, *Prison Notebooks*, on ideology in its "highest sense," p. 328; on "knotting," p. 241; and on the ideological convenience of contradiction, p. 405.

8. See *The Works of Alexander Pope*, ed. Whitwell Elwin and William J. Courthope (London: John Murray, 1881), III.121–22. It has of course been denied that the passage we are about to discuss contradicts itself—most notably, by Earl Wasserman, *Pope's "Epistle to Bathurst"* (Baltimore: Johns Hopkins University Press, 1960), pp. 29–40. Wasserman's argument is too detailed to be discussed in this essay. It may suffice to say that it seems to us that he does not allow sufficient weight to lines 161–66, and that finally his claim that the passage develops a consistent argument can be reduced to a claim that lines 155–78 are written within a discourse different from that employed in the paragraphs thereafter, and they *therefore* should not be regarded as inconsistent—whereas to us it is that very discursive shift which produces the contradiction that Courthope observed. Laura Brown, *Alexander Pope* (Oxford: Basil Blackwell, 1985), pp. 108–17, also sees a contradiction in this passage. We differ from her largely in analyzing this in terms of a discursive disjunction.

9. Warburton, quoted in *The Works of Alexander Pope, esq.*, ed. William Lisle Bowles (London: J. Johnson et al., 1806), III.297. Subsequently cited parenthetically in the text as "Bowles."

10. Anon., *The Art of Poetry on a New Plan* (London: J. Newbery, 1762), I.116.

11. *Art of Poetry*, I.137.

12. William Bowyer's note to his translation of Joseph Trapp, *Lectures on Poetry* (London, 1742), p. 189. The Lectures were first published in Latin, 1711–19.

13.   "An Essay on Virgil's Georgics," in *The Works of the Right Honourable Joseph Addison, Esq.* (London, 1721), I.249–50, 254.

14.   "De Poesi Didactica," a lecture delivered at Oxford in 1711, trans. in Richard Tickell, *Thomas Tickell and the Eighteenth-Century Poets* (London: Constable, 1931), pp. 202–03, 206–07.

15.   Trapp, *Lectures*, pp. 190, 192, 196, 201.

16.   Joseph Warton, "Reflections on Didactic Poetry," in *The Works of Virgil*, ed. Warton, 3rd ed. (London, 1778), I.156–235.

17.   William Enfield, *The Speaker* (London, 1797), p. 1.

18.   See James Thomson, *The Seasons*, ed. James Sambrook (Oxford: Oxford University Press, 1981), pp. 2–3 and 309.

19.   *The Seasons* (London, 1730), "Spring," lines 326–28, 785–95; Sambrook, *The Seasons*, p. 3.

20.   John Aikin, "An Essay on the Plan and Character of Thomson's Seasons," in *The Seasons, By James Thomson* (New York: George F. Hopkins, 1802), p. xliv. For eighteenth-century discussions of the unity of *The Seasons*, see Ralph Cohen, *The Art of Discrimination: Thomson's "The Seasons" and the Language of Criticism* (London: Routledge & Kegan Paul, 1964), esp. pp. 84–130.

21.   *The Works of Addison*, I.250–52.

22.   Warton, *Virgil*, I. 399, 401, 429.

23.   *Art of Poetry*, I.177, 233; and see Trapp, *Lectures*, p. 196.

24.   *Thomas Tickell*, pp. 205, 207–08.

25.   Edward Young, *Conjectures on Original Composition* (London, 1759), p. 38; Johnson, *Lives*, II.437.

26.   Quotations from *Night-Thoughts* are taken from the eighth ed. (London, 1749). Line numbers will be cited in the text.

27.   But to put it like this is to put it too simply. Within Book VIII as a whole, the civic discourse seems to function as an intrusion upon, and to emerge as digression from, what we call the "sublimated" or "recuperated" economic discourse. Within the digression on the Good Man, however, their positions appear to be reversed.

28.   See John Oldmixon, *An Essay on Critisicm* (London, 1728), pp. 27–40.

29.   See Pope, *Peri Bathous* (London, 1727), *passim*.

30.   Warton, *Virgil*, I, p. 401; *Art of Poetry*, I, p. 233; Jean-Baptiste Du Bos, *Réflexions critiques sur la poësie et sur la peinture* (Paris, edition of 1746), I.64.

31.   *Art of Poetry*, I.233.

32.   *The Diary and Letters of Madame D'Arblay, Edited by her Niece, Charlotte Barrett* (new ed., revised, London: no date), III.165.

33.   See *Goldsmith: The Critical Heritage*, ed. G. S. Rousseau (London and Boston: Routledge & Kegan Paul, 1974), pp. 76–87.

34.   See, for example, *The Beauties of the Poets*, ed. Thomas Janes, 6th ed. (London, 1799), p. 73; Enfield, *The Speaker*, p. 252.

35.   See, for example, Enfield, *The Speaker*, p. 254.

36.   See, for example, John Adams, ed., *The English Parnassus* (London, 1789), pp. 30–32.

37. *The Poetical Works of William Wordsworth*, ed. Thomas Hutchinson and Ernest de Selincourt (Oxford: Oxford University Press), p. 747.

38. We are grateful for the help of Peter De Bolla, who discussed with us the topic of this section of the essay, and made available to us his work in progress, "The Discourse of the Sublime."

39. Isaac Watts, *The Improvement of the Mind* (London, 1741), Chap. 4, section 8.

7. HETEROCLITES: The Gender of Character in the Scandalous Memoirs/Felicity Nussbaum

1. John Morris, *Versions of the Self: Studies in English Autobiography from John Bunyan to John Stuart Mill* (New York: Basic Books, 1966), p. 7; and Wayne Shumaker, *English Autobiography: Its Emergence, Materials, and Form* (Berkeley and Los Angeles: University of California Press, 1954), pp. 83, 23–24. For brief treatments of the scandalous memoirists, see John O. Lyons, *The Invention of the Self: the Hinge of Consciousness in the Eighteenth Century* (Carbondale: Southern Illinois University Press, 1978); and Donald A. Stauffer, *The Art of Biography in Eighteenth Century England* (Princeton: Princeton University Press, 1941). John Richetti, *Popular Fiction Before Richardson: Narrative Patterns 1700–1739* (Oxford: Clarendon Press, 1969); Patricia Meyer Spacks, *Imagining A Self: Autobiography and Novel in Eighteenth-Century England* (Cambridge: Harvard University Press, 1976); and Susan Staves, "British Seduced Maidens," *Eighteenth-Century Studies* 14 (1980): 109–34, provide critiques of the fictional memoirs. Only Spacks treats the nonfictional texts in any detail.

2. I have dealt with some of these issues in "Toward Conceptualizing Diary," *Studies in Autobiography*, ed. James Olney (Oxford and New York: Oxford University Press, forthcoming). For discussion of the "subject" see especially Mieke Bal, "The Rhetoric of Subjectivity," *Poetics Today* 5 (1984): 337–76; and Julian Henriques et al., *Changing the Subject: Psychology, Social Regulation, and Subjectivity* (London and New York: Methuen, 1984).

3. The philosophical controversies surrounding "identity" in the period are addressed in Christopher Fox's "Locke and the Scriblerians: The Discussion of Identity in Early Eighteenth-Century England," *Eighteenth-Century Studies* 16 (1982): 1–25. That women's autobiographical writing is less linear and more irregular than men's has been frequently reiterated. See Estelle C. Jelinek, *Women's Autobiography: Essays in Criticism* (Bloomington: Indiana University Press, 1980).

4. J. W. Smeed, *The Theophrastan 'Character': The History of a Literary Genre* (Oxford and New York: Clarendon Press, 1985), p. 54.

5. Henry Gally's essay is cited in Smeed, *The Theophrastan 'Character'*, pp. 263–64.

6. See, for example, A. J. Greimas and J. Courtés, *Semiotics and Language: An Analytical Dictionary*, trans. Larry Crist et al. (Bloomington: Indiana University Press, 1982), pp. 148–49.

7. Alexander Pope, *Epistles to Several Persons*, ed. F. W. Bateson, Twickenham Edition (London: Methuen, 1950), III.ii.46–74. This poem has been discussed in my *"The Brink of All We Hate": Satires on Women; 1660–1750* (Lexington: University of Kentucky Press, 1984); and Ellen Pollak's *The Poetics of Sexual Myth: Gender and Ideology in the Verse of Swift and Pope* (Chicago and London: University of Chicago Press, 1985).

8. By Feyjuo y Montenegro, translated from the Spanish of *El Theatro Critico* (London: 1774), pp. 217–18. Earlier editions were apparently printed in 1765 and 1768. Feyjuo y

Montenegro (1676–1764, also Feijóo), a Benedictine monk born in Spain, taught theology at Oveido University.

9. The title continues, *In Two Parts. First, Of the Ladies, Second, of the Gentlemen* (London, 1750), p. 13 and Preface. Subsequent references will be cited parenthetically in the text.

10. In *Miscellanies by Henry Fielding, Esq.*, ed. Henry Miller, Wesleyan Edition of the Works of Henry Fielding, I (Middletown, Conn.: Wesleyan University Press, 1972), pp. 153–78.

11. Mieke Bal, *Narratology: Introduction to the Theory of Narrative*, trans. Christine van Boheemen (Toronto: University of Toronto Press, 1985), pp. 79–83. Thomas Docherty, *Reading (Absent) Character: Toward a Theory of Characterization in Fiction* (New York: Oxford University Press, 1985), usefully questions the essential unity of character, though he limits the implications of his study to recent writing.

12. Roland Barthes, *S/Z: As Essay*, trans. Richard Miller (New York: Hill and Wang, 1974), p. 179. Joel Weinsheimer, "Theory of Character: *Emma*," *Poetics Today* 1 (1979): 185–211, provides a description of a semiotic approach. On eighteenth-century character, see Patrick Coleman, "Character in an Eighteenth-Century Context," *The Eighteenth Century: Theory and Interpretation* 24 (1983): 51–63; and Paul J. Korshin, *Typologies in England, 1650–1820* (Princeton: Princeton University Press, 1983).

13. As Mikhail Bakhtin has written, the ancient square "constituted a state. . . . the entire people participated in it . . . And in this concrete and as it were all-encompassing chronotope: the laying bare and examination of a citizen's whole life was accomplished, and received its public and civic stamp of approval," *The Dialogic Imagination: Four Essays*, ed. Michael Holquist, trans. by Caryl Emerson and Michael Holquist (Austin: University of Texas Press, 1981), p. 132.

14. Wendy Hollway's observations on gender restrictions, though addressed to the problems of contemporary women, are relevant here: "Gender difference is maintained, that is re-produced in day-to-day interactions in heterosexual couples, through the denial of the non-unitary, non-rational, relational [aspects of the] character of subjectivity," "Gender Difference and the Production of Subjectivity," in Henriques et al., *Changing the Subject*, p. 252.

15. Michèle Barrett, "Feminism and the Definition of Cultural Politics," *Feminism, Culture, and Politics*, ed. Rosalind Brunt and Caroline Rowan (London: Lawrence and Wishart, 1982, rpt. 1986), pp. 42, 39–40.

16. Catherine Belsey, *The Subject of Tragedy: Identity and Difference in Renaissance Drama* (London and New York: Methuen, 1985), pp. 191 and 221.

17. *London Magazine*, Vol. 20 (1751): 136.

18. Bonnell Thorton, *Have-at-you-all* (London, 1752), p. 29.

19. *The Tablet, or Picture of Real Life* (London, 1752).

20. Letters to Sarah Chapone, 6 December 1750 and 11 January 1751 in *Selected Letters of Samuel Richardson*, ed. John Carroll (Oxford: Clarendon Press, 1964), p. 173.

21. Carroll, ed., *Letters*, pp. 202–3.

22. Anon., *A Letter to the Right Honorable the Lady V—ss V—. Occasioned by the Publication of Her Memoirs in the Adventures of "Peregrine Pickle"* (London, 1751), p. 4.

23. Fielding, *Amelia*, ed. Martin C. Battestin, Wesleyan Edition of the Works of Fielding (Middletown, Conn.: Wesleyan University Press, 1983), IV.i.

24. *An Apology for the Conduct of A Lady of Quality, Lately traduc'd Under the Name of Lady Frail* (London, 1751), pp. 5 and 2.

25.   Virginia Woolf, *The Common Reader*, 1st and 2nd series combined (New York: Harcourt, Brace, and Co., 1948), p. 168.

26.   Patricia Meyer Spacks, "Ev'ry Woman Is at Heart a Rake," *Eighteenth-Century Studies* 8 (1974): 33, 38.

27.   Among those published in London during the eighteenth century were *Thérèse Philosophe* (c. 1748) by Jean-Baptiste, Marquis d'Argens; *Les Faiblesses d'une jolie femme, ou Mémoires de Madame de Vilfranc* (1785) by Pierre Jean-Baptiste Nougaret; *Félicia, ou mes fredaines* (1775); *The Secret History of Mlle Lubert* (1774); *La Nouvelle Madeleine, ou la Conversion* (1789); and *Justine, ou les Malheurs de la Vertu* (1791).

28.   Richetti, *Popular Fiction*, p. 123.

29.   R. Gill, II (London, 1802), Preface. See also *Trails for Adultery: or, the History of Divorces. . . . the Whole Forming a Complete History of the Private Life, Intrigues, and Amours of many Characters in the most elevated Sphere. . . . Taken in Short-Hand*, by a civilian (London, 1779).

30.   What had previously been private was made public when Charles II transferred criminal cases to the quarter sessions and assizes making publication of the trials possible. Peter Wagner, "Trial Reports as a Genre of Eighteenth-Century Erotica," *British Journal for Eighteenth-Century Studies* 5 (1982): 117–22, has noted a considerable decrease in trial reports between 1737 and 1770. But it seems possible that memoirs and fictions took up the space vacated by these reports.

31.   *An Apology for the Conduct of A Lady of Quality, Lately Traduc'd Under the Name of Lady Frail* (London, 1751), p. 6.

32.   Jay Fliegelman, *Prodigals and Pilgrims: The American Revolution against Patriarchal Authority, 1750–1800* (Cambridge: Cambridge University Press, 1982), and Avrom Fleishman, *Figures of Autobiography: The Language of Self-Writing in Victorian and Modern England* (Berkeley: University of California Press, 1983), especially p. 90.

33.   *Memoirs of the Late Mrs. Robinson.* Written by herself (New York, 1802), I. 96.

34.   She writes to "vindicate her Character from the Base Calumnies maliciously thrown upon it" in *An Apology for the Conduct of Mrs. Teresa Constantia Phillips*, 2nd ed. (London, 1748), I. 12. All subsequent references to this text are cited parenthetically.

35.   See James L. Clifford's edition, revised by Paul-Gabriel Boucé, of Smollett's *The Adventures of Peregrine Pickle in which are included Memoirs of a Lady of Quality* (Oxford and New York: Oxford University Press, 1983), p. 458. All subsequent references are cited parenthetically. The introduction includes a summary of events related to its publication and of a competing text, Dr. John Hill's *The History of a Woman of Quality: or, the Adventures of Lady Frail* (1751).

36.   *Memoirs of Laetitia Pilkington, 1712–50.* Written by herself, first pub. (1748–54), ed. Iris Barry (London: George Routledge and Sons, rpt. 1928). Born in Dublin, the daughter of a male midwife, she early married Matthew Pilkington, an Irish minister, who was soon unfaithful. Her own subsequent infidelity with painter James Worsdale became a public scandal. Excessive debt led to her imprisonment in 1748. Colley Cibber, in his seventies at the time, was instrumental in her release and encouraged her to write the memoirs. Subsequent references are to this edition.

37.   *A Narrative of the Life of Mrs. Charlotte Charke.* Written by Herself. Facs. of 2nd ed. (Gainesville, Fla.: Scholar Facsimile and Reprints, 1969). Charke's publications include a novel, *The History of Henry Dumont and Miss Charlotte Evelyn . . . with some critical Remarks on Comic Actors*, 2nd. ed. (London, 1756); *The Lover's Treat: or, Unnatural Hatred* (London, 1758); *The Mercer, or Fatal Extravagance* (London, c. 1755). Two plays, *The Carnival, or Har-*

lequen Blunderer (1735) and *Tit for Tat, or Comedy and Tragedy at War* (1743) were acted but never printed. *The Art of Management; or Tragedy Expelled* (London, 1735) is a satirical diatribe against Fleetwood's incompetent management of the Theatre Royal in Drury Lane. All subsequent references are to this edition.

38.   Introduction to the *Narrative of the Life of Mrs. Charlotte Charke*, Constable's Miscellany of Original Publications (London: Hunt and Clarke, 1929), p. 222.

39.   The Sally Paul case is described in *The Monthly Review* 22 (1760): 522. See also Terry Castle, "Matters Not Fit to be Mentioned: Fielding's *The Female Husband*," *ELH* 49 (1982): 602–22; and Sheridan Baker's "Henry Fielding's *The Female Husband*: Fact and Fiction," *PMLA* 74 (1959): 213–24.

40.   Hannah Snell, *The Female Soldier . . .* (London, 1750), p. 59.

8.   PRISON REFORM AND THE SENTENCE OF NARRATION IN THE VICAR OF WAKEFIELD/John Bender

1.   Roland Barthes, *Mythologies*, trans. Annette Lavers (New York: Hill & Wang, 1972), p. 45. This essay considers Goldsmith in light of ideas worked out in my book *Imagining the Penitentiary: Fiction and the Architecture of Mind in Eighteenth-Century England* (Chicago: University of Chicago Press, 1987). A few of the theoretical statements here are adapted from the book, but my treatment of *The Vicar of Wakefield* is new.

2.   Arthur Friedman, ed., *The Collected Works of Oliver Goldsmith*, 5 vols. (Oxford: Clarendon Press, 1966), V.292. Subsequent references (whether in notes or parenthetically in the text) are to this edition. On the critical fortunes of the novel see G. S. Rousseau, *Goldsmith: the Critical Heritage* (London: Routledge & Kegan Paul, 1974), especially pp. 9–13 and the critics cited there. Goldsmith, in his Advertisement to the novel, was the first to note the "faults" of the work and to defend any "absurdity" it might contain as subordinate to the "beauties" of the whole (IV.14). Mr. Burchell takes up the theme in chapter fifteen (IV.79).

3.   Mikhail Bakhtin, *The Dialogic Imagination*, trans. and ed. Michael Holquist and Caryl Emerson (Austin: University of Texas Press, 1981), p. 33. On Bakhtin's communicational, or semiotic, definition of "behavioral ideology" as abiding in the continuous formation and reformation of systems of meaning through linguistic and social communication see Bakhtin and Valentin Voloshinov, *Marxism and the Philosophy of Language*, trans. Ladislav Matejka and I. R. Titunik (New York: Seminar Press, 1973), esp. p. 91; and "Discourse in Life and Discourse in Art (Concerning Sociological Poetics)," in *Freudianism: A Marxist Critique*, trans. I. R. Titunik, ed. Neal H. Bruss (New York: Academic Press, 1976), Appendix I, pp. 93–116.

4.   See Anthony Giddens, *A Contemporary Critique of Historical Materialism* (Berkeley: University of California Press, 1981), especially pp. 1–25. My summary formulation closely paraphrases Eric Olin Wright's in "Gidden's Critique of Marxism," *New Left Review* 138 (1983): 12.

5.   Raymond Williams, *Marxism and Literature* (Oxford: Oxford University Press, 1977), p. 126. I also draw upon Louis Althusser, *Lenin and Philosophy*, trans. Ben Brewster (New York: Monthly Review Press, 1971); Terry Eagleton, *Criticism and Ideology*, (London: Verso Editions, 1978), Chap. 2, pp. 44–63, and "Ideology, Fiction, Narrative," *Social Text* 2 (1979): 62–80; Rosalind Coward and John Ellis, *Language and Materialism: Developments in Semiology and the Theory of the Subject* (London: Routledge & Kegan Paul, 1977), pp. 77–78; and Tom Bottomore, ed., *A Dictionary of Marxist Thought* (Cambridge: Harvard University Press,

1983), pp. 219–23. I cannot, however, accept the *a priori* aspects of some versions of Marxism that privilege the economic bases of production by granting them ultimate causal, or at least explanatory, force. I adopt, rather, a sympathetic but skeptical stance akin to that of Anthony Giddens.

6. Morris Golden, "Goldsmith, *The Vicar of Wakefield*, and the Periodicals," *JEGP* 76 (1977): 525–36.

7. Cesare Beccaria, *On Crimes and Punishments*, ed. and trans. Henry Paolucci (Indianapolis: Bobbs-Merrill, 1963), p. 9. This work was translated into French by the Abbé Morellet; the first English translation appeared in 1767. On Beccaria's life, work, ideas, and influence see Marcello Maestro, *Cesare Beccaria and the Origins of Penal Reform* (Philadelphia: Temple University Press, 1973).

8. On the French influence, see Pat Rogers, "The Dialectic of *The Traveller*," in *The Art of Oliver Goldsmith*, ed. Andrew Swarbrick (London: Vision Press, 1984), pp. 115–16 and citations; Arthur Lytton Sells, *Les Sources françaises de Goldsmith* (Paris: Édouard Champion, 1924); R.S. Crane and H.J. Smith, "A French Influence on Goldsmith's *Citizen of the World*," *MP* 19 (1921–22): 83–92; R.S. Crane and J.H. Warner, "Goldsmith and Voltaire's *Essai sur les Moeurs*," *MLN* 38 (1923): 65–76; and R.S. Crane and Arthur Friedman, "Goldsmith and the 'Encyclopédie'," *TLS* (11 May 1933) 331.

9. For detailed accounts of eighteenth-century prisons see John Howard, *The State of the Prisons* (Warrington: William Eyres, 1777); reprinted in *Prisons and Lazarettos*, ed. Ralph W. England, Jr., 2 vols. (Montclair, N.J.: Patterson Smith, 1973). Informative modern works on eighteenth-century prison reform include Leon Radzinowicz, *A History of English Criminal Law and its Administration from 1750*, Vol. I "The Movement for Reform, 1750–1833" (New York: Macmillan, 1948), pp. 165–493; Michel Foucault, *Discipline and Punish: The Birth of the Prison*, trans. Alan Sheridan (London: Allen Lane, 1977), Chaps. 2–3; Michael Ignatieff, *A Just Measure of Pain: The Penitentiary in the Industrial Revolution, 1750–1850* (New York: Pantheon, 1978), pp. 15–113, and his "State, Civil Society, and Total Institutions: A Critique of Recent Social Histories of Punishment," in *Crime and Justice, An Annual Review of Research*, Vol. 3, ed. Michael Tonry and Norval Morris (Chicago: University of Chicago Press, 1981), pp. 153–92; Seán McConville, *A History of English Prison Administration*, Vol. 1 (London: Routledge & Kegan Paul, 1981), pp. 49–134; Robin Evans, *The Fabrication of Virtue: English Prison Architecture, 1750–1840* (Cambridge: Cambridge University Press, 1982), pp. 1–236; and J.M. Beattie, *Crime and the Courts in England, 1660–1800* (Princeton: Princeton University Press, 1986), Chaps. 9–10.

10. On Goldsmith and Chambers see Ralph M. Wardle, *Oliver Goldsmith* (Lawrence: University of Kansas Press, 1957), p. 189; and John Ginger, *The Notable Man: The Life and Times of Oliver Goldsmith* (London: Hamish Hamilton, 1977), pp. 243–46. On Johnson and Chambers see E. L. McAdam, Jr., *Dr. Johnson and the English Law* (Syracuse: Syracuse University Press, 1951), pp. 65–122.

11. See Friedman, who says the novel was composed between 1760 or 1761 and 1762 (*Works*, IV. 3–4); and Ginger, who argues that Goldsmith was working on the novel as late as 1764 and that Chapters 19 and 27 were "written during or after 1763" (Appendix to *The Notable Man*, pp. 363–70).

12. Grant T. Webster, "Smollett's Microcosms: A Satiric Device in the Novel," *Satire Newsletter* 5 (1967): 34–37.

13. On the Rockingham Whigs see John B. Owen, *The Eighteenth Century, 1714–1815* (New York: Norton, 1976), pp. 179–85, 282–90; and Frank O'Gorman, *The Rise of Party in England: The Rockingham Whigs, 1760–82* (London: George Allen and Unwin, 1975). On the

issue of social class during the period see E.P. Thompson, "Eighteenth-Century English Society: Class Struggle Without Class?," *Social History* 3 (1978): 133–165.

14.   This phrase comes from "Of the Pride and Luxury of the Middling Class of People," which appeared in *The Bee*, Number 7, November 17 1759, (*Works*, I.486–87). The phrase, "middle order of mankind," comes from *The Vicar of Wakefield*, *Works*, IV.102. On Goldsmith's politics see R.W. Seitz, "The Irish Background of Goldsmith's Social and Political Thought," *PMLA* 52 (1937): 405–11, and "Some of Goldsmith's Second Thoughts on English History," *MP* 35 (1937–38): 279–88; Howard J. Bell, Jr., " 'The Deserted Village' and Goldsmith's Social Doctrines," *PMLA* 59 (1944): 747–72; Sven Bäckman, *The Singular Tale: A Study of The Vicar of Wakefield and its Literary Background* (Lund: G. W. K. Gleerup, 1971), pp. 66–67, 184–87; Robert H. Hopkins, "Social Stratification and the Obsequious Curve: Goldsmith and Rowlandson," in *Studies in the Eighteenth Century* 3, ed. R.F. Brissenden and J.C. Eade (Toronto: University of Toronto Press, 1976): 55–71; and Donald Davie, "Notes on Goldsmith's Politics," in Swarbrick, *The Art of Oliver Goldsmith*, pp. 79–89. For a related discussion see Raymond Williams, *The Country and the City* (New York: Oxford University Press, 1973), pp. 74–79.

15.   Owen, *The Eighteenth Century*, p. 169.

16.   Quoted by Roy Porter, *English Society in the Eighteenth Century* (Harmondsworth: Penguin, 1982), p. 130.

17.   Quoted by Isaac Kramnick, *Bolingbroke and His Circle: The Politics of Nostalgia in the Age of Walpole* (Cambridge: Harvard University Press, 1968), p. 79; see also pp. 230–35.

18.   E.P. Thompson, "Eighteenth-Century English Society: Class Struggle Without Class?," p. 140.

19.   *The Works of Jeremy Bentham*, 11 vols., ed. John Bowring (Edinburgh: William Tait, 1838–1843), IV.40, 44–46. For a full account of Bentham's Panopticon see Evans, *The Fabrication of Virtue*, Chap. 5.

20.   I refer in part to Pierre Macherey, *A Theory of Literary Production*, trans. Geoffrey Wall (London: Routledge & Kegan Paul, 1978), esp. pp. 59–60. For a considerable treatment of the subject, including discussion of Macherey, see Fredric Jameson, *The Political Unconscious: Narrative as a Socially Symbolic Act* (Ithaca: Cornell University Press, 1981), Chap. 1; and Terry Eagleton, *Criticism and Ideology*, Chap. 3, esp. pp. 89 and 100–1. I adopt Raymond Williams's idea of cultural "emergence" and his term "structure of feeling" (*Marxism and Literature*).

21.   Martin Battestin, *The Providence of Wit: Aspects of Form in Augustan Literature and the Arts* (Oxford: Clarendon Press, 1974), Chap. 7.

22.   J.R.S. Whiting, *Prison Reform in Gloucestershire, 1776–1820: A Study of the Work of Sir George Onesiphorus Paul, Bart.* (London & Chichester: Phillimore & Co., 1975), Appendices A and B.

23.   Ronald Paulson, *Satire and the Novel in Eighteenth-Century England* (New Haven: Yale University Press, 1967), pp. 269–75. My consideration of narrative technique and several other aspects of Goldsmith's novel has been influenced in part by the work of Marshall Brown, who made his chapter-length study from a forthcoming book on "pre-romanticism" available to me in manuscript.

24.   Frederick Cummings, et al., *Romantic Art in Britain: Paintings and Drawings 1760–1860* (Philadelphia: Philadelphia Museum of Art, 1968), p. 12.

25.   Dorrit Cohn, *Transparent Minds: Narrative Modes for Presenting Consciousness in Fiction* (Princeton: Princeton University Press, 1978), p. 100. See also Käte Hamburger, *The Logic of Literature*, trans. Marilynn J. Rose (Bloomington: Indiana University Press, 1973); Roy

Pascal, *The Dual Voice* (Manchester: Manchester University Press, 1977); and Ann Banfield, *Unspeakable Sentences: Narration and Representation in the Language of Fiction* (Boston: Routledge & Kegan Paul, 1982).

26. *The Letters of Gustave Flaubert, 1830–1857*, ed. and trans. Francis Steegmuller, 2 vols. (Cambridge: Harvard University Press, 1980–82), I.230. James Joyce, *A Portrait of the Artist as a Young Man* (New York: Viking, 1956), pp. 214–15.

27. Roland Barthes, "Introduction to the Structural Analysis of Narratives," in *Image-Music-Text*, ed. and trans. Stephen Heath (New York: Hill and Wang, 1977), pp. 112–13; reprinted in *A Barthes Reader*, ed. Susan Sontag (New York: Hill and Wang, 1982), pp. 283–84.

28. Other passages that might be similarly "translated" include the last paragraph of Chap. 13 (IV.71) and the opening of the first paragraph of Chap. 8 (IV.45).

29. The passage from Goethe's *Dichtung and Wahrheit* is reprinted in G.S. Rousseau, *Goldsmith: The Critical Heritage*, pp. 308–11.

30. Adam Smith, *The Theory of Moral Sentiments*, ed. D.D. Raphael & A.L. Macfie (Oxford: Clarendon, 1976), esp. pp. 82–85.

31. See G.S. Rousseau, *Goldsmith: The Critical Heritage*, pp. 9–13 and citations. The most extreme exposition of the satiric view is by Robert H. Hopkins, *The True Genius of Oliver Goldsmith* (Baltimore: Johns Hopkins University Press, 1969), Chap. 5.

32. See Pascal, *The Dual Voice*, pp. 2–32.

33. See, for example, the epigraph to this essay; also, Coward and Ellis, *Language and Materialism*, Chap. 4.

9. JOHNSON AND THE ROLE OF AUTHORITY/Fredric Bogel

1. Samuel Johnson, *A Dictionary of the English Language*, 2 vols. (London, 1755).

2. W. Jackson Bate, *Samuel Johnson* (New York and London: Harcourt, Brace, Jovanovich, 1977), pp. 8, 121–22, 379. Subsequent references are cited by page number in the text.

3. *The Rambler*, ed. Walter Jackson Bate and Albrecht B. Strauss, Vol. V of the Yale Edition of the Works of Samuel Johnson (New Haven and London: Yale University Press, 1969), p. 76. The Folio ed. of 1750–52 has "dictators exalted by their own authority."

4. James Boswell, *The Life of Samuel Johnson*, ed. G. B. Hill, rev. L. F. Powell, 6 vols. (Oxford: Clarendon Press, 1934–1964), I.73–74. Hereafter abbreviated as *Life* and cited in the text.

5. *Life of Milton*, in Samuel Johnson, *Selected Poetry and Prose*, ed. Frank Brady and W. K. Wimsatt (Berkeley and Los Angeles: University of California Press, 1977), p. 424.

6. Bowell, *Life*, IV.304. Johnson is, of course, paraphrasing *Paradise Lost*, IV.37.

7. Heinz Kohut, "Thoughts on Narcissism and Narcissistic Rage," in *The Search for the Self: Selected Writings of Heinz Kohut: 1950–1978*, ed. Paul H. Ornstein (New York: International Universities Press, 1978), II.643.

8. "PREFACE" to "Miscellaneous Poems and Translations" (1726), in *The Poetical Works of Richard Savage*, ed. Clarence Tracy (Cambridge: Cambridge University Press, 1962), pp. 265–69, 11. 32–37.

9. Samuel Johnson, *Life of Savage*, ed. Clarence Tracy (Oxford: Clarendon Press, 1971),

p. 90. Subsequent citations from this edition will be identified, by page number, in parentheses.

10. On the question of the ending of Johnson's *Life*, and on the opposition between "Nature" and "Fortune," see Frank Brady, "The Strategies of Biography and Some Eighteenth-Century Examples," in *Literary Theory and Structure*, ed. Frank Brady, John Palmer, and Martin Price (New Haven and London: Yale University Press, 1973), pp. 252–55.

11. *Life of Milton*, in Brady and Wimsatt, *Johnson Poetry and Prose*, p. 432. It may be significant that Johnson is here endorsing the statement of an earlier critic, John Clarke, who had brought the charge against Milton in 1731 (p. 432, n. 36).

12. In arguing that in the *Life of Savage* Johnson characteristically views situations in terms unavailable to their participants and thus establishes his "position as a knower," William Vesterman maneuvers Johnson into precisely the position that I am claiming he avoids. See "Johnson and *The Life of Savage*," *ELH* 36 (1969): 664.

13. Samuel Johnson, *The Complete English Poems*, ed. J. D. Fleeman (Harmondsworth: Penguin Books, 1971), p. 157.

14. William Lauder, "King Charles I Vindicated from the charge of Plagiarism, Brought against him by Milton, and Milton himself convicted of Forgery, and a gross Imposition on the Public," (London, 1754), p. 40. On Lauder, and on Johnson's relation to Milton, see Dustin Griffin, *Regaining Paradise: Milton and the Eighteenth Century* (Cambridge: Cambridge University Press, 1986), esp. chap. 11.

15. Bate, *Samuel Johnson*, p. 253. The best single account is in James L. Clifford, *Dictionary Johnson: Samuel Johnson's Middle Years* (London: Heinemann, 1979), pp. 57–70. See also the following series of articles by Michael J. Marcuse: "The Lauder Controversy and the Jacobite Cause," *SBHT* 18 (1977): 27–47; "The Pre-Publication History of William Lauder's *Essay . . . Paradise Lost*," *PBSA* 72 (1978): 37–57; "Miltonoklastes: The Lauder Affair Reconsidered," *Eighteenth-Century Life* 4 (1978): 86–95; "The *Gentleman's Magazine* and the Lauder Controversy," *Bulletin of Research in the Humanities* 81 (1978): 179–209; " 'The Scourge of Imposters, the Terror of Quacks': John Douglas and the Exposé of William Lauder," *HLQ* 42 (1979): 231–61.

16. William Lauder, "King Charles Vindicated . . ." (London, 1754), pp. 3–4.

17. For example, in "London," where the narrator's self-division stands in sharp contrast to the univocal—and fantasy-ridden—consciousness of Thales. See my brief discussion of the poem in *Literature and Insubstantiality in Later Eighteenth-Century England* (Princeton: Princeton University Press, 1984), pp. 58–61.

18. I suspect, in fact, that Johnson's disquiet over his initial response to Lauder's charges stayed with him for a long time. In his 1754 pamphlet, Lauder claims that his own acts of plagiarism were designed purely to rouse public indignation against the crime itself so that readers would be prepared to accept his real charge: that Milton interpolated into *Eikon Basilike* a prayer lifted from Sidney's *Arcadia* so that he could then (in *Eikonoklastes*) accuse Charles I of making impious use in a Christian context of what had been a pagan prayer. As the pamphlet's hysterical tone makes clear, Lauder is desperately attempting a second projection onto Milton in order to deflect the unbearable shame of having been found out in his first. (Modern scholarly opinion on Milton's alleged interpolation is summarized, and extended, by William Riley Parker in *Milton: A Biography* [Oxford: Clarendon Press, 1968], pp. 360–61, 964–66). Interestingly, in the *Life of Milton*, Johnson includes not only the charge of interpolation but also Lauder's criticism of Milton's Latin in the Salmasius controversy (Johnson, *Life of Milton*, in Brady and Wimsatt, *Johnson Poetry and Prose*, p. 400; Lauder, "King Charles I . . .," p. 38 and 38n.). Neither of these charges, of course,

belonged to Lauder or had been exclusively associated with him, but it is tempting to speculate that, in reproducing them and thereby identifying himself, however indirectly, with that rabid diminisher of Milton's reputation, Johnson was reenacting the penance he had undertaken in 1750 by dictating Lauder's confession for him.

19. *Papers Written by Dr. Johnson and Dr. Dodd in 1777*, ed. R. W. Chapman (Oxford: Clarendon Press, 1926), p. 23.

20. On the relation between Johnson and Chambers, see E. L. McAdam, Jr., *Dr. Johnson and the English Law* (Syracuse: Syracuse University Press, 1951), pp. 65–122; Thomas M. Curley, "Johnson's Secret Collaboration," in *The Unknown Samuel Johnson*, ed. John J. Burke, Jr. and Donald Kay (Madison: University of Wisconsin Press, 1983), pp. 91–112; Bate, *Samuel Johnson*, pp. 418–26, 486–87.

21. An eighteenth-century manuscript copy of the lectures is preserved at the British Museum as King's MSS 80–97. The paragraphs I quote are from Kings MS 80. I.2–4. The frequent, though inconsistent, use of "it's" for "its" has been silently corrected.

22. McAdam takes it to be "unmistakably Johnson's" (73, 81), and so—after reading through the lectures—do I. Strictly speaking, though, "unmistakably" is a word that cannot really be used in an undertaking, like ghost-writing, that aims precisely to mystify the question of authorship. There are interesting discussions of forgery, meaning the counterfeiting of a public record or deed by which property is conveyed, elsewhere in Chambers's lectures, e.g. in King's MS 89, X (Part II, Lecture X), 64–65, 80–82.

23. Martin Price, *To the Palace of Wisdom: Studies in Order and Energy from Dryden to Blake* (Garden City, N.Y.: Doubleday, 1964), p. 344.

24. Philip E. Lewis, *La Rochefoucauld: The Art of Abstraction* (Ithaca and London: Cornell University Press, 1977), p. 153. See also Isobel Grundy's interesting reflections on the Johnsonian maxim—in particular on the ways in which Johnson either qualifies its authority or embeds it in a sequence of reasoning that mutes its absolute character until the reader detaches it from that context—in "Samuel Johnson: Man of Maxims?" in *Samuel Johnson: New Critical Essays*, ed. Isobel Grundy (London: Barnes and Noble, 1984), pp. 13–30. Grundy draws attention to a pertinent remark of Emrys Jones in "The Artistic Form of *Rasselas*, *R.E.S.* n.s. 18 (1967): 398.

25. Richard A. Lanham, *The Motives of Eloquence: Literary Rhetoric in the Renaissance* (New Haven and London: Yale University Press, 1976), p. 21.

26. I allude to Bertrand Bronson's essay "Johnson Agonistes," available in *"Johnson Agonistes" and Other Essays* (Berkeley and Los Angeles: University of California Press, 1965); Roland Barthes, *Mythologies*, trans. Annette Lavers (New York: Hill and Wang, 1972), p. 18.

27. Barthes, *Mythologies*, p. 19, my emphasis; p. 25.

28. *Rambler* 208, ed. Walter Jackson Bate and Albrecht B. Strauss, Yale Edition of the Works of Samuel Johnson (New Haven and London: Yale University Press, 1969), V. 317, my emphasis.

29. Samuel Johnson, "Preface to A Dictionary of the English Language," in Brady and Wimsatt, *Johnson Poetry and Prose*, p. 285.

30. Samuel Johnson, *Diaries, Prayers, and Annals*, ed. E. L. McAdam, Jr., with Donald and Mary Hyde (New Haven: Yale University, 1958), p. 14, my emphasis. On narcissistic projection, doubling, and related topics see Otto Rank, *The Double: A Psychoanalytic Study*, trans. Harry Tucker, Jr. (Chapel Hill: University of North Carolina Press, 1971), esp. chap. 5; Sigmund Freud's essays "The Uncanny," "On Narcissism: An Introduction," and "Mourning and Melancholia" (*The Standard Edition of the Complete Psychological Works*, ed.

and trans. James Strachey [London: Hogarth Press, 1953–74] XVII, XIV); Jean Laplanche, *Life and Death in Psychoanalysis*, trans. Jeffrey Mehlman (Baltimore and London: Johns Hopkins University Press, 1976), chap. 4; Jacques Lacan, "The Mirror Stage . . .," trans. Alan Sheridan, in *Écrits: A Selection* (London: Tavistock, 1977), pp. 1–7; John T. Irwin, *Doubling and Incest/Repetition and Revenge* (Baltimore and London: Johns Hopkins University Press, 1975).

31.   The dream is in Samuel Johnson, *Diaries, Prayers, and Annals*, p. 67. Though he incorrectly adds a dramatic "always" to Johnson's text before "remember," Bate offers a brief and sensitive discussion of the journal entry, and of Johnson's relation to Nathaniel, in *Samuel Johnson*, pp. 160–62.

32.   John Guillory, *Poetic Authority: Spenser, Milton, and Literary History* (New York: Columbia University Press, 1983), p. x.

33.   Boswell, *Life*, I.348. On the topic of Johnson's particular sort of "heroism" in Boswell's *Life*, and the related topic of modern critical approaches to Boswell's image of Johnson, see pp. 173–94 of my *Literature and Insubstantiality*; and " 'Did you once see Johnson plain?': Reflections on Boswell's *Life* and the State of Eighteenth-Century Studies," in *Boswell's Life of Johnson: New Questions, New Answers*, ed. John A. Vance (Athens: University of Georgia Press, 1985), pp. 73–93.

34.   Pat Rogers, *Grub Street: Studies in a Subculture* (London: Methuen, 1972), p. 363.

35.   Rogers, *Grub Street*, p. 291.

36.   *Adventurer* 131, in *"The Idler" and "The Adventurer,"* ed. Walter Jackson Bate, John M. Bullitt, and L. F. Powell (New Haven and London: Yale University Press, 1963), p. 482.

37.   Grundy, *Samuel Johnson: New Critical Essays*, p. 23.

38.   Walter Jackson Bate, "Johnson and Satire Manqué," in *Eighteenth-Century Studies in Honor of Donald F. Hyde*, ed. W. H. Bond (New York: Grolier Club, 1970), p. 157.

10.   SENTIMENTALITY AS PERFORMANCE: Shaftesbury, Sterne, and the Theatrics of Virtue/Robert Markley

1.   All quotations are from the edition by Gardner Stout, Jr. (Berkeley: University of California Press, 1967), p. 188, and will be cited parenthetically in the text.

2.   See G. S. Rousseau, "Nerves, Spirits and Fibres: Towards the Origin of Sensibility," in R. F. Brissenden, ed., *Studies in the Eighteenth Century III* (Canberra: Australian National University Press, 1975), pp. 137–57; and John Mullan, "Hypochondria and Hysteria: Sensibility and the Physicians," *The Eighteenth Century: Theory and Interpretation* 25 (1984): 141–74.

3.   Donald Greene, "Latitudinarianism and Sensibility: The Genealogy of the 'Man of Feeling' Reconsidered," *Modern Philology* 75 (1977): 159–83. R. S. Crane's article, "The Genealogy of 'The Man of Feeling,' " appeared in *ELH* 1 (1934): 205–30. Greene had been attacked and Crane defended by Frans de Bruyn, "Latitudinarianism and Its Importance as a Precursor of Sensibility," *JEGP* 80 (1981): 349–68; de Bruyn, however, redefines "latitudinarianism" so broadly—as a "widespread 'supra-denominational' influence" (352)—that it encompasses virtually all forms of moderate and liberal Christianity. John K. Sheriff in *The Good-Natured Man: The Evolution of a Moral Ideal, 1660–1800* (University, Ala.: University of Alabama Press, 1982) notes perceptively that, given their differing descriptions of "latitudinarianism," the views of Greene and de Bruyn are "not necessarily contradic-

tory" (105n). As my discussion indicates, I am sympathetic to Sheriff's account of the tensions that exist between traditional Christian emphases on an active virtue and the sentimental self-absorption in one's own "good nature" as an end in itself. On this problem see also Louis Bredvold, *The Natural History of Sensibility* (Detroit: Wayne State University Press, 1962).

4.   See Sheriff, *Good-Natured Man*, pp. 1–18; and Chester Chapin, "Shaftesbury and the Man of Feeling," *Modern Philology* 81 (1983): 47–50.

5.   I have noted my disagreements with some of these critics in "Style as Philosophical Structure: The Contexts of Shaftesbury's *Characteristicks*," in Robert Ginsberg, ed., *The Philosopher as Writer: The Eighteenth Century* (Cranbury, N.J.: Associated University Presses for Susquehanna University Press, 1987). Two recent works are representative of this ahistorical approach to Shaftesbury's work: Robert Voitle's biography, *The Third Earl of Shaftesbury, 1671–1715* (Baton Rouge: Louisiana State University Press, 1984) and David Marshall's study, *The Figure of the Theater: Shaftesbury, Defoe, Adam Smith, and George Eliot* (New York: Columbia University Press, 1986), pp. 13–70. To make Shaftesbury conform to a clever but overworked thesis, Marshall highlights selected snippets about readers, writers, and actors but fails to consider Shaftesbury's comments on the theater and explicit vindications of his figurative language as defenses of the "Truth." Truth, for Shaftesbury, is always class-specific and ideologically delimited; his dialogues and images of the theater, in this regard, operate in what Bakhtin terms single-voiced or monological fashion. One valuable exception to the prevalent ahistorical readings of Shaftesbury is Lawrence Klein, "The Third Earl of Shaftesbury and the Progress of Politeness," *Eighteenth-Century Studies* 18 (1984–85): 186–214.

6.   All quotations from Shaftesbury's published works are from the sixth edition of *Characteristicks of Men, Manners, Opinions, Times*, 3 vols. (London, 1737–38), and will be cited by volume and page number in the text. This edition follows the authoritative second edition and includes the late but significant "Letter Concerning Design."

7.   See Voitle, *Shaftesbury*, pp. 75–76.

8.   See Mikhail Bakhtin, *The Dialogic Imagination*, ed. Michael Holquist; trans. Caryl Emerson and Michael Holquist (Austin: University of Texas Press, 1981), esp. pp. 264–66, 298–300. There are numerous discussions of Bakhtin's writings on the relationship between discourse and ideology. See particularly Susan Stewart, "Shouts on the Street: Bakhtin's Anti-Linguistics," *Critical Inquiry* 10 (1983): 265–69; Caryl Emerson, "The Outer Word and Inner Speech: Bakhtin, Vygotsky, and the Internalization of Language," *Critical Inquiry* 10 (1983): 245–64; Laurie Finke, "The Rhetoric of Marginality: Why I Do Feminist Theory," *Tulsa Studies in Women's Literature* 5 (1986): 251–72; and Robert Markley, *Two-Edg'd Weapons: Style and Ideology in the Comedies of Etherege, Wycherley, and Congreve* (Oxford: Clarendon Press, 1987), chap. 1.

9.   On Stubbe, see J. R. Jacob, *Henry Stubbe: Radical Protestantism and the Early Enlightenment in England* (Cambridge: Cambridge University Press, 1983). On Blake, see particularly David Gross, " 'Mind-Forg'd Manacles': Hegemony and Counter-Hegemony in Blake," *The Eighteenth Century: Theory and Interpretation* 27 (1986): 3–25.

10.   See Francis Hutcheson, *An Inquiry Concerning the Original of Our Ideas of Virtue or Moral Good* (London, 1725) for a defense of Shaftesbury's doctrine of innate goodness. Shaftesbury's *Characteristicks* went through eleven editions before 1790. For his influence on James Thomson, William Shenstone, and John Gilbert Cooper, see Chapin, "Shaftesbury and the Man of Feeling," pp. 47–50.

11.   See Chapin, "Shaftesbury" pp. 47–50; and Sheriff, *Good-Natured Man*, pp. 6–10, 16–17.

12. Terry Eagleton, *The Function of Criticism: From "The Spectator" to Post-Structuralism* (London: Verso, 1984), p. 11.

13. *The Plays of Richard Steele*, ed. Shirley Strum Kenny (Oxford: Clarendon Press, 1971).

14. The literary implications of this process in the eighteenth century have been studied by a number of critics. See particularly Ian Watt, *The Rise of the Novel: Studies in Defoe, Richardson, and Fielding* (London: Chatto & Windus, 1957); Maximillian Novak, *Economics and the Fiction of Daniel Defoe* (Berkeley: University of California Press, 1962); James H. Bunn, "The Aesthetics of British Mercantilism," *New Literary History* 11 (1980): 303–21; Michael McKeon, "Marxist Criticism and *Marriage à la Mode*," *The Eighteenth Century: Theory and Interpretation* 24 (1983): 141–62; and Richard Braverman, "Capital Relations and *The Way of the World*," *ELH* 52 (1985): 133–58.

15. *The Guardian* 137, 18 August 1713.

16. See Rousseau, "Nerves, Spirits and Fibres," esp. pp. 137–48; and Mullan, "Hypochondria," pp. 141–74.

17. G. A. Starr, "Sentimental De-Education," in *Augustan Studies: Essays in Honor of Irvin Ehrenpreis*, ed. Douglas Lane Patey and Timothy Keegan (Cranbury, N. J.: Associated University Presses for Delaware University Press, 1985), p. 254.

18. See particularly Michel Foucault's arguments in *The Order of Things* (New York: Pantheon, 1970), and Volume One of *The History of Sexuality*, trans. Robert Hurley (New York: Pantheon, 1978).

19. Virginia Woolf, introduction to *A Sentimental Journey* (rpt. London: Oxford University Press, 1967), pp. v–xvii; Arthur Cash, *Sterne's Comedy of Moral Sentiments: The Ethical Dimension of the Journey* (Pittsburgh: Dusquesne University Press, 1966); Melvyn New, *Laurence Sterne as Satirist: A Reading of "Tristram Shandy"* (Gainesville: University of Florida Press, 1969), pp. 43–46; Sheriff, *Good-Natured Man*, esp. pp. 49–53, 77–81; Jeffrey Smitten, "Spatial Form as Narrative Technique in *A Sentimental Journey*," *Journal of Narrative Technique* 5 (1975): 208–18, and his "Gesture and Expression in Eighteenth-Century Fiction: *A Sentimental Journey*," *Modern Language Studies* 9, 3 (1979): 85–97; Joseph Chadwick, "Infinite Jest: Interpretation in Sterne's *A Sentimental Journey*," *Eighteenth-Century Studies* 12 (1978–79): 190–205; Michael Seidel, "Narrative Crossings: Sterne's *A Sentimental Journey*," *Genre* 18 (1985): 1–22. For other important views of the novel see Eve Kosofsky Sedgwick, "Sexualism and the Citizen of the World: Wycherley, Sterne, and Male Homosocial Desire," *Critical Inquiry* 11 (1984): 238–44; Jonathan Lamb, "Language and Hartleian Associationism in *A Sentimental Journey*," *Eighteenth-Century Studies* 13 (1980): 285–312; Arnold E. and Cathy N. Davidson, "Yorick contra Hobbes: Comic Synthesis in Sterne's *A Sentimental Journey*," *Centennial Review* 21 (1977): 282–93; and Gardner Stout, Jr., "Yorick's *Sentimental Journey*: A Comic 'Pilgrim's Progress' for the Man of Feeling," *ELH* 30 (1963): 395–412.

20. *Complete Works and Life of Laurence Sterne*, ed. Wilbur L. Cross (New York: Taylor, 1904), VII.313–14.

21. *The Lounger*, 18 June 1785; cited in Sheriff, *Good-Natured Man*, p. 82. Sheriff provides a valuable reading of *The Man of Feeling* as a critique of sentimental excess, pp. 81–87.

22. See particularly Gerald R. Cragg, *The Church and the Age of Reason, 1648–1789* (New York: Atheneum, 1961); and, for the seventeenth-century background, Christopher Hill, *The World Turned Upside Down: Radical Ideas during the English Revolution* (rpt. Harmondsworth: Penguin, 1975).

23. On the survival of courtly forms of address in the eighteenth century see Carey McIntosh, *Common and Courtly Language: The Stylistics of Social Class in Eighteenth-Century British Literature* (Philadelphia: University of Pennsylvania Press, 1985), pp. 69–101.

24. See John Cannon's revisionist account of class relations in the eighteenth century, *Aristocratic Century: The Peerage of Eighteenth-Century England* (Cambridge: Cambridge University Press, 1984).

25. David Hume, *A Treatise of Human Nature*, ed. P. H. Nidditch (Oxford: Clarendon Press, 1978), p. 402. Seidel also calls attention to this passage.

26. On the problem of how audiences were intended to respond to dramatic characters in the late seventeenth and eighteenth centuries, see Rose Zimbardo, "Imitation to Emulation: 'Imitation of Nature' from the Restoration to the Eighteenth Century." *Restoration* 2 (1978): 2–9.

27. See Mackenzie's letter to Elizabeth Rose of 18 July 1769; quoted in Sheriff, *Good-Natured Man*, p. 89.

28. On the "private spaces" of the eighteenth-century novel see Christina Marsden Gillis, "Private Room and Public Space: The Paradox of Form in *Clarissa*," *Studies on Voltaire and the Eighteenth Century* 176 (1979): 153–68.

11. THE SPECTRALIZATION OF THE OTHER IN THE *MYSTERIES OF UDOLPHO*/Terry Castle

1. Philippe Ariès, *The Hour of Our Death*, trans. Helen Weaver (New York: Alfred A. Knopf, 1981), p. 606. All citations are from this translation; parenthetical notation refers to page numbers in this edition.

2. Sir Walter Scott, *Lives of Eminent Novelists and Dramatists* (London: Frederick Warne, 1887), p. 568.

3. Because Austen made it so difficult to take certain aspects of *Udolpho* seriously, modern critics have often refused to take any aspect of the novel seriously. Certainly Radcliffe can be vulgar in the extreme, but her impact on the modern life of the emotions cannot be dismissed. It is one aim of the present essay to read Radcliffe against the current Austenian caricature, and to restore to view the powerful current of feeling in her work, however awkwardly or crudely this feeling is expressed.

4. See Montague Summers, *The Gothic Quest: A History of the Gothic Novel* (New York: Russell & Russell, 1964), p. 139; J.M.S. Tompkins, *The Popular Novel in England 1770–1800* (Lincoln: University of Nebraska Press, 1961), p. 261; and Andrew Lang, *Adventures Among Books* (London: Longman's, Green & Co., 1905), p. 127.

5. All citations are from the World's Classics edition of *The Mysteries of Udolpho*, ed. Bonamy Dobrée, notes by Frederick Garber (Oxford: Oxford University Press, 1966). Parenthetical notation refers to page numbers in this edition.

6. See, for example, Robert Kiely, *The Romantic Novel in England* (Cambridge: Harvard University Press, 1972), p. 78; and among psychoanalytic and feminist critics, Norman Holland and Leona Sherman, "Gothic Possibilities," *New Literary History* 8 (1976–77): 279–94; Claire Kahane, "The Gothic Mirror," in *The (M)Other Tongue: Essays in Feminist Psychoanalytic Interpretation*, ed. Shirley Nelson Garner, Claire Kahane, and Madelon Sprengnether (Ithaca, N.Y.: Cornell University Press, 1985), pp. 334–51; Mary Poovey, "Ideology and 'The Mysteries of Udolpho,' " *Criticism* 21 (Fall 1979): 307–30; and Cynthia Griffin Wolff, "The Radcliffean Gothic Model: A Form for Feminine Sexuality," *Modern Language Studies* 9 (1979): 98–113.

7. See Robert Darnton, "Readers Respond to Rousseau: The Fabrication of Romantic Sensitivity," in *The Great Cat Massacre and Other Episodes in French Cultural History* (New

York: Random House, 1985), pp. 215–56. On *Udolpho's* contemporary appeal, see J.M.S. Tompkins, *Ann Radcliffe and Her Influence on Later Writers* (New York: Arno Press, 1980) and the Dobrée introduction to the Oxford edition.

8.   Tzvetan Todorov, *The Fantastic: A Structural Approach to a Literary Genre*, trans. Richard Howard (Ithaca: Cornell University Press, 1975), p. 114.

9.   Todorov, *The Fantastic*, pp. 116–17.

10.   Todorov, *The Fantastic*, p. 118.

11.   D.W. Winnicott, *Home is Where We Start From: Essays by a Psychoanalyst*, ed. Clare Winnicott, Ray Shepherd, and Madeleine Davis (New York: W.W. Norton, 1986), p. 30.

12.   Sigmund Freud, "The Uncanny" (1919), in *The Standard Edition of the Complete Psychological Works*, ed. and trans. James Strachey (London: Hogarth Press, 1955), XVII. 218–52.

13.   In "Imagery of the Surface in the Gothic Novel" (*PMLA* 96 [March 1981]: 255–70), Eve Kosofsky Sedgwick suggests that Gothic fiction typically presents "a (novelistic) world of faces where the diacritical code is poor"—i.e., where the differences between characters' physiognomies are so slight as to challenge the "fiction of presence" the novel also tries to ensure. One effect of this impoverished physiognomic code, she writes, is to create "unbounded confusions of identity along a few diacritical axes: any furrowed man will be confusable with any other furrowed man (Schedoni with Zampari with Zeluca, for example), and so forth" (p. 263). Sedgwick's rigorously poststructuralist perspective forbids her to interpret this phenomenon in any psychological sense (she treats it instead as a formal convention—part of the play of the "surface" in Gothic fiction), but a fruitful connection might nonetheless be made, following the developmental model of Freud and Piaget, between such "confusability" and the early stages of cognitive perception in the human infant.

14.   Todorov, *The Fantastic*, p. 148.

15.   See Ariès, *Hour of Our Death*, chaps. 10 and 11, esp. pp. 409–11 and 475–99. On the relocation of cemeteries see also Richard A. Etlin, *The Architecture of Death: The Transformation of the Cemetery in Eighteenth-Century Paris* (Cambridge, Mass.: MIT Press, 1985).

16.   Eve Kosofsky Sedgwick, in *The Coherence of Gothic Conventions* (New York: Arno, 1980), takes modern critics like Lowry Nelson and Robert Heilman to task for speaking of the sinister ambiance of Gothic fiction as "mere decor," "stage-set," "claptrap," and so on. In so doing, she argues, they fail to see that objects such as bloodstained veils, burial crypts, and open graves actually serve complex formal functions in the fictions in which they appear. While this is certainly true, Sedgwick misses a more obvious point: that the twentieth-century urge to trivialize may have something to do with the fact that the typical Gothic setting foregrounds precisely those artifacts—tombs, corpses, shrouds and so on—that modern society now views with particular fear and revulsion. The very assertion that such details are silly or melodramatic—or even as Sedgwick herself puts it, merely "formal" elements—suggests something of the extreme emotional defensiveness that the death-obsessed Gothic milieu now inspires. We have accustomed ourselves to finding hidden sexual plots in Gothic fiction (and indeed delight in them); we have still not reconciled ourselves, however, to its far more obvious concern with death and dissolution.

17.   Ariès's description of romantic mourning, it should be noted, is very close indeed to the picture of chronic or disordered mourning familiar to modern psychology. Freud spoke of the inability to let go of mental images of a dead loved one ("loss of interest in the outside world—in so far as it does not recall the dead one") as one of the classic symptoms of normal grief in his famous essay "Mourning and Melancholia" (1917). He

also noted, however, that this obsessional state might be unnaturally prolonged if the mourner possessed strongly ambivalent feelings toward the dead loved one. Modern clinicians, notably in Britain, have enlarged on this Freudian notion of chronic grief in a number of recent case studies. See in particular Geoffrey Gorer's *Death, Grief and Mourning in Contemporary Britain* (London: Tavistock Publications, 1965) and John Bowlby's magisterial *Attachment and Loss* (New York: Basic Books, 1980), 3 vols.

18.   Samuel Richardson, *Clarissa: or, the History of a Young Lady*, ed. Angus Ross (New York: Viking Penguin, 1985), p. 1403. Compare also Tony Tanner's comments on the theme of sentimental reunion in Rousseau in *Adultery in the Novel: Contract and Transgression* (Baltimore: Johns Hopkins University Press, 1979), pp. 144–46.

19.   Emily St. Aubert's sensation that her father's corpse still moves resembles the fantasy frequently held by children faced with death—i.e., that the dead body can somehow be made to move again. Likewise, the vision of the tomb as a home is also close to the projections of young children, who as Bowlby points out, often believe that by dying themselves they can be reunited with a dead parent. See *Loss: Sadness and Depression* (Vol. 1 of *Attachment and Loss*), pp. 274 and 354–58.

20.   Sigmund Freud, "Psychoanalytic Notes Upon an Autobiographical Account of a Case of Paranoia" (1911), in *Three Case Histories*, ed. Philip Rieff (New York: Macmillan Publishing Co., 1963), p. 155. For a further development of the notion that the cultivation of sublime emotion can be a paradoxical psychic mechanism for obviating loss or threats to the self, see Thomas Weiskel, *The Romantic Sublime: Studies in the Structure and Psychology of Transcendence* (Baltimore: Johns Hopkins University Press, 1976), pp. 17–18, 137–45, and 157–58; and Neil Hertz, "The Notion of Blockage in the Literature of the Sublime," in *The End of the Line* (New York: Columbia University Press, 1985), pp. 40–60.

21.   On Aquinian notions of mental imagery see Jonathan D. Spence, *The Memory Palace of Matteo Ricci* (New York: Viking Penguin, 1984), p. 13.

22.   See Frances A. Yates, *The Art of Memory* (New York: Penguin Books, 1969); and Spence, *Memory Palace*, pp. 1–23.

23.   Keith Thomas, *Religion and the Decline of Magic* (New York: Charles Scribner's Sons, 1971), p. 587.

24.   John Locke, *An Essay Concerning Human Understanding*, ed. and abr. A.D. Woozley (London: Wm. Collins Sons, 1964), pp. 123, 125, and 124–25.

25.   See M.H. Abrams, *The Mirror and the Lamp: Romantic Theory and the Critical Tradition* (London: Oxford University Press, 1953), pp. 62–63; and Weiskel, *The Romantic Sublime*, pp. 17–19.

26.   Burke, as Radcliffe probably knew, also wrote of the curious satisfaction to be found in grief: "The person who grieves, suffers his passion to grow upon him; he indulges it, he loves it: but this never happens in the case of actual pain, which no man ever willingly endured for any considerable time." And Burke too connected this pleasure with certain self-affirming mental operations: "It is the nature of grief to keep its object perpetually in its eye, to present it in its most pleasurable views, to repeat all the circumstances that attend it, even to the last minuteness . . ." See Edmund Burke, *A Philosophical Enquiry into the Origin of Our Ideas of the Sublime and Beautiful*, ed. J.T. Boulton (Notre Dame: University of Notre Dame Press, 1958), p. 37.

27.   I purposefully echo the title of Fredric Bogel's *Literature and Insubstantiality in Later Eighteenth-Century England* (Princeton: Princeton University Press, 1984). This rich discussion of "the perception of insubstantiality" in later eighteenth-century English literature relates in interesting ways to the concerns of the present essay.

28. Iconic images have always been used to inspire visions of the dead or absent. What have changed are the forms of commemorative imagery and the technological means by which such images are produced. In *Udolpho* characters habitually use small painted portraits of loved ones to evoke nostalgic thoughts: Du Pont steals a miniature picture of Emily and uses it throughout the novel as a sentimental *aide-mémoire*; St. Aubert keeps a miniature of his dead sister for a similar purpose; the nun Agnes has yet another miniature of the same woman, with whom she is obsessed. Because of its size and portability, the miniature had become the natural accessory to romantic mourning by the late eighteenth century: a talismanic device, so to speak, through which one might enter the idealizing space of the memory. As the capacity for image-reproduction improved in the nineteenth and twentieth centuries, with the invention of photography and similar processes, so undoubtedly was the spectralizing habit itself reinforced. What I am suggesting, however, is that the preference for mental imagery may in some sense have preceded and conditioned this new technology: that the very pattern of human invention was determined by preexisting emotional needs. On the role of commemorative objects in modern bourgeois culture, see also Susan Stewart, *On Longing: Narratives of the Miniature, the Gigantic, the Souvenir, the Collection* (Baltimore: Johns Hopkins University Press, 1984).

29. Sigmund Freud, *The Interpretation of Dreams*, trans. James Strachey (New York: Avon Books, 1965), p. 439.

30. The phrase "a conjuring into existence of a piece of real life" is from the essay "Recollection, Repetition and Working Through" (1914), trans. Joan Rivière, in *Therapy and Technique*, ed. Philip Rieff (New York: Macmillan Publishing Co., 1963), p. 162. Freud also uses the conjuring metaphor at several points in "Analysis Terminable and Interminable" (1937), reprinted in the Rieff volume. The phrase "psychical underworld" is from this last essay, p. 249.

31. Freud, "Dynamics of the Transference" (1912), trans. Joan Rivière, in *Therapy and Technique*, p. 114.

32. Freud, *An Outline of Psychoanalysis*, trans. James Strachey (New York: W. W. Norton, 1949), p. 31.

33. Freud, "Dynamics of the Transference," pp. 108–9.

34. Freud, *Outline of Psychoanalysis*, p. 34.

35. See Freud, "Analysis Terminable and Interminable," on "the still unresolved residues of transference," pp. 236–38.

36. Freud, "Analysis Terminable and Interminable," p. 242.

12. THE LITERATURE OF DOMESTIC TOURISM AND THE PUBLIC CONSUMPTION OF PRIVATE PROPERTY/Carole Fabricant

1. Jane Austen, *Mansfield Park*, ed. John Lucas (London: Oxford University Press, 1970), pp. 89, 74.

2. Austen, *Pride and Prejudice*, ed. Frank W. Bradbrook (London: Oxford University Press, 1970), p. 216.

3. *Pride and Prejudice*, pp. 212, 213. The outermost chronological limits of this form of tourism extended from the late seventeenth century to about 1840, although it is possible to isolate a somewhat shorter period—from the publication of the first comprehensive guidebook to an individual country seat in the mid 1740s through the first quarter of the nineteenth century—when country-house tours enjoyed their greatest vogue. The pop-

ularity of these tours was attested to by, among other things, the number of new and revised editions of guidebooks and other tourist literature published during this period. See John Harris, "English Country House Guides, 1740–1840" in *Concerning Architecture: Essays on Architectural Writers and Writing Presented to Nikolaus Pevsner*, ed. John Summerson (London: Penguin Press, 1968), pp. 58–74.

4. Esther Moir, *The Discovery of Britain: The English Tourists, 1540–1840* (London: Routledge & Kegan Paul, 1964), p. xv.

5. Dean MacCannell, *The Tourist: A New Theory of the Leisure Class* (New York: Schocken, 1976), pp. 14, 42.

6. In this connection we might recall the passage in *Windsor Forest* (401–12) where Pope, characterizing through the obverse side of foreign travel the English fascination with exotic but "safe" cultures and beings, presents the image of "the new World launch[ing] forth to seek the Old" (402) and alludes to the visit to England of four Iroquois Indian chiefs, who proved to be the London sensation of 1710, for both the London populace and the writers who exploited the event in print. See *The Twickenham Edition of the Poems of Alexander Pope*, I, ed. E. Audra and Aubrey Williams (London: Methuen, 1969), 191–92, for both the poetic text and the relevant footnote.

7. Antonio Gramsci's conception of the struggle for political and cultural hegemony and the creation of social consensus is relevant here. See Lynne Lawner's Introduction to Gramsci, *Letters from Prison*, ed. and trans. Lawner (New York: Harper & Row, 1973), pp. 42–45, 49–55. I'm using the term "culture industry" in a very general way, and obviously don't mean to evoke the authoritarian and dehumanizing associations it has come to have through Max Horkheimer's and Theodor Adorno's analysis of the commodification of modern-day mass culture. (See Adorno and Horkheimer, *Dialectic of Enlightenment*, trans. John Cumming [New York: Herder and Herder, 1972], pp. 120–67.) Certain aspects of this analysis, however, do have relevance for my discussion of eighteenth-century tourism—even more, for the institution of tourism in general—as Tom Bottomore's explanation makes clear: "the culture industry concerns itself with the 'predominance of effect.' It aims primarily at the creation of diversions and distractions, providing a temporary escape from the responsibilities and drudgery of everyday life. However, the culture industry offers no genuine escape. For the relaxation it provides—free of demands and efforts—only serves to distract people from the basic pressures on their lives and to reproduce their will to work. . . . The culture industry produces a 'social cement' for the existing order." See the entry for "Frankfurt School" in *A Dictionary of Marxist Thought*, ed. Bottomore (Oxford: Basil Blackwell, 1983), p. 186.

8. Raymond Williams, *Marxism and Literature* (Oxford: Oxford University Press, 1978), pp. 121–27. Subsequent references will be cited in the text.

9. For a discussion of the historical and socioeconomic implications of this trend toward greater privacy, exclusion, and separation of the classes as embodied in landscape and architecture, see Mark Girouard, *Life in the English Country House* (New Haven: Yale University Press, 1978), chaps. 5–7; and E. P. Thompson, "Patrician Society, Plebeian Culture," *Journal of Social History* 7 (1974): 389–90.

10. *Property: Mainstream and Critical Positions*, ed. C. B. Macpherson (Toronto: University of Toronto Press, 1978), p. 8. J. G. A. Pocock argues for the coexistence of several different views of property during this period. See *Virtue, Commerce, and History: Essays on Political Thought and History, Chiefly in the Eighteenth Century* (Cambridge: Cambridge University Press, 1985), esp. pp. 51–71.

11. For a reproduction of this painting, see John Harris, *The Artist and the Country House* (London: Sotheby Parke, 1979), p. 274, pl. 296.

12. David Solkin makes a similar point about the psychological and ideological appeal of eighteenth-century landscape painting. See *Richard Wilson: The Landscape of Reaction* (London: The Tate Gallery, 1982), pp. 103–5.

13. *The Torrington Diaries, Containing the Tours Through England and Wales of the Honorable John Byng (later Fifth Viscount Torrington) Between the years 1781 and 1794*, ed. C. Bruyn Andrews, 4 vols. (London: Eyre and Spottiswoode, 1934), II.380. Subsequent references are to this edition; page numbers will be cited in the text.

14. Sir Richard Joseph Sullivan, *Observations Made During a Tour Through Parts of England, Scotland, and Wales* (London, 1780), p. 81.

15. Neil McKendrick, John Brewer, and J. H. Plumb, *The Birth of a Consumer Society: The Commercialization of Eighteenth-Century England* (London: Europa, 1982), p. 11.

16. For a fascinating insight into the world of eighteenth-century advertising see McKendrick's study of George Packwood and his zealous promotion of the razor strop, in *The Birth of a Consumer Society*, pp. 146–94.

17. John Serle, *A Plan of Mr. Pope's Garden* (London, 1745), pp. 8–9. This enumeration suggests the links that could exist between domestic tourism and England's colonial and mercantile expansion in the eighteenth century. For a discussion of Pope in terms of the contemporary discourse of mercantile expansion and the Marxian concept of commodity fetishism, see Laura Brown, *Alexander Pope* (Oxford: Basil Blackwell, 1985), pp. 9–14.

18. See George C. Clark's Introduction to George Bickham, *The Beauties of Stow (1750)*, Augustan Reprint Society Publication #185–186 (Los Angeles: William Andrews Clark Library, 1977). Subsequent references to Clark's Introduction will be cited in the text. Subsequent references to Bickham will be to this edition; page numbers will be cited in the text.

19. Daniel Defoe, *Tour Through the Whole Island of Great Britain*, ed. G. D. H. Cole and D. C. Browning, 2 vols. (New York: Dutton [Everyman], 1962), I.77.

20. William Fordyce Mavor, *A New Description of Blenheim*, 2nd ed. (London, 1789), pp. vii–viii. Subsequent references to this edition will be numbered 2nd ed. and cited in the text.

21. Mavor, *A New Description of Blenheim*, 4th ed. (London, 1797), p. 146. Subsequent references to this edition will be numbered 4th ed. and cited in the text.

22. John Berger, *Ways of Seeing* (Harmondsworth: Penguin, 1977), p. 131.

23. *The Eaton Tourists; or, A "Colloquial Description" of the Halls, Grounds, Gardens, &c. at Eaton* (Chester, London, 1824), p. 5. Subsequent references will be to this edition; page numbers will be cited in the text.

24. James Woodhouse, *Poems on Sundry Occasions* (London, 1764), pp. iii–iv. Subsequent references to Woodhouse's "Elegy to Shenstone" will be to this edition; page numbers will be cited in the text.

25. *The Life and Poetical Works of James Woodhouse*, ed. R. I. Woodhouse, 2 vols. (London: Leadenhall Press, 1896), II.110–11.

26. *Life and Poetical Works of James Woodhouse*, I.17, 58.

27. Daniel Carless Webb, *Observations and Remarks, During Four Excursions, Made to Various Parts of Great Britain, in the Years 1810 and 1811* (London, 1812), pp. 178–79.

28. See Terry Eagleton, *Literary Theory: An Introduction* (Minneapolis: University of Minnesota Press, 1983), p. 17.

29. See Fredric Jameson, *The Political Unconscious: Narrative as a Socially Symbolic Act*

(Ithaca: Cornell University Press, 1982), pp. 76–87. The specific quotations appear on pp. 80, 76, and 85.

30. Pocock, *Virtue, Commerce, and History*, p. 71.

31. Alistair M. Duckworth makes the same point but uses it to support a traditional interpretation of *Mansfield Park* as a novel unambiguously affirming conservative values, especially the ideal of an inherited culture. See *The Improvement of the Estate: A Study of Jane Austen's Novels* (Baltimore and London: Johns Hopkins University Press, 1971), pp. 71–73. Those comprising the so-called "subversive school" of Austen criticism (e.g., Marvin Mudrick, D. W. Harding, etc.) tend, of course, to offer readings of Austen's novels that seem on the surface more congenial to my own. Yet, to the extent that these readings often explain the "subversive" elements of her novels in terms of biographical or temperamental factors, they bear little similarity to my discussion here.

32. Pierre Macherey, *A Theory of Literary Production*, trans. Geoffrey Wall (London: Henley, and Boston: Routledge & Kegan Paul, 1978), chaps. 13–14 (pp. 75–84).

33. John Barrell, *The Idea of Landscape and the Sense of Place, 1730–1840: An Approach to the Poetry of John Clare* (London: Cambridge University Press, 1972), p. 188.

34. Alice Walker, *In Search of Our Mothers' Gardens* (New York: Harcourt Brace Jovanovich, 1983), p. 58.

35. Quoted in MacCannell, *The Tourist*, p. 43.

36. MacCannell, *The Tourist*, pp. 39–40.

INDEX

CONTRIBUTORS

John Barrell is Professor of English at the University of Sussex. His most recent book is *The Political Theory of Painting from Reynolds to Hazlitt*. His *Poetry, Language and Politics* will appear in 1988.

John Bender is Professor of English and Comparative Literature at Stanford University. Fellowships from the Guggenheim Foundation, NEH, and the Huntington Library have supported research for his book, *Imagining the Penitentiary: Fiction and the Architecture of Mind in Eighteenth-Century England* (1987).

Fredric Bogel is Professor of English at Cornell University. He is the author of *Literature and Insubstantiality in Later Eighteenth-Century England* (1984) and *Acts of Knowledge: Pope's Later Poems* (1981). This essay represents the beginning of a new project on Samuel Johnson.

Laura Brown teaches English at Cornell University. She is the author of *English Dramatic Form 1660–1760: An Essay in Generic History* (1981), and *Alexander Pope* (1985), and is currently at work on a study of gender, capitalism, and imperialism in eighteenth-century England, of which the essay included here is a part.

Jill Campbell is Assistant Professor of English literature at Yale University. The essay published here is part of her book in progress, " 'Natural Masques': Gender, Identity, and Power in Fielding's Early Works."

Terry Castle's most recent work includes *Masquerade and Civilization: The Carnivalesque in Eighteenth-Century English Culture and Fiction* (1986). She is currently at work on a study of ghosts and apparitions in eighteenth- and nineteenth-century philosophical, psychological, and imaginative literature. She teaches at Stanford University.

Carole Fabricant is the author of *Swift's Landscape* (1982). Her essay "Binding and Dressing Nature's Loose Tresses: The Ideology of Augustan Landscape Design" (*Studies in Eighteenth-Century Culture* 8) was awarded the James L. Clifford Prize in 1978. An Associate Professor at the University of California-Riverside, her current project is on Pope, women, and landscape.

Harriet Guest is a Lecturer in English at University College, London. She has just completed a book on Christopher Smart. Her work in progress concerns the invention of the idea that there is something distinctive in women's experience.

Donna Landry, a recent recipient of an ACLS Fellowship, teaches at the University of Southern California. She has published essays on feminist theory and other topics, and is currently completing a book on eighteenth-century working-class women's poetry in Britain, "The Muses of Resistance."

Michael McKeon is the author of *Politics and Poetry in Restoration England: The Case of Dryden's "Annus Mirabilis"* (1975) and *The Origins of the English Novel, 1600–1740* (1987). He is a member of the English Department at Boston University.

Robert Markley teaches English at the University of Washington, Seattle, and is the editor of *The Eighteenth Century: Theory and Interpretation*. He is the author of *Two-Edg'd Weapons: Style and Ideology in the Comedies of Etherege, Wycherley, and Congreve* (1987). He is currently at work on the problems of gender and class in the eighteenth-century novel.

Felicity Nussbaum teaches at Syracuse University. She is the author of *The Brink of All We Hate: English Satires on Women, 1660–1750* (1984), and is completing a study of eighteenth-century autobiographical writing under the auspices of a Rockefeller Fellowship at the Institute for Research on Women, Rutgers University.

John Richetti is Professor of English at the University of Pennsylvania. His most recent book is *Philosophical Writing: Locke, Berkeley, Hume* (1983).